Canadian Natural Resource and Environmental Policy

Melody Hessing and Michael Howlett

Canadian Natural Resource and
Environmental Policy:
Political Economy and Public Policy

UBCPress / Vancouver

Printed in Canada on acid-free paper ∞

ISBN 0-7748-0614-1

Canadian Cataloguing in Publication Data

Hessing, Melody.
  Canadian natural resource and environmental policy

  Includes bibliographical references and index.

  ISBN 0-7748-0614-1

  1. Natural resources – Government policy – Canada. 2. Environmental policy – Canada. I. Howlett, Michael, 1955- II. Title.
  HC113.5H47 1997   333.7'09971   C97-910281-2

UBC Press gratefully acknowledges the ongoing support to its publishing program from the Canada Council for the Arts, the British Columbia Arts Council, and the Department of Heritage of the Government of Canada.

UBC Press
University of British Columbia
6344 Memorial Road
Vancouver, BC V6T 1Z2
(604) 822-5959
Fax: 1-800-668-0821
E-mail: orders@ubcpress.ubc.ca
http://www.ubcpress.ubc.ca

Contents

Figures and Tables

Acknowledgments

This book is the result of a multiyear collaborative effort. It draws on many sources, but especially on aspects of works previously published by the two authors. Thanks go to M. Ramesh, Jim Bruton, Jay Lewis, Jeremy Rayner, and Rebecca Raglon for helping to generate the ideas and data that have gone into this work. Comments and discussions in various forums and at various times with Jeremy Wilson, Colin Bennett, Alex Netherton, Jack Warnock, Ellen Baar, Robert Gibson, Robert Paehlke, Neil Nevitte, Bob McDermid, Tony Dorcey, Chad Day, Bob Varade, Bob Anderson, Catherine Murray, John Robinson, Ted Schrecker, Bill Andrews, Ann Hillyer, George Hoberg, and Kathy Harrison are also much appreciated. Thanks also go to the members of the Institute for Governance Studies at Simon Fraser University (especially Paddy Smith, David Laycock, Laurent Dobuzinskis, and Steve McBride) for their support over the years.

Research assistance on various aspects of the book was provided by Sonya Plater, Brad Hornick, Lynda Young, Wayne McIlroy, Bill Waddell, Natalie Minunzie, Bill Souder, Charlotte Cote, Ken Peacock, Paul Rose, Jeremy Dunn, Katharina Hutter, Laura Giroux, Zhang Yuo Guo, Les Banks, and Pat McClean. Grants from the Social Science and Humanities Research Council of Canada, the federal Department of Energy, Mines and Resources, the Dean of Arts at Simon Fraser University, Douglas College, the President's Research Grants at Simon Fraser University, and the Government of British Columbia Work-Study and Challenge grant programs are also gratefully acknowledged.

At UBC Press, thanks go to Holly Keller-Brohman, Randy Schmidt, Annette Lorek, and especially to Jean Wilson for bearing with us over the term of a lengthy project and to reviewers for their critiques and support.

Part 1:
Introduction

This section sets out the need to examine contemporary Canadian natural resource and environmental policy-making within its historical, socioeconomic, and political contexts. It also explores the evolution of resource and environmental policy in Canada and examines its political economy. This section identifies the central issues for resource and environmental policy analysis and locates them within a dynamic economic and institutional framework.

1
Canadian Natural Resource and Environmental Policy: Issues and Approaches

This book is a study of natural resource and environmental policy in Canada, historically the most significant area of Canadian economic activity. It discusses the evolution of Canadian resource policies from an early era of exploitation to the present era of resource management. This evolution represents a transition from the unfettered appropriation of resources by individuals and business interests to the more extensive involvement of the Canadian state in decisions about resource use and environmental protection.

The evolution of Canadian policy reflects part of a global shift toward concern for the greater conservation of the environment and the sustainability of existing resource bases. Increased demand for resources has escalated worldwide:

> Since 1950, the need for grain has nearly tripled. Consumption of seafood has increased more than four times. Water use has tripled ... Firewood demand has tripled, lumber has more than doubled, and paper has gone up sixfold. The burning of fossil fuels has increased nearly four-fold, and carbon emissions have risen accordingly ... The global economy is damaging the foundation on which it rests. Evidence of the damage to the earth's ecological infrastructure takes the form of collapsing fisheries, falling water tables, shrinking forests, eroding soils, dying lakes, crop-withering heat waves, and disappearing species.[1]

Increased recognition of the dependency of human and other species' survival on the diversity of complex ecosystems has aided the transition of resource policy from direct exploitation to an increasingly environmental focus. That is, policy increasingly addresses not only the conditions and amounts of resource appropriation but the larger biophysical context in which these activities take place. The increase in environmental problems, and the growing frequency of environmental 'events' of both an acute and a chronic nature, have contributed to the perception of an environmental crisis at the global level that has had significant consequences for national policy-making.

The accelerated pace and consequences of social impacts on environmental quality, their often irremediable character, as well as the lack of preventative measures to forestall these problems are perceived increasingly as a crisis of governance. Knowledge of the long-term, often indirect, and extensive impacts of resource use has prompted the call for more effective international and national policy regimes. It is expected that environmental crises will be the principal feature of national security and international action in the near future. As Robert Kaplan has argued, at the global level,

> It is time to understand 'the environment' for what it is: *the* national-security issue of the early twenty-first century. The political and strategic impact of surging populations, spreading disease, deforestation and soil erosion, water depletion, air pollution, and possibly, rising sea levels in critical, overcrowded regions like the Nile Delta and Bangladesh ... will be the core foreign-policy challenge from which most others will ultimately emanate, arousing the public and uniting assorted interests left over from the Cold War.[2]

Canadian resource and environmental policy warrants investigation and concern for a number of reasons. The size and wealth of this country alone are of global significance. Because Canada contains one of the largest land masses and longest coastlines on this planet, and has possessed enormous quantities of fresh water, timber, fish, mineral and petroleum resources, the policies generated within Canada have had, and will continue to have, a widespread impact on Canada and on other countries. Furthermore, Canadians are the second wealthiest citizens on Earth when the value of untapped resources and the relatively low population level are taken into account. A recent World Bank study indicates that 69 per cent of Canada's wealth stems directly from natural resources, with 9 per cent from industrial output and 22 per cent from human resources.[3] How these resources are utilized and managed has a direct impact on the well-being and quality of life of all Canadians.

As we will see in Chapter 2, traditional economic assessments of Canada's wealth did not incorporate the value of untapped resources of oil, natural gas, and minerals in their calculations. As a result, in such analyses, Canada tends to rank anywhere from the thirteenth to the sixteenth wealthiest nation on Earth, with an average per capita income of $20,670.[4] However, when the value of human and unused natural resources is included in traditional gauges of industrial output, productivity, and other economic activity, Canada's status rises dramatically. As Table 1.1 shows, when this measure is used, Canada ranks second among nations in terms of wealth.

Table 1.1

World's wealthiest countries, including ecological capital and population

Country	Wealth per capita (US$)
Australia	835,000
Canada	704,000
Luxembourg	658,000
Switzerland	647,000
Japan	565,000
Sweden	496,000
Iceland	486,000
Qatar	473,000
UAE	471,000
Denmark	463,000
Norway	424,000
United States	421,000
France	413,000
Kuwait	405,000
Germany	399,000

Source: Peter Morton, *Financial Post* (16 September 1995), 3.

This abundance of natural resources is globally significant and is sure to increase in significance as nations continue to alter their landscapes through intensive forms of resource extraction.

The amount of publicly owned, or Crown, lands in this country also makes resource and environmental policy internally significant. Crown land comprises 90.3 per cent of the Canadian land base, meaning that the stewardship of a vast majority of land is directly affected by government policy.[5] The common-property basis of other resources – fish, water, air – means that government policy decisions affect a large and diffuse number of interests in Canadian society.[6]

In recent years, the increase in numbers and types of resource users or stakeholders has precipitated heightened interest in Canadian resource and environmental policy processes.[7] The broad impact of resource use on the public – ranging from employment in resource industries to the health effects of pollution – has expanded the basis of public interest in these activities. The increase in stakeholders has resulted in the expansion of policy networks and communities concerned with resource and environmental issues. Increased demand on resources by competing interests has also occasioned increased levels of conflict between stakeholders, reflected in, and mediated by, the policy process.[8] Furthermore, heightened demand for more direct public input into policy processes has intensified concern for the responsibility and legitimacy of public institutions involved in resource and environmental policy-making.[9]

Demographic changes in Canada have also contributed to a greater concern for the maintenance of environmental quality, while they have increased pressures on the availability and character of resource use. The size of the Canadian population, its distribution, and its density all affect the quality of the environment. In the 130 years since Confederation, the Canadian population has grown from 3.7 million to 28.1 million persons.[10] Although the fertility rate has generally declined and stabilized over the past century, immigration has contributed significantly to population growth. Population has also been moving west. Higher rates of growth in Alberta, British Columbia, the Yukon, and the Northwest Territories and declines in population growth rates in the Atlantic provinces both reflect and impact upon resource availability and the landscape. Human settlement has transformed ecosystems from grasslands, wetlands, and forests into agricultural production and urban areas. Urbanization has increased from 19 per cent of the Canadian population in 1871 to 76.6 per cent in 1991,[11] and it has created additional pressure on systems ranging from waste disposal to air quality and the preservation of biodiversity.

In Canada, the rate of population growth has accelerated in recent decades, with an increase of 27.7 per cent between 1971 and 1991 alone (from 22 to 28.1 million people).[12] Acceleration in rates of population growth and economic activity puts pressure on the amount and quality of resources upon which these activities are based. As we approach the millennium, today's economy is six and a half times larger than that of fifty years ago, and it places additional demands on the environment, especially in regard to industrial processes, resource use, energy consumption, and transportation.[13]

Despite its large size and relatively low population, Canada is not immune from the types of resource and environmental pressures now demanding attention and action throughout the world. The increased scarcity of some resources – as illustrated by the closure of the East Coast cod fishery, declines in the West Coast salmon fishery, the acceleration of the number of endangered species, and predicted shortfalls in timber allotments – indicates the inadequacy of our past policy efforts.[14] In addition, 20 per cent of Canada's farmland is deteriorating as a result of modern agricultural practices, 13 per cent of our forests can no longer be considered productive, and much of the best farmland in the country is being converted into urban uses.[15]

Better understanding of the negative health effects of pesticide use, industrial contaminants, and toxic wastes has also prompted concern about the potential adverse effects, to humans and other species, of pollution, whether industrial, agricultural, or otherwise. In Canada, related health issues ranging from mercury poisoning at Grassy Narrows,[16] the exposure of agricultural workers to pesticides, the burning of PCBs at Saint Basile le Grand, to chronic concerns about the quality of drinking water and air have led many observers to question the effectiveness of current policies and the processes by which they have been developed.

As a result of these issues and concerns, increases in the number of stakeholders, greater knowledge of the consequences of environmental degradation, and a better understanding of ecological complexity, Canadian resource and environmental policy has been subjected to increasing criticism. The inadequacy of existing policy measures is reflected in deteriorating environmental conditions and increasing resource scarcity. Critics allege that policies have been developed without due regard to the public interest or ecological concerns and that 'special interests,' especially business, are given preferential treatment in the policy process. These criticisms have not only succeeded in delegitimizing many aspects of the existing system of regulation but have led to demands for new policies and new mechanisms to implement them.[17]

One barrier to analysis has been the complexity and fragmentation of policy issues and jurisdictions that deter efforts at a comprehensive and unified analysis. Resources include energy and mineral reserves, fish and wildlife, agricultural and forest lands, as well as water and air. Consider, for example, the difficulty of comparing charges for timber harvesting licences in the Temagami region of Ontario to provisions for regulating toxic discharges of chemicals into the St. Lawrence River or fines for poaching bighorn sheep in national parks in Alberta. The land base itself is varied, representing a large number of distinct geographic ecosystems, most of which do not conform to the numerous municipal, regional, provincial, and territorial political boundaries that formally demarcate them. Different levels of government, and a range of ministries, administrative arrangements, and statutes, comprise a significant barrier to a comprehensive policy analysis. Changes in government and in constellations of participatory politics also make it difficult to understand general trends in the actors and interests represented in the policy-making process.[18]

Another difficulty is that resource policy has been traditionally located within the context of economic activity, and its analysis has largely been directed toward concerns of the marketplace.[19] The relatively recent expansion of resource policy-making to encompass broader environmental concerns, however, affords a different perspective on the subject.[20] Nevertheless, ecological databases often continue to reflect economic indicators rather than document the character and change of ecological systems.[21] A lack of consistent and integrated indicators from which to trace and project resource use continues to obscure changes in environmental quality and resource supplies.

Moreover, resource and environmental policy has not often been publicly debated because such exposure in the past has served the interests of neither the state nor resource industries. Public clamour about the issuing of timber licences or pollution regulations slows down a policy process that industry views as already mired in bureaucracy. The technical and legal nature of many resource and environmental issues also contributes to the complexity of the discussion and may obscure the political issues and decisions on which they are based, distancing policy discussion from the public.[22]

Additional geographic, economic, and sociocultural factors have also constrained the development of critical resource and environmental policy analysis. Historically, the large size of the Canadian land base and the relatively small population, especially within a global context of far greater human-to-land densities, have curtailed concern for environmental degradation, resource supplies, and environmental carrying capacities. The southern and urban concentration of human settlement in Canada also distances the majority of citizens from direct experience with, and concerns about, the impacts of resource extraction. Indeed, 68 per cent of Canadians live within 100 kilometres of the Canada-United States border. Only 10 per cent of the country is permanently settled, and only 1 per cent of the land is used for urban residential and industrial activity.[23]

As scholars of Canadian literature and culture such as Northrop Frye and Margaret Atwood have suggested, the 'Canadian experience' has been characterized as a struggle of survival against an alien and antagonistic environment.[24] In this context, Canadians' historical lack of concern over issues of environmental degradation is consistent with concerns for the maximization of conditions for resource exploitation.

Finally, a tradition of economic dependency on large-scale resource exports has reinforced a laissez-faire approach to resource and environmental policy in this country. With many jobs provided by resource extraction, both labour and governments may be relatively quiescent toward the demands of industry for permits, licences, and exemptions from regulations. The export of resources by 'free-range' transnational corporations is viewed as contributing to national survival, while the threat of losing corporate investment deters dissent.[25]

Nevertheless, Canadian resource and environmental policy is evolving and policy analysts must attempt to overcome these and other barriers to its understanding. This evolution reflects changes in the social, economic, and political fabric of the country, as well as shifts in our understanding of the interests served by resource extraction. Resource and environmental policy is forged by a variety of policy actors dealing with constantly changing knowledge, information, and technology. It is not surprising, given this complexity of actors and variables, that the identification of typical Canadian ways of dealing with resources and the environment – the Canadian resource and environmental policy style – and the specification of how and why that style changes should be a challenge. Yet it is important that we rise to that challenge, given increased pressures on natural systems, additional numbers of stakeholders, and the accelerating impact of transnational actors and global forces on the Canadian landscape, all of which call for policy responses.[26]

Overview of the Book

This book takes on the difficult challenge of attempting to identify characteristics of Canadian resource and environmental policy, based on historical references, contemporary examples, and smaller case studies, and to provide a critical framework for the study of emerging resource and environmental policy issues.

The discussion will show how Canadian resource and environmental policy has evolved to become increasingly interventionist and extensive. Governments have shifted from espousing the unfettered exploitation of resources to a more active, if evolving, conception of environmental stewardship. These changes occurred slowly as the resource sector developed and, in the modern period, as existing Canadian resource and environmental policies were challenged by environmental activists and other emerging stakeholders. The book discusses this evolving political economy of resource production in Canada, outlining the significant political actors, their motivations, and their actions in bringing about changes in policy.

From a political economy perspective, public policy-making is an activity of government that fuses knowledge and interests.[27] Policy-making in the resource and environmental area is largely about the struggle between different societal actors attempting to establish, maintain, or increase their share of the material wealth created by human activity, wealth generated to a great extent by resource extraction and use. But policies also reflect the struggle between adherents of different perspectives on the ways in which social life should be conducted, the character of relations between humans and their physical environment, and the quality of that environment. The analysis of policy-making requires that we know what material interests exist in a sector, what sets of ideas compete for prominence, and what actors and processes are engaged in policy formation.

In this regard, it is important to note that conflicts over knowledge and interests are reconciled, or mediated, through political institutions and the policy processes of government. In order to aid in the understanding of policy-making, the book introduces the student to the notion of a 'policy cycle': a staged, sequential, and iterative model of the policy process. It explores the character of Canadian resource and environmental policy-making at the different stages of the policy cycle and asks about the potential for, and directions of, policy change.[28] In so doing, it focuses attention on constellations of policy actors who participate in resource and environmental policy-making, including civil servants, industry representatives, members of environmental organizations, and others. The role that these actors, processes, and institutions play in creating a unique policy style is highlighted in order to make comprehensible the pattern of policy change – and the lack of it – in this area of government activity.

The text emphasizes five themes in the study of this significant sector of Canadian life. It adopts a political economic perspective on the general context and development of Canadian resource and environmental policy. It provides a theoretical analysis of the different ideological perspectives and material interests that motivate policy actors and that both generate and legitimate policies in this sector. An administrative concern with the development and implementation of resource and environmental policies is developed, and the text explores the substantive issues in policy analysis that pertain to resource and environmental policy-making. Finally, it considers the future directions of policy within the context of dynamic social, economic, and ecological systems.

Analyzing Environmental Policy-Making: Political Economy and Public Policy

Natural resources are, of course, at the origin of the production of goods for human consumption. Most of these goods are produced from the application of capital and labour to the materials found in the natural world.[29] Neoclassical models of economic activity make a number of assumptions about activities that govern the conversion of ecological components into resources. These assumptions are usually taken for granted in market economies, when forests are translated into timber allotments or when a salmon run is reduced to fishery quotas, openings, and closures. The traditional context of resource policy analysis has been a model in which the costs and benefits of resource extraction, processing, and sales are understood primarily as market transactions and measured by standard accounting practices.[30] Political economy, however, understands the economic process as socially and politically driven. It examines the way in which power and authority are derived, transmitted, and channelled through economic processes.

Within a resource and environmental context, a political economic perspective explores the ways in which multiple and often conflicting interests are activated and impacted differentially by economic transactions. Such a perspective attempts to 'situate' an exploration of policy in a dynamic context of evolving material and ideological interests. This approach to resource and environmental policy begins with an understanding that ideas and perspectives are materially grounded. It emphasizes both complementary and conflicting economic interests among the multiple actors involved in resource extraction. It understands resource and environmental issues as emanating in part from economic transactions but recognizes that actors are differentially situated with respect to the costs and benefits of those exchanges. In contrast to the neoclassical market paradigm, in which the interests of economic actors are viewed as complementary, a more critical perspective, endorsed by many political economists, understands these interests as potentially conflictual.

A political economic approach poses a number of questions to be addressed in any consideration of a nation's resource and environmental policy. A first set of questions deals with the origins of existing resource and environmental policies and with their capacity for change. What interests does any given policy regime represent and serve? Which actors were represented in its creation and implementation? Which were excluded or marginalized? Another set of questions is related to our understanding of the state's role in this process. Given the priority of economic transactions in market capitalist societies, for example, is it possible for the state to act as an impartial arbiter in decision-making? In what ways do policy processes reflect values such as fairness and neutrality? How does the state maintain autonomy from economic interests?

Yet a political economic approach also raises problems, especially for the consideration of environmental issues. A tendency toward economic determinism accompanies such an approach. Must environmental interests be rooted only in market-driven economic processes, or is it possible for extra-economic forces to generate policy change? A predominantly political economic focus may work to dismiss extra-economic claims or reduce them to material interests. It could tend, for example, to interpret indigenous land claims simply as a challenge to other productive interests rather than as issues of fundamental justice or spiritual relations to the landscape.

Furthermore, while political economy is critical of the social distribution of effects of resource activities among human populations, it remains essentially anthropocentric. That is, environments are perceived in human-centred terms with no, or little, concern for intrinisic ecological value. Concerns over environmental integrity are articulated only within the context of their ability to generate or impede market activity. Watching the setting sun becomes a Kodak moment, or a postcard, rather than a moment of peace, reconciliation with nature, or spiritual affirmation.

As many of its students have noted, policy-making involves more than simply the struggle over the distribution of costs and benefits involved in production.[31] It also involves a related struggle in which actors in addition to those with direct material interests in a given process or sector clash over the accumulation and application of knowledge to the area concerned.[32] In most areas of government activity, there is an effort to apply scientific as well as moral knowledge to policy-making, a process that is inherently conflictual because knowledge is rarely objective or universally endorsed. Scientific knowledge is rarely achieved independently of moral issues. For instance, funding for research is allocated in response to political pressure, as has been witnessed in terms of public health issues such as AIDS, heart disease, breast cancer, and smoking. Data for testing are often submitted by companies with a direct interest in the activity in question, for example, while limitations on experiments with various types of subjects may be mandated by law. Moral or normative judgments, by their very nature, remain subjective. Public policy analysis undertaken from a political economic perspective helps us to conceptualize and clarify this struggle over ideas.

In this context, it is important to recall that the concept of 'resources' represents a particular socioeconomic construction of ecological systems. The primary idea driving natural resource use in Canada in recent years, and hence significantly affecting environmental policy discourse, has been that of resource management as the allocation of public resources to private industry. In Canada, unlike in many other countries concerned with issues such as urban pollution or toxic wastes, the key environmental issues have been related to resource management. These issues have included the designation and protection of wilderness areas and wildlife habitat, pollution regulation, herbicide and pesticide management, and disputes over extraction methods in the timber, fishing, and mining industries.

Resource management has included the monitoring, facilitation, and negotiation of resource consumption patterns, ranging from simple extraction to other, and increasingly 'multiple,' uses such as tourism. Resource management has been treated in Canada, as in other nations, as an 'applied' science, oriented to ecological research and its application by different administrative agencies.[33] But much of the research on which government policies have been based has been produced by industry, and – as we will see throughout this book – the private sector has been extensively involved in the policy process in various capacities.

From a political economic perspective, the transition in Canada from resource to environmental policy reflects not only changing material conditions but also evolving ideological perspectives. Resource and environmental policy-making encompasses a wide range of issues, often concerning multiple resources in the context of an integrated form of development or use. Its concerns are not exclusively those of humans, but include other species, in a range of activities that often extend beyond the marketplace.[34] While resource policy may have been identified solely in terms of mineral reserves or timber allocations, environmental policy also incorporates the impact of mining or logging on salmon habitat or on human health, among other issues.

Contemporary Canadian resource and environmental policy reflects a number of considerations that have been raised through this introductory discussion. First, because Canada has a large land mass and a relatively small population, the country has avoided, or postponed, many of the sharp confrontations over pollution and degradation of the urban environment that have been a feature of smaller or more populous countries. Second, because Canada has relied on natural resources to generate much of its economic wealth, this reliance has distinctly coloured Canadian attitudes toward the environment. Resource extraction and processing supports a good deal of the labour force, and efforts at environmental protection or mitigation in Canada begin with the understanding that resource harvesting enjoys a great deal of public support. Third, despite these domestic factors, international events have had a major impact on Canadian environmental policies, organization, and attitudes. Canada has been heavily influenced by events and organizations in the United States, organizations that have periodically moved into Canada and brought with them a range of new ideas and sentiments, as well as new concepts of regulations and laws designed to address resource and environmental problems.[35] More recently, events at the international level, specifically at the United Nations, have also had a major impact on Canadian policy-making. Nevertheless, the Canadian mix of policies and attitudes is not an exact copy of the American, and international initiatives have not been adopted *holus bolus*. Rather, Canada has developed a distinctive approach to the environment conditioned not only by the examples of its powerful neighbour and by international pressures but also by its own unique social, cultural, political, and economic experiences.

A policy analysis rooted in political economy allows us to better understand the conditions under which resource activities take place, as well as the consequences of their development for environmental policy-making. This approach allows us to better understand the origins of policy change and to better predict what future policy changes might occur.

Understanding the Evolution of Canadian Resource and Environmental Policy

Who should be managing Canadian resources, in what way, and on whose behalf? Numerous types of resource and environmental policies are possible. The World Resources Institute, for example, has identified at least five common models of resource management, which place varying emphasis on socioeconomic and ecological factors. These models include frontier economics, resource management, sustainable development, selective environmentalism, and deep environmentalism, and together help to characterize the general pattern of evolution of Canadian policy in this sector.

The first level, frontier economics, characterizes much of the Canadian legacy. In this model,

the industrialized world tended to see the environment as an infinite supply of resources and a bottomless sink for wastes ... The economy was seen to exist in almost complete isolation, separate from the environment. Resources were seen as being abundant. So, for example, an increased demand for forest products could be met simply by building a new mill. The more pressing problem ... was the scarcity of human capital, not of resources. Consequently, the destruction of the environment made little difference ...[36]

The second model marks the emergence and development of a resource management approach. At this stage, the interdependence of humans and the environment was recognized, and increasing concern about environmental degradation, such as pollution, was voiced. The need for the conservation of resource stocks was identified. A broader, more ecological approach was introduced in the sectoral sciences, recognizing interdisciplinary approaches as well as the interconnections between different flora and fauna and their supporting environments. As well, 'policies were introduced to make polluters more accountable for the damage they caused ... and the environmental implications of resource extraction were assessed to mitigate or limit environmental damage.'[37]

In contrast are two models that emphasize environmental over economic factors. Selective environmentalism, the first, reflects a largely voluntary approach to exercising environmentally friendly options in both the production and the consumption of resources. Buying 'green' products that have been and can be recycled, reducing amounts and concentrations of effluents, and planning for the future of the environment are examples of policies congruent with this model. It assumes that market forces will respond to consumer demand with some small degree of state encouragement. More extreme is the model of deep environmentalism, which calls for the priority of environmental concerns over market forces. From the perspective of 'deep ecology,' humans are only one species among others, and ecological integrity is the necessary foundation for all human activity. It is concerned less with economic than with ecological viability, and requires a dramatic overhaul or replacement of the current market economy.

The midrange perspective identified in this schema is sustainable development, which incorporates both ecological and economic factors. 'The sustainable development approach holds that resources must be treated on the basis of their future, as well as their present, value, and offers genuine hope of economic development without environmental decline.'[38] As we will see throughout this book, this principle captures the essence of an emerging Canadian resource and environmental perspective: an attempt to reconcile the needs of humans with those of other species and to provide for future ecological as well as human preservation. Whether it can be realized in practice, however, is another matter, at least partially determined by the political economy of Canadian resource use.

There is a broad spectrum of opinion in this country about the prerogatives and interests involved in developing and affecting the contents of any new Canadian approach to resource and environmental management. While government's role in resource management is authorized by the formal definition and allocation of powers, many believe that the management of resources should only include those who have a vested interest in the resource involved. While many Canadians believe that Crown lands reflect a public ownership guaranteeing the future prosperity of the timber resource, others believe that private ownership of lands and forests would better ensure long-term protection and avoid a 'tragedy of the commons' – the collective and cumulative devastation of commonly owned property.[39] Many Canadians believe that Native peoples should bear responsibility for managing their traditional lands, yet land claims remain unresolved and contentious. At the heart of these debates is the question 'Management by whom and for whom?'

Canadian natural resource policy has changed over the past several decades to emphasize multiple use and integrated resource management.[40] The overall principle governing this use remains, however, an anthropocentric utilitarianism, the belief that human use remains central to the organization of resource and environmental management. From this perspective, as Max Oehlschlaeger argues, 'the wilderness in whatever guise is effectively reduced to an environment, a stockpile of matter-energy to be transformed through technology, itself guided by the market and theoretical economics, into the wants and needs of the consumer culture.'[41] The conservation of resources under this model assumes a reliance on science to alter and control natural systems. It also ignores the inequalities associated with the distributive mechanisms of the market economy as 'consumption is equated with pleasure, and high rates of economic throughput are thus equated with the good life.'[42]

This 'resourcist' paradigm has increasingly come under attack from environmentalists promoting new sets of ideas about nature. These ideas range from the tenets of deep ecology to those of sustainable development, and they include the ethically acceptable relationship of human beings with the natural world.[43] These conceptions take into account more fully the links between different systems, including economic, ecological, and social, and attempt to meet these integrated systemic demands in resource and environmental policy-making. They also attempt to temper anthropocentrism with biocentrism as a fundamental perspective from which policies and their results are to be formulated and evaluated. For instance, clearcut logging and ensuing habitat loss are understood to be a threat to the survival of species such as the marbled murrelet, thereby introducing additional, non-market factors into public policy-making. What was previously understood as primarily an economic activity becomes an issue of the preservation of biodiversity, the maintenance of aesthetic values, the intrinsic value of all living things, and other broad environmental concerns.

The continued support of resource management regimes that foster the maximization of commodity production, despite the emergence of new ecological ideas and actors, represents a conundrum for Canadian resource and environmental policymakers. The increasing diversification of the Canadian economy has introduced new and competing interests into existing economic equations but has not yet fundamentally altered their configuration. What is required to move the Canadian policy style toward a more ecologically sensitive paradigm? What are the constraints impeding policy change?

It is the aim of this book to illuminate the elements of Canadian policy-making in this critical sector and to provide answers to some of these key questions. It will do so by outlining both the political economy of this sector and the nature of the policy discourses that have emerged, as well as the manner in which both knowledge and power, or interests and ideas, are brought together in the public policy process. By examining both material interests and policy ideas in this sector, we can better understand the complexities of government policy-making and, in doing so, grasp the essential dynamics of policy processes and the potential for policy change.

Part 2:
The Context(s) of
Canadian Natural Resource and
Environmental Policy

This section sets out the socioeconomic and institutional contexts within which Canadian resource and environmental policy is made. It discusses the continued relevance of the resource sector to the operation of the domestic Canadian economy and examines the complex situation concerning jurisdiction over resources and the environment in a federal state. The impact of international treaties and organizations on Canada's domestic policy-making is also discussed.

character, its regional differences, its status relative to international economies, as well as the pace and direction of its evolution are fundamental to understanding and predicting policy change. The long-term shift away from a staples, or resource community-based, economy is arguably the most significant factor driving the evolution of Canadian resource and environmental policy.

The Fundamentals of a Staples Economy

A staple refers to a raw, or unfinished, bulk resource commodity sold in the market. Timber, fish, and minerals are staples, extracted and sold without, or prior to, significant amounts of processing.[1] This extraction of natural resources without processing or finishing takes place in the *primary sector*. The significance of exporting unfinished goods, to the understanding of economic structures and activities, lies not only in their location and availability but also in their lack of value-added. Value-added refers to the utilization of additional labour or capital in a product and the subsequent derivation of additional income from the sale of that product. For instance, rather than, or in addition to, exporting unfinished lumber, value-added production also includes the conversion and processing of timber into finished products – chairs, tables, and houses. Lower value-added activities are very vulnerable to competition in international markets, and staples economies remain vulnerable to fluctuations in international commodity prices.

Staple theory, derived by H.A. Innis and expanded by others, explains how the character and development of the Canadian economy are linked to its strong resource base.[2] The reliance on staples has, of course, been fed by the continuing global demand for Canadian resources. Yet the export of staple goods has been accompanied by the import of finished goods from other countries, thus indirectly supporting labour in other countries and forgoing the stability associated with a more diversified economy.

Having a staples economy raises several overlapping problems for resource and environmental policy-making in Canada. If faced with resource scarcity, as is the case with the closure of the cod fishery in Newfoundland, what is the prognosis for economic diversification and change? What are the conditions that would contribute to such diversification? What are the impediments to this change? In what ways is this economic base unique among industrialized nations? How has Canada's economic heritage been affected by today's international economic realities?

While most observers would agree that historically Canada can be characterized as a staples economy, there is considerable disagreement over whether or not it has completed a transition to an industrial or post-industrial economy and over its future economic capabilities.[3] This debate parallels the global economic debate concerning the speed and consequences of a more general economic transition of preindustrial countries to industrialization and beyond. One version of this process was propounded by W.W. Rostow, an American economist, in the 1960s. Rostow argued that economies pass through five identifiable stages in their transition to a mature economy (see Figure 2.1).[4]

We can apply Rostow's model to the Canadian economy, but not without difficulties.[5] The *traditional* stage would be that concerned exclusively with the extraction of staples in the early 1800s, especially fish, fur, and, increasingly, timber. The *preconditions* period would be that of the mid-1850s to Confederation and would include the shift of resource exports to the United States after the Civil War. *Economic takeoff* occurred from the turn of the century to the First World War, with early industrialization. The *drive to maturity* took place in the context of continuing industrialization and culminated in the post-Second World War years with the expansion of the service sector and the *age of high mass consumption*. From this model, it could be argued, the Canadian economy has matured from being dependent on resource extraction to being more diversified, industrial, and increasingly postindustrial.

Figure 2.1

Rostow's stages of economic growth

1 **Traditional society:**
   Land is the basis of wealth
   Low agricultural productivity, high employment
   Hierarchical society

2 **Preconditions period:**
   Externally triggered transition
   Increased commercialism, new elites, investment
   Higher agricultural productivity releases labour and capital for other uses

3 **Takeoff:**
   Period of intensive growth
   Increase in investment rates
   Development of leading sectors
   New sociopolitical framework promoting change

4 **Drive to maturity:**
   Economic growth is self-sustaining
   New sectors evolve from old, diversified economy

5 **Age of high mass consumption:**
   The culmination of the drive to maturity

Source: W.W. Rostow, *The Stages of Economic Growth: A Non-Communist Manifesto* (Cambridge: Cambridge University Press 1960).

However, the picture is much less certain than might appear at first glance. The actual picture of Canadian be discerned from an analysis of the *sectoral structure* of the country's economy. This analysis looks at the amount and nature of goods and services produced in each of the three major sectors of the economy: the primary, secondary, and tertiary sectors.[6] The *primary sector* is composed of economic activities associated with the extraction and production of natural resources. According to the United Nations system of Standard Industrial Classification (SIC), these resources relate to agricultural, forestry, fishing, mining, and oil and gas exploitation. The *secondary sector* is composed of activities oriented toward the processing of natural resources and manufacturing. The *tertiary sector* is composed of various goods and services provided to facilitate or organize the primary and secondary sectors; it includes activities such as construction, transportation, finance, real estate, insurance, public administration, wholesale and retail trade, and many others.

In most older industrialized countries, the historical trend has been for economic activity to shift from the primary to the secondary sector and finally to the tertiary, or service, sector.[7] This is the logic behind Rostow's model and, at first glance, appears to have been the case in Canada, as the figures in Table 2.1 indicate.

Both the amount of goods and services produced in different sectors and the number of people employed in each sector have shifted decisively toward the service sector. Over the last century, in fact, on a national basis, the primary and tertiary sectors have shifted locations as sources of economic production. This shift has primarily been caused by the rapid decline in agricultural activity and employment, which fell from 32 per cent of GNP and about 46 per cent of employment in 1880-91 to between 3 and 4 per cent of each in 1983-4. Most of the slack has been picked up by the tertiary sector, especially in the provision of various kinds of services, which rose from 23 per cent of GNP and employment in 1880-91 to between 67 and 68 per cent in 1983-4.

Table 2.1

Sectoral distribution of Canadian economic activity

	(% GNP/GDP)		(% Employment)	
Sector	1880	1992	1891	1992
Primary	43.5	5.6	49.2	5.0
Secondary	18.9	29.2	14.7	12.8
Tertiary	37.6	65.2	36.1	82.2

Source: Statistics Canada, *GDP by Industry 1992*, Catalogue No. 15-203 (Ottawa: Supply and Services 1992); K.A.H. Buckley and M.C. Urquhart, *Historical Statistics of Canada* (Toronto: Macmillan 1965); and Statistics Canada, *The Labour Force July-December 1992*, Catalogue No. 71-001 (Ottawa: Supply and Services 1993).

This is not to say, however, that the Canadian economy is any less reliant on natural resource-based production. Much of Canada's manufacturing base is in fact the production of resource-based commodities such as lumber or pulp and paper and various mineral- and oil-based products that are commonly thought of as 'primary production' but that the United Nations SIC system refers to as 'manufacturing industries.' About one-quarter of domestic manufacturing capacity is accounted for by the wood, paper and allied, primary metal, non-metallic, and petroleum and coal products industries. An additional $25 billion was produced from the generation of electricity. In fact, in 1994, almost $80 billion – or about one-sixth of Canada's GDP – was directly accounted for by various kinds of resource-related activity (see Table 2.2).

Closely related to these natural resource activities are other economic activities, such as rail and truck transportation of resources and resource products and many construction projects. In addition, resource activities generate many indirect effects, from banking and financial arrangements associated with large-scale capital projects to the food, vehicle, and other expenditures made by workers earning their salaries in the resource sector. In all, resource and resource-based activities generate as much as fifty cents of every dollar produced in Canada.[8] This continued reliance of the Canadian economy on primary resources and resource-based manufacturing puts it at odds with economies in many other large, modern nation-states, especially the United States, and has significant consequences for Canadian resource and environmental policy-making.

Table 2.2

Resource component of the Canadian economy, 1994

Activity	Component ($000,000)	% GDP
Primary SIC (Agriculture, fisheries, mining, and forestry)	38,183.7	7.17
Manufacturing SIC (Wood industries, paper and allied, primary metal, non-metallic mineral products, petroleum, and coal products)	24,818.3	4.66
Utilities SIC (Electric power)	24,818.3	3.14
Total	79,776.5	14.98

Source: Statistics Canada, *Provincial Gross Domestic Product by Industry 1984-1994*, Catalogue No. 15-203 (Ottawa: Supply and Services 1995).

Although there has been a move in the Canadian economy away from a complete dependence on resources, it has not taken place at the speed or to the extent that it has in other nations, such as the United States or Japan. The continuing high profile of resource sectors, the relative lack of non-resource-based industrialization in this country, and the high degree of foreign ownership explain our lack of conformity with the Rostow model.

Moreover, many analysts would argue that the original dependence on staples export and the lack of value-added, or processing, activities are self-perpetuating phenomena. In understanding the 'development of underdevelopment' in Canada, it is often argued, the structural relations of capitalism must be examined to illustrate the ways in which transnational corporations perpetuate a flow of capital from corporate headquarters to branch plants, from the centre to the periphery. Theorists such as André Gunder Frank have explained the condition of underdeveloped nations and regions not in terms of the lack of cultural capital or due to technical incompetence but as a reflection of a precise type of exploitation, 'which focused upon the extraction of resources to fuel imperial development, while simultaneously retarding and distorting the internal development of the regions themselves.'[9]

The Canadian Economy: Resource Industries and Economic Development

Four significant aspects of the contemporary structure of the Canadian economy affect resource and environmental policy considerations. First, the production of wealth in Canada as a whole has been and remains dependent on resource extraction. This fact has coloured Canadians' attitudes toward the environment as well as the configuration of actors involved in the formulation of Canadian resource and environmental policy. Second, not all regions of the country are dependent on the export of the same resources, nor to the same extent, which has resulted in different patterns of resource and environmental interests and actors in different parts of the country. Third, most Canadian resource commodities are exported to international markets, increasingly to the United States. This exporting results in a small, open economy in Canada subject to international pressures in a variety of areas, including resource trade issues.[10] Fourth, regional economies based on resource exports in a small, open economy are inherently unstable and result in significant inequalities in wealth and incomes in the various regions of the country. These regional economies, and indeed the Canadian economy in general, are subject to fluctuations in world commodity prices over which Canadians have little control. This instability results in Canadian government efforts to offset these inequalities through large-scale public expenditures, efforts that often focus on job creation and employment issues and that can clash with those related to environmental protection.[11]

The Canadian Economy and Resource Trade

Canada was colonized by Europeans so that its natural resources could be sold in the world market.[12] The proceeds from the exports paid for the importation of goods consumed by the settlers. So, from its very beginning, Canada has been a trading nation. Reflecting the importance of trade, Canada established its Trade Commissioner Service as far back as 1892, long before the establishment of its own diplomatic service.[13] The importance of international trade to the Canadian economy has fostered Canadian participation in most major international trade arrangements, such as the General Agreement on Tariffs and Trade (GATT), the International Monetary Fund (IMF), the World Bank, the G7 group of industrial nations, the United Nations Organization and its various specialized agencies, and the Canadian and North American Free Trade Agreements (CAFTA and NAFTA).[14]

Canada's dependence on international trade for the generation of wealth in Canadian society is quite marked. As the figures presented in Table 2.3 indicate, Canadian trade dependence has always been high among OECD nations and by 1992 accounted for one out of every four dollars generated in the economy.

Until the turn of the century, the economy was based on exports of fish, fur, and, later, timber and wheat. In the twentieth century, as industrialization swept the world at an unprecedented speed, demands increased for Canada's natural, especially mineral, resources. In fact, this country has been one of the world's largest exporters of natural resources throughout this century. Yet even today, less than half of Canadian exports are fully-manufactured goods, the remainder being semimanufactured products, unprocessed crude materials, and farm and fish products.[15]

Table 2.3

Canadian trade dependence in international perspective

	Exports as a per cent of GDP	
	1965	1992
Canada	15.6	24.5
France	10.2	17.4
Japan	9.5	10.2
UK	13.3	21.0
US	3.9	7.9
West Germany	15.6	24.0
OECD average	9.0	22.1

Source: Canada, External Affairs, *A Review of Canadian Trade Policy* (Ottawa: Supply and Services 1983), 20; and *Europa World Yearbook*, 1995.

There are many resource sectors whose very survival depends on exports. The figures provided in Table 2.4 demonstrate the extent to which the actual goods that Canada exports in order to generate such a large proportion of its GNP are primarily resource goods, either in a raw state or in only slightly processed form.

In contrast, Canadian imports throughout history have consisted mainly of manufactured goods. Imports are especially high in the high-technology and capital-goods sectors, the sectors regarded by some as essential to the long-term competitiveness of Canadian industries and, indeed, the Canadian economy.[16] In such products, Canada has traditionally experienced huge trade deficits. The policy of *import substitution* pursued vigorously in the late nineteenth century and throughout most of this century has made almost no difference to the strength of the Canadian manufacturing sector, except in a few industries such as automobiles and telecommunications.[17]

While the level of manufactured exports increased dramatically between 1960 and 1994, most of this increase occurred in a single sector, that of automobiles, which accounted for about 27 per cent of Canadian exports in 1994. This sector, however, has been covered by special trading arrangements, including the Canada-US Autopact, the Canada-US Free Trade Agreement, and the North American Free Trade Agreement. Although automobile exports are significant, large numbers of assembled automobiles and auto parts are also imported into the country under the terms of these agreements. The figures in Table 2.5 illustrate the extent to which Canada's positive balance of trade in merchandise items remains reliant on natural resource exports. Note that forest and energy exports generate almost five times the surplus accumulated through automobile production.

Table 2.4

Percentage of Canadian exports by commodity group

Commodity group	1960	1994
Agricultural goods	18.8	8.2
Crude materials	21.2	26.1
Fabricated materials	51.9	16.4
Manufactured goods	7.8	49.3

Source: Canada, External Affairs, *A Review of Canadian Trade Policy* (Ottawa: Supply and Services 1983), 26; Statistics Canada, *Canadian International Merchandise Trade,* Catalogue No. 65-001 (Ottawa: Supply and Services 1994).

Table 2.5

Canadian merchandise trade balances, 1994

Product	Trade balance ($000,000,000)
Agricultural/Fish products	5.3
Energy products	12.8
Forest products	26.8
Industrial goods	-0.8
Machines and equipment	-19.0
Automobile products	8.2
Consumer goods	-17.3

Source: Statistics Canada, *Canadian Economic Observer,*
Catalogue No. 11-010 (Ottawa: Supply and Services 1995).

In fact, in 1994 the total primary processing sector generated an annual trade surplus of close to $45 billion. This sum is sufficient to pay for all the deficits incurred importing highly manufactured machinery and equipment and consumer goods. This surplus also helped to cover part of the large deficit Canada runs virtually every year on services trade – mainly as a result of the large sums flowing out of the country in dividend and interest payments, as well as in areas such as tourism.

The dominance of resources in Canadian exports and of manufactured goods in imports has played a critical, if contradictory, role in shaping Canada's international trade objectives. The abundance of marketable natural resources in Canada determined right from the beginning that the reduction in foreign trade barriers to their export would be Canada's main foreign economic policy objective. This goal was problematic, however, because Canada's demand for reductions in foreign barriers generated corresponding demands from other countries that Canada lower its own barriers to imports, which were particularly high on manufactured goods. Meeting this demand was difficult because Canada wanted to grow out of its role as a 'hewer of wood and drawer of water,' by nurturing its manufacturing industries behind tariff walls until they were strong enough to take on the world market. But many industries – including textiles, clothing, and footwear – failed to grow out of their infancy over the years and needed continued protection. The large number of workers that they employed, often in economically depressed regions in Ontario and Quebec, made the removal of protection even more difficult. Canadian policymakers have thus been led to pursue the somewhat contradictory goals of negotiating reductions in barriers to exports while attempting to retain Canada's own barriers to imports. Particularly since World War II, Canada has been under increasing pressure from the United States to lower its import barriers as the price for gaining increased access to the US market for its exports.[18]

This pressure underlines the fact that a vital aspect of Canada's resource trade concerns the markets to which Canadian exports are destined. Although in the past Canada had two major markets (the United States and the United Kingdom), this situation has changed dramatically since World War II. Since 1940, the US market has emerged as the major destination for all Canadian exports. This growing dependence on the US market is illustrated in Table 2.6.

As the table shows, Canadian trade has steadily shifted away from the United Kingdom and toward the United States, to the point where the latter alone now accounts for more than four-fifths of all Canadian exports and is by far the largest single market for Canadian goods. The North American Free Trade Agreement, signed in 1993 by Canada, the United States, and Mexico in the effort to regulate this trade, will be discussed in Chapter 12.[19] While the economic and environmental consequences of the treaty for Canada are still not clear, the treaty will likely exacerbate existing trends rather than counter them. The effects of this growing dependence on the US market are far-reaching. The international trading system has a significant impact on the policies that Canadian governments can follow toward altering the terms of trade or the nature of domestic production in ways that might then affect the country's major trading partner.[20]

Canada's Resource Economy and Regional Development Issues

Canada's regional variations in resources and population have contributed to regional differences in wealth and production, but also to different demands on governments in different areas of the country. The figures in Table 2.7 provide a breakdown of GDP by province and the percentage that each province contributes to the national total.

Table 2.6

Direction of Canadian export trade, 1900-94 (as a per cent)

	1900	1920	1940	1960	1980	1994
US	38.3	37.4	41.1	55.8	66.2	81.4
UK	52.3	39.4	35.5	17.4	4.0	1.5
Japan	0.1	0.6	2.5	3.4	5.4	4.5
Other Europe	2.9	13.8	6.3	8.3	10.7	5.0
Developing	–	–	–	7.9	11.9	6.6
Other	6.4	8.8	14.6	7.2	1.8	1.0

Source: M.C. Webb and M.W. Zacher, 'Canada's Export Trade in a Changing International Environment,' in D. Stairs and G.R. Winham, eds., *Canada and the International Political/ Economic Environment* (Toronto: University of Toronto Press 1985), 88-9; and Statistics Canada, *Total Exports from All Countries*, ESTAT CD-ROM.

As these figures show, there is a wide range in GDP between the provinces. More significantly, about 63 per cent of Canadian economic activity takes place in the two central provinces of Quebec and Ontario. The four provinces of Atlantic Canada account for only 6 per cent of Canadian production, while the four western provinces account for about 30 per cent.

These aggregate statistics can be misleading in an estimation of the relative wealth of different jurisdictions because they do not take into account the fact that different provinces have different populations. All things being equal, we would naturally expect Ontario and Quebec, with their large populations, to produce more than other less populated provinces. A better measure of wealth is not simply GNP or GDP but GNP or GDP per capita. These figures are provided in Table 2.8.

Although these figures include income transferred by the federal government to the poorer provinces, it is important to note that, even with these transfers, there are significant variations in wealth between the provinces and regions of the country. With the exception of Saskatchewan, the central and western provinces enjoy per capita incomes of 90 per cent or greater of the national average, while the provinces of the Atlantic region have incomes below 85 per cent of the national figure. In fact, even with substantial transfer payments included, the average per capita income in Newfoundland is only about three-quarters that of the highest provinces, Ontario and British Columbia.[21]

Table 2.7

Provincial GDP and share of national GDP, 1994

Province	GDP ($000,000)	Share of national GDP (%)
Newfoundland	7,803	1.3
Prince Edward Island	1,934	0.3
Nova Scotia	14,864	2.5
New Brunswick	12,038	2.0
Quebec	134,684	22.5
Ontario	238,576	40.0
Manitoba	19,841	3.3
Saskatchewan	18,951	3.1
Alberta	71,073	11.9
British Columbia	73,652	12.3
NWT/Yukon	2,368	0.4

Source: Statistics Canada, *Provincial Economic Accounts,* Catalogue No. 13-213 (Ottawa: Supply and Services 1995).

Table 2.8

Provincial per capita incomes, 1994

	Per capita income ($)	National average (%)
Newfoundland	17,467	79
Prince Edward Island	17,746	80
Nova Scotia	18,917	85
New Brunswick	17,939	81
Quebec	21,020	95
Ontario	23,666	106
Manitoba	20,156	91
Saskatchewan	18,621	84
Alberta	22,603	102
British Columbia	23,432	106
National average	22,143	100

Source: Statistics Canada, *Economic Reference Tables,* Catalogue No. 13-213p (Ottawa: Department of Finance 1995).

The second important regional aspect of Canada's continued dependence on resource-based economic activities concerns the unequal nature of resource dependence found in different parts of the country. Although the Canadian economy as a whole never experienced the shift into manufacturing industries that orthodox theories of economic development envisioned, the economies of Ontario and, to a lesser degree, Quebec did do so. As the figures in Table 2.9 show, by the early 1990s there was a very unequal distribution of sectoral economic activities between the regions of the country.

As these figures indicate, in past decades the western Canadian provinces had a high share of Canadian primary production, that is, agri-

Table 2.9

Distribution of sectoral economic activity by region, 1992 (% national GDP)

Region	Primary	Secondary	Tertiary
Atlantic	4.4	3.8	7.2
Central	22.5	72.8	61.3
West	73.1	23.4	31.5

Source: Statistics Canada, *Provincial GDP by Industry,* Catalogue No. 15-203 (Ottawa: Supply and Services 1992).

cultural and natural resource production. Central Canada, on the other hand, completely dominated manufacturing activities in the country. Not surprisingly, the Atlantic provinces, given their relatively small economies, were marginal producers in all three sectors of the national economy. More specifically, the figures presented in Table 2.10 show that provinces such as Prince Edward Island, Saskatchewan, and Alberta continue to rely heavily on their natural resources and agricultural sectors to generate economic wealth.

These figures, however, fail to include the significant component of provincial manufacturing activity – in sectors such as oil refining, smelting, sawmills, or pulp and paper production – that are resource-based. The figures in Table 2.11 show the extent to which regional manufacturing relied on natural resources in the early 1990s. As these figures illustrate, both the Atlantic region and especially British Columbia were heavily dependent on resource activities for their economic well-being. Only Quebec and Ontario had diversified economies that were not entirely resource dependent – although even in those provinces substantial economic activity was still directly associated with resource extraction and processing.

Thus, many inhabitants of the western and Atlantic provinces gain their living from natural resource and agricultural activities, which, because of their dependence on uncontrollable foreign markets and the large amounts of capital invested in them, are inherently less stable than the

Table 2.10

Primary sector component of provincial GDP, 1994

Province	(%) GDP
Newfoundland	6.0
Prince Edward Island	10.5
Nova Scotia	5.0
New Brunswick	5.8
Quebec	3.3
Ontario	2.4
Manitoba	6.0
Saskatchewan	23.1
Alberta	25.0
British Columbia	6.4

Source: Statistics Canada, *Provincial Gross Domestic Product by Industry 1994,* Catalogue No. 15-203 (Ottawa: Supply and Services 1995).

Table 2.11

Regional resource-based manufacturing activity, 1992

Region	% Resource based
Atlantic	50.5
Quebec	42.6
Ontario	34.4
Prairies	45.0
British Columbia	75.5
Canada	42.9

Source: Statistics Canada, *Provincial Gross Domestic Product by Industry 1992,* Catalogue No. 15-203 (Ottawa: Supply and Services 1993).

manufacturing activities located in central Canada. Canada has a monopoly or near monopoly on the production of only a few resources or agricultural goods, and Canadian producers must sell at prices set by international conditions of supply and demand. They are not price-makers but *price-takers* in international markets. While international demand for most resources – outside of wartime – has increased at a relatively steady but low rate, world supplies of particular primary products have been highly variable. A good harvest, the discovery of significant new reserves of minerals or oil, or new production capacity in the fishery or forest products sectors can quickly add to world supplies and drive down world prices until demand slowly catches up and surpasses supplies, resulting in sudden price increases. It is these fluctuations in international supplies that account for the *boom and bust* cycles prevalent in most resource industries and, by implication, most resource-based economies like Canada's.

The instability of regional resource-based economies generates personal and regional disparities in incomes. Resource-dependent regions of the country may experience periods of high or low incomes, depending on how international supply and demand affects the prices of the resources on which their economies are dependent. Given the orientation of most resource exports toward the US market, in effect this means depending on the state of international supplies and US demand. Any increase in international supplies or any decrease in US demand can devastate a regional economy, while the reverse situation can bring newfound prosperity.

Both aspects of regional economic health, of course, remain largely outside the control of Canadian governments.[22] However, these governments will receive demands for ameliorative action made by residents of affected regions whenever economic downturns occur. These demands may directly contradict other demands for resource conservation or environmental protection.

In conclusion, then, the significance of the structure of the Canadian economy for resource and environmental policy includes the following: (1) the prosperity and continuing existence of many regions of Canada are dependent on resource extraction, whether forests, coal, fish, fur, oil, or minerals; (2) primary industries are export oriented and subject to fluctuations in international demand; (3) little secondary industry or value-added component has developed in hinterland areas; (4) although resource dependent, these regions are geographically different from one another, but all tend to support the urban, industrial centres and are largely controlled from outside the region; (5) regional differences are dynamic and subject to both internal and international influences that may further improve or degrade the regional situation; and (6) regional variations in employment and income are the focus of many policy initiatives, ranging from social redistributive measures to industry subsidies and regulations.[23]

The Social Dimensions of Canada's Resource Economy

In addition to regional, national, and international differences in the economics of resource use, social differences are relevant to Canadian resource and environmental policy formation and implementation. Incomes, wealth, and power vary significantly in Canada not only by region, but also by class, gender, and ethnicity. These factors affect the definition of actors in the political process and help shape the context of policy-making.

Social differences permeate processes of production and consumption, but they are also significant in terms of environmental consequences. Social actors absorb the costs and share the benefits of resource development in different ways. Jobs and incomes are unevenly distributed and the effects of economic development are not imparted equally to everyone. The uneven allocation of economic rewards and the diffuse, indirect, and often negative social and ecological consequences of regionally resource-based economic development lead many to question the benefits of Canada's historic pattern of economic development.[24]

Significant Aspects of the Canadian Demography

Several characteristics of the Canadian population are relevant to resource and environmental policy-making, as we mentioned in Chapter 1: the relatively small population, the southern concentration of population, the uneven distribution of population within the provinces, and high levels of urbanization.

These demographic factors have several implications for policy. Canada's large land mass, low population density, and high degree of urbanization (over three-quarters) mean that Canadians may be less likely to perceive resource scarcity or degradation as problematic than residents of more industrialized, and often smaller, countries, such as Japan and Great Britain (see Table 2.12).

Table 2.12

Population density per 1,000 hectares, 1993

Australia	23
Bangladesh	9,388
Canada	30
China	1,292
France	1,043
Germany	2,308
Japan	3,319
Mongolia	15
Netherlands	4,502
Namibia	19
Nigeria	1,310
Russian Federation	88
Sweden	211
UK	2,393
US	281
World average	427

Source: World Resources Institute, *World Resources 1994-95*, Table 17-1 (New York: Oxford University Press 1994), 284-5.

The increasing urbanization of Canada precedes and parallels the transition from resource dependency to increased economic reliance on urban-based, tertiary, or service sector, employment. The southern and urban concentration of the population creates a physical and symbolic distance from hinterland areas of resource extraction and economic wealth creation.

Class, Social, and Ethnic Inequalities

Social inequalities permeate Canadian society and are significant to resource and environmental policy by shaping the policy process as well as social consequences. Social class, often identified in terms of socio-economic status, is defined by political economy in terms of one's relation to the means of production. Differences in power and authority are tied to the unequal distribution of wealth and also shape access to the decision-making processes in both the private and public sectors.

Canada is a class-differentiated society, with a disproportionate share of wealth and power held by a small corporate elite. This elite represents only about 3 per cent of the population, including a small concentration of ownership families and a larger executive group. In 1990, the richest 20 per cent of Canadians owned 70 per cent of the wealth, while the poorest 40 per cent owned less than 1 per cent. In terms of annual income, the top one-fifth of income earners earned over 35 per cent of total income, while the bottom one-fifth earned about 7 per cent (see Table 2.13).

Furthermore, the growing gap between those living in wealth and those living in poverty reflects social differences that are of increasing concern for policymakers. While the United Nations has ranked Canada as the best country in which to live, in the past decade there was increasing polarization between social classes, especially for families. Using Statistics Canada data from 1981 to 1993, the Canadian Council on Social Development found that even after redistributive action by the state (income taxes and social programs), the poorest 40 per cent of families became poorer within this period while the richest 40 per cent became richer.[25] These socioeconomic factors, while rarely explicitly addressed as such in the policy process, are relevant to understanding which policy actors are included in the subsystem and how policy affects a variety of actors and interests in different ways.

While there is a high degree of urbanization in Canada, there is also a pattern of single-industry or resource communities that have been and continue to be vital to resource industries. Class, gender, and ethnic differences permeate Canadian social structure, not only within urban areas but also within resource communities. Many such communities are isolated and lack adequate social services and a diverse pool of employment opportunities. For resource industries, the centralization and concentration of business administration in urban centres perpetuate a productive division between urban owners and management and a hinterland labour force. For workers in resource communities, employment is heavily dependent on forces external not only to their region but also to their class.

Decisions by the economic elite, who reside elsewhere and have interests in other regions or countries, effectively control the existence and nature of resource-based jobs.[26] Employment opportunities in resource industries for local residents are also restricted by the increasing technological

Table 2.13

Quintile shares of family income after taxes, 1981-92

Quintile	1981 family income (%)	1992 family income (%)
Top	35.3	36.0
Second	23.6	23.9
Middle	18.8	18.8
Fourth	14.5	14.1
Bottom	7.8	7.2

Source: Statistics Canada, *Income after Tax, Distribution by Size in Canada, 1992*, Catalogue No. 13-210 (Ottawa: Supply and Services 1993).

aspects of the work, aspects that upgrade skill requirements while also reducing the demand for labour. In addition, when hinterland economic activity requires participation by corporations from the centre, persons from the industrial heartland are sent to the hinterland as managers and supervisors. This constrains outlying regions by providing few opportunities for local advancement.[27]

Ethnicity has been and continues to be a factor in resource-based economies. Ethnic minorities have been both a significant source of labour in resource development and a primary source of economic exploitation. The historical economic exploitation of agrarian Francophones by an urban British business class, for example, is a common theme in the separatist argument in Quebec. Some elements of western antipathy to Ontario and eastern Canada can be traced to discrimination against early settlers to the region from Eastern Europe. The exploitation of racial minorities in railroad construction and maintenance was also a key characteristic of British Columbia's economic and social development.

Canadian resource-based economic development has also exploited indigenous peoples and expropriated their land and resources. Sylvia Hale notes:

> It may have well been inevitable that Native hunting and gathering economies would decline with the influx of white settlers ... But there was nothing inevitable about the nature of the treaties imposed upon many Native bands or about the fact that, while European settlers were allocated 160 acres of farmland per family, Native families were allocated 10 acres or less. Nor was it inevitable that Indian reserves were located on lands unsuitable for agriculture ... Later when gold and other minerals were found in the North or when hydro-electric power projects were set up, Native lands were expropriated with minimal compensation. Such events reflect the fact that Native peoples are not represented within the centres of economic and political control in Canadian society where such decisions are made, and hence that their interests are not taken into account.[28]

While many First Nations people are employed in resource industries, they also experience more poverty and a lower socioeconomic status than do other ethnic groups in Canada. They are underrepresented not only in government policy bodies but in corporate decision-making as well. Their claims to resource control and ownership, and to a history of more successful and sustainable stewardship of land and resources make their continued marginalization, if not exclusion, from policy circles additionally problematic.[29]

Gender Issues in the Resource Economy

Gender is an issue for resource and environmental policy because women have been underrepresented in policy-making and because they, too, are impacted by resource activities and decisions that affect employment, resource communities, and environmental quality. In Canada, one-third of women under sixty-five, almost one-half of senior women, and 60 per cent of female single parents live in conditions of poverty in which their living and working environments are substandard and inadequate.[30] Women continue to be employed in short-term work and are at the low end of a spectrum of wages. A 1994 National Action Committee on the Status of Women report points out that, when we take into account all full- and part-time wage earners, 'women's average wages are just $18,050, compared to $29,328 for men. All working women, on average, earn 61.5 percent what men earn.'[31]

Resource industries represent traditionally heavily male-dominated economic sectors. Women continue to be strongly overrepresented in clerical, educational, health, and service work and underrepresented in work in the primary sector. In occupational terms, women comprise only 15.9 per cent of mining employees and 14.9 per cent of forestry workers and they are often employed in support functions in their sectors.[32] Women's significant roles in resource industries are often completely ignored or treated as marginal, as Martha MacDonald notes in regard to debates in Nova Scotia about fishery policy:

> The actors in these discussions always seem to be the companies, the fishermen, and the government. Where are fish plant workers, the majority of whom are women? The fishing industry runs on the unpaid and low paid work of women: as wives of fishermen, helping to outfit the boat, sell the fish and cook for the men; as fish plant workers doing the most tedious, low-paid jobs; and as workers in the service sector earning enough to enable their husbands to keep fishing for low returns.[33]

Women's lack of equal access to corridors of both economic and political power reinforces their marginality. Women have been excluded and underrepresented in formal decision-making bodies and processes, and their lack of access to public and corporate power has limited their ability to influence policy change. At the federal and provincial levels of government, women continue to exercise less power and control than their male counterparts in portfolios such as industry and finance, which impact directly on economic activity. Few Canadian cabinet ministers have been women, and half of them have held health care, social service, tourism, or culture portfolios. In terms of corporate decision-making, only 2 per cent of chief executive officers in Canada, and between 2 and 3 per cent of top

American executives, are women.[34] Resource-based economic activity thus not only reflects but also reinforces social disparities by mediating employment opportunities, incomes, and power relations in terms of class, race, and ethnicity, but also in terms of gender.

Nevertheless, the traditional gender-based division of labour in the resource sector is being challenged by feminist practices, changes in family composition, and other factors related to the general advancement of women. These all point to the need for increased gender representation and awareness in resource and environmental policy-making.

The Ecological Dimensions of Canada's Resource Economy

Besides highlighting the significance of economic, demographic, and social factors in resource and environmental policy-making, a political economic approach to the formation of policy has the potential to make explicit the ecological processes central to production. That is, ecological processes are understood to have economic functions and consequences, as do economic activities.[35] The ecological consequences of demographic and economic systems are enormous, but have usually been ignored, externalized, or understood in terms of an economic framework that distorts and devalues their significance.

Ecological Systems as Resource Systems

The ecological context is the fundamental and basic foundation in which all other systems operate and are contained. Resources are located in elements of the ecosphere (air, water, soil, and organisms ranging from subparticulates to humans to polar bears) and in subterranean and subaquatic areas. These resources may be classified into four groups: renewable, replenishable, non-renewable, and non-replenishable.[36]

Renewable resources consist of organisms capable of reproduction, such as microorganisms, plants, animals, and human beings. They use the ecosystems around them to reproduce and support themselves. Replenishable resources are non-organic and include air, water, soil, and climate. They compose the webs of ecosystems that support renewable organisms. Below the earth are found non-renewable resources such as fuel and radioactive elements. Fossil fuels have been particularly significant to industrialization and to contemporary lifestyles, yet they are non-renewable. Non-replenishable resources consist of minerals that are converted into marketable products, becoming unavailable for future use unless recycled. Both non-renewable and non-replenishable resources are finite and non-regenerative, and they exert environmental damage by releasing hazards such as acid rain, ozone depletion, global warming, toxicity, and pollution.

The general problems resulting from misuse or overuse of these resources fall into two categories. The first is overuse of renewable and replenishable resources beyond their reproductive or restorative capacities. These problems range from overgrazing to deforestation to species extinction. The second is the use and release of non-renewable and non-replenishable resources, ranging from the dumping of hazardous wastes to the mercury poisoning of a river, from the adverse health effects associated with asbestos mining to decreased urban air quality from the release of carbon dioxide.

Ecosystems and Policy

Ecological systems are often considered solely in terms of their supply of economic resources, but they are also politically constructed through policy regimes that do not conform to or reflect their composition or boundaries. Existing political systems enable the comparison of ecosystemic features across political borders. The boreal and taiga shields, for instance, extend from Newfoundland to the Yukon, and one would expect that provincial and territorial legislation regulating economic activity such as logging and mining in Newfoundland and the Yukon would be compared as a means of identifying the most effective policies.

However, the classification of Canada's environment has evolved through several phases, many of which were geared to the identification of specific resources by the relevant resource-management ministries. Forest regions were identified by Forestry Canada, for example, while physiographic regions were categorized by Energy, Mines and Resources Canada. Ecological classifications set out jurisdictions and issues that are then incorporated into the policy process. Only recently has the Canada Committee on Ecological Land Classification produced national standards for the classification of ecological profiles, consisting of tiers of ecosystems ranging from large-scale 'ecozones' to site-specific 'ecoelements.'[37] These fifteen zones are Tundra cordillera, Boreal cordillera, Pacific maritime, Montane cordillera, Boreal plains, Taiga plains, Prairie, Taiga shield, Boreal shield, Hudson plains, Mixed wood plains, Atlantic maritime, Southern Arctic, Northern Arctic, and Arctic cordillera.

At present, there is little reference to the distinct character of these ecosystems in resource and environmental policy-making. Provincial boundaries may be viewed as an impediment to the accumulation and exchange of information relevant to ecosystemic disorganization, because provinces may not use transferable databases nor exchange relevant information with one another. Without similar policies and the exchange of relevant information, environmental degradation may persist and be transferred from one area to another. For some, ecozone-based analysis could contribute to a better understanding of resource and environmental policy issues. The concept of 'bioregionalism,' for example, argues that political boundaries and other forms of social organization should be based on ecosystem character.[38] For instance, Cascadia as a political boundary would include the area encompassed by the North Cascades, transcending current boundaries of Oregon, Washington, and British Columbia. State of the Environment reporting has already begun to use these ecologically based classifications, usually based on river drainage systems, to measure environmental changes within an ecosystem.

The process of economic development, especially industrialization, has numerous environmental and ecological implications. While both preindustrial and industrial societies have exceeded local ecological capabilities, the latter have the potential for doing so in a more accelerated, intensive, and large-scale manner. While preindustrial societies have sometimes been praised for their limited patterns of resource use, most have also exceeded the carrying capacity of their agricultural bases through the overharvesting of natural resources such as trees or animals. Extensive resource extraction in industrial societies typically results in substantial resource depletion. In mining, there may be greater reliance on lower-grade ores; in forestry, second- or third-growth timber and less accessible timber stocks may be recruited; and in the fishery, the depletion of certain stocks shifts extraction to less desirable and other more ecologically precarious stocks.

While the key resource issues for a preindustrial society include resource availability, especially on a per capita basis, for industrial societies, economic activity can have more immediately harmful environmental impacts that result from manufacturing processes or final product disposal, such as air and water pollution, waste disposal, or toxic contaminants. Industrialization requires the extraction of ever increasing amounts of natural resources and the mass production of elements injurious to natural environments. Tertiary sector, or service-based, activities can be less harmful, but they include activities such as electricity generation, which can result in large-scale environmental change and habitat alteration, and various forms of wasteful consumerism.

There has been little ecological interpretation of existing models of economic transition. One central problem of economic development is that social benefits (at least to certain segments of society) have taken place at the cost of ecological integrity. While the transition to an industrial society is accompanied by accelerated environmental disorganization, it is not yet clear that the transition to a postindustrial society will relieve the ecological burden. Ecological costs may be transferred increasingly to the hinterland, rather than absorbed by the metropolis. These problems raise numerous questions for policy. In what ways can ecological needs be represented by policy? How do we identify ecological concerns? In what ways is it possible for ecological needs to override economic needs? Which actors can represent ecological needs that are not human centred? What are the possibilities for expanding the policy model to incorporate ecological concerns?

Conclusion

In Canada, internal inequalities in economic development are frequently explained with reference to the assumptions of orthodox development theory. Studies of the Maritimes and of Newfoundland have emphasized traditional cultural and institutional barriers as impeding economic development and diversification.[39] This market deficiency perspective explains regional inequalities in terms of constraints on productivity and efficiency, including factors such as 'local cultural values, lack of valuable resources, geographical distance from markets, inadequate infrastructure, e.g., inferior roads, harbours, educational facilities, etc., low levels of capital investment in new and productive technology, an inadequately skilled labour force, widely dispersed settlement patterns, and even government interference with "natural" market forces.'[40]

The staples approach developed by Innis and others, however, recognizes that the initial comparative advantage provided by large resource supplies in staples economies may result in a staples *trap* – when the over-concentration of capital and other resources in the primary sector prevent economic diversification. While this approach does not explain how regions or countries with similar resource industries have developed in different ways, it provides an approach to understanding these differences.

In the 1970s, many Canadian academics began to explain the Canadian situation in these terms. Canada's colonial heritage and continuing trading advantages with Great Britain, as well as its proximity to, and primary trading relationship with, the United States, were reinterpreted in a 'staples-dependency' vein. Evidence cited to bolster the claim that Canada was, and would remain, an underdeveloped nation as a result of the resource-based nature of the economy included 'the initial dependence of a staple region on a foreign industrial supplier, the fact that Canada and her regions first began as imperial colonies, the frequent unequal and exploitative trade relations governing international exchanges, and the periodic cyclical swings from boom to bust embedded in a staple economy.'[41]

However, while dependency approaches help us to understand Canada's semiperipheral status among industrialized nations, they remain inadequate to explain the extent, character, and variation of Canada's development in relation to the lesser-developed world. Many new approaches have emphasized the *nature of production* – the combination of technology, organization, values, and class relationships – as the core determinant of economic development. This 'postdependency' approach emphasizes specific historical circumstances as well as the ways in which political and economic forces shape an industry, province, region, or nation. Figure 2.2 identifies some of the policy implications that emerge from adopting these different approaches.

Regardless of the type of analysis adopted, however, it is important to note that these theories share the insight that the stage of economic development of a society has a number of implications for policy, among which are the ecological consequences of this development. Countries with different economic structures are expected to have, among other things, different sets of environmental and resource concerns.

Industrial societies generally can exceed ecological limits through the mass production of goods and the introduction of increased quantities and higher concentrations of wastes than can be absorbed by the environment. The mass production of goods requires the extraction of increasing amounts of natural resources, while production processes often increasingly emit toxic by-products.

But because of the wide discrepencies present in the availability of resources, levels of industrialization, and population concentrations of different countries and regions, the consequences of industrialization vary. Highly urbanized service sector economies such as those in Japan or Western Europe may be most concerned with questions of resource availability and environmental degradation, pollution, and contamination associated with service and manufacturing activities. Countries with abundant resources and widely dispersed populations, such as Canada, New Zealand, or Australia, will exhibit a different set of concerns and policy responses pertaining to, for example, wilderness protection and resource harvesting regulations.

These basic socioeconomic and ecological facts affect all aspects of state policy-making, including resource and environmental policy-making, elevated to high status in Canada due to the nature of the Canadian economy and society. The Canadian situation is quite complex and will be discussed in greater detail in succeeding chapters. Yet at a basic level, Canadian government responses to resource and environmental concerns are seriously constrained by the resource export and dependent nature of the production of wealth in this country. Some of these constraints are simply due to the nature and consequences of production activities undertaken in Canada, but others originate in the integration of the domestic political economy into the international system of trade and production. All must be taken

Figure 2.2

Approaches to persistent regional inequality: Causative factors and policy implications

Approach	Critical causes	Policy implications
Market deficiency	• Lack of entrepreneurship • Fragmented infrastructure • Dispersed population • Income support dependency • Geographical isolation	• Promote education • Small/medium business promotion • New roads, harbours, airports • Lessen income supports • Growth centres • Relocation incentives/industry
Staple	• Fragmented settlement • Low-linkage development • Poor production function • Staple mentality/trap	• Integrated transportation • Incentives for technology use • Taxes: personal income growth • Encourage diversification
Dependency	• Aborted capital accumulation • Collaboration of elites • High levels of foreign ownership and control	• Sever exploitative links • Replace imported with local goods • Social revolution
Postdependency	• Combined external and internal factors • Different modes of production coexist	• Promote capitalist development • Prognosis not optimistic for redistribution of wealth

Source: Adapted from Lawrence Felt, 'Regional Disparity and Unequal Accumulation,' in P.S. Li and B.S. Bolaria, eds., *Contemporary Sociology: Critical Perspectives* (Toronto: Copp Clark Pitman), 258.

into account in an analysis of Canadian natural resource and environmental policy.

A political economic perspective makes a number of contributions to the analysis of resource and environmental policy. It understands alterations in the traditional staple base as significant in determining new directions and levels of social, economic, and ecological activity. In spite of its continuing resource emphasis, the diversification of the Canadian economy has progressed in the centre, in urban areas, and most recently in the western provinces. A political economic approach understands this process in terms of the unequal flow of capital from the hinterland to the metropolis, increasing concentrations of wealth, continuing patterns of extensive foreign ownership and control, as well as increasing dependence on international trade and globalization. Furthermore, it understands that significant inequalities in wealth and power within and between regions, and accompanying divisions of class, ethnicity, and gender, reflect differences in the production and distribution of wealth and have significant ecological consequences. All of these factors are significant aspects of the context(s) of Canadian resource and environmental policy-making.

3
The Institutional Context: The Canadian Constitution, Aboriginal Rights, and International Agreements Affecting Resources and the Environment

The socioeconomic context of natural resource production in Canada has had a great impact on policy decisions. Resources and natural environments are located within an economic framework based, in contemporary Canada, on a market economy with some state regulation. The state is active in establishing and maintaining conditions for the accumulation of capital, and the Canadian governments' ability to act on various resource and environmental issues is severely constrained by the reliance of the economy on resource production and international trade in bulk commodity resources.

This is not the only constraint that governments face, however. The state must also maintain its legitimacy by appearing to act on behalf of all citizens and to conform to liberal characterizations of its independence and fairness. A policy analysis adopting a political economic perspective understands the relationship between the economic systems of the society and its governments as one of 'relative autonomy.'[1] Rather than viewing governments, courts, and laws as completely independent from economic activities, the laws, values, and institutions of the society are understood to be derived from and to reflect this material base of production.

The state subsidizes industries, provides business incentives, contributes to a stable labour climate, and negotiates international trade agreements. The state also receives fiscal support from economic interests, both individual and corporate, in forms ranging from stumpage fees and fishing and game licences to taxes. From a political economic perspective, the functions of the state are thus derived from its economic footings, but have changed historically with the incorporation of less sector-specific revenues.[2]

The Evolution of Canadian Resource and Environmental Policy
State functions have evolved dramatically over the course of Canadian history, reflecting a number of changes in the institutions, processes, and actors in the resource and environmental policy sector. These include four stages of policy culminating in the contemporary era. In these stages,

government policy has moved from (1) inaction to (2) a concern with resource rents, then to (3) a concern with resource conservation, and finally to (4) the current resource and environmental management regime.

The Era of Government Inaction: Pre-1800

In the colonies of Great Britain in the northern half of North America, it took several decades for governments to realize that they should take action on behalf of natural resources. Although some key resources of great financial or military value (such as gold or tall trees suitable for the masts of wooden sailing ships[3]) were reserved for the use of the Crown, other resources were simply used by settlers for their own purposes.

The first actions taken by governments involved their securing different forms of property rights, which ensured early mining and forestry operations that they would have a secure supply and the exclusive right to remove the resources located on the lands that they owned or leased. While land in some parts of the country (notably the Maritimes and some parts of Quebec) was sold to private owners, elsewhere the overwhelming majority of land was never 'alienated' but retained as Crown land. Resources located on private land (with the exception of those mentioned above subject to prerogative rights) required little regulation save surveying and title registration. Surveyor generals in most colonies were charged with making and keeping such lists.[4] However, the idea of securing removal or harvesting rights on public lands required the development of more complex systems of leases (such as those required for timber or mineral resource extraction). By about 1800, most colonies had created commissioners of Crown lands to replace surveyor generals. These commissioners were charged with surveying and with title and lease registration.[5] Once the demand for timber, mineral, or other resource 'concessions' grew, it was possible for governments to begin to charge different kinds of rent for the use of their lands and resources, and Canadian government policy entered a new era.

The Era of Revenue Generation: 1800-80

The second period lasted for almost 100 years as governments in Canada developed a host of legislation containing a bewildering variety of charges for resource use.[6] They included annual rents for mineral claims or timber limits, the development of extensive royalty or stumpage charges for the extraction of resources, and the development of embryonic taxation schemes levied against company profits.

It was during this era that the first government departments were established to deal with resources. These 'lands and forest' departments actively abetted the pillaging of Canadian resources by issuing many and cheap licences to companies willing to extract resources at a rapid rate.[7] By Confederation, when most lands and resources were retained by the provinces, royalties from their sale by far amounted to the largest proportion of provincial government revenues.[8]

This great revenue made control over resources a subject of much intergovernmental competition. Between 1867 and 1900, the federal government attempted to use its powers over trade, commerce, and fisheries and other means to extend its control over provincial resources. By 1900, however, it had lost three major constitutional battles with the provinces over the delineation of the Ontario-Manitoba border, concerning the validity of the Ontario Rivers and Stream Act, and in a judicial interpretation of the validity of Ontario's forest 'manufacturing condition,' which restricted its role to controlling resources located on federal lands.[9]

The Conservation Era: 1880-1950

By the 1880s, the negative aspects of the policies of revenue enhancement were obvious in the deforestation of much of central and eastern Canada. In addition, due to technological improvements such as the development of the pulp and paper industry and large-scale oil-drilling rigs, governments were increasingly called upon to moderate the rate of resource extraction and to secure supplies for industries and towns over the long term and not simply on an annual basis. These calls led to the development of new administrative arrangements embodied in regulatory agencies (such as forest services and mines departments) and long-term tenures (such as pulpwood leases).[10] It was also during this era that Canada's system of national parks and forest reserves was created.[11]

After 1900, having lost its constitutional battles with the provinces, the federal government had to be content to administer its own lands through the Department of the Interior and to attempt to influence provincial policy through reason and persuasion. This influence was accomplished, for instance, in Sir Wilfrid Laurier's convening of the first National Forest Congress in 1905 and by the efforts made by both the Laurier and Borden governments to promote conservation through federal participation in the long-standing Commission of Conservation and through the provision of assistance for the formation of various professional associations such as those created for foresters, agronomists, and forestry and mining engineers.[12] Only the imposition of federal controls on resource production and prices during the two world wars brought any alteration to this policy, because concerns about conservation were put aside during the war efforts.

The constitutional arrangements for the distribution of federal and provincial authority over natural resources during this period also established the framework within which policies aimed at environmental protection have since been created. As Rankin notes, when the Constitution was adopted in 1867, '"the environment" was not perceived as a coherent subject for the legislators' attention ... The jurisdiction of the federal and provincial governments for the protection and enhancement of environmental quality is not explicitly addressed.'[13]

Prior to World War II, environmental functions, including resource management, pollution regulation, wilderness and species preservation, and parks services, were allocated to different ministries, legislated and administered largely at the provincial level. Administrative provisions for environmental protection were minimal, fragmented, and framed primarily in terms of human economic and organizational requirements. Regulations were primarily intended to limit the spread of infectious diseases, and most such policies, accordingly, were administered by health authorities.[14]

The Management Era: 1950 to the Present

After the Second World War, federal reconstruction efforts targeted expansion of the national economy through resource development. Although the federal role remained limited by the constitutional division of powers and provincial resource ownership, the King and St. Laurent governments attempted to influence the direction of provincial resource policies through the utilization of the federal spending power. This approach was embodied in the enactment of initiatives, such as the Canada Forestry Act in 1949, that authorized the federal government to enter into shared-cost, conditional grant programs with the provincial governments.[15]

Throughout this period, efforts were also made at the provincial level to secure long-term resource conservation. This initiative involved long-term land zoning – such as the creation of forest and mineral reserves – as well as the establishment of new boards and agencies to secure resource supplies – such as those established in Alberta to regulate oil and gas production.

Following the resource development orientation of the Royal Commission on Canada's Economic Prospects, the Diefenbaker government attempted in 1960 to establish a direct federal presence in the resource sector through the creation of specific federal departments of forests, energy, and resources.[16] However, provincial opposition to this jurisdictional intrusion stymied Diefenbaker's plans. Federal expenditures in resource sectors continued to be made, however, but now took the form of regional development incentives. Grants to the resource sector under various regional development programs accounted for a large percentage of total regional development expenditures between 1965 and 1971.[17]

Over this period, the consolidation and force of environmental activity, in both legislative and administrative character, accelerated dramatically.

The administrative structure for Canadian environmental protection was the focus of considerable attention. These changes reflected two major developments: an overall increase in the role and powers of the state in regulatory processes, and a corresponding increase in the complexity of legislation and administrative structures to facilitate this movement. In this period, environmental protection essentially underwent a transformation from *de facto* self-regulation by industry to more sophisticated state supervision of the regulatory process.

Governments at both federal and provincial levels began to establish mechanisms to regulate pollution, although, as a whole, environmental management continued to reflect a narrow and fragmented mandate. While this was a time of significant economic and demographic expansion, it was also an era in which increased scientific documentation of the effects of pollution and a surge in environmental events elicited government responses. Regulatory models were adapted from many countries, especially the United States, where a flurry of postwar regulatory legislation was directed not only to pollution but also to wilderness and species preservation.[18] Regulatory statutes guiding an environmental licensing system were passed in a number of provinces; examples are the British Columbia Land Act and Water Act, and the Ontario Air Pollution Control Act. Independent bodies, such as the Pollution Control Board in British Columbia, the Water Authority in the Maritime provinces, and the Water Resources Commission in Ontario, were established to administer this legislation. Most of these regulatory initiatives were taken at the provincial level, although the federal Trudeau government in 1970 faced growing pressure to move into the environmental arena.[19]

The creation of new regulations often involved the transfer of powers from existing government structures and was resisted by existing ministries, especially at the provincial level, so that new 'environmental' agencies were often added to resource mandates. Thus, these agencies did not represent an entirely new slate of organizational systems; they merely shifted the existing resource framework in a number of ways. This approach contributed to the division of administrative resource and environmental functions, both vertically between different levels of government and horizontally between different agencies and departments with overlapping jurisdictions.[20]

Developments in the contemporary era include the amalgamation of much existing environmental legislation and passage of additional and more extensive environmental legislation, at both senior levels of Canadian government. The establishment of ministries of the environment at both federal and provincial levels represents the formal recognition of an environmental agenda that both transcends and, to a limited extent, appropriates the responsibilities of existing resource departments. At the federal level, Environment Canada, whose jurisdiction included both resource management and pollution prevention, was created in 1971 by the Trudeau government.[21]

The establishment of Environment Canada brought together existing agencies having responsibility for various aspects of environmental protection and renewable resource management and featured a new Environmental Protection Service for pollution control and the protection of air, water, and soil quality. However, it was 'to achieve its conservation and protection objectives by influencing and co-ordinating the activities of other departments.'[22] Desfosses notes that, while a significant number of functions was transferred to the Department of the Environment from other ministries,[23] other environmental activities continued to be performed under their previous departments.[24] While Environment Canada created a structure under which considerable responsibility for environmental protection was amalgamated, 'substantial powers were still left in the hands of the established departments.'[25]

Departments of the environment were created at the provincial level throughout the 1970s and 1980s, although they provided primarily environmental regulatory, rather than resource management, functions. The technique of the environmental impact assessment was introduced. Provincial legislation and administration was significant in its extension of regulatory provisions and its increased 'get tough' policy, with greater punitive sanctions available for enforcement. Yet the legacy of structural fragmentation in jurisdiction and regulatory standards continues to make resource and environmental administration a complex and difficult process.

The Canadian Institutional Structure
The analysis of Canadian resource and environmental policy-making, must take into account not only historical changes but the institutional order that establishes the basic political structure within which governments in Canada operate.[26] This order, broadly defined, is composed of two legal regimes. The first is the constitutional order in Canada itself. As will be discussed below, the fact that Canada is a democratic, parliamentary, and, above all, federal country has a significant impact on determining how governments act in response to any set of their own or public concerns. The basic constitutional order determines which government is responsible for which area of legislative activity and, within governments, which branch or level of government is able to make authoritative and binding decisions. The second regime is the set of international treaties, organizations, and rules that sovereign states have agreed should set the broad para-

meters within which domestic governments will operate. These *international regimes* exist in virtually every area of government activity and can have a significant impact by limiting or otherwise constraining the policy choices available to governments.[27] This is as true of the natural resource and environmental sector as it is of many other areas of state activity.[28]

The Constitutional Structure of Canadian Government

Canadian governments make public policy. However, it is the Canadian constitution that determines exactly which actors are entitled to make policies and decisions for the Canadian state. Like the international order, the constitutional structure of a country is an important component of the institutional context of policy-making.

The Canadian constitution creates a democratic parliamentary system similar to that found in Great Britain. This 'Westminster' model of parliamentary democracy has several characteristics that affect how policies are made.[29] The most significant characteristic relates to the strength of the executive in such systems. Unlike in many countries, notably the United States (where the powers of the executive are offset by powerful legislatures), in Canada the Westminster-style governments – the legislature and the executive – are merged in a single body: Parliament. This fusion, all other things being equal, gives the executive much latitude in ensuring that its wishes become law.[30] In this regard, Canada has a strong form of executive government in which major decisions are made by political leaders and administrative officials and debated or publicized in legislative bodies.

Not all the aspects of Canada's parliamentary style of government are identical to those found in the United Kingdom. The most significant difference is that Canada has two distinct levels or orders of government, rather than one. While the United Kingdom is a 'unitary' or centralized state, Canada is a *federal* system. That is, it has two levels of government – the federal and the provincial – that are sovereign within their established jurisdictions.[31] This division of powers is significant for policy purposes because it determines which government will actually be entitled to make policy decisions in a particular area. Resource and environmental policy has been a significant locus of federal-provincial struggle, an arena in which power between levels of government may be contested. To a great extent, as is discussed below, the question of the division of powers regarding Canadian environmental policy flows from that relating to resources.[32]

The Division of Powers over Natural Resources and the Environment before 1982

Prior to 1982, the division of federal and provincial powers over natural resources and the environment was determined by colonial practices, the enactment of the British North America Act (1867), and subsequent judicial and parliamentary activities.[33]

The constitutional arrangements for the distribution of federal and provincial authority over natural resources at the time of Confederation established the framework within which policies aimed at environmental protection have since been created. At the time, the environment was not perceived as a coherent subject for the legislators' attention.[34]

At Confederation, the British North America (BNA) Act followed British colonial practice – itself with a history extending back to the Norman conquest – of according jurisdiction over natural resources to the level of government that controlled the territory in which they were located. Hence, Section 109 of the BNA Act awarded ownership of land and resources to the provincial governments, while Sections 92(5) and 92(13) awarded provincial governments the exclusive right to legislate concerning the management and sale of public lands and resources and, more generally, 'property' within the province, including privately owned land and resources.[35]

The only significant exception to this rule concerned the fisheries, which, under Section 91(12), fell into exclusive federal jurisdiction. This exception, of course, befitted the nature of the ocean and anadromous fisheries, which transcended provincial boundaries and prevented the provinces from delimiting property relations. This was also in keeping with a second tenet of the BNA Act, which was to place interprovincial matters within federal jurisdiction – as occurred, for example, with interprovincial ferries and other forms of interprovincial transportation and communication. The fact that fisheries installations were private property and that some inland fisheries did not cross provincial boundaries, however, was not lost on the provinces, which quickly engaged the courts in upholding their rights in these areas. This resulted in the attenuation of the 'exclusive' federal power and the emergence of a complex jurisdictional situation in this area. At present, some activities (ocean fisheries) are exclusively federal, some are exclusively provincial (aquaculture), and some are joint (recreational fisheries).[36]

The terms of Confederation also gave the federal government the right to control resources on its lands. Although these lands were minor at the time of Confederation and restricted to Indian reserves, military installations, and the like, in 1869 they were greatly expanded by the purchase of Hudson's Bay Company lands by the federal government. British

2
The Socioeconomic Context: Canadian Resource Industries and the Postwar Canadian Political Economy

A political economic analysis of resource and environmental policy diverges from conventional approaches in several ways. In contrast to models that view state and economic institutions as inherently independent, for example, it explores the structural integration of economic and political forces and the alliance of these actors in the policy process. And it notes that the social and economic relations of production, as well as distributive processes, are factors shaping policy-making. The production and distribution of wealth at regional, national, and global levels are investigated as factors influencing the ways in which resource and environmental policy is made.

As discussed in Chapter 1, a political economic approach perceives environmental and resource policy as the product of the interplay of interests and ideas in the policy process. Interests are economic but also display social, technical, ideological, and, especially, political aspects. Relevant actors thus include governments and a variety of stakeholders representing different sectors and relations in the process of production. These actors have different ideological perspectives, cultural beliefs, and technological expertise, all of which enter into policy deliberations.

From this perspective, policy-making is seen as a dynamic process, subject to pressures by actors representing a spectrum of ideas and holding different stakes in the policy process and its outcomes over time. The potential for policy change, from a political economic perspective, is derived from shifts in these forces and relations of production. This chapter begins the analysis of the political economy of Canadian resource and environmental policy by identifying its fundamental economic, social, and political characteristics.

Understanding Canada's Resource-Dependent Political Economy

Central to the understanding of Canadian resource and environmental policy is an understanding of the operation of the Canadian economy. Its

Columbia, Prince Edward Island, and Newfoundland entered Confederation on much the same terms as the original provinces of Nova Scotia, New Brunswick, Quebec, and Ontario and consequently owned and controlled their resources. However, this was not the case with the three provinces carved out of the federally owned Northwest Territories. Manitoba, Saskatchewan, and Alberta did not receive jurisdiction over their land and resources until this power was conveyed to them by the federal government in 1930.[37] The federal government still retains jurisdiction over the land and resources of the remaining Yukon and Northwest Territories, although it has begun to transfer some responsibilities in these areas to the two territorial governments in recent years. This pattern is likely to continue in 1999 when the new territory of Nunavut is carved out of the existing Northwest Territories.

In addition, the federal government, citing international treaty obligations in the area of nuclear materials, invoked its little-used 'declaratory power' (Section 92[10c]) in 1945 to assume full responsibility for the control of uranium production and the nuclear industry.[38] The federal government was also the beneficiary of a 1967 Supreme Court of Canada decision that awarded the offshore regions to it and not to the provinces. As part of the 'Canada Lands,' resources located offshore – such as oil and gas but also including some significant mineral deposits – are the sole responsibility of the federal government.[39]

Exclusive federal powers in the areas of trade and commerce and wide-ranging powers in the area of taxation have also limited provincial constitutional supremacy in many resource matters.[40] Control over the natural resource industry has often been debated as a question of the provincial right of ownership versus the federal right to regulate trade and commerce, a right contained in Section 91(2) of the Constitution Act (1867). This has been the case because of the high percentage of Canadian natural resources destined for interprovincial or international markets. These resources elude provincial property-based jurisdiction and enter into the federal domain as soon as they cross provincial boundaries.[41]

In the area of taxation, the provincial governments have also had to defer to the more extensive federal powers in this area. Although provinces are granted the exclusive right under Section 109 to levy royalties on resources in their territories, these royalties relate only to the extraction stage of the natural resource production process. Revenues arising at later stages of the process can be appropriated by both levels of government. At this point, however, provincial governments were restricted under Section 92(2) to levying 'direct' taxes (that is, taxes paid directly to the government by the taxpayer), while the federal government's powers under Section 91(3) are unlimited.[42]

The result of this tangled constitutional situation prior to 1982 was for both levels of government to respect a slowly developed and court-regulated natural resource *modus vivendi* in which the hallmark of Canadian natural resource decision-making was provincially led intergovernmental collaboration.[43] This occurred first in bilateral dealings with the federal government and, since World War II, in multilateral forums such as the Canadian Council of Resource and Environmental Ministers (CCREM) and the Canadian Council of Forest Ministers (CCFM).[44]

The Division of Powers over Natural Resources and the Environment after 1982

In 1982, a major round of constitutional negotiations climaxed in the patriation of the BNA Act and the creation of the Constitution Act. The only change to the division of powers between the federal and provincial governments invoked at the time affected natural resources. This was the establishment of Section 92a of the Constitution Act, 1982.

The six clauses of Section 92a address all the main issues of Canadian natural resource constitutional politics since Confederation: federal/provincial jurisdiction and ownership, control over extraprovincial trade and commerce, and the division of taxation authority. First, Section 92a(1) provides an exclusive provincial right to legislate in the areas of non-renewable natural resource exploration, development, conservation, and management, including the generation of electrical energy. Section 92a(5) defines natural resources as those described in the Sixth Schedule to the Act, while Section 92a(6) assures that the new language will not be interpreted in such a manner as to restrict preexisting provincial legislative rights. Second, Section 92a(2) provides for an extension of provincial legislative jurisdiction to include interprovincial exports, subject to the caveat that 'such laws may not authorize or provide for discrimination in prices or in supplies exported to another part of Canada.' Provincial legislative authority is further limited by the establishment of federal paramountcy in Section 92a(3).[45] Third, Section 92a(4) establishes a provincial right to tax non-renewable natural resources, and electrical energy and facilities, by any mode of taxation whether or not these goods are exported from the province, but subject to the caveat that 'such laws may not authorize or provide for taxation that differentiates between production exported to another part of Canada and production not exported from the province.'[46]

The provisions of Section 92a reaffirm previous provincial powers, allow provinces to levy indirect taxation on natural resource revenues, and provide provincial legislatures with control over interprovincial resource and energy exports, subject to several non-discriminatory caveats and federal paramountcy.[47] In terms of resource regulation, the caveats contained in Section 92a(2) provide that a province may discriminate between products destined for intraprovincial markets and those destined for interprovincial trade, but the caveats insist that each province treat all extraprovincial Canadian markets equally. In terms of resource taxation, the caveats contained in Section 92a(4) prohibit discrimination between intraprovincial and interprovincial exports.

The most significant difference between the two sections, however, concerns provincial control over international exports. Provincial regulatory control over natural resource trade is explicitly limited by Section 92a(2) to that concerning the 'export from the province to another part of Canada.' The regulation of international trade hence remains an area of exclusive federal jurisdiction. Provincial taxation requirements, however, are not limited to those affecting exports to domestic markets. Instead, Section 92a(4) refers more generally to 'whether or not such production is exported in whole or in part from the province.'

Thus, Section 92a represents, in the convoluted fashion typical of Canadian constitutional debate, a significant rearrangement of the pre-1982 federal-provincial *modus vivendi*. It not only reaffirms provincial control over many important aspects of natural resource management but also, subject to several caveats protecting the national interest, gives the provincial governments additional powers in the areas of interprovincial regulation and resource taxation, which had previously formed part of the established federal jurisdiction.[48]

Subsequent rounds of constitutional talks in Canada have, of course, failed to alter the constitutional status quo. While discussions have focused on the possibility of the increased devolution of responsibility for the environment to the provincial level, this has not occurred.[49] Some aspects of federal powers have been undermined by court decisions, especially the effort by the federal government to impose its authority on the provinces in the area of water pollution under the purview of the Fisheries Act.[50] Other aspects of federal powers, however, including the ability to authorize environmental assessments in areas of provincial jurisdiction, have been strengthened.[51]

This situation has led to a patchwork response to environmental concerns by both levels of government in Canada.[52] Different aspects of environmental problems are dealt with by different levels of government in accordance with resource ownership and jurisdiction as initially laid out in 1867 and modified in 1982. While the federal government is able to deal with some problems that have a national scope, the most effective problem-solving is often accomplished through intergovernmental agreement rather than legislative dictates.[53]

Aboriginal Jurisdiction

Another significant element of the post-1982 Canadian constitutional situation relates to aboriginal rights to, and jurisdiction over, lands and resources.[54] Although the claims and rights of First Nations in Canada date back to the initial contacts with European colonizers and subsequent seventeenth, eighteenth, and nineteenth century treaties and administrative arrangements,[55] they began to receive explicit constitutional status binding the actions of Canadian governments only after 1982.[56]

Parallelling developments in Alaska and elsewhere,[57] in the 1960s Native groups began to challenge the restricted interpretations of Native rights contained in Canadian jurisprudence. These groups engaged in numerous activities – such as demonstrations, court challenges, and media campaigns – aimed at changing the political and administrative status quo.[58] A persistent lobbying effort in the following decade contributed to an improved climate for, and visibility of, Native concerns. In the early 1970s, Canada's aboriginal organizations managed to secure a place at the constitutional negotiating table as the federal government grappled with an unrelated crisis provoked by threats of Quebec's secession.

Although they were eventually left out of the eleventh-hour bargaining that resulted in the 1982 Canada Act and amendments to the Canadian constitution, Natives did secure several provisions in the new document entrenching existing treaties. They also secured a promise that the next round of constitutional discussions would focus entirely on their aspirations, which had come to be recognized as instances of collective identity and rights similar to those of Quebec.[59] While the promised aboriginal round ended in failure in 1987, it did serve to place Native demands for self-government high on political, public, and constitutional agendas.[60]

While First Nations may have failed at the constitutional negotiating table, they did manage to effectively use the courts to expand their control over many areas of life, including lands and resources. Beginning with the *Calder* decision in 1973, legal challenges by aboriginal organizations began to produce results as the Supreme Court of Canada affirmed the continued existence of aboriginal title even in areas in which that title had often been considered extinguished.[61] At about the same time, other courts began to grant injunctions against various projects slated for construction on lands subject to claims disputes, notably in the case of the massive James Bay hydroelectric project in northwestern Quebec.[62]

These actions ultimately resulted in the establishment of a new land claims policy by the federal government and the successful negotiation of six claims covering most of northern Canada and Quebec between 1974 and 1995, as well as the beginnings of negotiations over additional claims covering British Columbia, Labrador, and the remaining areas of the

Northwest Territories.[63] The successfully negotiated 'modern treaties' include two land claims in Quebec, three in the Northwest Territories, one in the Yukon, and a self-government arrangement in British Columbia.[64] Native claims, of course, have included not only these 'comprehensive claims' but also those covering Métis lands and smaller or 'specific claims' arising out of disputes over the implementation of existing treaties.[65]

By the late 1980s and early 1990s, court decisions clarifying the 1982 constitutional changes had come down in favour of a broad interpretation of aboriginal rights in many areas, especially rights to the fishery.[66] However, due to recurrent constitutional setbacks, the proposals made by First Nations for additional rights to self-government have not yet been successfully institutionalized. Discussions clarifying the nature of aboriginal self-government, rights, and title continue,[67] however, they have only resulted in some tentative steps toward implementation, and even these efforts came to a halt with the failure of the Canadian public to endorse the self-government provisions of the Charlottetown Accord on the Constitution in October 1992.[68]

The current situation concerning aboriginal land and resource jurisdiction is thus complex. In areas covered by treaties, First Nations control a variety of aspects of resource management, depending on the nature of the treaty involved. With treaties signed prior to the 1970s, Native peoples usually have complete control over land and resources on Indian reserves established by the federal government, although they are unable to alienate these lands except through an extremely cumbersome political-administrative process. Some bands, such as those located in parts of southern Alberta with substantial oil and gas reserves, do very well from the sale of resource rights – although, again, control over the expenditure of funds remains governed by complex arrangements between local bands and federal 'Indian' administrators.

Most reserves, however, are small and contain few resources; in most cases having been established in the nineteenth century with the potential for future Native agricultural pursuits in mind. One of the few resources accessible to bands on many reserves is the fishery, and a protracted court battle is under way in this area. To date, it has provided Native bands with a greater role in catches and fishery management, subject to government conservation measures and the need to establish, on a case-by-case basis, the existence of an aboriginal right to a commercial – as opposed to a food – fishery.[69]

For treaties signed after 1970, the situation is very different. Many of these treaties cover vast areas of land (especially in the Yukon and Northwest Territories) and are extremely dense and complex. Following loosely the precedents set by Native land settlements in Alaska, these agreements contain provisions concerning educational, political, social, and cultural life, as well as those relating to the economy and environment of the area covered by the treaty.[70]

Although each agreement is unique, the general tendency has been for the First Nations involved in each land claim to receive a small area of land for which they have all surface and subsurface rights. They have also received larger areas over which they may exercise only various specified surface and subsurface rights. Because most of these agreements have covered areas in Canada's far north, forestry issues have not received a great deal of attention (although this situation is bound to change as agreements are signed in British Columbia), and the most attention has been paid to mineral, oil, and gas rights and, especially, to hunting and trapping rights. In Quebec, issues related to hydroelectric generation have also been key.[71]

For the most part, First Nations have traded control over minerals, oil, gas, and hydroelectricity for financial compensation, recognition of aboriginal title, and protection of hunting and trapping rights.[72] Nevertheless, the manner in which hunting and trapping rights intersect with provisions governing resource project approvals – especially entrenched treaty rights related to habitat and environmental protection – has given aboriginal groups a major voice in many resource policy areas. Thus, Native groups may not actually control a mineral resource, for example, but they may control access to the resource across lands dedicated to hunting and trapping.[73]

Thus, although aboriginal jurisdiction remains a dynamic, evolving entity, in certain areas of the country covered by modern treaties, aboriginal groups play a major role in resource development and environmental protection. Traditional aboriginal pursuits such as hunting, trapping, and fishing have been defined by the courts or old treaties as Native rights. In these areas, First Nations can also play a major role regardless of the part of the country in which these pursuits are undertaken. Both federal and provincial governments in recent years have begun to take aboriginal concerns much more seriously than in the past and in these areas aboriginal rights and title act as significant constraints on government actions.[74] As we will see in Chapter 7, however, the extent of Native participation in areas not explicitly covered by land claims or aboriginal rights remains very limited.

Significant Federal and Provincial Environmental Legislation

While most resource and environmental laws and regulations are implemented under provincial authority, there are several federal acts currently of particular significance to environmental protection. As we have seen, federal regulatory activity is constitutionally 'limited to international and interprovincial contamination, federal lands and developments and controlling the import, manufacture, use and ultimate disposal of toxic substances.'[75] Federal legislation most significant in dealing with environmental issues includes the Canadian Environmental Protection Act (CEPA), the Canadian Environmental Assessment Act (CEAA), the Fisheries Act, the Canada Shipping Act, and the Transportation of Dangerous Goods Act.

The CEAA, passed in 1992, provides for the planning, monitoring, and evaluation of projects that have an environmental impact. The CEPA was proclaimed in 1988, and it governs activities under federal jurisdiction such as international or cross-border air pollution (e.g., acid rain), the dumping of substances into oceans and navigable waterways, and the regulation of toxic substances. The Fisheries Act pertains to fish habitat and its harmful alteration or destruction. This statute has been especially relevant to concerns with pulp mill and other water pollution. Other federal statutes that are sometimes relevant to environmental matters are included in Figure 3.1.

The Department of the Environment (DOE) has been the federal agency primarily responsible for environmental matters. It has administered elements of a number of statutes, including those derived from federal powers over fisheries, such as the Fisheries Act and the Fish Inspection Act, both used extensively to control water pollution, as well as newer statutes such as the Canada Water Act, the Clean Air Act, and the Environmental

Figure 3.1

Significant federal environmental legislation

Name of act	Governs (if unspecified)
Canadian Environmental Protection Act	International air pollution
	Ocean and waterways
	dumping
	Toxic substances
Canadian Environmental Assessment Act	
Fisheries Act	Protection of fish habitat
Canada Shipping Act	Shipping, fuel, ballast, cargo, pollution
Canada Water Act	
Transportation of Dangerous Goods Act	
Arctic Waters Pollution Prevention Act	
Navigable Waters Protection Act	
Migratory Birds Convention Act	
Atomic Energy Control Act	
Hazardous Products Act	
Pest Control Products Act	

Source: Statistics Canada, *Human Activity and the Environment,* Catalogue 11-509E (Ottawa: Ministry of Industry, Science and Technology 1991), 34-5.

Contaminants Act.[76] Other federal departments also administer statutes for environmental protection, primarily to regulate federally owned or administered lands or activities. The Department of Indian and Northern Affairs, for example, has administered the National Parks Act, while the Department of Transport has administered several statutes, including the Canada Shipping Act, the Railways Act, the Aeronautics Act, and the Navigable Waters Protection Act. The Department of Energy, Mines and Resources has been responsible for the independent Atomic Energy Control Board, which operates the Atomic Energy Control Act.[77]

While the establishment of Environment Canada anticipated its direct involvement in regulatory activity, the administration of regulatory standards set forth in federal legislation is, for the most part, in the constitutional domain of the provinces. Federal activity is geared to the establishment of policies and guidelines for provincial regulatory standards, the coordination of provincial activities, and scientific research.[78] Many different instruments are utilized to carry out these functions.

Various provincial and territorial statutes also deal with environmental protection, either directly or indirectly. This legislation has primarily focused on 'the environmental effects incidental to manufacturing, natural resource and economic development projects, and contamination of land within the province.'[79] Differences in statutory provision for environmental protection are reflected in Figure 3.2, which identifies the most significant statutes in the provinces.

International Agreements, Canada's Resources, and the Environment

Governments operate within the context of the international system of states. While the activities of domestic governments affect the nature of the international system, events and actions in the international system can also have a major impact on the activities of domestic states.[80] Foreign military or environmental crises are good examples of the links between national and international actors, but the interaction continues on a day-to-day basis because of treaties, understandings, and commitments made by states to various international organizations.[81]

The nature of international agreements in the resource and environmental policy area is of significance, because they can restrict the choices of governments on policy issues.[82] Once again, these agreements tend to reflect the Canadian interest in resource exploitation rather than environmental protection per se, although this emphasis has been changing in recent years.

Figure 3.2

Significant provincial statutes governing environmental protection

Jurisdiction	Act
Newfoundland	Department of Environment Act
Nova Scotia	Environmental Protection Act
	Water Act
	Dangerous Goods Transportation Act
	Beverage Containers Act
Prince Edward Island	Environmental Protection Act
New Brunswick	Clean Environment Act
Quebec	Environment Quality Act
Ontario	Environmental Protection Act
	Ontario Water Resources Act
Manitoba	Environment Act
Saskatchewan	Environmental Management and Protection Act
Alberta	Clean Air Act
	Clean Water Act
	Environmental Protection and Enhancement Act
British Columbia	Waste Management Act
	Environment Management Act
	Health Act
	Pesticide Control Act
	Litter Act
Yukon and	Area Development Act
Northwest Territories	Northern Inland Waters Act

Source: Roger Cotton and Kelley M. MacKinnon, 'An Overview of Environmental Law in Canada,' in G. Thompson, M.L. McConnell, and L.B. Huestis, eds., *Environmental Law and Business in Canada* (Aurora, ON: Canada Law Book 1993), 8-11.

International Trade Agreements: From Empire to NAFTA

Great Britain's move toward free trade through the repeal of the Corn Laws in 1846, with its inadvertent effect of terminating the Canadian producers' preferred access to the British market, can be seen as the beginning of Canada's efforts to develop its own resource trade policy. The British action signified that Canada's interests were no longer a factor in the mother country's trade policies. Consequently, the five colonies forming British North America signed the Reciprocity Treaty with the United States in 1854, offering preferred access to each other's markets. The treaty was terminated in 1866 at the request of the American government. The reasons for its abrogation included Canada's huge trade surplus, pressures from US interests that were adversely affected by Canadian exports, and Britain's support for the South in the American Civil War, which caused much resentment in the eventually victorious North.[83]

The end of the treaty led Canadian policymakers to search for alternative means of establishing access to a large market for Canadian producers, one of the results of which was Confederation in 1867. At the same time, the newly established Canadian government continued to pursue another reciprocity agreement with the United States, but to no avail. Frustrated with the American government's lack of interest in negotiating a trade deal, the Canadian government under Macdonald announced the National Policy in 1879, the cornerstone of which was a drastic increase in tariffs on imports.

One reason for this measure was to exert pressure on the American government to negotiate reciprocal reductions in tariffs. Another was to foster industrial development by protecting Canadian 'infant industries' from imports and by encouraging foreign manufacturers to establish plants in Canada in order to avoid tariffs. The second goal was largely accomplished, as many manufacturing plants, both Canadian and foreign (mostly American), were established toward the end of the century. However, the goal of negotiating reciprocity with the United States remained as elusive as ever. Nonetheless, the efforts continued, covertly by the Conservatives and overtly by the Liberals. The 1879 offer of preferential access to imports from Britain remained similarly unreciprocated by the British government.[84]

The goal of a free trade agreement with the United States was almost reached in 1911, when the Liberal government under Laurier announced that it had reached an agreement to reduce tariffs on a reciprocal basis on a range of natural products and some manufactured products. It was clearly designed to support western and eastern agricultural and primary producers, while only marginally reducing the protection afforded central Canadian manufacturers. But 1911 was an election year, and the Conservatives, in cohort with business and labour in the manufacturing sector and with staunchly anti-American British loyalists, mounted a bitter campaign that ended in a humiliating defeat for the Liberal Party. The lesson from the election was not lost on either main party, and neither dared raise the topic for several decades.[85]

The anti-American, pro-British sentiments that marked the 1911 election were out of tune with the time, however, for the United States was rapidly emerging as the world's foremost military and economic power. Despite the rejection of the free trade deal, Canada's trade with the United States continued to expand, and increasingly large amounts of American capital poured into the country. Canada was on the march toward closer integration with the US economy, punctuated only by the Great Depression in the 1930s. In 1935, the two nations signed an agreement to lower their tariffs substantially; this was the first trade pact between the two neighbours since 1854. It was followed by further attempts to reduce tariffs, and in 1938 an agreement was reached between the United States,

Great Britain, Australia, New Zealand, and South Africa to provide easy access for each other's goods. The process of multilateral reductions in trade barriers had begun, and it gained momentum after World War II.

The United States emerged from the war as clearly the dominant technological, economic, and military power in the world. It was in its interest to organize an open world trading order, and this goal was supported by Canada, which also emerged from the war as a beneficiary of increased world trade. The American efforts led to the negotiation and signing of the General Agreement on Tariffs and Trade (GATT) between twenty-three nations in 1947. This agreement, which has expanded considerably in both membership and scope since its inception, still forms the basis for trade between the non-Communist nations.[86]

The postwar international economic order has been characterized by *multilateralism*, a principle fully supported by Canada. Canadian leaders, aware of the nation's high degree of trade dependence, have recognized that a multilateral arrangement provides the best guarantee against protectionism and the economic and diplomatic powers of the larger nations. This guarantee explains the active Canadian participation in all the rounds of GATT negotiations and its support for other international institutions such as the World Trade Organization (WTO), created to succeed GATT following the Uruguay round of trade talks.

While Canada's commitment to multilateralism is beyond doubt, in practical terms the multilateral framework has worked mainly toward expanding Canadian trade with the United States.[87] The purpose of GATT/WTO is to promote a liberal international economic order based on the principle of comparative advantage. The organization establishes reciprocal rights and obligations among its members to reduce barriers to international trade, and it offers exporters opportunities to sell in the markets of member nations. But it also imposes an obligation not to erect barriers to imports, except under special circumstances provided for in the agreement. This obligation has been problematic for Canada, which, as we have seen, has wanted to reduce foreign barriers to its exports while maintaining its own barriers to imports of manufactured goods.[88]

Since the establishment of GATT, the value of world trade has increased more than six times. During this period, the growth in exports has been higher than the rate of economic growth in most developed and developing nations. While GATT cannot be credited with all the expansion in international trade, it certainly played a key role in facilitating the expansion.

GATT was critical in promoting international trade and increasing the economic prosperity of trade-dependent nations such as Canada, but by the 1980s there were justified fears about its future. For one thing, its membership had increased fourfold since its inception, making multilateral negotiations difficult because of the wider variety of interests that had to be accommodated. Moreover, there was no nation that could act as the United States did between the 1940s and the 1960s to prod negotiations and enforce discipline. In fact, a gigantic trade deficit had made protectionism politically popular in the United States even though it was the architect of GATT and the modern liberal trading order. The European Community's preoccupation with integration in Western Europe and its disregard for the interests of the nations outside the region also did not bode well for the future of GATT.

The fear that GATT might not be as effective in the future as it was in the past had led many countries to look for alternatives. After the Uruguay round, GATT was restructured, emerging as the WTO. But Canada had already shifted its focus toward solidifying and furthering its already relatively open trade relations with the United States. The Mulroney government, soon after its election in 1984, declared its intention to pursue free trade with the United States. The agreement was reached in October 1987 and came into effect on 1 January 1989.[89]

The Canada-US Free Trade Agreement (CAFTA) signified the *de facto* recognition of Canada's special trade relations with the United States, which had existed for almost a century, and reflected a sense of resignation among policymakers that it is not possible to utilize state actions to diversify Canada's trade relations to any substantial degree from the pattern imposed by the international marketplace. In 1992, this agreement was extended to Mexico in the North American Free Trade Agreement (NAFTA).[90] Talks are under way to extend membership to Latin American nations in a new Free Trade of the Americas (AFTA) agreement, while other talks have centred on the creation of a new free trade area in the Pacific Rim under the aegis of the Asia-Pacific Economic Council (APEC).[91]

The free trade agreements have affected many areas of Canadian resource policy, although their effects on environmental policy-making have been less significant.[92] The provisions regarding the energy sector, in particular, have been some of the most far-reaching and contentious in Canada. Energy production is undoubtedly a vital sector in the Canadian economy: about 14 per cent of total Canadian investment is in this sector, which accounts for about 10 per cent of total Canadian exports.[93] The United States is the world's largest consumer and importer, as well as producer, of energy, and Canada is currently its largest foreign supplier. Many of the Trudeau government's measures to Canadianize the sector under the terms of the National Energy Program (NEP) were a major irritant to the United States, and it is doubtful whether the American government would have signed the FTA without an assurance that such measures would not be repeated.

The energy sector as defined in the agreements includes oil, natural gas, light petroleum gas, coal, uranium, and electricity. The FTAs eliminate almost all barriers to trade in these commodities. The agreements explicitly prohibit measures that make export prices higher than domestic prices, measures such as the export tax imposed under the NEP by the Trudeau government. Moreover, the agreements, while not prohibiting restrictions on the amount of energy exports to the United States in times of shortage, require that Canada permit American importers to purchase an amount no smaller than that used in the past thirty-six-month period. The US interest in insisting on this provision was to secure a guarantee that in times of shortage the Canadian government will introduce cuts that will affect consumers on both sides of the border equally. While this provision is in keeping with those implicit in GATT (Article 20) and with Canada's obligations under the International Energy Agreement pertaining to oil, the FTAs go further by explicitly specifying the proportion of supplies to be shared. Critics allege that, insofar as the Canadian government cannot reduce supplies to American consumers in times of shortage without hurting Canadian consumers as well, this is a serious erosion of Canada's sovereignty.

International Environmental Organizations and Structures

The GATT/WTO and CAFTA/NAFTA treaties are probably the most significant international commitments made by Canadian governments in the resource policy area.[94] While most of these treaties deal only indirectly with the environment, Canada does participate, with the United States and Mexico, in the (North American) Commission on Environmental Cooperation (CEC), an organization set up to mitigate the environmental aspects of North American free trade through the North American Agreement on Environmental Cooperation (NAAEC). Canada has specific exemptions from several practices of the NAAEC because of its federal structure, which exempts the provinces unless they choose to participate.[95]

Other international organizations and treaties have had a more direct impact on Canadian environmental policy-making.[96] Canada participates in all major international organizations with an environmental focus and has taken a lead role in the major international organization devoted to the environment, the United Nations Environmental Program (UNEP), which originated at a conference led by a Canadian and which has been headed by Canadians.[97]

In addition, Canada belongs to the World Bank, which, along with the International Monetary Fund (IMF), plays a major role in financing industrial development in many countries, and is a member of organizations such as the Organization for Economic Cooperation and Development (OECD) and the G-7, which can affect the environment through their role in establishing international investment patterns and activities.[98] Canada is also a member of international organizations such as the World Meteorological Organization (WMO), the International Maritime Organization (IMO), the International Union for Conservation of Nature and Natural Resources (IUCN), and the World Health Organization (WHO), which also deal with environmental concerns in the course of their activities.[99]

Canada is a major participant in the international environmental regime and is a signatory to treaties such as the Rio Declaration on Bio-Diversity, the Montreal and Helsinki Protocols on Ozone Depletion, and the Agenda 21 proposals for environmental action into the next century.[100] Other major international agreements include the United Nations Economic Commission for Europe-sponsored Convention on Long Range Transboundary Air Pollution (LTRAP); protocols on sulphur emissions, nitrogen oxides, and volatile organic compounds; the United Nations Framework Convention on Climate Change; the UNESCO Convention for the Protection of the World Cultural and Natural Heritage; the UNESCO Convention on International Trade in Endangered Species of Wild Fauna and Flora; the Basel Convention on the Control of Transboundary Movements of Hazardous Wastes and Their Disposal; and the International Convention for the Prevention of Pollution of the Sea by Oil. Major bilateral agreements with the United States also cover areas such as air quality and acid rain, migratory birds and caribou, the Great Lakes, and waterfowl management.[101]

All of these treaties and agreements commit the governments of Canada to observing certain rules and principles of conduct. In its own way, each establishes minimum standards for national conduct and, with beneficial intent, limits the options open to governments in addressing domestic policy issues.[102]

Conclusion: Institutional Constraints on Government Action

Just as resource and environmental policy-making is affected by the socio-economic context in which it occurs, so it is affected by the broad institutional context of government. How a country fits into the international system of states, and the dynamics of this international system, influence both domestic and international policies. The ways in which the political institutions of a country are constructed, and the shifts in the powers of central and local governments relative to one another, are also significant components of the context of public policy-making. Furthermore, the powers of government(s) relative to those of the private sector must be considered, especially in an era when transnational corporations exert such extensive influence on domestic politics.

The aspect of Canada's position in the international system of states that is most significant for resource and environmental policy-making is the open nature of its resource-based economy. Canada is one of the most trade-dependent nations in the world, and its high degree of trade dependence, coupled with its small population compared with some other nations, makes it very vulnerable to international pressures. The types of goods produced and the prices at which they are sold are determined by international market forces, which diminish Canada's capacity to control its political economy. As such, the international arena imposes an enduring constraint on Canada. The country has, as a result, negotiated a series of treaties and participated in the creation of a series of institutions designed to minimize uncertainty stemming from international conditions. Likewise, Canada has participated in a series of environmental treaties and arrangements, although they do not have the same singularity of purpose and the broad scope of trade arrangements.

On the domestic front, the most important aspect of Canada's institutional structure is its federal nature, which has resulted in the situation whereby more than a dozen senior governments make resource and environmental policy in this country. Environmental considerations per se were not dealt with in the British North America Act and remain the subject of divided authority and complex jurisdictional debate. Although the nature of Canadian federalism has changed over the years, the original division of powers set out in 1867 has largely been retained. Resources were originally divided between the provinces and the federal government on the basis of land ownership. As the federal land base has decreased over the years, so too has the federal government's ability to affect resource policy-making. The progressive decentralization of powers, the privatization of many previously public functions, and increasing funding constraints all exert pressures on government regulatory capacity. Conversely, areas of the country under the jurisdiction of aboriginal land claims have grown, as has the role of aboriginal organizations in land, resource, and environmental policy-making.

As the discussion in Chapter 8 emphasizes, this governing arrangement has some significant disadvantages for Canadian resource and environmental policy-making. Probably the most significant disadvantage is the need for intergovernmental cooperation for the most crucial policy provisions. Agreement is not always forthcoming, and cross-sectoral intergovernmental bargaining, more often than not, loses sight of fundamental environmental objectives. This process can also be time-consuming and subject to innumerable delays as a result of elections and other political events in Canada's thirteen (and soon to be fourteen) major jurisdictions.[103]

Part 3:
Analyzing Natural Resource and Environmental Policy

This part sets out several of the key concepts utilized in the study of resource and environmental policy-making. It discusses, in general terms, the nature of the actors who collectively contribute to Canadian resource and environmental policy-making, and it outlines several methods to capture the manner in which the ideas and interests expressed by these actors are incorporated into the policy-making process. It also critically surveys several frameworks that have been used to assess the key factors motivating these actors. From this review of policy actors, interests, and models, it argues that a staged, sequential, and iterative model of the policy process best captures the dynamics of public policy-making in this sector.

4
Policy Actors: Resource and Environmental Policy Subsystems

Identifying the contexts within which governments operate is only the first step in understanding policy development and change. Before a systematic analysis of the policy process can be undertaken, it is necessary to identify exactly who makes public policy. That is, who are the key actors whose activities should be analyzed and assessed? Are all resource and environmental interests represented by policy actors? Do they all have similar access to the policy process?

Democratic political systems are usually thought to represent and be accountable to their citizens. Accordingly, the development of Canadian resource and environmental policy is often thought to be generated, although indirectly, by the public, whose elected representatives are responsible for initiating appropriate government action. Such systems are thought to be additionally and directly driven to action by processes such as lobbying, public education, and media campaigns, all of which further encourage the development of policy.

Yet while public involvement does occur in many aspects of Canadian resource and environmental policy, many would criticize this model of democratic politics and policy-making as unduly idealistic. The lack of accountability of elected officials, the complexity of issues and processes, and the differential access to financial and technical resources enjoyed by competitive interests are just some of the barriers that discourage effective public involvement. Indeed, the diffuse and discretionary character of much of what is perceived as 'public' involvement counters the notion of an active public embodying a civic culture. The institutional and economic advantage of actors with productive interests in resource activities typically exceeds that of those representing non-productive interests. This imbalance curtails the opportunities for, and the effectiveness of, public involvement in the resource and environmental policy process.

These criticisms reveal the need to analyze Canadian resource and environmental policy-making in a more critical and systematic fashion. As will be discussed below, a significant component of such analysis revolves around the notion of a *policy subsystem*, which is comprised of a group of actors bound together by some combination of material interests and policy ideas. It plays a significant role in determining the content and context of sectoral policy decisions. The membership of policy subsystems, the degree to which they are accessible to other actors, and their internal dynamics have considerable impact on the policies to be developed.

How does the composition of policy actors influence decisions made in resource and environmental policy? In this chapter, we will set out, in general terms, the range of actors in the policy process and examine the character of their involvement. In Chapter 7, the specific configuration of actors in the Canadian natural resource and environmental policy subsystem is examined.

Policy Subsystems, Policy Communities, and Policy Networks

The membership and dynamics of the policy subsystem have long attracted the attention of students of public policy-making. Identifying who the key actors in public policy-making are, what brings them together, how they interact, and what effect their interaction has on policy are the key objectives in this tradition. Scholars have developed a variety of models to address these questions.[1] A useful way to think about this issue relates to the idea of various policy subsystems working within the overall political system, processing policy issues in parallel form in order to ease the informational and decisional load placed upon the central institutions of democratic government.[2] In this context, the resource and environmental subsystem refers to actors involved in, and impacted by, governmental decision-making in this sector.

Let us consider some of the ways in which subsystems have been conceptualized before discussing them within the context of resource and environmental policy-making (see Chapters 6 and 7). Doing so will allow us to identify the primary characteristics of policy subsystems and to ascertain to what degree the public or any other actor is active in the resource and environmental policy subsystem. Discussion of different models of the policy subsystem will help establish a framework to which we can apply a political economic analysis and will become the basis for explaining our empirical observations on resource and environmental policy-making in Canada.

Empirical research into the nature of these policy subsystems has led to ever more precise specification of their contents and activities. The general trend in this research has been to displace an early emphasis on direct connections between subsystem members in relatively permanent and stable exchange networks. Rather, there has been increasing agreement that many subsystems operate in a much more dispersed and dynamic manner and that the bonds of ideas as well as those of material interests are critical to the forging of a subsystem. A brief review of the evolution of the concept will demonstrate this development.

The oldest conception of a policy subsystem involved the notion of a 'subgovernment' consisting of groups of societal and state actors in routine patterns of interaction.[3] This concept was developed in the United States in the 1950s based on the observation that interest groups, congressional committees, and government agencies there had developed a system of mutual support in the course of constant interaction over legislative and regulatory matters. These three-sided relationships in areas such as agriculture, transportation, and education were often dubbed 'iron triangles' because of their iron-clad control over many aspects of the policy process.[4] These groups were condemned by many observers for having 'captured' the policy process, that is, subverting the principles of popular democracy by ensuring that their own interests prevailed over those of the general public.[5]

Further research into the American case in the 1960s and 1970s, however, revealed that these subgovernments were not all-powerful and that, in fact, their influence on policy-making varied across issues and over time.[6] Soon a more flexible notion of the policy subsystem evolved, called the *issue network*.[7]

Building on his earlier work on social policies in Britain and Sweden,[8] Hugh Heclo argued that, while some areas of political life were organized in a heavily institutionalized system of interest representation, others were less so. As he put it, 'Preoccupied with trying to find the few truly powerful actors, observers tend to overlook the power and influence that arise out of the configurations through which leading policy makers move and do business with each other. Looking for the closed triangles of control, we tend to miss the fairly open networks of people that increasingly impinge upon government.'[9] Heclo conceptualized policy subsystems as a spectrum, with iron triangles at one end and issue networks at the other. He explained the differences between iron triangles and issue networks in the following way:

> The notion of iron triangles and subgovernments presumes small circles of participants who have succeeded in becoming largely autonomous. Issue networks, on the other hand, comprise a large number of participants with quite variable degrees of mutual commitment or dependence on others in their environment; in fact it is almost impossible to say where a network leaves off and its environment begins. Iron triangles and subgovernments suggest a stable set of participants coalesced to control fairly narrow public programs which are in the direct economic interest of

each party to the alliance. Issue networks are almost the reverse image in each respect. Participants move in and out of the networks constantly. Rather than groups united in dominance over a program, no one, as far as one can tell, is in control of the policies and issues. Any direct material interest is often secondary to intellectual or emotional commitment.[10]

Issue networks were thus much less stable, had a constant turnover of participants, and were much less institutionalized than iron triangles.[11]

The notion of a range of policy subsystems is useful for policy analysis because it provides a tool for classifying the different sets of actors present in policy-making as well as the nature of their interactions. However, in itself, this concept fails to deal with the realities of the roles played by political power and specialized technical knowledge in the policy process. That is, while belief systems and ideas may determine what policies subsystem members will seek to have adopted, the ability of actors to succeed in this endeavour is affected by resources such as 'money, expertise, number of supporters, and legal authority.'[12] The 'public,' for example, has neither the direct power over jobs and resources enjoyed by business nor the direct control over technical knowledge enjoyed by government officials. Any conception of the actual workings of policy subsystems must take into account the advantages enjoyed by business and government in the policy process of modern liberal governments.

In recent years, the idea has developed that policy subsystems can usefully be divided into two components to understand the unequal resources enjoyed by different actors in the policy process of democratic states. In one component, actors are bound together by common material interests that lead to significant ongoing interaction within a general framework of policy ideas. In the second, the material interests promoting regular contact may be lacking, but common policy knowledge continues to create a subset of significant policy actors.

The first subset of actors is usually referred to as a *policy network*. In his comparative study of foreign economic policy, Peter Katzenstein referred to policy networks as those links that join the state and societal actors in the policy process,[13] while in Britain R.A.W. Rhodes argued throughout the early 1980s that interaction between various departments and branches of the government and between the government and other organizations in society constitute policy networks that are instrumental in formulating policy.[14] Rhodes argued that networks vary according to their level of 'integration,' which is a function of their stability of membership, restrictiveness of membership, degree of insulation from other networks and the public, and the nature of the resources that they control.[15] Similar attributes were specified in the United States by Keith E. Hamm, who argued that subgovernments could be differentiated according to their 'internal complexity, functional autonomy, and (levels of internal and external) cooperation or conflict.'[16]

All of these conceptions envisioned policy networks as being essentially interest based: that is, participants were assumed to enter these networks in order to further their own ends, which were seen as essentially material and 'objectively recognizable' from outside the network. In the context of resource use, for instance, a policy network dealing with the fishery would include representation from the Department of Fisheries and Oceans; provincial governments; commercial, Native, and sports fishers; the United Fisheries and Allied Workers Union; and the processing industry. It is this emphasis on common material interests that sets policy networks apart from 'policy communities,' which might include the more diffuse interests of environmentalists, other government agencies, consumers, and others.

Stephen Wilks and Maurice Wright defined a 'policy community' as including all those involved in policy formulation, and they restricted the term 'policy network' to a subset of community members who interact with each other in the exchange of interests. In their view, 'policy community identifies those actors and potential actors drawn from the policy universe who share a common policy focus. Network is the linking process within a policy community or between two or more communities.'[17] Within the context of pulp mill regulation, for example, the policy community might include both productive and non-productive interests: pulp and paper manufacturers, fishery representatives, labour, health officials, representatives from all levels of government, First Nations, the media, academics, local residents, and environmentalists among others. The network, in comparison, would include those who more routinely interact in the formation and implementation of policy. Networks are more restrictive and enjoy a more direct pipeline to the policy process.

This conceptual distinction has proved useful in subsequent studies.[18] Its main advantage lies in the manner in which it integrates two different levels of motivations guiding the actions of those involved in policy formulation: the policy community holding knowledge of, or expertise in, an issue and the policy network, subset of the larger community, which holds a material interest.[19] Thus, two different aspects of the process of policy formulation come into sharper focus.[20]

Membership in Policy Subsystems

While subsystem membership is expected to vary across policy issues and sectors and over time, it is possible to outline a basic inventory of policy actors from whose ranks members of specific subsystems will be chosen. At their most general level, policy actors and potential subsystem members in democratic polities can be divided according to their location inside or outside political institutions. That is, some will be state actors, while others will be societal actors. Such a distinction, of course, overemphasizes the boundaries between state and society, boundaries that are much more permeable than this conceptual division would allow. This distinction may also obscure the complexity and character of relations within these categories, especially the latter. Yet this division is useful as a basis for assessing the degree to which actors external to the state are capable of influencing policy-making.

Societal Actors: Public and Productive Interests

A variety of potential subsystem members exist outside state institutions. They generally fall into two types: those representing aspects of the 'public' interest in the successful production and reproduction of society, and those representing interests directly tied to the production of specific goods and services in society ('productive' interests).

Public Interests

Various policy actors directly represent the public in the policy-making process. For our purposes in this text, we will use 'the public' to mean non-state actors who do not represent productive interests. In this context, the public becomes an inclusive term, used by a variety of actors to represent a spectrum of interests. In the most general sense, the public is an amorphous and passive entity whose pulse is measured by attitudinal surveys. But the public also has the capability to mobilize itself to act on issues of collective concern. Public interest organizations represent non-productive interests, including – in the resource and environmental context – health, recreational, community, gender, First Nations, environmental, and educational concerns. As we will discuss in Chapter 6, even industry may take on the guise of a public interest actor as a means of extending or constructing its political representation beyond traditional lobby groups.

Typically, the diffuse public is viewed as a barometer of the overall political process, while organized public groups direct pressure to certain policy objectives. However, individual citizens can express their concerns and opinions to governments through a variety of procedures that facilitate and supplement established political and policy processes. These procedures include public opinion polls, a host of other survey instruments, public and media education, and the lobbying of elected representatives through party politics.

Public opinion polls are a source through which elected MPs, bureaucrats, and others can assess the political 'pulse' of the country. Public opinion surveys are mechanisms through which the views of the electorate are assessed, directing elected representatives to appropriate action and political parties to the articulation of policy that will reflect popular sentiment. By themselves, of course, surveys are not policy actors, but they generate information that can be used by actors, whether they represent government, productive, or other interests. Polls are relatively easy to administer and provide a cost-effective and immediate means of assessing the political and environmental pulse of the citizenry. They may also be used as marketing or public relations instruments by the private sector. They are a way of finding out if, what, and how members of the public view environmental issues.

Interest in public perceptions of environmental concerns has increased in the postwar years, accompanying increased public knowledge about environmental issues, the participatory fervour of the 1960s, and growing criticisms of science. It should be noted, however, that observers are divided in their assessment of the increase in public environmental awareness. Some point to survey evidence indicating a growing public awareness of environmental degradation accompanied by an increasing and durable public concern. Others see awareness and concern as more sporadic and anomalous, often accompanying a specific event such as a chemical spill.[21]

Even if the public indicates a strong degree of environmental concern, it does not necessarily act accordingly, because other factors – such as traditional voting allegiance, media coverage, and personalities – may intervene. As one British analyst observed, 'Unless God opens an ozone hole directly above the place of Westminster, or melts the polar ice-cap just enough to bring the Thames lapping round the chair-legs in the Members' Bar, "Green" issues will never rank with the central concerns of British politics.'[22] Just as attitudes and actions are distinct and often contradictory in everyday life, so they are in attitudinal assessments.

The media play a more active role both influencing and reflecting public opinion. They influence the formation of policy by generating public concern and thereby political pressure, thus encouraging political actors to take action on a particular issue.[23] Media coverage not only raises public perceptions and concerns about environmental issues but also constructs the issues by defining them as economic or political, social or personal, radical or conservative. What gets reported, how it gets reported, who does the reporting, and the medium of the reporting all have implications for the message to the public.[24] The lack of media coverage allocated to environmental events, the negative portrayal of environmentalists and issues, and the corporate bias in environmental coverage have been experienced by many environmental groups. Journalists also encounter constraints in resources, time, space, management support, and the 'traditional practices and economic interests of their employers,' which act to the detriment of their ambition to cover many environmental issues.[25]

According to most views of the resource and environmental policy process, public concerns regarding specific environmental issues are both expressed and shaped through the media, resulting in appropriate action by elected delegates and political parties. Yet while the public's concern with resource and environmental issues has risen and fallen, these social indicators may be correlated only generally with the rise and fall in legislative efforts to enhance environmental protection. They are only one factor in the formation of the policy agenda.[26]

There are several additional constraints to the media's role in the policy process. Many chronic issues remain unnoticed or undeveloped by the media and not yet identified as critical by scientific research. Media bias on behalf of productive interests has resulted in inadequate coverage or presentation of issues and fewer resources allocated to coverage. Furthermore, the media is an often erratic barometer of public opinion and does not necessarily reflect the ability to sustain momentum toward political change. Moreover, even when concern is registered by the public, there is no guarantee that appropriate action will be taken by governments. Thus, while the media may be treated as a motivating force in the policy process, they may also be ineffective in resource and environmental policy formulation.[27] They remain members of policy communities but not of policy networks.

Political parties comprise another vehicle that shapes public opinion. But they are also vehicles for the election of leaders and governments, and often they play only a minor role in specific policy issues. They are a means through which opposing views can compete to attain political power through the electoral system. Parties articulate political platforms, and candidates for political office are elected largely on the basis of their party affiliation. In parliamentary systems like Canada's, the party that has received the majority of seats becomes the party in power, and its leader becomes the prime minister. The party receiving the next highest number of seats becomes the official opposition.

When a strong majority is held by one political party, it is easier to enact proposed legislation and thus to make the decisions espoused by the leading party. With a smaller majority, it is more difficult to implement decisions. Thus, parties can play a significant role in the policy-making process, both in the design and articulation of policy and in the implementation of that policy through the decision-making process. But the influence of political parties on decision-making is much more than a 'numbers game' of adding votes or seats in Parliament. The substance of party policy reflects the accommodation of numerous factors on any issue, such as the pressures of competing lobbies, the maximization of political gains, public accountability, the tradition of existing policy measures, prospects of reelection, the position of the official opposition, and differences between party members themselves. Party members must negotiate their way through these varied and competing factors to articulate policy in the form of campaign promises. When in power, they must continually negotiate both internally and with other politicians and lobby groups to pass and enact legislation. Sometimes decisions are made by inactivity, by the failure to implement a law or to revise a statute.

While political parties can provide access to the corridors of power or to the locus of public policy decision-making, they are less than directly responsive to the public, a factor that becomes especially important in environmental protection. As Vaughan Lyon observes, the representative character of electoral politics and the party system were established 'in an era when the commitment to democratic values was relatively weak, populations were more deferential ... and demands on government modest.'[28] Thus, while parties have evolved to represent competing political perspectives, they do not provide a means for representing all emerging views on a public issue. The unwillingness of political parties to incorporate new environmental perspectives into their proposals for legislation and government, for example, reflects not only the political and economic agendas of specific parties but also larger institutional constraints related to the operation of parliamentary democratic governments.

This discussion shows that the means and actors that exist to directly represent the public interest in policy-making are limited in their ability to do so. Political parties and the media exist on the outskirts of the policy process, exerting little direct influence on the policy network. The indirect representation of the public through various organizations that serve to aggregate and articulate public sentiments has the potential to be a more salient force in policy-making. These organizations include interest groups, pressure groups, and peak associations of various kinds, many of which form the backbone of sectoral policy networks.

Members of the public organize pressure groups to influence the political agenda of a government. Strategies of pressure groups include the lobbying of elected political representatives, educational campaigns geared to influence politicians as well as the general public, protests, and 'direct action' through which members may engage in non-sanctioned activities. Some groups are directed toward general objectives, while others are formed in response to specific issues or conditions. Some are short term and issue specific; others are active for decades. Fund-raising mechanisms differ between groups, as do leadership and procedural questions, strategies, and objectives.

In the resource and environmental policy sector, environmental groups can mobilize and organize support outside the political arena and then pressure existing political forces to work toward enhanced environmental protection. Such groups have been especially successful in their educational activities. Many groups form links with other groups to address issues with large-scale impacts. In the United States, for example, CATS, Citizens Against Toxic Sprays, has been successful in recent decades in opposing pesticide use. A Canadian success story is that of The Pulp Pollution Campaign in Vancouver, which was mobilized in the late 1980s by the West Coast Environmental Law Foundation and other groups. It included a wide range of over fifty environmental and other public interest groups, and its public education and lobbying efforts have been effective in pressuring government to tighten pulp pollution regulations in British Columbia.

Environmental non-government organizations, or ENGOs, have several advantages in resource and environmental policy-making that are not enjoyed by other indirect means of representing the public interest. The use of the media in expanding a base of public support is one example. The strategic use of the media by Greenpeace in efforts to stop the sealing industry and to remove nuclear submarines from Canadian waters, for instance, has been especially effective in mobilizing public support. Smaller, issue-specific groups are able to manoeuvre well in anticipation of, and response to, industry edicts and government proclamations. The often local or grassroots composition of environmental groups carries a political message to both politicians and project proponents.

Yet environmental organizations, while representing a means by which the public can initiate and influence the policy process, are also limited by a number of factors. While pressure groups have increasingly gained access to policy networks in Canada in recent years, the uncertainty of funding, the temporary and issue-specific nature of many groups, and their organizational instability restrict their success in dealing with other network actors. Struggles between and within ENGOs have also dissipated activists' morale and energy, while public support may ebb and flow in response to a variety of socioeconomic factors.

Rather than playing a proactive role in the policy process, public interest groups are in practice typically reactive, responding to specific projects or problems. Furthermore, the consequences of their activities are rarely clear. While these activities have symbolic and educational value, the ability of groups to penetrate the corridors of political power and to have a voice in policy formation or decision-making remains limited.[29]

Productive Interests

A second set of societal actors is motivated to participate in policy-making, usually by having a direct material interest in state activities in a particular sector. This is true of most areas of economic life in which productive interests and actors exist. The end of all commodity production is ultimately the satisfaction of human needs and desires, and in a market economy this activity will only be undertaken if it generates a return to the producer that is above the costs of production. In most manufacturing and service activities, a division of surplus is made between the profits that accrue to the owners of capital and the wages that are earned by the owners of labour.

The economics and politics of the natural resource sector, however, are different from those found in most other areas of human productive activity because there are three, rather than two, general categories of interests involved in the process of the creation of commodities and in the distribution of surplus from such production. When a surplus is generated from resource extraction and production, it goes to 'landowners' (in Canada, those agencies that issue mineral, oil, or timber rights or fishery or trapping licences) in the form of 'rents' as well as (if they are separate actors) to those whose equipment and labour are utilized in extracting the resource.[30] So the interests of capital in maximizing profit, of labour in securing and enhancing wages and employment, and of landowners in collecting rents are contested and negotiated in the policy process.

This important distinction helps us to establish the nature of productive interests in the natural resource area. That is, the fundamental productive interests involved in the natural resource sector have their origins in the creation of surplus from natural resource production and will tend to conflict with each other over the distribution of that surplus.[31] Thus, for example, conflicts might arise between truck loggers and mill owners over log prices, or between the Ministry of Forests, which allots timber licences, and the forestry companies that need and pay for them. Furthermore, because the Canadian state is a 'landowner,' collecting rents from resource extraction, it has a productive interest in the generation of surplus.[32]

In order to pursue their interests, productive actors create a variety of specialized pressure groups and peak associations. Among interest groups, business is generally the most powerful, with an unmatched capacity to affect public policy. A capitalist economy, by definition, entails a market form of economic organization in which ownership of the means of production is concentrated in the hands of the capitalists. This fact lies at the root of the unparallelled power of business.[33]

The increasing globalization of production and financial activities due to improvements in communication and transportation, and the gradual removal of controls on international economic transactions, have contributed tremendously to the power of capital in recent decades. It is possible for many businesses to respond, if they so wish, to any unwanted government action by removing capital to another location. Although this mobility is limited by a variety of factors, including the availability of suitable investment opportunities in other countries or jurisdictions, the potential loss of employment and revenues is a threat with which the state must contend in making decisions. Because of the negative consequences that this removal entails for state revenues, capitalists – both domestic and foreign – have the ability to 'punish' the state for any action that it might take of which they disapprove.[34]

The financial contributions that businesses make to political parties also influence policymakers. Elections can often turn on relatively short-term issues and personalities and thus necessitate large budgets to influence voters through extensive media advertising campaigns. In such situations, political parties supported by contributions from businesses are in a better position to run media campaigns and thus to influence voting behaviour. This support can lead political parties and candidates running for office to accommodate business interests more than those of other groups. Similarly, the financial contributions that businesses often make to research institutions and individual researchers further entrench their power. The organizations and individuals receiving funds tend to be sympathetic toward business interests and can provide business with the intellectual wherewithal often required to prevail in policy debates.

The ability of individual firms and capitalists to pressure the government to serve their interests can lead – if the government succumbs to the pressure – to incoherent and short-sighted policies. Endemic conflicts between various business groups only aggravate such situations. The problem may be offset, however, if business has cohesive central organizations that are able to thrash out the differences and come up with consistent policy proposals.

Such an organization is able to adopt a bold position if necessary and to convey it to the government, without incurring serious opposition from its rank and file. It must therefore be a peak association with the authority to impose sanctions and discipline on its members. The state must have confidence that, once a commitment has been made by the association, it can expect adherence to it by individual businesses. Moreover, if the state is confident of the strength of the business association, then it can delegate some business-related responsibilities to the business association itself. Generally speaking, the United States is regarded as having the weakest business organization in the industrialized world and Japan the strongest, with Britain and Canada being closer to the US model and

France, Germany, Austria, and Sweden being closer to the Japanese model.[35]

Labour can also occupy a powerful position among groups, though not as much as business. However, unlike the latter, which can enjoy considerable weight with policymakers even at the level of the individual firm, labour needs a collective organization, a trade union, to have its voice heard in the policy subsystem. In addition to bargaining with employers on behalf of their members, trade unions engage in political activities to shape government policies affecting them.[36] The role of trade unions in the public policy process is rooted in late-nineteenth-century democratization, which enabled workers, who formed a majority in every industrialized society, to have a say in the functioning of the government. Given the voting clout afforded them by democracy, it was often easier for them to pressure the government to meet their needs than to bargain with their employers. The formation of labour or social democratic parties, and eventually such governments, in many countries reinforced labour's political capacity.

As with business, the nature and effectiveness of the trade unions' participation in the policy process depend on a variety of institutional and contextual factors. The structure of the state itself is an important determinant of union participation in the policy process. A weak and fragmented state will not be able to secure effective participation by the unions because the latter would see little promise that the government would be able to keep its side of any bargain. Weak business also inhibits the emergence of a powerful trade union organization because the need for it is less immediate.

State Actors: Governments

A very significant role is played by elected and appointed government officials in public policy subsystems. These officials include members of the executive, legislators, members of the judicial system, and administrators. These actors gain their ability to influence policy directly from their structural location at the centre of policy networks.[37]

While political parties articulate policy and play an active role in getting the policy 'ball' into play, individual officials are often important in keeping it in play and in directing it to possible goals. The prime minister, members of cabinet, and members of Parliament are all directly involved in the formation of policy through their attention to, and influence on, the decision-making climate.

Political leaders can play a role in promoting environmental protection, but they may also act to promote resource extraction. They develop legislation and vote on bills, and their public presence, media skills, and engagement in policy discourse may actively promote or discourage resource and environmental policy options. In a culture in which the strong role of the media and the personality of leaders contribute to the personalization of decisions, leadership in the political sphere can be crucial. Similarly, the absence of leaders whose attention is primarily directed to resource or environmental issues can impede the formation of stronger or better policies.

Appointed officials dealing with public policy and administration are often collectively referred to as the 'bureaucracy.' Their function is to assist the executive in the performance of its tasks, as is suggested by the terms 'civil' and 'public' servants used to describe them. However, the reality of modern government is that their role goes well beyond what one would expect of a servant. Indeed, bureaucrats are often the keystones in the policy process and the central figures in many policy subsystems.

Most of the policy-making and implementing functions once performed by legislatures and the political executive are now performed by the bureaucracy since the functions of modern government are too complex and numerous to be performed by a small number of elected politicians. The bureaucracy, in contrast, consists of a large number of specialists who have the time and expertise to deal with a policy issue on a continuing basis.[38]

In modern governments, the degree of freedom enjoyed by officials is circumscribed by a host of rules that govern each administrative office and constrain the actions of each office holder. These rules range from the country's constitution to the specific mandate conferred on individual officials by various laws and regulations.[39] The rules usually set out not only which decisions can be made by which government agency or official but also the procedure that they must follow.

As Graham T. Allison and Morton H. Halperin have noted, such rules provide decisionmakers with 'action channels' or a regularized set of procedures for producing certain types of decisions.[40] While the purpose of the rules is to circumscribe the freedom available to decisionmakers and to force them to record their deliberations in a fashion that allows for subsequent evaluation, considerable discretion remains with individual decisionmakers to arrive at their own judgments of the best course of action to follow in specific circumstances. Exactly what process is followed and what decision is considered 'best' vary widely across decisionmakers and the contexts in which they operate.

The bureaucracy's power and influence are based on a range of resources.[41] First, the law itself often provides for certain crucial functions to be performed by the bureaucracy. It often confers wide discretion on individual bureaucrats to make decisions on behalf of the state. Second, bureaucracies have unmatched access to material resources for pursuing their own organizational, even personal, objectives if they so wish. The government is the largest single spender in most (if not all) countries, a situation that gives its officials a powerful voice in policy areas involving significant government expenditure. Third, the bureaucracy is a repository of a wide range of skills and expertise, resources that make it a premier organization in any country. It employs a large number of various professionals hired due to their status as experts in their areas of specialization. That they deal with similar issues on a continuing basis endows them with unique insights into problems. Fourth, modern bureaucracies have access to vast quantities of information on the different aspects of society. At times, the information is gathered deliberately; at times, it comes to the bureaucracy simply as part of its central location in the government. Fifth, the permanence of the bureaucracy and the long tenure of its members give it an edge over its superiors, the elected executive. And sixth, the fact that policy deliberations occur, for the most part, in secret within the bureaucracy denies other policy actors the opportunity to mount opposition to its plans.

However, we must avoid exaggerating the role of the bureaucracy. The political executive is ultimately responsible for all policies, an authority that it does assert at times. High-profile political issues are likely to involve higher levels of executive control. This control is also likely to be higher if the bureaucracy consistently opposes a policy option preferred by politicians. Moreover, the bureaucracy itself is not a homogeneous organization but a collection of organizations, each with its own interests, perspectives, and standard operating procedures that make arriving at a unified position difficult. Even within the same department, there are often divisions along functional, personal, political, and technical lines. It is not uncommon for the executive to intervene in order to resolve intra- and interbureaucratic conflicts.[42]

Such disputes and many others, however, can end up before the courts – the third major 'branch' of the political system. The judicial system is designed to provide a reasonably impartial means of adjudicating issues defined by statute or the common law. It also provides for the evaluation of policy through its decisions on matters brought before the courts, a subject which is discussed in Chapter 10. If the courts find the party at fault, an array of punitive actions and remedies may be invoked. While the judicial process emphasizes the implementation of policy, it constructs a context in which ongoing policy efforts are directed and therefore can affect which policy options are considered and which are not.

Taxonomies of Policy Subsystems

By the end of the 1980s, efforts turned to developing consistent methods for classifying and analyzing policy subsystems based on their membership and activities.[43] The analytical separation of community and network set out above aids in the conceptualization of a workable subsystem taxonomy.

Policy communities may be united around a set of core policy beliefs or a *policy paradigm*,[44] or they may be characterized by disagreement over the fundamentals of policy-making in a particular sector. While the notion of a 'community' would seem to connote a shared perspective, membership in a policy community does not necessarily suggest shared perspectives. Basic policy community configurations are set out in Figure 4.1.

In this model, four types of policy communities can be said to exist. When policy community members are in basic accord with a dominant set of policy ideas, a *hegemonic community* is found. This may occur in a number of cases: when there is excessive state domination with little room for opposing views, when policy ideas themselves represent an extension of the status quo, or when there has been no need or opportunity for alternative perspectives to emerge. At the opposite extreme, when there is no dominant set of ideas and policy community members are divided, the result is a *chaotic community*. In this case, there is no affinity or strategic liaison between differing positions, little opportunity for forging new policy ideas, and much possibility for maintaining the status quo or veering toward anarchy.

When policy community members are united but behind a small number of competing sets of ideas, one can expect a *fractious community* to exist. Similarly, when there is a dominant set of ideas but policy community members differ on its merits, one can expect to find a divided or *bifurcated community*.

Figure 4.1

A taxonomy of policy communities

		Number/Type of ideas	
		One major idea	Two or more
	Yes	*Hegemonic community*	*Fractious community*
Community members in agreement			
	No	*Bifurcated community*	*Chaotic community*

Source: Adapted from M. Howlett and M. Ramesh, *Studying Public Policy: Policy Cycles and Policy Subsystems* (Toronto: Oxford University Press 1995).

Within each of these communities, one would expect some form of regular interaction between a subset of members with material or productive
interests – a policy network – to develop. In terms of resource and environmental policy, for instance, state actors will be in routine communication with industry actors to determine licensing agreements and to
evaluate regulatory compliance. Policy networks will vary according to the
number and type of participants and their relations with each other, as set
out in Figure 4.2.

On the basis of the criteria of location of policy-relevant network actors
in states or societies, we find eight basic types of policy subsystems. At first
glance, we can see that some networks are state dominated while others
are society dominated, and that some represent few groups and interests
while others represent many. A *bureaucratic network* represents the
extreme case in which the principal interactions between subsystem
members take place exclusively within the state. For instance, issues related to national security and defence, such as the siting of nuclear power
plants, will be discussed, at least on a preliminary basis, within a largely
bureaucratic network. At the other extreme, an *issue network* is one in
which, as Heclo suggested, the principal interactions take place between a
large number of societal actors. While we might assume that the term
'societal actors' reflects a balance from a full spectrum of competing interests, business and productive interests have traditionally been the primary actors in this category.

Between the two extremes are six other possibilities. *Participatory networks* are those in which state agencies play a strong role but are dominated by diffuse societal actors. Planning issues in national parks provides
one example of such a subsystem. *Pluralist networks* are those in which

Figure 4.2

A taxonomy of policy networks

State/Societal relations within network	Number/Type of network participants			
	State agencies group	One major societal group	Two major societal groups	Three or more
State directed	Bureaucratic network	Clientelistic network	Triadic network	Pluralistic network
Society dominated	Participatory network	Captured network	Corporatist network	Issue network

Source: Modelled after Frans Van Waarden, 'Dimensions and Types of Policy Networks,'
European Journal of Political Research 21, 1-2 (1992): 29-52.

many actors are involved in the subsystem but in which state actors are dominant. These networks include recent attempts to expand access to decision-making through the creation of environmental round tables, for instance. When there is only one major societal actor, usually a business interest, facing the state, two common types of networks exist. In *clientelistic networks,* the state dominates the societal actor; in *captured networks,* the reverse is true. The traditionally strong involvement of industry in the regulation of pulp pollution is an example of the latter, while the subsystem related to Native peoples has often been considered an example of the former. When two societal actors face the state and the state dominates the subsystem, it can be termed a *triadic network.* Wilderness protection groups working with representatives from the forestry industry, for example, form a triadic network in the Protected Area Strategy developed by the British Columbia government. When societal actors such as business and labour dominate the state, the policy network is more akin to a traditional *corporatist network.* This type occurs, for example, when business and the Native fishery interest work together against the state in establishing fishery quotas. This typology presents a means of examining the relative access to the policy-making process enjoyed by different actors, assessing the openness or exclusivity of the policy process, and better understanding its responsiveness and potential.

What type of subsystem exists in a given sector or issue area is of major significance in understanding the dynamics of policy formulation within that area. Which policy options will be considered seriously for adoption is largely a function of the nature and motivation of key actors arrayed in the subsystem. This discussion of the composition of policy subsystems provides us with some key tools with which to examine the resource and environmental policy sector. It provides a basis for describing who the various policy actors are as well as the character of their relations with other actors.

We distinguish between state and societal actors, and between productive and non-productive actors, as a means of identifying multiple and potentially divergent interests in the policy process. In distinguishing between policy communities and networks, we recognize the differential access to decision-making that some actors may enjoy. This informal division between policy insiders and outsiders also has implications for the kinds of policy developed. We also note the range and combinations of networks that may impact the policy process in various ways. This range of actors and network relations is especially important to the resource and environmental sector. It reflects the potential for policy innovation, as seen in the emergence of new interests and perspectives, while it acknowledges the force of traditional alliances in maintaining past policy styles.

Of course, analyzing the role that actors actually play in the policy process, as opposed to the role that they should or might play, requires an empirical analysis of the interactions that actually exist between all of the actors cited above in a particular sector. Exactly what type of policy subsystem exists in Canada in the resource and environmental sector will be discussed in greater detail in Chapter 7. The implications of this configuration for the nature of Canadian resource and environmental policy-making and its propensity for development and change are set out in Part 4.

5
The Resource and Environmental Policy Process: An Analytical Framework

The historical, socioeconomic, and international contexts of policy are important elements in the analysis of any sector. Establishing the nature of the policy subsystem is also significant. But such an analysis must be placed within the context of an analytical framework if the relevant influences of various contextual factors upon policy subsystems are to be understood.

The principal aim of this chapter is to discuss the strengths and weaknesses of the frameworks so far proposed for the study of resource and environmental policy-making and to suggest an alternative model that can serve to elevate these frameworks from a taxonomical to a conceptual or theoretical level. The chapter proceeds from the observation of commonalities among natural resource politics to the level of a testable theory of why those politics exist. Through the introduction of a policy cycle model, it provides the basis by which we can examine how Canadian resource and environmental policy is actually made.

Understanding Canadian Resource and Environmental Policy-Making

Because Canada has long had a natural resource-based economy, analyses of the Canadian political economy have long dealt with policy issues. The examination of the domestic and international effects of a trade-reliant, resource-based economy on Canadian community development, on government infrastructural development, and on Canadian policies toward the world economy have all merited the attention of successive generations of Canadian scholars working within the political economic tradition.[1]

While these analyses all have much to say about the operation of the Canadian political economy, they have much less to say about government policy processes. This reflects the tendency of many studies in the political economy tradition to ignore or, at best, undertheorize, state activities. Rather, state actions were usually assumed to be determined by either the technological or economic prerequisites of large-scale natural resource extraction activities.[2]

The bulk of the existing literature is composed of numerous case studies of specific natural resource industries. Major efforts have been made to analyze the economics of virtually every natural resource industry, and some efforts have been made to at least review and summarize government regulatory and legislative activities in these areas. Much duplication exists however, and, despite the multiplicity of such case studies, several significant gaps in coverage remain. These gaps are mostly the result of the somewhat arbitrary restriction of most case studies to specific time periods and often to specific jurisdictions. The result has been, of course, that certain eras and jurisdictions have received much more attention than others – in Canada, usually the post-World War II period and the activities of the federal government.[3] Even works that have attempted to provide an overview of a specific sector have tended to focus on events occurring within specific time periods and, in generalizing from the study of these periods to developments in other periods, have tended to provide less than accurate descriptions of developments outside their periods of focus.

The failure to systematically evaluate the conclusions of case studies on a cross-sectoral or cross-national basis has seriously affected the generalizability of most of these conclusions.[4] Elements of resource activity idiosyncratic to one industry, jurisdiction, or province have often been extrapolated, and sometimes mistakenly characterized, as representative of a more general pattern. As a result, faulty generalizations about the course of policy development have been made.

Despite the tendency toward single-industry case studies, a number of studies have recognized similarities between industries and have attempted to treat the sector as a whole. Drawing on the insights of many case studies, these works represent a theoretical advance, but they have tended to restrict analysis to the legal or economic aspects of sectoral activities and have failed to consider the links between the two.[5] Many of these studies have been undertaken by economists concerned with the economic 'efficiency' of industrial or regulatory activities and have failed to examine all but the most obvious political aspects of this question in areas such as conflicts over pricing, land use, or international trade relations. Similarly, many legal analyses have been undertaken by lawyers or legal scholars who have tended to focus on partial issues such as constitutional jurisdiction and property rights or, more recently, policy instruments utilized by governments in the area.

In general, few works have systematically examined the overall Canadian natural resource and environmental policy process. Despite a large literature on a variety of aspects of the natural resource sector and government policies toward the sector and its environmental aspects, the study of Canadian natural resource policy-making remains under-developed.

Two Frameworks for Resource Policy Analysis

Two frameworks were put forward in the 1980s in the attempt to overcome the limitations of many of the existing studies discussed above. Both began the process of developing taxonomies of relevant economic and political variables in the Canadian natural resource and environmental policy sector. One is a 'public choice' or 'rational choice' framework developed by Mark Sproule-Jones,[6] while the other is an 'institutional-ideological' framework developed by G. Bruce Doern and Glen Toner in their work on the Canadian National Energy Program.[7]

The analysis put forward by Sproule-Jones is based on the notion that natural resource policy is determined by individual decisionmakers, working within a context of institutional structures and processes, who must deal with the additional constraints imposed by the natural characteristics of resource-based economic activities in making their decisions. One aspect of this approach that represents an advance over the case studies and single-factor analyses concerns its effort to link together the economic, political, and decision-making aspects of the overall policy process concerning natural resources. The classification of the policy-relevant aspects of the resource base – 'type of resource,' 'abundance,' 'technology' of production, and 'interdependencies' with other resources – is also useful.

Like most works in the public choice vein, however, that of Sproule-Jones is preoccupied with justifying the deductive application of the principles of methodological individualism to policy analysis. It is assumed that the appropriate unit for analysis is the individual decisionmaker and that the costs and benefits of policy decisions must also impact on the individual citizen, 'rather than on groups, corporate bodies, or governments.'[8] Such theoretical speculations, of course, should not be imposed on considerations of the sector but be inductively developed from the observations and findings of the case studies and other works in the field that have highlighted the salience of these sets of actors to resource and environmental policy-making.

A second and more inductive framework was outlined by Doern and Toner, who, like Sproule-Jones, note that the basic physical characteristics of resources form fundamental and often ignored constraints on government policy-making. Their list of critical variables is quite different from that produced by Sproule-Jones, however, and includes spatial location, geological realities, transportation and distribution issues, climate, location in the global economy, and (for Canadian goods) location vis-à-vis the US market. Although this perspective is derived from an in-depth case study of a major resource sector and policy initiative, their list has no apparent organizing principle and is, at best, ad hoc.

Like Sproule-Jones, Doern and Toner recognize that the institutional context of natural resource politics is crucial to the understanding of political processes in the area. They note that natural resource policy development takes place within the context of a capitalist economy, a federal constitution, and the institutions of representative government, and they correctly note that the question of policy 'interests' with which these institutions deal must be addressed if policy outcomes are to be comprehended. However, unlike Sproule-Jones, who relies on a public choice conception of rational self-interest maximization to understand the motivations of individual decisionmakers and other key policy actors, Doern and Toner attempt to define these interests based on a weakly defined sense of the 'ethical and procedural norms and values' that 'relevant' actors bring to the political process.

Both frameworks are laudable attempts to develop a conceptual apparatus for understanding natural resource policy-making, and both advance studies of the subject beyond single-sector or period case studies. Both rightly stress the constraints placed on public policy decisionmakers by the fundamental nature of natural resource production and the concomitant ability of political conflicts to affect certain aspects of those economic constraints. And both correctly emphasize the fundamental role played by the institutional structures and processes of politics in this regard. They can thus be seen to effectively synthesize not only many of the observations made by specialized industrial case studies but also the contributions of economists and legal-constitutional scholars to Canadian natural resource and environmental policy literature.

However, certain problems exist in attempting to utilize either framework as a conceptual tool for informing research and building theory. First, the economic and political variables that the two frameworks present are similar but different, reflecting the somewhat idiosyncratic nature of each. Second, both frameworks have difficulty establishing the roles played by interests and actors in the policy-making process.[9] Taken together, the two frameworks highlight the significance of rational calculations of actor self-interest and policy ideas, ethics, and values. Yet taken individually, neither is able to capture the entire range or nuances of policy-making activity. Third and most importantly, neither generates a clear sense of where to begin and how to proceed in the process of analyzing policy-making in this sector.

Policy Cycles and Policy Styles: A Process Model of Public Policy-Making

A more consistent and usable framework for natural resource and environmental policy analysis can be derived from the general model of the public policy-making process devised over the past forty years by students of the subject.[10] The application of this model to Canadian natural resource and environmental policy avoids many of the problems associated with the idiosyncratic sectoral models set out above.[11]

The essence of this approach is to simplify public policy-making by breaking the policy process into a series of discrete stages and substages. The resulting sequence of stages is referred to as the 'policy cycle.'[12] This simplification has its origin in the earliest works on public policy analysis, but it has received slightly varying treatment by different authors over the past half-century. Although the names and order of particular stages or substages remain somewhat controversial, there has been slow progress toward the establishment of a common model, or at least a common logic, for elaborating the order of the stages. In what follows, a description of the stages of the cycle is presented, along with the logic for dividing the process into these components.

The Policy Cycle Model

The idea of simplifying public policy-making by breaking the process into discrete stages was first broached in the work of Harold Lasswell.[13] For Lasswell, the policy process begins with intelligence gathering, that is, the collection, processing, and dissemination of information to those who participate in decision-making. It then moves on to the promotion of particular options by those involved in the decision-making. The third stage sees those decisionmakers actually prescribe a course of action. In the fourth stage, the prescribed course of action is invoked, meaning that a set of sanctions is developed to penalize those who fail to comply with the prescriptions of the decisionmakers. The policy is then applied by the courts and the bureaucracy and runs its course until it is terminated or cancelled. Finally, the results of the policy are evaluated against the aims and goals of the original decisionmakers.

This model was highly influential in the development of the policy sciences. Although not entirely accurate, it did reduce the complexity of studying public policy by allowing each stage to be isolated and examined before putting the whole picture of the process back together. It formed the basis for later models that viewed policy-making as a process of applied problem-solving, which is, in effect, a five-stage process.[14] It involves (1) recognition of a problem, (2) proposal of a solution to the problem, (3) choice of a solution, (4) putting the solution into effect, and (5) monitoring the effects of the solution upon the problem.[15] This approach introduced the notion of the policy process as an ongoing cycle. That is, it recognizes that most policies do not have a definite life cycle – moving from birth to death – but seem to endlessly recur as one policy succeeds its predecessor with minor or major modifications.

Based on this problem-solving logic, it is possible to derive a five-stage model of the policy cycle. Of course, substages exist within each stage, and they will be discussed in later chapters. The general five-stage model and its underlying logic are found in Figure 5.1.

In this model, 'agenda-setting' refers to the process by which problems come to the attention of governments. This is the earliest stage in the sequence, when a problem initially emerges. This stage is characterized by incomplete or partial definitions of the problem and the existence of various proposals for its solution. These proposals will also often be ill conceived or inappropriate at this point. This stage only ends when a problem is reconceptualized or redefined in such a way that a range of feasible solutions becomes imaginable.

'Policy formulation' refers to the process by which policy options are formulated within government. In this second stage, estimations concerning the calculation of the risks, costs, and benefits associated with each solution raised in the earlier stage are made. This process involves both technical evaluation and normative choices. The object of this stage is to narrow the range of plausible choices by excluding the non-viable ones and to rank the remaining options in terms of desirability.

'Decision-making' refers to the process by which governments adopt a particular course of action or inaction. The actual decision on a particular course of action to follow is made at this selection stage. This can involve the adoption of one, none, or some combination of the solutions remaining at the end of the formulation stage.

Figure 5.1

A five-stage model of the policy cycle

Phase of applied problem-solving	Stage in policy cycle
1 Problem recognition	1 Agenda-setting
2 Proposal of solution	2 Policy formulation
3 Choice of solution	3 Decision-making
4 Putting solution into effect	4 Policy implementation
5 Monitoring results	5 Policy evaluation

Source: M. Howlett and M. Ramesh, *Studying Public Policy: Policy Cycles and Policy Subsystems* (Toronto: Oxford University Press 1995).

'Policy implementation' refers to the process by which governments put policies into effect. This fourth stage involves executing the policy option selected at the decision-making stage. Policy implementation uses the traditional tools of public administration concerned with implementing policy and with ensuring a proper match of policy tool and policy context to successfully execute the chosen policy.

Finally, 'policy evaluation' refers to the processes by which the results of policies are monitored by both state and societal actors, leading to the reconceptualization of policy problems and solutions. Here the results of the entire process, especially including the results of the implementation phase, are monitored in order to attempt to determine if the policy option chosen has successfully addressed the initial problem, if the management of the implementation process was effective, and if the evaluation process itself has been conducted according to appropriate criteria. The adjustments to policy that can result from evaluation may be broad or narrow. That is, they could involve minor tinkering with the implementation effort; they might lead back to a reconsideration and redefinition of the problem that the policy was supposed to address; or they could involve a reassessment of some option rejected at an earlier stage of the policy process.

Advantages and Disadvantages of the Cycle Model

There are several advantages and disadvantages that stem from utilizing a model of the policy process as a staged, sequential cycle in the analysis of Canadian resource and environmental policy-making. For the most part, however, the advantages of so doing far outweigh the disadvantages, which can be minimized by keeping in mind an important point about models of all kinds in social inquiry.

The advantages of the policy cycle method are many, several of which have already been mentioned. First, the most important is the manner in which such an approach reduces the complexity of public policy-making by breaking down that complexity into any number of stages and substages, each of which can be investigated alone or in terms of its relationship with any or all of the other stages. This is a key advantage, because it not only allows numerous case studies and comparative studies of different stages to be undertaken and integrated but also aids in the process of theory-building.

Second, the notion of the policy cycle integrates theoretical and practical issues in a manner envisioned by the founders of the policy sciences but unrealized by other approaches. This is because the cycle model helps identify the key characteristics of policy-making at different stages of the process. This approach acknowledges the complexity and dynamics of policy processes and actors while providing a common basis for their comparison. For resource and environmental policy, the policy cycle provides a framework within which different sectors as well as different levels of government can be examined in a similar manner. It also specifies where and how each of the decisions involved in the public policy-making process is made. This specification allows a number of tests to be developed to examine theories of the policy-making process. Whether public policy-making is an 'automatic' or 'deterministic' process, or whether it is a highly contingent one, for example, are questions that can be operationalized and tested using this method.

There are several disadvantages to the cycle model, however, some of which are philosophical, others methodological. First, it can be argued that the model is overly rational. That is, it is based on a model of applied problem-solving and assumes that democratic governments go about solving problems in a more or less systematic fashion and that policymakers are capable of learning from their successes and failures. It can be argued, of course, that this is the case neither with individuals nor with complex organizations such as governments. In both cases, the identification of problems and the development and implementation of solutions can be viewed as a more or less ad hoc and idiosyncratic process in which decisionmakers simply react to circumstances and do so in terms of preset ideological dispositions and interests.[16] However, even if this were the case, a model that postulates some rational norm for policy-making from which actual policymakers diverge would be essential in order to understand the divergence.

Methodological concerns are directed primarily to the temporal logic of the model and its application to actual policy-making practice. Events that occur at any stage of the process not only affect the current policy process but may become the basis for emerging issues as well. While the notion of a cycle may be fine in the abstract, in practice the stages of the cycle are often compressed, skipped, or followed in a different order from that specified by the logic of applied problem-solving. Thus, the cycle is arguably not a single iterative loop but is composed of a series of smaller loops. The results of past implementation decisions regarding pesticide registration, for instance, will have a major impact on future policy formulation, regardless of the specifics of the agenda-setting process in the case concerned. These concerns underscore the complexity of the policy process and the need to constantly examine and refine any theory on the basis of empirical investigations.

In addition, the model requires a more or less transparent decision-making arena in which not only the objectives of governance but also the means of influencing them are open and visible. Imbalances in power and political access tend to be obscured. The consequences of political decisions that may affect the survival of an industry, a community, or even a species may also be ignored, only to become visible much later on.

The criticisms point out the need to remember at all times that the cycle 'model' is exactly that. The notion of the policy cycle is a simplifying heuristic that is intended not to capture all of the complexity of public policy-making but to reduce it for analytical purposes. That actual policy-making is more complex than the model should not be surprising or unexpected. It is the model, however, that both allows the 'exceptions' to be uncovered and aids in the investigation of the complexity.[17]

Conclusion: Explaining Policy Change and Development

The use of a disaggregated and sequential model of the public policy process – the policy cycle – helps us to understand the dynamic nature of public policy-making and to organize the complex relations binding actors, institutions, and policy instruments. However, while the disaggregation aids in the detailed examination of the policy process, it begs the question of what that process looks like when all of its constitutive pieces have been reassembled. That is, is there a pattern of policy development and change that is 'typical' of policy-making in liberal democratic states?[18] Or does each issue, sector, and country develop and change policies in a different and idiosyncratic fashion?[19] If so, what is the general pattern of Canadian resource and environmental policy development?

Studies of public policy-making have shown that there are in fact two typical overall patterns of policy change.[20] One, the more 'normal' pattern, involves relatively minor tinkering with established policies and policy processes. The second is more substantial and involves the fundamental transformation of policies and policy processes.

With regard to the first pattern, it has often been observed that there is a surprising degree of continuity in most public policy-making. There is ample empirical evidence in literally thousands of case studies of disparate policy sectors and issues in a multitude of countries that most policies made by governments are usually, in some way, a continuation of past policies and practices.[21]

This pattern of modest policy change can be explained in several ways, but most analyses attribute this continuity in policy-making to the fact that the same set of actors is typically involved in the policy process over a long period of time. In his pathbreaking analysis of 'incremental' decision-making over three decades ago, for example, Charles Lindblom attributed this propensity for limited policy change to the marginal differences between existing and proposed policy options. Policymakers must bargain between themselves to arrive at a decision and are therefore unlikely to overturn agreements based on past negotiations and compromises.[22] More recently, Frank Baumgartner and Bryan Jones argued that subsystems tend to construct 'policy monopolies' in which the interpretation and general approach to a subject are more or less fixed. Only when this monopoly is broken by the emergence of new members of subsystems can a policy be expected to change in any significant way.[23]

Both interpretations suggest that in normal circumstances a policy problem or issue will be dealt with in the context of an existing approach to the problem or issue in question, or what has been described in some studies as a 'policy style.'[24] Several studies have applied this concept with great facility to policy-making in various nations and sectors.[25] Some have dealt with long-term patterns in details of policies, such as the rigid and legalistic nature of American environmental regulations compared with the flexibility and self-regulation that characterize their counterparts in Britain.[26] Others have found patterns at a broader level, such as in the American preference for regulation in instances in which other countries employ public enterprises (e.g., in the areas of transportation and utilities).

The second type of typical policy change is much more dramatic, what some observers have called a change in *policy paradigms*.[27] Peter Hall has defined a policy paradigm as establishing

> the broad goals behind policy, the related problems or puzzles that policy-makers have to solve to get there, and, in large measure, the kind of instruments that can be used to attain these goals. Like a gestalt, this framework is all the more powerful because it is largely taken for granted and rarely subject to scrutiny as a whole. It seems likely that policy-makers in all fields are guided by some such paradigm, even though the complexity and coherence of the paradigm may vary considerably across fields.[28]

A policy paradigm is thus closely linked to a policy subsystem, and a change in paradigm is often linked directly to a change in subsystem membership and composition.[29] It is essentially a set of ideas held by relevant policy subsystem members – a doctrine or 'school' of thought, such as Keynesianism or Monetarism in the area of government fiscal policy – that shapes the broad goals policymakers pursue, the way they perceive public problems, the kinds of solutions they consider for adoption and the instruments they use to implement their decisions.

The notion of a paradigm shift as a metaphor for describing significant policy change is a recent development in the discipline.[30] It was developed to capture the process of fundamental long-term change in the underlying beliefs, values, and attitudes connected with public problems and the solutions to them on the part of policymakers. However, as we discuss in this text, paradigm shifts also reflect alterations in material interests. Different combinations of economic actors, changing productive relations and consumptive activities, and changes in the configuration of state power and its relations to societal actors all have significant impacts on how policies change.

In Part 4, Canadian resource and environmental policy-making is subjected to detailed analysis, using the policy cycle method. That is, the policy process in this sector is broken down into five stages, and each stage is examined in order to determine current Canadian resource and environmental policy style.

As we shall see, the debate and flux between predominant ways of thinking about policy problems, or 'policy discourses,' have become increasingly important in expanding the resource paradigm into an environmental one. Given a complex set of conflicting, materially driven actors in the existing policy subsystem, some leeway is provided to new actors to develop and articulate ideas that can challenge the existing policy orthodoxy. But the configuration of network and community actors has resulted in a subsystem that remains resistant to change, one that is adapted to negotiative patterns and administrative closure that deters policy rehabilitation.

The following chapters provide an analysis of the stages through which resource and environmental policy moves from its inception to its evaluation, as it is shaped by events, actors, ideology, and changes in material conditions. As has been seen, Canadian natural resource and environmental policy has changed very slowly but has proceeded through a number of distinct periods since its inception. The following chapters will demonstrate that it continues to evolve within the current policy paradigm, but again very slowly, with some portents of dramatic change ahead, but also with many signs that such changes may take years to be realized.

Part 4:
The Canadian Natural Resource and Environmental Policy Process

This section examines Canadian resource and environmental policy using the concepts and framework developed in the preceding chapters. The analysis draws its inspiration from classical political economy as well as from more recent studies in the policy sciences. It combines the political economic notion of a fundamental material interest of certain actors in resource exploitation with the analysis of policy actors, interests, and ideas developed in the policy sciences. As the chapters in this part of the book will show, the political economic context of resource production in Canada inserts issues of production and distribution into policy-making within the structure and processes of Canadian representative political institutions. Detailed examination of the stages of the policy cycle in this sector reveals how and why new ideas and discourses emerging in policy communities have so far been unable to exert much influence and thus to challenge traditional actors dominating existing policy networks. This section outlines the fundamental elements of the Canadian resource and environmental policy style, as well as its capacity for future adaptation and change.

6
Agenda-Setting: The Role of the Public in Resource and Environmental Policy Formation

The first, and perhaps the most critical, stage of the policy cycle is agenda-setting, in which issues emerge on the government agenda for action. Although often taken for granted, the means by which concerns become candidates for government action are by no means simple.[1] Issues are generated by a variety of factors and must undergo complex transformations before they are considered seriously for resolution. Resource and environmental issues compete with one another for government attention both within and across sectors, and they compete with social and economic issues 'with a human face' that have traditionally garnered, and continue to claim, more immediate state attention. What happens at this stage has a decisive impact on the entire policy process and its outcome. As Roger Cobb and Charles Elder put it:

> Pre-political, or at least pre-decisional processes often play the most critical role in determining what issues and alternatives are to be considered by the polity and the probable choices that will be made. What happens in the decision-making councils of the formal institutions of government may do little more than recognize, document and legalize, if not legitimize, the momentary results of a continuing struggle of forces in the larger social matrix ... From this perspective, the critical question becomes, how does an issue or a demand become or fail to become the focus of concern and interest within a polity?[2]

The manner in which problems are recognized, if they are recognized at all, is an important determinant of how they will ultimately be addressed by policymakers. Demands for the resolution of some public problems come from the society, and, in the context of resource and environmental policy, they come particularly from environmental organizations. Greenpeace, for instance, has been tremendously successful at 'targeting' certain audiences and specific issues to mobilize public support on behalf of issues such as whaling, seal hunting, predator control programs, and underground nuclear testing. Other issues emerged on the agenda in response to government initiatives, for instance the use of consultative tribunals such as royal commissions to focus attention on issues ranging from forestry practices to the health of the fishery and mining industries.[3] Similarly, the demand for resolution of some problems (e.g., wilderness areas) through public policy may have a great deal of public support at a given time, while others (e.g., reform of toxic regulations) may not.[4]

At its most basic, agenda-setting is about the recognition of a problem on the part of the government. Many of the early works on this subject are American and are deeply imbued with the pluralist sentiments prevalent in mainstream American political science.[5] Thus, for example, agenda-setting has been defined as 'the process by which demands of various groups in the population are translated into items vying for the serious attention of public officials.'[6]

Such definitions are closely linked with the idea that public policy-making is driven by the actions of social groups. But this is by no means certain or obvious. Discussion concerning the nature and degree of public involvement in the political process has been central to political theory from classical Greek concepts of direct political participation to those supporting the large-scale electoral practices of contemporary government.[7] Current liberal versions of representative democracy assume that the concerns of constituents will be relayed down the field of political action by elected representatives, assisted by lobbyists and media exposure, passed as appropriate legislation and enshrined in law. Citizens concerned about air quality or the location of toxic waste disposal sites, for example, will notify their MPs or MLAs, who will introduce and/or support legislation or make other appropriate decisions regarding the issue. Thus, while the public's role in policy-making is generally preliminary and informal, the representation and accountability inherent in the political system is supposed to ensure the production of appropriate policy responsive to public needs and concerns.

Other perspectives, however, accord a much more limited role to the public.[8] Elitist approaches to political life, for example, assume the existence of a large and apathetic population whose locus of political activity is the electoral, and not the policy, process.[9] The existing system of political accountability in democratic states, it is argued, restricts direct public involvement in the policy process. This limited involvement actually works to the benefit of the public, because the increased scientific and bureaucratic complexity of much public policy-making has created a 'knowledge gap,' separating the general public from a technocratic elite composed of activists and experts.[10] Allowing experts in government to deal with experts in policy matters could in principle prevent an ignorant public from continually making errors of judgment.

On the other hand, not all observers are satisfied that rule by experts or elites is always beneficial. Contemporary arguments for greater public involvement in government include concerns for the protection of individual property rights against state action, the need to legitimize the political process, and the general desire to counter tendencies toward strong government. While public participation has been traditionally oriented toward refining and supplementing the electoral process, precedents for more extensive and direct public involvement in government have reemerged in many policy sectors, including resource and environmental policy-making. Indeed, the diffuse nature and widespread social consequences of environmental issues, it has been argued, are consistent with the desire to repopularize contemporary representative democracy.[11]

Given the ample empirical evidence that the policy process in Canada is often initiated not by the public but by members of governments,[12] a better definition of agenda-setting is one closer to the more 'neutral' one provided by John Kingdon:

> The *agenda*, as I conceive of it, is the list of subjects or problems to which governmental officials, and people outside of government closely associated with those officials, are paying some serious attention at any given time ... Out of the set of all conceivable subjects or problems to which officials could be paying attention, they do in fact seriously attend to some rather than others. So the agenda-setting process narrows this set of conceivable subjects to the set that actually becomes the focus of attention.[13]

This chapter explains the process by which issues are most likely to become part of the resource and environmental policy agenda in Canada. In so doing, it discusses a number of related questions. Which issues have priority on the agenda? How do they compete with those of other sectors, both internally and externally, to get a place in the agenda spotlight? What are the origins of the politicization process through which issues become identified as appropriate for the policy agenda? Are issues predominantly materially defined and market driven, such as timber allocations and fishery quotas? Or can they be idea-generated, as in the introduction of growth management criteria and wilderness protection? To respond to these questions, let us first consider the different means or venues through which issues are defined.

Setting the Resource and Environmental Agenda in Canada: Actors and Interests

To understand agenda-setting, we must comprehend (1) how demands for a policy are made by various policy actors, (2) how the government responds to these preliminary demands, and (3) the conditions under which these demands emerge and are articulated. Toward this end, we need to understand how the material interests of social and state actors coincide with their knowledge of policy issues and with the various institutional and ideological constraints under which they operate. We need to identify the ways in which policy actors construct their activities as representing material – or other – interests and the factors that facilitate or constrain this articulation of interests.

From a political economic perspective, material interests generate, or at least influence, ideological perspectives, and together they generate bases from which the consolidation of the public into organized interest groups takes place. This chapter explains the ways that these material interests are constructed so as to be represented by organized actors in the policy subsystem. As was shown in Chapter 4, the two basic sets of interests are those related to the process of producing marketable commodities from resources (productive interests) and those related to non-market aspects of resource and environmental use ('public' interests).

Productive, or production-based, interests usually refer to market-driven resource extraction processes, and they are typically grouped around industrial organizations, such as businesses and labour unions involved in mining, energy, fishing, or logging activities. Their interest is to develop or maximize the economic surplus generated from these activities, whether in the form of profits, wages, or reductions in the cost of adhering to various government policies. These material interests are supported by ideological perspectives that usually argue the social benefits of private enterprise and that uphold the notions of a free-market system, a laissez-faire regulatory climate, and the preeminence of industrial and extractive interests in resource management. However, new productive interests are emerging in the resource and environmental policy subsystem. Economic diversification reflects the growth of tourism and the advent of new industries, such as oyster farming or aquaculture, whose interests may run against traditional extractive interests. Competition with international producers also expands membership in the competitive arena or at least introduces additional concerns into the policy arena. Thus, productive interests are complex and dynamic.

Not all material concerns are market driven, nor do all market processes have equal impacts on environmental quality. That is, a widespread public concern for environmental integrity has contributed to the base from which environmental organizations have been initiated. The 'new environmental paradigm'[14] enunciated by most contemporary environmental organizations also represents a material interest, even if these groups are not directly aligned with productive activities. Changes in demographics, employment, especially increased tertiary-sector employment, and urbanization are materially based and account for much of the rise of contemporary environmentalism. Environmental approaches to resource use based on ecological perspectives also reflect a fundamental material interest in the continued well-being of the biophysical systems on which human and other life is based. The contributions of these systems – water, air, photosynthesis – remain external to most economic transactions, but environmental interests in them are material nonetheless.

Contemporary Canadian resource and environmental agenda-setting, to a great extent, represents a continuing clash between public and productive interests. However, the dominant discourse has been developed by productive interests, centred on the idea of the exploitation of publicly owned resources for private profit.[15] This exploitation has been carried out largely by private companies, and thus business is a prominent societal actor, which plays an active role in agenda-setting. Because most of this exploitation has been carried out on public land, however, the state has also been closely involved in this process.

State Actors

Various state actors and institutions are involved in Canadian resource and environmental agenda-setting although the material interests of the state have been obscured by both the policy on political institutions and policy processes as well as the diffusion of state revenues. State actors include municipal and regional governments, but primarily the provincial and federal levels of jurisdiction, as discussed in Chapter 3. Within these levels, especially at the upper tiers, functional differences ensure the representation of legislative, executive, judicial, and administrative actors. In addition, sectoral diversity, legislative fiat, and redundancy often ensure representation of multiple ministries, such as ministries of forests, ministries of the environment, and ministries of lands or parks. Many policy issues may garner input from all these levels and components of the state apparatus.

As we have seen, exactly what role officials play in agenda-setting is circumscribed by the constitutional and institutional arrangements within which politicians operate, as well as by the sets of rules governing the structure of government agencies and the conduct of officials. Parliamentary systems, for example, tend to concentrate authority in the elected executive officials and the bureaucracy, permitting only minor roles to the legislature and the judiciary in the early stages of the policy cycle.

This is because the task of the legislature in a parliamentary system of government is to hold governments accountable to the public rather than to formulate or implement policies.[16] Legislatures are public forums in which social problems are highlighted and proposals to address them are put forward and publicized. In parliamentary systems, however, most laws are proposed by the executive and subsequently adopted by the legislature. Legislators belonging to the governing party are always expected to support the government, and private members have only limited opportunities to initiate legislation. This function permits only limited opportunities for legislators to influence the policy agenda.

On the other hand, government administrative agencies, by providing 'advice' to government ministers, are well placed to initiate policy discussions and to dominate the agenda-setting process. These agencies have become extremely sophisticated in recent years. In the resource sector, every jurisdiction in Canada developed single- or dual-purpose agencies in the early years of the twentieth century to administer specific resource sectors. These agencies have put great effort into monitoring and controlling resource policy-making, including agenda-setting.[17] In the recent past, organizational changes in many governments led to the creation of omnibus natural resource ministries that increased efforts, not always successfully, to integrate resource planning activities with environmental planning in general.[18] These government agencies are usually large and well funded, have considerable discretion in the introduction and implementation of legislation, and are the focal point for many policy debates.[19]

Market-Based Productive Interests

Capital in the natural resource sector in Canada is overwhelmingly private, although Crown corporations exist in virtually every sector.[20] The only sector dominated by public corporations, however, is hydroelectric generation. Private capital employed in the other sectors is diverse, being composed of independent commodity producers, small competitive capital, and large, often transnational, capital in major resource manufacturing industries. All of these resource-dependent businesses have an interest in resource and environmental agenda-setting, as does tourism, which relies upon the preservation of nature, and other emerging environmental industries, which extend traditional resource use to additional ends, such as value-added and restorative processes.

In Canada, although divided by both sector and jurisdiction, the resource industries – and especially the manufacturing components of those industries – have articulated their interests in maintaining and enhancing profits through strong business associations. These associations have continually resisted efforts to regulate industrial behaviour and have urged private sector solutions to any problems that they encounter.[21] They have resisted any effort to expand subsystem membership, contesting the legitimacy of environmental groups, for example, to participate in allocating resource lands and organizing local industry supporters to counter grassroots environmentalism.

Labour in the resource sector is mostly organized into large trade unions, although many small operations are non-union. The labour unions in this sector are among the largest in Canada and have a long history of militant activity.[22] They also have an interest in Canadian resource and environmental policy-making, an interest often closely aligned with business in a desire to preserve jobs and improve wages and working conditions for union members.[23]

Although the resource sector tends to be highly unionized, these unions are divided by sectoral representation, by regional location, and by national affiliation. Thus, in the mid-1980s, for example, the four largest pulp and paper unions were the Canadian Paperworkers Union (CLC), with 70,000 members in 296 locals; the Federation of Paper and Forest Workers (CNTU), with 169 locals and 14,000 members in Quebec; the Pulp and Paper Workers of Canada (CCU), with seventeen locals and 7,200 members in British Columbia; and the United Paperworkers International Union (AFL-CIO-CLC), with four locals (three in Ontario and one in Manitoba) and a total of 1,750 members.[24] In the woods industry, the International Woodworkers of America had sixty-five locals and 51,216 members in 1985. The Lumber and Sawmill Workers Union had about 17,000 members, mostly in Ontario and Newfoundland. Woodworkers in Quebec were split into three unions in addition to those in the Federation of Paper and Forest Workers Union – about 2,500 in the National Federation of Building and Woodworkers Union (CNTU), 3,422 in the Quebec Woodworkers Federation (independent), and a small number in the one Montreal local of the National Brotherhood of Joiners, Carpenters, Foresters and Industrial Workers (CLC). Small associations of fewer than fifty members exist in British Columbia, such as the Northern Interior Woodworkers Association and the Cariboo Woodworkers Association, some in company unions and some loosely affiliated with the 6,513-member Christian Labour Association of Canada (independent).[25]

A union movement fragmented along any or all of possible regional, linguistic, ethnic, religious, industrial versus craft, foreign versus domestic, or import-competing versus exporting lines will also experience difficulties in influencing any stage of the policy process, including agenda-setting. Fragmentation among labour organizations tends to promote local and sporadic industrial strife and an incoherent articulation of labour's interest in the policy process.[26] As a result, labour has not emerged as a major player in Canadian policy-making, focusing its efforts at the firm, rather than the policy, level through the collective bargaining process. In the Canadian resource sector, labour plays a relatively minor role in the agenda-setting process compared to industry or government.

Other Environmental Interests and Actors

The pattern in Canada of private utilization of public resources has led to the involvement of the public in policy debates surrounding resource use and associated environmental issues. While the role of government officials and industrial corporations and associations in resource and environmental agenda-setting in Canada is historical and readily observable, the role that non-market actors play at this stage, and the incentives provided to encourage this participation, remain much less obvious.

While the mobilization of the entire society around specific issues is both impossible and institutionally undesirable, some portion of the public may be mobilized to ensure the representation of certain interests or perspectives on the political agenda. This participation reflects the existence of multiple stakeholders in resource and environmental issues and ensures the balance of divergent views on different political matters. Public participation offers an opposition and hence a balance to productive forces, and it enhances the inclusion of alternative approaches to an issue.[27]

Public participation, then, does more than contribute to the policy debate: it frames the debate and even ensures that it takes place. Perhaps even more significantly, the involvement of the public confirms assumptions of a democratic policy process and helps to legitimize the role of the state as open and fair, as an independent arbitrator of competing interests. Thus, in the environmental context, public participation ensures not only that issues such as pesticide contamination appear on the policy agenda but also that their presence there in turn (re)confirms the competence and neutrality of the state.

In 1977, a Canadian conference on public participation entitled Involvement and Environment[28] reflected this heightened concern for the extension of citizen involvement in environmental policy. Efforts to increase the instruments for, and power of, citizen involvement in environmental policy have continued to accelerate, especially in the context of citizen-generated organization, the move to increased statutory provisions for citizen involvement, and increased citizen activity in the administrative sphere. In 1987, the UN-inspired Brundtland Report called for increased recognition of 'the right of individuals to know and have access to current information on the state of the environment and natural resources, the right to be consulted and to participate in decision-making on activities likely to have a significant effect on the environment, and the right to legal remedies and redress for those whose health or environment has been or may be seriously affected.'[29]

Avenues for public involvement in environmental policy reflect changes in perceptions of the role of the public, the popularity of government, and the degree of concern over environmental issues. The instruments for public participation have evolved not only in the context of a dynamic political climate but also in a period of dramatic regulatory development, with new Canadian legislation and environmental processes that offer the potential for more extensive and empowered citizen involvement.

Criticisms concerning the ineffectiveness of the political system in ensuring environmental stewardship, and the limited role of public participation in existing political processes, have contributed to an expanded participatory ethic. The delay of bureaucratic processes, the increase in conflict concerning the allocation and use of resources, the rise in perceptions of environmental crisis, the extension of the state's regulatory powers into new areas of land-use planning, the question of the neutrality and capability of the state, and the environmental politicization of the public have encouraged the development of extra-electoral mechanisms to enhance the policy process by extending and strengthening the options for public participation.

Increased public knowledge about environmental problems, and the emergence of a more diversified economic base, have also contributed to the mobilization of the Canadian public. The ecological dimensions of resource policy are now considered to have not only economic but also significant aesthetic, social, health, community, and political consequences.[30]

Ronald Inglehart has argued that ideological shifts, and especially the evolution of a 'postmaterialist' culture as a result of generational change, are conducive to environmental protection through enhanced citizen involvement.[31] A number of surveys have documented the growing public concern about environmental protection in Western societies. These analyses of public attitudes have been directed toward two primary goals: exploration of the values associated with 'environmentalism'[32] and discussion of the politicization of environmentalism and its significance for traditional electoral politics.[33]

Increased social affluence, economic diversification, cultural diffusion, demographic expansion, and accelerated environmental degradation have joined with other factors to generate environmental perspectives oriented toward a greater biocentrism and preservationism among sections of society. These actors are often referred to as members of 'new social movements' because they increasingly challenge older, more directly market-driven sets of resource owners, managers, and workers.

While observers generally agree that environmentalism has become a public concern, there is less agreement about its source of support and its future appeal. While some would argue that there has been a gradual extension and broadening of environmental concerns, Buttel argues that deteriorating economic concerns will overshadow them.[34] Yet as Jones and Dunlap report, the social factors underlying environmental support (higher levels of education, youth, political liberalism, and urban residence) remained more or less the same from 1973 to 1990, as did the levels of environmental support.[35] Bakvis and Nevitte note the precipitous drop in environmental support in Canada (to 4 per cent in 1991 from 14 per cent in 1990), adding that 'It is probably not coincidental that at about the same time the federal government quietly placed its Green Plan on the back-burner.'[36]

Thus, public support for environmental issues may continue to grow in Canada along with continuing trends of economic diversification, high education, and urbanization. Nonetheless, this growth will be countered by economic downturns, restructuring and unemployment, and continuing regional dependence on a resource-based economy.

The Structures of Canadian Resource and Environmental Agenda-Setting

In earlier eras, agenda-setting took place largely through the activities of governments and resource industries with little participation by the public.[37] During the earliest phase, naturalist organizations such as the Audubon Society (1886) and Sierra Club (1892) in the United States, and the Federation of Ontario Naturalists (1931) in Canada, promoted the appreciation of nature. Continuing organized public concern about environmental protection did not surface on the policy agenda in Canada until the second half of the twentieth century. While public interest in the natural environment, and recognition of its degradation, grew dramatically in the post-Second World War period, protests continued to be sporadic, event motivated, and directed toward finite activities.[38] It was not until the 1960s that active and continuing government lobbying on environmental issues by non-productive interests took place.[39]

However, in more recent years, the environmental 'movement' has increasingly directed public and political attention toward environmental issues. The rise of environmental groups may be attributed to a number of factors, including the success of the environmental movement in specific areas and with respect to specific issues, the increased education of the Canadian public concerning the seriousness of many resource and environmental issues, better laws for access to information, and the improved organizational capabilities of environmental groups themselves. The increased severity of, and variation in, environmental issues has also contributed to the growth and influence of environmental groups.[40]

These groups bring their concerns to the attention of the public and policymakers through a variety of means. Public education disseminates information so that the public is made aware of specific issues. The organization of protests is also an effective means of bringing issues to public attention through the media. Groups such as Greenpeace have been especially successful in mobilizing public support for environmental issues through widespread campaigns. Other groups direct their attention to political lobbying or legal reform. While most of these groups must raise funds from donations and other fund-raising activities, some receive funding from the government and professional associations, which has implications for the types of activities undertaken.[41] Yet in spite of the growth in the numbers and capabilities of environmental groups in recent decades, policies of fiscal restraint and a climate of economic downsizing have restricted financial support for environmental groups in the 1990s, and the climate for support remains unsettled.[42] Thus, what counts as participation, in form, content, and support continues to evolve.

Preorganizational Societal Agenda-Setting: Petitions, Protests, and Civil Disobedience

At its most elementary stage, public participation is relatively passive, requiring only a response to a political survey or the endorsement of environmental positions put forward by political parties, interest groups, or other individuals. There is widespread public recognition of the existence of environmental issues, although attitudes reflect a number of factors, including gender, social class, political persuasion, and geographical location.[43] Bakvis and Nevitte have documented a relatively high level of 'green' or environmental consciousness among the Canadian public.[44] Expressed rather diffusely through the electoral process, however, these sentiments must compete with a range of others for government attention.

This low level of public involvement in agenda-setting may escalate to organizing letter-writing campaigns, neighbourhood petitions, or study sessions on a specific issue, or to picketing, protesting, and other forms of violent or peaceful civil disobedience. These actions can have a significant effect on policy-making in specific regions or issues. But while policymakers are interested in the larger diffuse perceptions of the public, and must take acts of civil disobedience seriously, these expressions of the public interest tend to be issue-specific, ad hoc, and idiosyncratic. This is not to say that public protests are ineffective; rather, they often capture the attention of the media and can be pivotal in forcing political attention to an issue.

While such forms of public participation may succeed in bringing attention to, and sometimes altering decisions already made on, for example, the siting of toxic waste dumps or new resource projects, more long-term forms of public participation are required to fundamentally alter policy processes. This alteration occurs when public participation is organized to lobby decisionmakers, focus media attention, or educate other members of the public about topics such as environmental risks and hazards.

Organized Societal Agenda-Setting: Nongovernmental Organizations

In general, the evolution of a non-market public environmental interest has been characterized by a transition from preoccupation with ad hoc, reactive, and transitory forms of citizen input to better-organized, longer-term, and increasingly 'proactive' activities. Environmental organizations have become a significant force in political lobbying, especially in demanding increased public involvement in resource and environmental decision-making. Environmental groups have had a rapid increase in membership in Canada. As Jeremy Wilson noted:

> The Canadian environmental movement comprises at least 1,800 groups ... [that] vary in size from small, local ones ... to large national groups like Greenpeace with over 300,000 members and the Canadian Wildlife Federation, which claims 620,000 'members, supporters and affiliates.' In between these poles we find major national groups like the Canadian Nature Federation with 36,000 members and the Friends of the Earth with 25,000, along with large provincial and regional organizations such as the Western Canada Wilderness Committee with over 25,000 members and Pollution Probe with 20,000 ... It seems safe to conjecture that over one million Canadians belong to at least one group.[45]

Of course, organized groups often conduct forms of public protest and short-term action as part of their long-term strategies. Large-scale, well-organized campaigns such as the continuing struggle over logging and mining in the Temagami area of Ontario or the Christmas Mountains of New Brunswick, or the Clayoquot Sound protests against logging on Vancouver Island in the early 1990s, in which over 800 people were arrested, have been especially instrumental in highlighting public concerns for government.

Nongovernmental organizations embody the environmental and public interest in varied ways. The 'environmental movement' now embraces nationwide groups ranging from early natural history or conservation organizations such as Ducks Unlimited to those such as Greenpeace that advocate more 'direct action' on environmental issues. While Greenpeace has Canadian roots, many organizations are spin-offs of American and other global organizations. Still others are local in membership and objectives. These organizations often promote specific environmental ideologies and serve not only to define new strategies and objectives concerning specific issues but also to articulate new directions for conceptualizing existing and future relations between humans and the natural world.

Environmental organizations have been instrumental in raising public and political consciousness about an extensive array of environmental problems. Wilderness preservation has been pursued by the Sierra Club, Western Canada Wilderness Committee (WCWC), and other organizations, while pollution and recycling have been addressed by Pollution Probe, the Society Promoting Environmental Conservation (SPEC), and others. Some organizations, such as the David Suzuki Foundation, conduct independent research, while others, such as the West Coast Environmental Law Association, Canadian Environmental Law Association, and Sierra Legal Defense Fund, offer legal skills and information to members of the public and engage in a wide variety of environmental and legal reform issues. Thus, organizations represent either single or multiple issues, may be local, national, or international, and engage in a multiplicity of activities.

There is considerable variation in funding, resources, and political strategies as well. The majority of environmental organizations are funded primarily by member donations, grants, and returns from specific projects, and, as a consequence, they continue to represent a rather impermanent influence on the policy process. Both the impermanence and the amount of funding deter the lobbying potential of environmental groups. Again, as Wilson has noted: 'no Canadian environmental group has resources adequate enough to cover all of the government officials who play significant roles in the typical policy process.'[46] Thus, the lack of funding and organizational stability, in addition to other factors, tends to reinforce the front-end, agenda-setting role of environmental groups.

Environmental organizations follow numerous strategies in their activities, which both directly and indirectly impact the agenda-setting stage of the policy process. Their actions encompass two major trends: public-oriented activism, and political-institutional lobbying. As Wilson observes, 'Many groups ... practise a kind of dual politics, mixing the pressure group's pragmatism with the social movement's commitment to the goals of societal transformation and its sensitivity to co-optation.'[47] Given the pragmatic and ideological limitations that they face in accessing the policy process, many groups feel that their energies and talents are better spent in public education. This approach provides a feedback loop within the first policy stage, redirecting policy concerns back to the general public, from whom they can then be more forcefully articulated and directed toward agenda-setting. This then contributes to a groundswell of public support for new environmental initiatives, and it may also mobilize individuals and additional groups around certain issues.

Institutionalized Societal Agenda-Setting: Public Inquiries, Task Forces, Round Tables, and Environmental Assessments

Over the past several decades, new avenues for public participation – various kinds of boards, commissions, and tribunals – have provided more institutionalized means for citizen involvement. The 1990s have ushered in a number of new instruments through which the public's participation is actively sought by the state. Environmental task forces, round tables, land-use planning commissions, and other advisory instruments have been created by governments in various provinces, while new environmental legislation – embodying processes such as mandatory environmental assessment reviews – has created an additional instrument mandating public participation. In the following section, we will review the predominant forms through which the state has elicited and directed public participation and the limitations of these forms of resource and environmental agenda-setting.

As we shall see, institutionalized forms of citizen involvement in resource and environmental policy-making attempt to replace agenda-setting by only those actors intimately involved in project or policy proposals with a process in which 'outsiders' as well as 'insiders' can promote new and alternative perspectives on these issues. Advisory committees, commissions, task forces, and round tables are government-appointed bodies that exercise a policy function in considering environmental issues and resource development. The appointment of members of the public to these and other institutional bodies is also, in itself, a means of increasing the representation of the public, both at the agenda-setting stage of the policy process and, perhaps increasingly, throughout the entire process.

Consultative processes include both short-term and long-range mechanisms to provide recommendations to government concerning environmental policy. Increasingly, the role of the public in these processes has expanded to include participation in the design of the consultation process as well as in making policy recommendations to government. Following the tabling of a commission's recommendations, public participation may also be extended to administrative activities. Mandated by legislation to form regional resource boards or similar regulatory instruments, for example, appropriate levels of government will often elicit public involvement in administrative activities such as regulatory monitoring and environmental impact assessment.

Public Inquiries

Consultative hearings are conducted within the framework of public inquiries to investigate issues of concern, make recommendations, and formulate policy. Theoretically, the commission of inquiry supplements and shortcuts the electoral process by securing information and making recommendations that are then taken into account by the appropriate branch of government. Although not binding on government, recommendations are rarely completely disregarded and are typically submitted to the legislature, becoming public documents. The subject matter of the inquiry is typically urgent, of concern to more than one ministry and level of government, and is the subject of some controversy. The public inquiry is invoked at the discretion of government and is subject to political, economic, and social pressures. Indeed, the very initiation of the tribunal is likely to be the product of pressure by public interest groups. Thus, while the consultative tribunal may not be the first step in agenda-setting, it may be considered a formal means of recognizing that the issue is officially on the agenda.[48]

A number of consultative inquiries serve as benchmarks in the area of resource and environmental policy. Perhaps the best known was the Mackenzie Valley Pipeline Inquiry headed by Mr. Justice Thomas R. Berger in the mid-1970s to assess the desirability of building a gas pipeline through the Mackenzie River Valley.[49] This inquiry was instrumental in changing the concept of public participation by emphasizing the necessity for, and validity of, community involvement. This inquiry also considered other related issues, including the status of public participation in the decision making process and the consideration of the social and cultural context of the proposed pipeline. Berger created a precedent by extending the concept of public participation, providing funding for public participants and establishing both community and formal hearings through which aboriginal participation was fostered. The success of the tribunal, not only in reconsidering and deferring the construction of the pipeline but also in reaffirming the social traditions of indigenous peoples and local communities, elevated public participation to a more effective and official form of involvement in the policy process. While the costs of public participation were extensive, the expenditure of '$5.3 million of public funds represents a small fraction compared to the total social and environmental costs associated with the project, most of which would have to be borne by the indigenous people of the North.'[50]

Other inquiries have followed this tradition, confirming the importance of public involvement in natural resource consultation. The Alaska Highway Pipeline Inquiry (Lysyk Commission) called in its 1977 report for guarantees of public participation in the regulatory process. The West Coast Oil Ports Inquiry (Thompson Commission), although prematurely terminated, continued this emphasis on high-profile, community-based public participation. With regard to uranium mining, a number of public inquiries have been held in Canada, all of which have had provisions for public involvement. The Bayda or Cluff Lake Board of Inquiry in Saskatchewan in 1974 addressed questions that ranged from the specific plans proposed for uranium mining to the dangers of nuclear proliferation. The British Columbia Royal Commission of Inquiry into Uranium Mining, convened in British Columbia in 1979, also solicited input from public interest groups and provided funding to facilitate their participation.

At both federal and provincial levels, consultative inquiries have provided a means by which the public can be heard in the formulation of environmental policy. Yet while the climate for public participation in the 1970s led some observers to note the development of a 'tradition' of participation in natural resource issues, the ad hoc nature of these commissions and the paucity of successors in later decades leads us to question their long-term viability as agenda-setting institutions.

Environmental Task Forces

Environmental task forces have been created for planning, consultation, or conflict resolution concerning specific environmental issues. The task force may be invoked by a government when there is an arena of environmental conflict in which different groups have different interests and perspectives regarding the allocation or designation of the environment. In British Columbia, for instance, the Clayoquot Sound Task Force was one of several such bodies created by the provincial government to resolve the dispute between logging and preservationist interests in several ecologically and politically 'sensitive' areas of the province.

Commissions are also created as instruments to consult a variety of interests with regard to environmental planning. Increased diversification of the economy, the rapid expansion of service industries such as tourism, and accelerated technological change have led to increased demands on the natural environment. The development of new planning and regulatory functions has created opportunities for increased public involvement. Recent planning initiatives, such as the Commission on Resources and Environment (CORE) established in British Columbia in 1992, addressed the need for, and process of, citizen involvement in land-use policy. In several years of operation prior to its cancellation in 1996, CORE engaged in a number of activities, which included large-scale regional planning initiatives in three regions of the province. Extensive public consultation and negotiations between multiple interests took place in each region.

The CORE process reflected many of the new directions for citizen involvement in environmental policy. The Commission on Resources and Environment Act, which set out the mandate of the commission, required:

(1) the development, for public and government consideration, of a BC-wide strategy for land use and related resource and environmental management;
(2) the development, implementation, and monitoring of
    • regional planning processes to define the uses to which the areas of the province may be put
    • community-based (local) participatory processes to consider land-use issues
    • a dispute-resolution system for land-use and related resource and environmental issues;
(3) assurance of effective and integrated management of the resources and environment of the province by
    • facilitating the coordination of initiatives within the government
    • encouraging the participation of aboriginal peoples.[51]

The establishment of CORE reflected several innovative initiatives in Canadian resource and environmental policy. CORE included mandated citizen participation; it was directed toward land-use planning in an anticipatory rather than a reactive manner; and it was given a strong policy role in developing both a provincial land-use strategy and local and regional aspects of that strategy. The act was also unique in that it provided for 'the independence of the office from the ministries and agencies of government with which it deals, full investigative and public hearing powers akin to a standing commission of inquiry, and the responsibility to report to the legislature and the public as well as to the executive branch.'[52]

While the CORE process was successful in generating public participation and in contributing to interaction between interested parties, it also experienced a number of problems. Its lack of decision-making and adjudicating authority undermined its effectiveness, and its selection of representatives from different sectors and interests was criticized from all positions. Yet in spite of these critiques, CORE's emphasis on a more widespread, participatory, and preliminary process of institutionalized land-use planning was indicative of continuing changes in resource and environmental agenda-setting.

Round Tables

Most Canadian jurisdictions moved to establish environmental round tables between 1988 and 1990. However, the tasks specified for these round tables have differed, as have their membership and their success. In some jurisdictions, round tables were expected to act as legitimation devices, educating the public about the merits of conservation strategies developed elsewhere. In others, round tables were mandated to develop conservation strategies but were given little control over their implementation. Only a few were given the ability to formulate a conservation strategy and directly affect its implementation.[53]

Significantly, the round tables have varied greatly in composition. Members have come from various locations in Canadian society and include an array of government representatives, corporate executives and members of business associations, representatives of labour and farmers' unions and associations, representatives of environmental groups, members of Native bands and organizations, and members of the 'interested public' or 'policy community' (including professors and university administrators, private consultants, members of private and public policy 'think tanks,' and the public at large).

On an aggregate basis, however, government and corporate officials have dominated the round tables, together accounting for half of total initial membership in the 1988-90 period. Environmental groups accounted for only 15 per cent of total membership. Labour, farming, and First Nations groups comprised less than 10 per cent of membership, while a variety of members of the policy community not included in these groups accounted for about one-quarter of total membership.[54]

All the round tables formed to date share several characteristics, regardless of the nature of their composition and mandates. First, all were clearly designed to raise the public profile of government environmental efforts, and all, at a minimum, addressed the need to relegitimate environmental policy-making through public education. Second, all report directly to cabinet if not to the first minister in the jurisdiction in which they were formed. Yet most round tables have attempted to go beyond the level of public education and pure legitimation and to involve previously disenfranchised groups in new patterns of policy formulation and implementation. The recent dissolution of several round tables, however, casts some doubt on their ability to acheive these objectives.

Environmental Assessment Review Processes

While commissions, task forces, round tables, and other processes have been initiated in response to emergent – and often contentious – issues or to specific environmental activities and regions, there have been other attempts to statutorily provide for more routine public participation with regard to environmental policy. Perhaps the most well known of these efforts have been the federal environmental assessment review process (EARP) and its provincial counterparts, which have been evolving for the past twenty years.[55]

These processes represent attempts to legislate public participation in a routine manner as a formal stage in the policy process. They confirm the importance of planning as an anticipatory, rather than a reactive, means of environmental management. Involvement in the EARP process combines features of consultative and administrative tribunals. Initiation of the process reflects its administrative origins in that environmental assessment has been legislated and prescribes certain routine features of public participation, but the relatively relaxed procedures of EARP hearings and the information-gathering functions attest to its consultative status. Although these reviews can help to set agendas, they also have a major role to play in the implementation of project decisions, thus extending public involvement to a greater administrative role. Given their significance to the overall Canadian resource and environmental policy process, we will discuss the formulation and implementation of federal environmental assessment review legislation in a case study in Chapter 8.

Limitations on Societal Agenda-Setting

All of these agenda-setting instruments – ad hoc, organizational, and institutional – attempt to enhance the public's access to the policy process. Most reflect efforts to expand and empower public participation by 'retrofitting' existing instruments, although some involve developing additional venues of involvement.

Yet public involvement in this initial phase of the policy cycle continues to be limited by a number of fundamental constraints. Many of the activities of the environmental movement, of course, are directed to more general goals, such as public education, or are too general, diffuse, radical, or philosophical for incorporation into specific policy agendas. Many environmentalists are suspicious of consultative policy processes, as well, and intentionally engage in organizational strategies that follow the beat of a different drum. Direct action and media coverage are perceived by some groups to be more effective vehicles for influencing the policy process than inclusion on various boards, commissions, or tribunals. But even if groups and individuals choose to participate in institutional processes, they face numerous hurdles in attaining their ends.

Typically, appointments to consultative bodies, and often the bodies themselves, are short term rather than ongoing. The establishment of a commission may therefore serve to postpone or divert public attention from the issue. Members of public interest groups may find themselves co-opted by the terms of reference, the influence of other board members, or the procedures themselves. Energy devoted to approved participatory venues channels participation into positions of cooperation and compromise and detracts from both a hard bargaining position and other forms of resistance that some believe are more effective. Finally, the appointed body typically lacks substantive power to implement decisions, restricting its impact upon later levels of the policy process.[56]

The Issue of Representation: Who Speaks for What Interest?

The discretionary character of contemporary practices of public involvement may be inadequate to ensure the inclusion of all interests. There is not yet a mechanism for ensuring that a range of environmental perspectives is represented or that their relative importance to, or impacts on, the environment are assessed. An environmental 'tokenism,' may result in the selection or appointment of a limited number of environmental representatives. In fact, in many instances, the public interest is often identified by default as any antagonist to a proponent's development plans. Furthermore, the anthropocentric bias of political institutions, also restricts the consideration of all related issues and interests. For instance, a task force on air quality may include industrial producers, Ministry of Health officials, and organizations representing human health interests, while the health and survival of other species may remain unaddressed.

As we have seen, environmental interests themselves reflect a broad spectrum of concerns, including those of biodiversity, health protection, and contamination. Yet due to inevitable funding shortages, many environmental groups may be required to work together in order to participate, resulting in what Alistair Lucas refers to as 'inappropriate coalitions' that can diffuse the activities of the individual groups.[57] The assumption that all 'environmental' interests are 'non-productive' is incorrect, as when an industry coalition, such as SHARE in British Columbia (a thinly camouflaged vehicle of the forest industry), purports to reflect a broad spectrum of environmental interests.[58]

The representation of a variety of interests through public involvement in environmental policy formation is further limited by social class, ethnicity, and other factors, as it is in other political arenas. While many environmental impacts often affect marginalized groups disproportionately, these groups have few resources to expend in resistance. The geography of poverty locates the poor near toxic waste and other sites of environmental degradation, while the employment of minority groups as cheap sources of labour poses additional health risks to those desperate for work. While the environmental movement is sometimes dismissed as a Western, middle-class phenomenon, this characterization is in part the very product of participation in state-directed processes. The institutional requirements of such activity – expenditures of temporal, financial, educational, and verbal resources – reinforce representation from those most likely to possess the right types of economic and human capital.

While it is possible to generate a more representative participation, as the Berger Commission demonstrated, most environmental processes continue to represent less than a full spectrum of both social and environmental interests. Biases that reflect class, gender, race, and other factors within the environmental arena can be viewed as rationales for further extending and democratizing those forums.

Not only the substantive identification of interests but also the economic genesis of their participation are factors in representation. Environmental groups typically represent diffuse aggregate interests, and the relatively small and extra-economic interest of individual members acts as a disincentive to participation. Consider, for example, the application of a smelter to expand its physical plant, which would increase the amounts of effluent in surrounding air and water. The motivation for this expansion is economic – increased production will generate jobs and greater corporate profit. In contrast, citizens who live in the area may oppose this application because they are concerned about adverse health effects to humans as well as other species. While some may be motivated because they represent competing economic interests (e.g., fishing or tourism), others are active because the proposed development is perceived as deleterious to themselves, to others, and to other species. The diffuse benefits of participation will not directly or financially compensate their efforts, while the lobbying and participation of project proponents yield immediate economic benefits.

The Lack of Resources and Support for Public Involvement

In spite of considerable publicity, Canadian public interest groups remain underrepresented in regulatory and policy proceedings compared to producer groups.[59] Representational imbalances are not an anomaly but the product of government instruments and regulatory processes in which, typically, highly concentrated interests with direct economic and political stakes in an issue (those of corporate or state proponents) initiate activities to which informally organized citizen groups may not have the resources to respond.[60] As noted above, while proponents' interventions are often tied to the ongoing efforts at regulatory compliance of the agency or industry, expenditures for public interest intervention lack an economic incentive as well as a base.

Accordingly, one of the major issues around public participation is that of funding. With the increase in formal instruments for public participation, and the extra-economic (e.g., ecological, spiritual, health) genesis of much environmental participation, the issue of financial support for participants has come to the forefront. The traditional notion of self-generating and discretionary participation assumes that finances are the responsibility of the organization itself. From bake sales to door-to-door soliciting, the onus of funding the activities of citizen groups in affecting policy rests with the group itself.

This is often considered proper, because only if the public is highly motivated and well organized will it direct resources to influence policy-making. Hence, this form of 'market-based' funding is often viewed as acting as a kind of control against frivolous environmental action.[61] But while many successful environmental campaigns – from those against clearcut logging in British Columbia to those opposing spruce budworm spraying in New Brunswick and Nova Scotia – have been conducted in this manner, the appropriateness of self-funding for environmental organizations is questionable.

Two significant organizational constraints to public participation are the 'free rider' issue and the problem of high transaction costs involved in maintaining large memberships. While members of the public may benefit from their representation by an environmental group, their rewards are not primarily financial, and there is little direct motivation for their contribution to its support. Thus, public involvement is directed toward the 'public good,' and members of the public become 'free riders,' reaping the rewards of any such actions. Furthermore, transaction costs expand with the number of people represented, because the indirect benefit of public involvement is not directly shared, either socially or financially, with others. Thus, in addition to the organizational and legitimation requirements of public participation, free rider and transaction costs provide a strong rationale for increased funding of public interest groups.

The ad hoc and discretionary nature of the funding mechanisms currently used to fund the majority of public participation processes is a problem for additional reasons. Inadequate funding is a problem because it directly affects the character of the submission or intervention that citizens can provide. Funding may limit access to experts, restrict the amount of time available for the analysis of documents, and curtail the preparation of organizational facilities and the training of individuals for the processes at hand. Inadequate funding may result in the formation of inappropriate coalitions, through which positions are diluted and information is 'mainstreamed' in the search for common ground.[62]

These and other arguments lead many observers to suggest that there is a need to increase government funding of public participants in environmental agenda-setting. While such funding has become increasingly difficult in an era of intense fiscal restraint, increases in legitimation crises may tempt the state in this direction. While many environmental groups are self-supporting, state funding of an organization or activity is often necessary to get an environmental issue on the agenda and to influence the policy process on its behalf. Funding is central to the performance of basic activities: photocopying, telephone calls and other liaison work, media contact, membership drives, and day-to-day administrative tasks. With more formal and legal venues, funding supports additional services, such as expert witnesses, who may be recruited to prepare submissions, testify, or otherwise aid in the policy process. At the present time, many commissions and other institutional forums for public participation have some discretion in allocating funds to participants. Unfortunately, some participants have used this discretion to exclude or favour other participants. Some agencies, such as the National Energy Board, have rejected funding applications on the ground that there is no legal authority to require them. Recent legislation, such as environmental assessment laws, is thus moving toward increasing delineation of mechanisms for funding public interest participation.

Today in Canada, many citizen groups raise funds to support themselves, while others receive grants from government to fulfil their various mandates. Single-issue groups may be more successful in achieving funding than umbrella organizations, which must endure upswings and downturns in public concern. When specific instruments (e.g., task forces, consultative hearings) for public participation are identified, funding is often attached as a means of ensuring the representation of the public. Kenneth Engelhart and Michael Trebilcock strongly urge the support of public interest groups in regulatory decision-making by either a government grant program or a tax credit in general activities, and by ad hoc cost awards by regulatory agencies for formal representation of the public. They caution: 'Failure to take such steps ... will fuel a persistent and ultimately corrosive social perception of the regulatory process as a game played by regulator and regulatee, with an empty chair as symbol of the fact that other interests, while centrally affected by its outcomes, are systematically disenfranchised from effective participation in that process.'[63]

Procedural and Technical Issues Discouraging Public Involvement

As avenues to public participation in the policy process have increased, questions of procedural fairness have emerged and contributed to additional concerns surrounding the public's role in agenda-setting. Increased formalization of public access to policy agendas brings with it procedural issues that emerge in the process of participation. These issues reflect the public's disadvantage in procedural and substantive expertise, as well as the very structure of participation itself. In spite of precedents set by the Berger Commission and other royal commissions of inquiry to promote more equitable access to members of the public, citizen 'performances' in public forums are discouraged both by cultural norms and by informal sanctions that may be applied. One participant in the Royal Commission into Uranium Mining in British Columbia observed that the setting was adversarial and formal enough to intimidate community members from speaking.

> We found ourselves in a physical arrangement which, in our opinion, was not designed to encourage dialogue or maximize participation. The position of the Commissioners on a raised platform facing the assemblage suggested adversaries rather than comrades in a common search for truth. The necessity of being called upon and of walking to a microphone before one could speak discouraged spontaneity and overlooked the fact that many people are more comfortable with speaking off the cuff than reading a prepared statement ... What we are getting at is the process ... seems formal enough to intimidate some people.[64]

In consultative tribunals, quasijudicial or other standardized formats provide, in theory, a parallel basis of participation for all participants. While the procedures may at first appear to be similar to all participants, an unequal basis of participation emerges under more careful scrutiny. Problems include difficulties ensuring access to technical knowledge and to specific information relevant to projects or proposals under consideration. In the traditional professional, technical, and bureaucratic resource decision-making process, scientific knowledge and methodology are shared by those with similar training and perspectives. Greater representation of the public in the policy-making process requires greater access to information, knowledge, and skills.

General Technical Knowledge

But mere inclusion in policy processes does not provide public representatives with scientific backgrounds and educations similar to those enjoyed by bureaucrats and project proponents. Resource and environmental issues, while reflecting ethical and social concerns, are scientific and economic issues and are defended with reference to appropriate expertise. Participation thus assumes specialized knowledge of an issue by members of the public and their ability to construct the issue as problematic. In contrast to proponents whose daily work relies on an educational background or administrative familiarity with the issue at hand, members of the public are typically employed in a range of occupations with no direct relation to the issue.

Preparation for lay participation thus involves an education in the technical aspects of the issue of concern, and it may extend to networking with other environmental organizations or involve extensive research in the technical aspects of the area of interest. New or alternative positions must be justified on grounds acceptable to the tribunal. Members of the public must secure and understand information that leads them, first, to identify an issue as problematic and, second, to be able to support their position in the face of well-informed adversaries.

Access to Specialized Project or Proposal Information
This raises another problem of access to specific technical or administrative information. Proponents have available considerable information generated in standard practices of development applications or resource extraction. This information is often considered to be either private property or, if released, a competitive disadvantage to the proponent.

This situation was reflected in the community hearings of the British Columbia Royal Commission of Inquiry into Uranium Mining. In this case, the identification of sites in which uranium exploration was taking place was restricted by existing mining regulations. While hearings were scheduled in communities of interest to mining companies, the public did not know the location of exploration and proposed mining sites and thus could not assess the geographical aspects of the issue. Members of the public perceived the lack of knowledge imparted to them as an impediment to participation, as one participant indicated:

There are 54,000 people living on the west side of [the] Okanagan Lake system from Summerland to the border ... Up until a few weeks ago, I would hazard a guess that 99 percent of these people did not know there was any uranium exploration going on in the immediate area. Those who did know were probably prospectors, mining company officials, those working for the Mining Division of the Provincial Government and the Federal government ...

Why was such a large segment of the population ignorant about uranium exploration in the area? Was it, one, because we were all very stupid or unwilling to learn anything; or, was it because the British Columbia Government and/or the Federal Government, and the Mining Fraternity were being very careful to keep the matter as quiet as possible?[65]

Thus, the identification of an issue, its perception as problematic, the articulation of possible solutions or strategies, and the mobilization of resources are all brought into play in order for the agenda-setting process to occur.

Whose Agenda, Which Style? Rethinking Agenda-Setting

In the formal study of agenda-setting, a distinction is often made between the *systemic* or unofficial public agenda and the *institutional* or official agenda. The systemic agenda 'consists of all issues that are commonly perceived by members of the political community as meriting public attention and as involving matters within the legitimate jurisdiction of existing governmental authority.'[66] This is essentially a society's agenda for the discussion of *public* problems, such as crime or health care, water quality or wilderness preservation. Thus, while we use the notion of 'agenda-setting' as if there were only one agenda, and one process of inclusion, there is a distinction between the larger 'net' of all possible issues and the 'catch' of those issues counted and included as the official agenda at the end of the policy day.

Each society has literally hundreds of issues that concern some citizens, who would have the government do something about them. However, only a small proportion of the problems on the public or systemic agenda are actually taken up by the government for serious consideration. Once the government has accepted that something needs to be done about a problem, it can be said to have entered onto the institutional agenda, which is comprised of issues to which the government has agreed to give serious attention. In other words, the public agenda is an agenda for discussion, while the institutional agenda is an agenda for action, indicating that the formal policy process for dealing with the problem in question has begun.

As a way of explaining the dynamics of this stage of the policy cycle, in the case of Canadian resource and environmental agenda-setting, we will focus on the role played by state and societal actors in moving issues from the systemic to the institutional agenda. Over twenty years ago, the American political scientists Cobb, Ross, and Ross developed a model of typical agenda-setting styles. In their analysis, they argued that three basic patterns of agenda-setting could be discerned, distinguished by the origins of the issue as well as by the resources utilized to facilitate their inclusion on the agenda.

In the *outside initiation* model, 'issues arise in nongovernmental groups and are then expanded sufficiently to reach, first, the public [systemic] agenda and, finally, the formal [institutional] agenda.'[67] In this model, issues are initiated when some part of the public articulates a grievance and demands its resolution by the government. The aggrieved groups attempt to expand support for their demand, a process that may involve submerging the specific complaint within a more general one and the formation of alliances across groups. Finally, these groups join and lobby with others in attempting to get the expanded issue onto the formal agenda. If they have the requisite political resources and skills and can outmanoeuvre the advocates of other issues and actions, they can often succeed in having their issue enter the formal agenda. Thus, as Cobb, Ross, and Ross summarize it, 'The outside initiative model applies to the situation in which a group outside the government structure 1) articulates a grievance, 2) tries to expand interest in the issue to enough other groups in the population to gain a place on the public agenda, in order to 3) create sufficient pressure on decision makers to force the issue onto the formal agenda for their serious consideration.'[68]

Some examples of outside initiation can be seen in Canadian resource and environmental policy-making. The Pulp Pollution Campaign in British Columbia in the 1980s is one. In this instance, over fifty environmental groups joined forces and engaged in public education and lobbying to pressure the government to enact tougher antipollution regulations. They fought for stronger standards and a tougher enforcement protocol, and they were successful in achieving both.

The *mobilization* model is quite different and describes 'decision-makers trying to expand an issue from a formal to a public agenda.'[69] In this model, issues are simply placed on the formal agenda by the government with no necessary preliminary expansion from a publicly recognized grievance. There may be considerable debate within government over the issue, but the public may well be kept in the dark about the policy and its development until its formal announcement. The policy may be specified in detail, or it may just establish general principles whose specification will be worked out later.

Expansion of support for the new policy is important in this model, however, because successful implementation depends on a favourable public reaction to the policy. Toward this end, government leaders may hold meetings and engage in public relations campaigns aimed at mobilizing public support for their decisions. As the authors put it, 'The mobilization model describes the process of agenda building in situations where political leaders initiate a policy but require the support of the mass public for its implementation ... The crucial problem is to move the issue from the formal agenda to the public agenda.'[70] Examples of mobilization in Canadian resource and environmental policy can be seen in many government-sponsored consultative processes, which range from the planning process concerning Banff National Park to the recent provincewide CORE land-use planning exercise in British Columbia.

In the third, or *inside initiation*, model, influential groups with special access to decisionmakers initiate a policy and do not necessarily want it to be expanded and contested in public for technical and/or political reasons. In this model, initiation and specification occur simultaneously as a group or government agency enunciates a grievance and specifies some potential solution to the problem. Expansion is restricted to specialized groups or agencies with some knowledge of, or interest in, the subject. Entrance is virtually automatic due to the privileged place of those desiring a decision. According to Cobb, Ross, and Ross, 'Proposals arise within governmental units or in groups close to the government. The issue is then expanded to identification and attention groups in order to create sufficient pressure on decision makers to place the item on the formal agenda. At no point is the public greatly involved, and the initiators make no effort to get the issue on the public agenda. On the contrary, they try to keep it off.'[71]

Despite examples of other agenda-setting styles in Canada,[72] it is our contention that the majority of resource as well as environmental issues in this country originate within the context of inside initiation. Stumpage rates, changes in park regulations, the licensing of hunters and guides, pollution regulations, and waste disposal siting are among the policy issues that reflect the process of inside initiation. This is not due to an intentional conspiracy between productive and state interests, nor does it reflect the total exclusion of the public from agenda-setting. It does, however, reflect the existing government institutional structure, which, as this chapter has shown, is geared to evaluate and respond to external changes and to internal pressures without public participation.[73]

Conclusion: The Canadian Resource and Environmental Agenda-Setting Style

From the above discussion, it should be apparent that two of the most critical factors in identifying a typical pattern of agenda-setting in any policy area are the level and extent of public participation, and the response or 'preresponse' of the state in directing and accommodating this activity.[74] That is, the manner in which state and societal actors interact within policy subsystems is a crucial component of a sectoral agenda-setting style. A key element in the process of agenda-setting revolves around the creation of 'policy monopolies' in which specific sets of policy actors grouped together in policy subsystems gain the ability to control the interpretation of a problem and thus the manner in which it is conceived and discussed.[75]

As the discussion in this chapter has shown, in the Canadian resource and environmental area, public participation has been extended over the past several decades, parallelling and perhaps preceding the emergence of environmental policy in a sector previously devoted almost exclusively to resource exploitation. Among the major developments are an extended profile of public participation with respect to (1) the range of policy decisions, (2) formal entitlement or inclusion, (3) increased financial support, and (4) the extent and duration of the policy process.[76]

Yet many observers would argue that these developments are primarily symbolic and have not led to a major shift in the overall direction of policy from its traditional resource exploitation orientation. We have discussed the range of constraints encountered in the representation of the public interest. These constraints mean that in contrast to an orthodox pluralist approach ensuring the representation of multiple competing interests, the public in fact plays a more limited role in the agenda-setting process. Support for this view is found in the fact that the rhetoric of public participation is primarily geared toward discretionary forms of public consultation rather than mandatory and adequately supported inclusion on formal agenda-setting bodies. This situation is due to the economic and institutional advantages of productive and state actors, which are able to overcome most of the disincentives that public interest groups face. Limited and sporadic participation, short-term and discretionary institutional venues for involvement, inequalities of access to the policy arena, procedural limitations, and lack of power in decision-making all act as deterrents to effective public interest representation in the policy process.

Demand for an increased role of the public in policy formation in the 1960s and 1970s resulted in an expanded public presence on boards, tribunals, and councils. At present, however, the effectiveness of this increased profile of public participation continues to be constrained by a number of forces, as discussed above. While the public is a factor in the generation of resource and environmental policy, the criticisms raised in this chapter reveal the serious limitations that govern the extent and effectiveness of both diffuse and organized publics in formal policy processes.

With the increased emphasis on public involvement in administrative processes, and the reactive nature of much public activity with regard to environmental concerns, it can be argued that the policy agenda in general continues to be established through traditional actors and channels designed to expedite resource extraction – that is, through a process of inside initiation – with only temporary examples of other forms of agenda-setting in particular situations. This is consistent with the *de facto* preoccupation of the policy process with administrative concerns, reflecting not only a preference for existing institutional (organizational) processes but also for a traditional negotiative policy style, as we will observe in Chapter 7.

Despite much lip service paid to public participation, the public is often prevented from actively participating in the policy process or from articulating its grievances in a policy-relevant manner. At best, the public is mobilized from time to time by state officials seeking sanction and support for their initiatives. Even the record of mobilizations such as the ill-fated federal Green Plan of the early 1990s has illustrated the continued dominance of the inside initiation style. The development activity initiated by both private and state proponents, and the regulatory processes accompanying this development, are in practice the key elements of agenda-setting in this sector.

Over twenty years ago, C.G. Morley wrote, 'There are no laws which require that the public be involved in the determination of the broad policies relevant to environmental quality generally and resource management specifically.'[77] In the intervening years, new environmental legislation has been designed and implemented, and the provision of extralegal mechanisms enhanced, not only in response to a climate of growing environmental populism but also as increasingly institutionalized public participation indirectly bolsters the legitimacy of the state. While environmental organizations have joined the public interest roster and have been successful in raising public consciousness on environmental issues, their peripheral position and restricted capabilities limit their contributions to the policy process. In Canadian resource and environmental agenda-setting, it appears that *plus ça change, plus c'est la même chose*. The public, although an increasingly visible force in agenda-setting, remains secondary to traditional state and productive actors.

7
Policy Formulation: Identifying the Canadian Resource and Environmental Policy Subsystem

The resource and environmental subsystem comprises both the larger community of actors and interests as well as the more powerful networks that are engaged in the policy process. The preceding chapter discussed both the potential of, and the constraints to, public participation in agenda-setting. The potential for the representation of emerging interests, especially those represented by non-market actors, is a feature of Canadian democracy, and, as we have discussed, these interests have become more visible, especially at a symbolic level, in agenda-setting. Yet significant obstacles to public participation limit its potential to emerge fully as a mainstream player in the policy process. Given the popular belief that democracy is 'rule by the people,' this raises important questions about who, if not the public, is actually making Canadian resource and environmental policy and to what ends this policy is directed.

On the basis of observations about the Canadian natural resource and environmental policy subsystem – the principle actors and their interactions with each other – we can say a great deal about the nature of the policy options placed before governments to resolve issues that have made it onto the official agenda.[1]

Chapter 6 identified a range of potential and actual subsystem members, including a variety of state and societal, and market and non-market, actors. In this chapter, we will describe these actors in greater depth and examine the nature of their interaction. As the discussion in this chapter will show, analyzing the structure of the policy community and the policy network present in a given policy area reveals a great deal about the propensity for new and/or radical options to be developed.[2] To put it another way, an analysis of subsystem members and their interaction helps us to understand why significant change is rarely forthcoming in Canadian natural resource and environmental policy-making.

Defining Policy Formulation

In accordance with the cycle model of public policy-making set out in Chapter 5, after a public problem has entered onto the official or formal agenda, some course of action for resolving the problem must be proposed. The definition and exploration of the various options available for addressing governing problems form the basis of policy formulation.

Like agenda-setting, policy formulation is a diffuse and dynamic process, difficult to reduce to any one event or stage of activity. According to Charles Jones, the distinguishing characteristics of policy formulation are:

(1) Formulation need not be limited to one set of actors. Thus there may well be two or more formulation groups producing competing (or complementary) proposals.
(2) Formulation may proceed without clear definition of the problem, or without formulators ever having much contact with the affected groups ...
(3) There is no necessary coincidence between formulation and particular institutions, though it is a frequent activity of bureaucratic agencies.
(4) Formulation and reformulation may occur over a long period of time without ever building sufficient support for any one proposal.
(5) There are often several appeal points for those who lose in the formulation process at any one level.
(6) The process itself never has neutral effects. Somebody wins and somebody loses even in the workings of science.[3]

Policy formulation often originates directly in agenda-setting as problems and potential solutions are placed simultaneously on the government agenda. Or solutions may be developed after a problem has been accepted for response by the government. In all cases, the range of available options needs to be considered and narrowed down to those that policymakers can accept or consider feasible.[4] This process of defining, considering, and accepting or rejecting options is the substance of policy formulation.

In terms of resource and environmental policy, we might expect Canadian policymakers to identify a number of policy options that range from the more radical and less market-driven options expressed by non-productive interests to the more conservative and market-based preferences of industry and project proponents. Why certain types of options are often proposed in this policy sector and why others appear much less frequently are questions addressed in the discussion below.

Canadian Resource and Environmental Policy
Subsystem Membership

In Chapter 4, the discussion of policy subsystems identified generic subsystem members. They include societal actors not directly related to the productive process, such as members of community and environmental groups, the media, and political parties. Also included as societal actors are representatives of economic interests, such as labour, management, and others, whose stake in resource use derives from concerns for productivity.

The second major category of subsystem members includes state actors involved in the process of resource and environmental management and in the public ownership of most resources. In Chapter 6, we argued that the highly symbolic nature of public representation often obscures the strength of economic and state actors in the resource and environmental policy subsystem, which remains largely inaccessible to non-traditional and non-productive social actors.

In this chapter, we will explore the continuing articulation of policy options within the subsystem, demonstrating how policy formation is socially and politically constructed. The specific character of the Canadian natural resource and environmental subsystem will be examined. After discussing the characteristics of the general types of actors, and their location within the Canadian political and economic structure, we will introduce survey research to describe the nature of knowledge and interaction between sectoral subsystem members. This analysis will allow us to characterize the nature of the resource and environmental policy community and policy network and to draw several conclusions about policy formulation in this sector.

Societal Members of the Canadian Resource and Environmental Policy Subsystem

As we noted in Chapter 6, representation of a public interest in environmental protection has been attempted through the use of a variety of instruments designed to facilitate public participation in the policy process. The need for public participation in policy formulation as well as in agenda-setting is often invoked as a remedy for government ineffectiveness or to offset the legitimation problems caused by the increased emphasis on bureaucracy rather than democracy in modern society. As one careful observer of the sector put it,

Due to the extraordinary demands on government and the increasing complexity of society over the last several decades, we have delegated more and more authority ... Our political system appears increasingly unrepresentative ... Our judicial system has become irrelevant to many citizens through the excessive cost and delay of participation and through its inability to deal with dynamic, multi-party, public policy disputes which simply cannot be adjudicated on a right versus wrong basis ... And our administrative agencies are often seen as hierarchical structures ... that focus the attention of public servants upwards towards the source of authority and accountability, rather than towards the individuals directly affected.[5]

Increased recognition of the role of social and ethical considerations in scientific and technical decisions has also validated the role of the public in environmental policy. Public participation, by including social and ethical dimensions, is viewed as a means of tempering the tendency of administrators and governments to put forward only scientific and technical proposals for resolving resource and environmental problems.[6]

The Public

We have seen that a variety of institutional, procedural, and administrative constraints limit the capabilities of public participation in the resource and environmental policy subsystem. In effect, the public is like a cluster of bees buzzing around an already occupied hive, garnering attention but generally unable to obtain access to the policy subsystem. This is not to say that members of the public are never successful, or that they do not influence the general climate of policy formation, but that the public's capability to directly affect policy-making is more limited than might be surmised at first glance.

Representation of Non-Producer Interests

The representation of the public interest by non-producer groups in resource and environmental policy formulation provides countervailing perspectives in the production of policy options to be considered by governments, especially following an inside initiation process of agenda-setting. Competition between heterogeneous, independent, and organized interests in the formulation of policy options helps to provide diverse points of view. Participation by environmental groups can oppose or neutralize the perspectives of entrenched interests and/or project proponents who may already have a formal position in decision-making. As David Lenny has noted:

Pressure from the public may also prod members of the bureaucracy towards a much stronger position in terms of environmental protection. Public involvement will tend to lessen regulator 'capture' by regulatees, and will therefore produce more 'balanced' decisions ... Since the administrative agency must take an objective position, it is necessary for the public ... to become involved so that some voice apart from the industry's will be heard, and therefore the traditionally 'unrepresented' interests will have an influence on the decision-makers.[7]

Specialized interest or pressure groups, media coverage of environmental issues, and political party representation of public sentiments are some of the means by which specific policy proposals reflecting the public interest are formulated. As we have discussed, none of these actors is able to significantly influence the articulation of policy problems. Chapter 6 acknowledges the heightened profile of public interest groups in the policy process but confirms their general lack of success in initiating the institutional agenda-setting process.

While much of their effort involves lobbying politicians, public education about the merits and potential for ecologically sound solutions to Canada's environmental problems is a primary objective of Canadian environmental groups, and the media are a primary instrument used for this purpose. While environmental groups have increased their public profile, media coverage of resource and environmental issues has shifted over the past three decades. The tendency of the media to highlight specific events rather than to cover chronic problems discourages the in-depth analysis of multilayered problems such as environmental degradation and the formulation of long-term policy options for dealing with such problems.

The alliance of the media with productive interests also poses problems for resource and environmental policy formulation. The high concentration of media ownership in Canada, and the connections between economic elites, do not produce a conducive climate for impartial coverage or the promotion of non-status quo policy alternatives. The low profile given to environmental coverage, for example, is at least partially a reflection of this bias. Parlour and Schatzow, in their study of media reportage of environmental issues from 1960 to 1972, also identify as problems the individual basis of editorial decision-making concerning environmental issues, the lack of scientific support for reporters, and the reactive, as opposed to proactive, nature of their coverage of environmental problems.[8]

To what extent have non-status quo policy options been incorporated into party platforms and in the decisions endorsed by mainstream political parties? In Canada, for example, environmental concerns have been introduced with limited success by the major political parties. Both the Liberal Party of Canada and the Progressive Conservative Party of Canada have traditionally endorsed a role for the state in supporting 'free enterprise,' albeit with growing, if reluctant, acceptance of its regulatory and social welfare roles. However, while they have introduced and approved environmental measures, they have been reluctant to include such concerns in more than a symbolic fashion in their party platforms.

The Liberal Party, which has governed Canada at the federal level throughout most of the twentieth century, has been generally more favourable to state intervention in social and economic spheres than its Progressive Conservative Party counterparts, who directly mirror the private sector in their platforms and their support. Yet for both parties, the incorporation of environmental options represents more extensive economic regulation – a direction not eagerly embraced by the private sector and its supporters. In Chapter 8, we will review some of the recent environmental initiatives launched by these two parties while in office and reflect on their limited success.

The New Democratic Party (NDP), a social democratic party traditionally representing labour, has been more critical of corporate activity and more likely to sponsor increased state intervention, especially with regard to social welfare and other redistributive issues. The traditional social justice role of the NDP provides the potential for environmental leadership, yet the NDP's strong affiliation with labour has restricted environmental attachment, because increased environmental regulation has often been interpreted as a threat to jobs in the resource sector.

The early-1990s stint of the NDP in British Columbia is an example of the party's ambivalence to environmentalism. Its heavy-handed treatment of environmental protesters during the Clayoquot logging dispute led to the withdrawal of support for the party by many environmentalists. In an effort to recapture green votes, the party adopted a stronger environmental profile, illustrated by the establishment of the Commission on Resources and Environment (CORE) land-use planning process, the doubling of parks and wilderness areas, and the enactment of the Forestry Practices Code. Yet while the BC NDP may have taken on a slightly more environmental hue during its first term in office, the shift of both federal and provincial NDPs to the centre and their heightened affiliation with the private sector have precluded their enunciation and support for more radical environmental proposals.[9]

The lack of traditional party response to environmental concerns, in a global context, has often encouraged the formation of a Green Party with an explicit environmental mandate. While Green parties have been more successful in Europe and Australia under systems of proportional representation than in North America, they have nonetheless exerted some pressure on Canadian political parties. Green parties were established at both federal and provincial levels in the early 1980s to confront environmental issues. Yet they experienced numerous internal problems of organization and ideology that inhibited their success.[10]

The Green Party's platform and activities have not been restricted to environmental objectives as such; they also reflect an ideological position that challenges standard links between social organization and environmental degradation. In rejecting hierarchical forms of social organization, the party has adopted decision-making by consensus, while the selection of candidates reflects an attempt to achieve gender equality. Platforms include an array of social goals, with positions on labour, technology, housing, and other issues. Rather than sticking to environmental objectives in a narrow sense, then, the Greens have preferred to propose changes to the entire social and political system. Their strategies and processes have become so extensive and time-consuming that many activists have become disillusioned, opting once again to apply pressure to existing parties around specific environmental issues. Still others have criticized the Greens for their amalgamation of environmental with social objectives.

This is not to say that Green parties have failed in Canada solely due to internal machinations. Additional constraints have discouraged their success in Canadian politics.[11] These constraints include the tendency of voters to maintain their alliance with a given party over time; the ability of existing parties to command resources, especially media coverage; and the advantages of incumbents in galvanizing continuing support.

Representatives of Productive Interests

Unlike non-productive social actors, market-based actors are very active in policy formulation, and various organizations representing business have often been successful in developing policy options eventually adopted by governments. However, this success should not be overstated. As we saw in Chapter 6, for example, a significant productive interest, labour, has generally avoided the policy realm and focused its energies at the level of the firm or the industry, bargaining over wages and working conditions.

Similarly, the impact of sectoral and jurisdictional cleavages in diffusing industrial representation in policy formulation should be noted. The pulp and paper industry, for example, has been represented since 1913 by a national organization, the Montreal-based Canadian Pulp and Paper Association (CPPA).[12] While this organization has been able to speak with authority to governments concerning the interests of this industry, the same has not been true of many other equally significant resource sectors.[13] The lumber industry, for example, has not had an authoritative national organization until recently,[14] tending instead to rely on provincial associations to carry out its lobbying and other activities. Thus, the most important organization representing lumber industry concerns to government and elsewhere over the last half-century has been the Council of Forest Industries of British Columbia (COFI), whose membership is dominated by the large, integrated operators in the coastal region.[15] Other resource industries are similarly divided, often resulting in a wide range of policy proposals being developed for government, rather than a monolithic one.

Conflicts, in fact, are endemic to the Canadian resource and environmental policy subsystem because the foundations of market-based resource extraction and processing contain the seeds for such conflict in the way in which economic surplus is generated and distributed. Maximizing surplus requires plentiful, accessible raw materials; efficient, low-cost processing; and high demand and high prices in final sales markets. However, while this might appear as a common general principle behind natural resource politics, landlords, labour, and capital in fact have different interests in determining exactly how a surplus will be 'maximized' and who will bear the costs or enjoy the benefits of this process. Disputes arise between competing enterprises, between capital and workers over shares of profits and wages,[16] between landlords and capital over shares of profits and rents,[17] and between landlords and workers over shares of rents and wages.[18] These conflicts almost always result in different producer groups developing and supporting different policy options within existing policy processes.

State Members of the Canadian Resource and Environmental Policy Subsystem

Not only societal actors are involved in proposing options for government. As is the case with agenda-setting, government officials themselves can play a major role in policy formulation.

In theory, legislators can play a significant role in policy formulation through initiating and revising legislation. Legislators must approve the government bills enacting policies and the government budgets funding their implementation. These bills and budgets must be initiated in the legislature, and only legislature members can begin this process. In addition, legislators can demand changes to existing policies and affect the content of bills as they pass through the legislative approval process. However, as is the case with agenda-setting, in parliamentary systems such as Canada's, the legislature's policy formulation potential is usually not realized.[19]

In the resource and environmental sector, this is virtually always the case. Technical issues in resource management or environmental protection, for example, are unlikely to involve legislators because they may not fully understand the problems or solutions proposed, or they may see little political benefit in pursuing these matters. Issues related to national security and foreign policies are usually handled behind a shroud of secrecy outside the legislature. Similarly, policies dealing with problems perceived to be crises are unlikely to involve the legislature very much because of the time it takes to introduce, debate, and pass a bill.

In Canada, as in many contemporary legislative democracies, what policy formulation there is in representative assemblies is performed not on the floor of the legislature but in parliamentary committees established along functional lines to review proposed legislation. Committees often build considerable expertise in the areas with which they deal, and the extent to which this happens enables the legislature to exercise influence over not only formulating but also implementing policies. In order to build expertise, however, the members need to serve on the committees over a relatively long period of time. Committee members must also not necessarily vote along party lines if their autonomy and assertiveness are to be maintained.

As a result of the limitations mentioned above, legislatures generally play only a small role in Canadian resource and environmental policy formulation. While some legislators may, on the basis of their expertise or special interest in the problem, be included in the policy subsystem, legislatures as a whole are not significant actors in resource and environmental policy formulation.[20]

Unlike the legislature, the executive (the cabinet and the bureaucracy) is one of the key players in the policy process. Its central role derives from its constitutional authority to govern the country. While there are other actors involved in the process, in Canada, the authority to develop and introduce policies rests ultimately with the executive.

In addition to its prerogative in policy matters, the executive possesses a range of other powers that strengthen its dominant position in policy formulation. Control over information is one such critical resource. The executive has unmatched information that it withholds, releases, or manipulates in ways that bolster its preference and weaken the case of those opposed to it. Control over fiscal resources is another asset favouring the executive because legislative approval of the budget usually permits a wide area of discretion for the government. The executive also has unparalleled access to mass media in publicizing its positions and undermining those of its opponents. Moreover, it has the bureaucracy at its disposal to provide advice and to carry out its preferences. It can, and often does, use these resources to control and influence societal actors such as interest groups, mass media, and think tanks.[21] In many countries, as well, the government has important powers allowing it to control the timing of the introduction and passage of laws in the legislature. This power confers a great deal of control of the political process on the executive.[22]

Canadian politicians at both federal and provincial levels, however, have tended not to exercise their power to enhance environmental pro-

tection or regulation. At the federal level, perhaps the strongest environmental advocate in recent years has been Lucien Bouchard, who served as
ambassador to France and minister of the environment in the Mulroney
government prior to his political reincarnation as leader of the Bloc
Québécois. A backer of the Green Plan and an outspoken environmental
advocate, Bouchard supported environmental issues in a Conservative
administration. Nevertheless, he was quick to abandon them in favour of
his more controversial support for Quebec sovereignty in the wake of the
failure of the Meech Lake constitutional accord, eventually abandoning
federal politics altogether to become premier of Quebec.

Other resource ministers have also enjoyed a high profile – and have just
as readily abandoned their portfolios. In 1995, for example, Brian Tobin,
then federal minister of fisheries and oceans in the Chrétien Liberal government, attracted international attention for his role dealing with the
Newfoundland cod issue. Tobin authorized the boarding of a Spanish ves-
sel for fishing off the Grand Banks, an area considered by Canada to be off-
limits to other nations for conservation purposes. The ensuing political
debate, part of the ongoing struggle to secure European compliance with
Canadian resource policy, placed Canada – and Tobin – in the international spotlight. Tobin soon left federal politics, however, to become premier of Newfoundland.

At the provincial level, political leaders have also endorsed environmental issues. In British Columbia, for example, Environment Minister
Moe Sihota had strong support from environmental factions during the
NDP's reign in the early 1990s, and his charismatic reputation was viewed
as an effective aid to environmental causes such as the expansion of
provincial parks. Yet modern governments tend to rotate ministers
through different portfolios over a cycle of two to three years, and initiatives begun by one minister are often dropped by successors.

At the provincial level especially, an initiative must often be taken by
the premier, rather than by a cabinet minister, if it is to be assured success.
Such strong support for environmental alternatives to existing resource
policies however has not been readily forthcoming.

The power of provincial premiers in directing policy, and the influence
of productive interests in directing executive decisions, for example, were
made apparent in 1989 when, at the last minute, British Columbia's Social
Credit premier Bill Vander Zalm reversed his minister's position on tougher
regulations for pulp mill pollution. In May 1989, Environment Minister
Bruce Strachan stated that AOX (organochlorine) levels would be set at 2.5
kg per tonne of pulp by the end of 1991 and at 1.5 kg per tonne by the end
of 1994. By December, the BC cabinet had approved the 1.5 AOX limit, and
John Reynolds, then environment minister, announced this regulation.

Three days later, after consultations with industry leaders, Premier Vander Zalm vetoed the new regulations, citing concern about job loss. This prompted the resignation of Reynolds, who stated, 'I don't think big business should be dictating the province ... The (1.5 kg) regulations ... truly represent the standards that are required.'[23] On December 14, the government limited AOX levels to the 2.5 kg per tonne level. As staff counsel from the West Coast Environmental Law Association noted at the time:

> The premier's decision is an unmitigated environmental disaster. The difference between what the government promised and what the premier has now implemented is approximately 15 metric tonnes of toxic organochlorine contamination every day. If that amount of pollution were to spill unexpectedly, just once, it would be treated as a major environmental emergency. Yet the pulp companies will be allowed to dump this extra amount ... for years to come.[24]

While the political executive is powerful, as we saw in Chapter 6 in the context of agenda-setting, the tremendous growth in the size, scope, and complexity of government functions over the recent past has, in many sectors, effectively prevented generalist politicians from controlling, or often even being aware of, the specific activities of government officials nominally under their control.[25] It is those officials who exercise the greatest control on resource and environmental policy formulation.

In Canada in recent years, there has been a tendency for larger, omnibus departments of natural resources to emerge at both the federal and provincial levels, encompassing regulatory authority for a variety of natural resource sectors, including forests, mines, and energy. This is only a general pattern, however, because there have also been efforts to combine national resource administration with areas such as tourism, water resources, or parks or to combine resource administration with environmental protection. At the federal level, reflecting the ambiguous nature of the federal role in resource and environmental policy formation, a variety of idiosyncratic organizational forms have been used – from the original Department of the Interior at the time of Confederation to the more recent ministries of state for forests and mines. The mandates, personnel, and traditions of different ministries affect their reception to new ideas. Those with explicit environmental protection mandates, for example, may be more open to the positions of environmental groups than their resource development-oriented counterparts, such as departments of energy, forests, or mines.

The need for greater coordination of increasingly sophisticated policy regimes has also been evident in efforts made at the intergovernmental level to develop effective resource and environmental governing structures. At this level, resource and environmental issues have been addressed since 1960 both in the context of other natural resource issues in the Canadian Council of Resource and Environment Ministers (CCREM) and its off-shoots and in the creation of specific councils for forests, energy, environment, and mines.

Each ministry, department, or agency employs hundreds, if not thousands, of specialists. They monitor social actors and other state agencies on a day-to-day basis and act as the major point of contact for actors interested in resource and environmental policy formulation.[26] Given their direct links to the political executive, they can heavily influence the nature of the resource and environmental policy options put forward by governments.[27]

Charting the Canadian Resource and Environmental Policy Subsystem

The above discussion identifies the principal societal and state actors involved in resource and environmental policy formation in Canada. However, the discussion has not revealed very much about how these actors interact within the subsystem.

As we saw in Chapter 4, these actors comprise a policy subsystem composed of a policy community (those actors who share some policy-relevant knowledge) and a policy network (those actors who also interact with each other on a routine basis). Characterizing the nature of the subsystem requires empirical research into the ideas, attitudes, and actions of its members.

The importance of resources to the Canadian economy, geography, culture, and society ensures that many of the actors cited above have the level of knowledge of policy issues required to qualify for policy community membership. Thus, it should not be surprising that a large, vibrant, and well-organized community exists in this area of government activity in Canada.

Characterizing the nature of the policy network in this sector is more difficult. This task requires empirical research examining the interactions between network actors. As will be discussed in the concluding section of this chapter, the configuration of actors in communities and networks, and the relationship between the two levels of the subsystem, reveal a great deal about the types of options that are considered in policy formulation and why.

Charting the Policy Community

The discussion above and in previous chapters identified five general categories of membership in the resource and environmental policy community, ranging from state to societal actors and including productive as well as non-market based societal actors. They are representatives of government, business, labour, environmental groups, and First Nations organizations. Although the exact configuration of these actors varies by resource sector, these general categories have emerged in many places in recent years, including, for example, membership on round tables on the environment and economy.

Bruton and Howlett cite evidence of the activities of the four major non-government members[28] of this community gathered through a mail survey of 537 Canadian environmental groups, corporations, labour unions, and Native tribal councils carried out in late 1990.[29] Their research has shown that the contemporary policy community is quite divided in its perceptions of environmental issues and strategies.

Table 7.1 demonstrates that there is nothing even approaching a consensus between policy community members as to the nature of the most important resource and environmental problems that Canadians face. Among respondents who thought that environmental issues were 'very important' to their organization, thirty-six major problems were identified.

Table 7.1

Policy community perception of major problems facing society
Percent of respondents indicating environmental issue as 'very important'

Air and/or water quality	9.1	Ignorance and apathy	1.8
Global warming	6.7	Bureaucratic inertia	1.2
Pollution	5.5	Anthropocentrism	1.2
Public attitudes	5.5	Loss of wildlife, habitat	1.2
Waste management, garbage	5.5	Resource exploitation	1.2
Toxic pollution	4.9	Greed	1.2
Overconsumption, waste	4.3	Lack of citizen participation	1.2
Water pollution	4.3	Wilderness preservation	1.2
Resource, soil sustainability	4.3	Auto emissions	.6
Ozone depletion	4.0	Costs of cleanup	.6
Growth-based economy	4.0	Hunting	.6
De-reforestation	4.0	Poverty, inequality	.6
Third World poverty	2.4	Intergenerational equity	.6
Energy consumption, waste	2.4	Tragedy of the commons	.6
Air pollution	2.4	Achieving consensus	.6
Acid rain	1.8	Objectivity in risk assessment	.6
Population growth	1.8	Complexity of problems	.6
Resource megaprojects	1.8	Multiple (all of above)	1.8
Missing	14.0	(N = 64)	

Source: J. Bruton and M. Howlett, Environmental Survey, 1990-1.

This lack of a clear definition of the environmental 'problem' is common to all representative categories of policy community membership, as Table 7.2 shows. Within each group, there are many different definitions of the key resource and environmental problem, although a general concern with pollution ranks quite high among corporate, labour, and First Nations groups. Even in this aggregated form, however, only one-third of the groups identified pollution as a serious environmental problem.

Table 7.2

Policy community perceptions of major problems facing society (aggregated)
Percent of respondents indicating environmental issue as 'very important'

	Environmental	Corporate	Labour	Native	Total
Pollution	35	38	41	35	33
Resource, soil sustainability	10	8	14	22	12
Global warming	10	14	14	9	11
Overconsumption	15	3	7	4	9
Public attitudes	14	11	3	9	10
Waste management, garbage	2	14	10	–	6
Wilderness preservation	6	–	–	9	4
Other	8	12	11	12	15
Total	100	100	100	100	100

Source: J. Bruton and M. Howlett, Environmental Survey, 1990-1.

Not only do the different social actors disagree on the nature of the problem that governments are expected to address, but there is also no single definition of the problem common to any group. This is a reflection of the complexity of the resource and environmental problems that confront Canada. But the multiplicity of views within the policy community makes policy-making more complex, because governments cannot simply respond to an existing consensus on the nature of the problem that policy should address.

Such disagreements also have an immediate effect on policy formulation, for groups disputing the definition of a problem will unlikely be satisfied with any government efforts to resolve them. This fragmentation or lack of a common perspective on the nature of fundamental policy problems is a significant factor in Canadian resource and environmental policy-making. While the policy community may have been more united in the past, and representative of a smaller spectrum of interests, at present it is clear that a *chaotic policy community* exists in this sector.

But to what extent are these groups active in policy formulation? What is the nature of their relations with one another? We can see from the following that not all the actors in the policy community are actively engaged in the policy network.

Charting the Policy Network

Because the policy community is so large and fragmented, more significant in the case of Canadian resource and environmental policy-making is the policy network. As was discussed in Chapter 4, the existence and nature of a policy network within the larger policy community are significant to policy analysis, because of the potential for the network to either bring harmony to a discordant set of policy actors or upset an apparent consensus within the larger community. That is, policy networks can sometimes bring a reasonable level of consensus to the selection of a policy option, even when the policy community is fractured and divided over the source of a problem.

Bruton and Howlett have shown that different components of the resource and environmental policy community exhibit different levels of interest in policy matters in this sector. As might be expected, environmental groups are the most likely to attach importance to resource and environmental issues, to be aware of such issues, and to be involved in the policy process in this sector. Corporations share similar high levels of interest and involvement. Native groups, however, tend to see resource and environmental issues as significant but are likely to be less aware of existing government programs in this area and therefore less involved in their deliberations. Labour is much less involved in the process than are environmental and business respondents, largely attributable to the fact that almost 60 per cent of labour respondents did not even see environmental issues as being particularly important to their organization – by far the lowest rate among these groups.

The survey results presented in Table 7.3 indicate that, in the area of Canadian resource and environmental policy, a triadic policy network exists. That is, evidence of labour apathy and First Nations exclusion from the policy network lends credence to the notion that a regulatory triangle has evolved in most areas of Canadian resource and environmental policy. This triangle involves government regulators and two competing interest groups in policy formulation. Such a pattern of state-group interaction allows both politicians and officials some latitude in determining the content of policies to fit their own electoral, partisan, or bureaucratic interests, rather than simply responding to the demands of interest groups.[30]

Table 7.3

Frequency of intra- and interorganizational contacts (% 'frequent')

	Environmental	Corporate	Labour	Native
Environmental	88	35	44	44
Corporate	46	88	47	39
Labour	26	55	84	17
Native	33	13	23	85
(N =)	(64)	(40)	(32)	(25)

Source: J. Bruton and M. Howlett, Environmental Survey, 1990-1.

Policy Formulation and the Canadian Resource and Environmental Policy Subsystem

The divided and fractured nature of the Canadian resource and enviromental policy community influences the shape of the discourse within which policy options are formulated.

As the data presented in Table 7.4 show, major disagreements over both the goals and means necessary to rectify resource and environmental problems continue to characterize the politics of policy-making in this sector. This is especially the case with the policy option of sustainable development or the simultaneous adjustment of economic development and environmental protection. Some groups think this is an attainable goal, while others do not.[31] As the figures illustrate, business and labour demonstrate higher levels of commitment to sustainable development than do other subsystem members. Moreover, the mechanisms through which sustainable development will be attained are interpreted very differently by these groups.

Even though subsystem members may not always agree on the problem to be resolved, they can sometimes agree on the desirability of certain

Table 7.4

Policy community disagreements over policy options
Percent of respondents indicating environmental issue as 'very important'

	Environmental	Corporate	Labour	Native	Total
Support sustainable development	50	85	76	9	66
Support additional regulation	88	58	100	83	83
Require plant closures	66	55	33	50	64
(N =)	(60)	(39)	(33)	(22)	(154)

Source: J. Bruton and M. Howlett, Environmental Survey, 1990-1.

forms of government activity. Some groups may not oppose government responses to policy problems even when they disagree on the nature of the problem that the action is intended to address. The figures presented in Table 7.4 show that, while environmental groups are divided on whether or not sustainable development is possible, they generally share the notions that additional government regulation will be required to protect the environment and that attainment of this goal will probably require the closure of existing plants and factories.

Business groups are especially likely to support the idea of sustainable development. However, the business community is divided over the issue of whether or not additional government regulations and plant closures are required to implement this policy. Businesses and business associations are much more likely than any other group to oppose additional government regulations.

This division between the principal societal members of the policy network reinforces rather than overcomes the difficulties arising from a fractious policy community. The existence of environmental groups in the policy network reflects the increased and continuing access of the public interest to the policy subsystem. However, the potential for closer working relationships, and the opportunity for improved communications between network members, are affected by the divergent positions of productive and non-productive actors. The different political and economic origins of these interests mean that they will not be easily resolved in the process of developing options for governance. Rather than simply endorse a subsystem consensus, governments must often choose between conflicting visions of, and solutions to, current problems.

Conclusion: The Nature of Canadian Resource and Environmental Policy Formulation

Canadian resource and environmental policy-making is influenced by the fundamental political economy of resource production, which, in turn, influences the nature of the existing policy subsystem. The subsystem is composed of a variety of actors who have fundamentally different interests in resource and environmental activities and hence tends to be conflict riddled.

The conflicts between productive and non-productive interests include not only significant divisions between those concerned about environmental impacts, such as toxicity in pulp effluents, and those concerned primarily with surplus, profitability, and paycheques. Jeremy Wilson describes how environmental groups imperil 'the unwritten code of speculative rights at the heart of the ... capitalist ethos, threatening a system that has long legitimized a profitable traffic in rights to Crown resources.'[32]

Conflicts also reflect differences in people's circumstances, especially their jobs, and other aspects of their lifestyles, as mediated by education, gender, and political persuasion.

State actors also face significant challenges from societal actors. The ability of landlords to collect rents and determine resource usage can be challenged on a variety of legal and ethical grounds. These challenges have occurred with increasing frequency in recent years in cases involving Native land claims, private property rights,[33] or concerns for environmental protection and sustainable development pressed by environmental groups against both private and public landlords.[34]

Finally, the state itself, as we have seen, is not a monolithic actor but is also challenged from within. That is, conflicts occur regularly between government ministries, agencies, and jurisdictions.[35] All of these conflicts can adversely affect a government's willingness and ability to mediate conflicts between societal actors or develop its own consistent proposals for governing resource use.[36]

While there may have been some general agreement in the past over the basic elements of resource and environmental management, at present the policy community is divided over the nature of the problems that government should address. This large, chaotic policy community is coupled with a smaller triadic policy network in which environmental groups have managed to disturb an old pattern of bilateral government-industry relations. The subsystem now allows a great deal of autonomy to state actors in formulating policy, but it also has the potential to generate multiple policy conflicts and substantial public controversy.

Policy community membership extends to just about anyone who has some knowledge or expertise in the area concerned. At minimum, it includes state policymakers (administrative, political, and judicial), members of non-governmental organizations (NGOs) concerned with the subject, members of the media who report on the subject, academics who follow or research the area, and members of the general public who, for whatever reason, have taken an interest in the subject.[37] In resource and environmental issues, the policy community also involves members of other organizations such as businesses, labour unions, and formal interest groups or professional associations concerned with government actions in the sector. In some cases, international actors such as multinational corporations, international governmental or non-governmental organizations, or the governments of foreign states can also be members of sectoral policy communities.[38]

The subset of actors who interact within more formal institutions and procedures of government are members of sectoral policy networks.[39] These networks include representatives from the community but are 'inner circles' of actors, those who effectively hold power and forge the policy paradigm. In the resource and environmental sector in Canada, only state actors, such as business and environmental groups, are significant members in the sectoral policy network.

What does this subsystem configuration tell us about the likely nature of policy options developed at this stage of the Canadian natural resource and environmental policy process? For options that radically depart from the status quo to come forward, there are two preconditions that must be met. First, there must be some change in the policy community. That is, there must be some new interests or ideas present in the subsystem. Otherwise, by definition, options will contain only knowledge or ideas already encompassed by the status quo.

Hence, the results of policy formulation are contingent upon the configuration of the policy subsystem in the specific sector concerned. In the case of Canadian resource and environmental policy-making, the evolution of a triadic policy network from a traditional bilateral 'corporatist' or 'clientelist' industry-government one and the shift from a hegemonic to a chaotic policy community is significant in several ways.

First, within the policy community, there are new ideas in circulation, reflecting the emergence of new interests. The shift from anthropocentric to biocentric resource management discourse that has begun to appear in Canada, for instance, reflects relatively new perspectives about how to manage and value resources.[40] It contrasts sharply with the previously hegemonic commodity production paradigm,[41] which remains dominant among network members. Disputes over the meaning of resource and environmental policy, as a result, have now become a major source of friction between policy networks and policy communities and affect the nature of the policy options they develop.

Ambiguity and disagreement surrounding the central goal of resource and environmental policy is especially important given the triadic character of the policy network. When network members agree on the overall goals of policy, they tend to settle minor policy differences as a series of technical questions, successfully excluding the concerns of the wider policy community as irrelevant to the smooth implementation of a settled policy. Major disagreement over policy goals, however, such as exist between ENGOs and business in the Canadian resource and environmental policy network, cause tension within the network and may tempt members to recruit allies from the wider community.

These disagreements politicize technical management disputes and can bring in to the network previously excluded members of the wider policy community. Undoubtedly, much of the pressure for resource and environmental policy change is animated by a powerful set of competing ideas

emerging behind criticisms of the existing resource management paradigm and reflecting transnational concerns about sustainable ecosystem
management.[42] This pressure reflects the democratization of the policy
process as new actors (and interests such as those of the tourist industry or
a wilderness preservation group) emerge in the subsystem. Yet while the
policy network reflects greater heterogeneity, the power of different actors
within it remains strongly differentiated and the representation of non-
productive interests remains underdeveloped.

It is no longer the case in this sector that only status quo options are
being proposed and considered in policy formulation. To a great extent at
present, policy networks in the resource and environmental policy sector
in Canada exist in considerable tension with the policy communities in
which they are embedded. New ideas are circulating in opposition to old
paradigms, and new actors representing emerging interests are willing to
articulate a different vision of resource and environmental policy. Yet
institutional advantages to productive interests in policy networks have
been forged through decades of policy style from which the presentation
of public and 'environmental' interests in the triadic network marks a significant shift in the policy community. These new actors remain weak,
though, and decision-makers have tended to co-opt elements of new ideas
that continue to serve the interests of dominant and older network members. This situation may change over time, however, as the subsystem continues to develop.

8
Decision-Making: The Politics of Canadian Resource and Environmental Policy

The discussion in Chapters 6 and 7 highlighted two features of Canadian resource and environmental policy-making: the expansion and diversification of the policy community, and the restricted institutional arena in which policy options continue to be formed. Chapter 6 described the array of interests as well as the heightened public awareness of, and desire to contribute to, resource and environmental issues, but it argued that agenda-setting remains largely a matter of inside initiation. In spite of its increased presence, the public continues to be circumscribed and largely nominal. Items move onto the official agenda more as a result of internal government initiatives than as a response to public pressure. Chapter 7 outlined the contours of the Canadian resource and environmental policy subsystem and discussed the nature of the policy community and policy network in this sector. We argued that a large and chaotic policy community now exists in this sector, characterized by interaction between multiple market and non-market interests with few ongoing alliances. This interaction has encouraged the emergence of a variety of ideas relating to sustainability and other 'green' concepts, thus challenging a formerly hegemonic approach to resource management for purely exploitative purposes.

The open nature of the policy community, and the largely symbolic increase in public participation in institutional agenda-setting, we argued, obscure the fact that a much smaller policy network (which continues to be dominated by business and government) generates policy options and controls the process of policy formulation. While environmental groups have managed to make their presence felt in the network, their lack of connections to business and the difficulties they encounter articulating extra-economic interests restrict their influence. A triadic policy network provides the government with some autonomy in resisting the influence of industry. But governments' own economic interests and the tradition of, and institutional predilection for, a market-based system of resource exploitation continue to favour policy options put forward by productive actors.

The previous two chapters set out the basic nature of the initial phases of the policy cycle and helped to explain why policy-making in this sector has tended to develop slowly, with little change in general orientation. That is, due to the limited nature of public input and the dominance of closed policy networks driven by the self-interest of actors engaged in resource production, it is very difficult for new ideas or alternative approaches to penetrate the policy process.

As the discussion in this chapter will show, the limitations on the types of ideas and issues flowing through to governments are accentuated by the constraints encountered by government decisionmakers themselves in the settings or contexts in which public policy decisions are made. Combined, these sets of influences reinforce the tendency of the policy-making system to provide decisions of a reactive and incremental nature.

Definitions and Issues in Resource and Environmental Policy Decision-Making

Decisions are made at numerous stages in the policy cycle, with different consequences for the development of policy. They range from the enactment of legally binding and sanctioned legislation and the announcement of official government policy to the more unofficial discourse of campaign promises and the informal statements of politicians covered by an increasingly pervasive media. Decisions also vary in their impact and are subject to revision. Although we tend to think of decisions as final and authoritative, the fluidity, complexity, and overlap of decision-making with other stages of the policy cycle are prominent features of contemporary policy-making.

Gary Brewer and Peter DeLeon describe the decision-making stage of the public policy cycle as

> the choice among policy alternatives that have been generated and their likely effects on the problem estimated ... It is the most overtly political stage in so far as the many potential solutions to a given problem must somehow be winnowed down and but one or a select few picked and readied for use. Obviously most possible choices will not be realized and deciding not to take particular courses of action is as much a part of selection as finally settling on the best course.[1]

This definition makes several key points that are relevant to Canadian resource and environmental policy. First, decision-making is not a self-contained stage, or a synonym for the entire policy-making process, but a moment in policy-making rooted firmly in the previous stages of the policy cycle. It involves choosing from among a relatively small number of alternative policy options identified in the process of policy formulation to resolve a problem. Second, this definition underlines the point that decision-making is not a technical exercise (although it may concern technical issues or evaluate issues using technical measures) but an inherently political process. Resource and environmental policy decisions create 'winners' and 'losers,' including and beyond human interests, even if the decision is to do nothing or to retain the status quo.

It is problematic to address decision-making as a single event, such as a vote approving the passage of legislation, because other factors are also significant to this stage. Decision-making is rarely reduced to one decision; rather, it is based on a policy tradition that in itself reflects the sedimentation of years of approved legislation and ensuing administrative activities.[2] While political attention is usually directed to the passage of specific new legislation, less attention is paid to the policy precedents that have formed the status quo. Furthermore, the bureaucratic manipulation that actually shapes political decisions is only rarely visible and accessible to the public. Elizabeth May describes the gauntlet of decision-making after her experience as a policy adviser to the federal minister of the environment:

> There are powerful gatekeepers throughout the bureaucracy. People near money – Treasury Board and Finance. People near decision-making – the Department of Justice and the Privy Council Office. All those nameless, faceless bureaucrats who advise the chairmen of cabinet committees about which departmental memoranda have achieved sufficient consensus in 'the system' to be placed on a cabinet agenda ... Cabinet committees were carefully managed and choreographed by the 'central agencies.' An original idea would be as out of place at a cabinet meeting as a Ouija board ... If through some miracle of tenacity and political pressure an idea does make it to cabinet committee for a decision, the ministers around the table will respond, based on the script of criticism advanced by the Minister's own senior bureaucrats.[3]

Other strains, such as the pressures of decentralization, fiscal crisis, or international economic competition, also influence policy decisions in ways not always directly visible. Making resource and environmental decisions is not only complex, occurring at multiple levels of government and in both informal and formal venues, but also subject to numerous constraints, and these factors must be taken into account in attempting to model decision-making.

The decision-making stage of the policy cycle received the most attention in the early development of the policy sciences, when analysts borrowed heavily from models of decision-making in complex organizations.[4] The majority of these new conceptual models criticized traditional emphases on the neutrality and the pragmatic aspects of decision-making, and by the mid-1960s discussions about public policy decision-making had ossified in the debate surrounding two competing general models: the 'incremental' model, which postulated a limited form of decision-making in which affected actors bargained over outcomes, and the 'rational' model, in which decisionmakers attempted to optimize outcomes through a more 'scientific' form of analysis.[5]

The stalemate between adherents of the two models led to efforts in the 1980s to develop alternative models.[6] Some attempted to synthesize the rational and incremental models, while others focused on the irrational elements of organizational behaviour in order to arrive at some third path beyond rationalism and incrementalism.[7] A critical model challenging the neutrality of the state and the fairness of decision-making processes also evolved. This model questioned the premise of equality of access to, or representation in, decision-making and acknowledged the disproportionate power of some, primarily economic, interests in this process.

In this critical view, the extent of state autonomy within a policy subsystem is a crucial issue in public policy decision-making. Critical approaches view regulatory decisions as being directly affected by the context of decision-making and by the configuration of state and societal actors involved. From this position, the climate in which Canadian resource and environmental policy decisions have traditionally been made with the joint input of civil servants and industry representatives, for example, is understood to be biased, political, and bilateral, rather than neutral, rational, and open.

Utilizing these insights, John Forester has argued that there are at least five distinct decision-making styles associated with a variety of decision-making conditions and contexts.[8] According to Forester, 'what is rational for administrators to do depends on the situations in which they work.'[9] That is, the decision-making style and the type of decision made by decisionmakers vary according to issue and institution. As he put it in a 1984 article,

> Depending upon the conditions at hand, a strategy may be practical or ridiculous. With time, expertise, data, and a well-defined problem, technical calculations may be in order; without time, data, definition, and expertise, attempting those calculations could well be a waste of time. In a complex organizational environment, intelligence networks will be as, or more, important than documents when information is needed. In an

environment of inter-organizational conflict, bargaining and compromise may be called for. Administrative strategies are sensible only in a political and organizational context.[10]

Forester suggests that, for decision-making to take place along the lines suggested by the rational model, the following conditions must be met.[11] First, the number of *agents* (decisionmakers) will need to be limited, possibly to as few as one person. Second, the organizational *setting* for the decision will have to be simple and closed off from the influences of other policy actors. Third, the *problem* must be well defined; in other words, its scope, time horizon, value dimensions, and chains of consequences must be well understood. Fourth, *information* must be as close to perfect as possible: it must be complete, accessible, and comprehensible. And fifth, there must be no urgency for the decision; that is, *time* must be available to the decisionmakers to consider all possible contingencies and their anticipated consequences. Only when these conditions are met, Forester argues, can rational decision-making be expected to prevail.

He further argues that, to the extent that these five conditions are not met, as is almost always the case, other styles of decision-making will predominate. Thus, the number of agents can multiply greatly; the setting can include many different organizations and can be more or less open to external influences; the problem can be ambiguous or susceptible to multiple competing interpretations; information can be incomplete, misleading, or purposefully withheld or manipulated; and time can be limited or artificially constrained and manipulated.

Recasting Forester's variables allows us to develop a simple but effective model of public policy decision-making that we can apply to Canadian resource and environmental issues. 'Agent' and 'setting,' for example, can be discussed as elements of how decisionmakers are situated vis-à-vis policy subsystems, while the notions of 'problem,' 'information,' and 'time' can all be seen as relating to the types of constraints placed upon decisionmakers. Examining who dominates the policy subsystem and the nature of the resource constraints under which decisionmakers operate, as will be discussed below, allows us to accurately characterize the types of decisions typical of a policy sector such as Canadian resource and environmental policy-making.

Two Case Studies in Modern Canadian Resource and Environmental Policy Decision-Making

While decision-making is popularly understood as the 'highest' or major event in the policy process, it is difficult to identify specific decisions for analysis. Decisions in the resource and environmental sector can encompass a range of actions from the passage of legislation defining and implementing new agencies to a variety of regulatory processes that bear on the physical environment. Also, as noted above, decisions are typically located within a continuum of events and are rarely produced idiosyncratically. And in Canada in particular, relatively little attention has been focused on the mechanics of decision-making, due mainly to the fact that many records and documents of cabinet or federal-provincial deliberations remain unavailable to investigators.[12]

As a result, rather than present a survey of existing cases, we will illustrate the principal elements of the Canadian resource and environmental decision-making style through the presentation of two case studies dealing with elements of federal and federal-provincial decision-making. Because of the number of decisions that have affected resource and environmental policy historically, we will focus on decisions made over the past decade at the federal level. We can thus compare the relative influence of factors such as government ideology over a time period in which both Conservatives and Liberals were in power[13] and the impact of Canada's federal system of government on decision-making.

The two major federal decisions that will be examined are the adoption of the 1992 Canadian Environmental Assessment Act and, at a sector-specific level, the 1987 National Forest Sector Strategy. These initiatives share several features. They represent federal initiatives and illustrate some of the difficulties encountered in harmonizing provincial environmental processes and coordinating provincial resource strategies. They also reflect the influence of international environmental policy initiatives, including proposals for increased national planning and local government action promoted by several prominent international organizations. Moreover, both represent efforts to develop a more extensive and interventionist role for the state in addressing resource and environmental concerns in Canada.

As the discussion below will show, these cases amply illustrate several major constraints to decision-making in this sector. The complex division of power between the provinces and the federal government, while contributing to a flurry of provincial initiatives, has also impeded the potential harmonization of various Canadian efforts. The instability and regression of the economic climate, heightened by the restructuring and downsizing of Canadian industry under the terms of the Canada-US and North American Free Trade Agreements, have also impeded public policy decision-making, because increased momentum to decentralize federal decision-making powers deters the potential for significant new federal legislation. Bureaucratic pathologies ranging from internal administrative power struggles to duplications of effort, or from problems of communication to institutional conservatism, have further hampered the speed and scope of many decisions and are features of both cases.

The Canadian Environmental Assessment Act

As was discussed in Chapter 6, environmental assessment involves not only the identification of proposed projects anticipated to have an environmental impact but also a review of these projects, including the terms under which they will be accepted. At the federal level, the Environmental Assessment Review Process (EARP) has been applied to 'federal projects' initiated by federal departments and agencies, using federal funds and involving federal lands and jurisdiction. Doern estimates that about 10,000 project decisions have been made by government on an annual basis.[14] When a government agency initiates a project that will have an impact on the environment, assessments made under the provisions in EARP guidelines determine the viability of the project and the measures that must be put in place to accommodate its impacts.

Prior to the evolution of the environmental assessment process, Canada, like other Western democracies, had largely avoided taking the environment into account in project planning and implementation. The modern era of natural resource development led to the opening of Canada's hinterlands on a massive scale, and the federal government encouraged these developments through various policies, programs, and projects intended to foster regional development, national integration, and job creation.[15] However, in the traditional encouragement of economic development, impacts on the environment – on the health of aboriginal peoples and others, on the protection of natural habitat – were not addressed. The costs of mitigation, if identified, were externalized to other departments and to the population at large. Environmental assessments were proposed as a means of anticipating and internalizing the environmental costs of resource and economic development.

In the early 1970s, the groundwork for the Canadian Environmental Assessment Review Process began. In 1969, the National Environmental Policy Act (NEPA), mandating environmental project assessments, had been passed by the Nixon government in the United States. By 1972, the Trudeau government had announced that future Canadian government projects would be subject to environmental evaluation. Yet Canadian officials were leery about following the US precedent, which emphasized litigation, had considerable scope, and was accordingly very costly and time-consuming.[16]

Early efforts to formulate the scope, representation, and administrative support for environmental assessment reflected the ambivalence shown in the December 1973 cabinet decision introducing the Federal Environmental Assessment Review Office (FEARO). It was established to assess environmental projects either undertaken or funded by the federal government or to be carried out on federal lands.[17]

FEARO was established by cabinet decision without any enabling legislation passed by Parliament. Furthermore, it called for 'self-selection' as a means of identifying potential projects through which the proponent could initiate an assessment, rather than wait for a central agency to make that decision. In other words, a federal ministry initiating a project could decide that its development was not of significant magnitude, duration, or impact to require an environmental assessment. Federal government departments and agencies were to develop their own screening procedures and apply them to their own proposals. Crown corporations and key regulatory agencies would only be invited to participate, and policy adopted by cabinet would not fall under the assessment process. Projects deemed to have potentially significant environmental impacts were to be referred to the minister of the environment for review, but the assessment panel was to comprise only bureaucrats from the Department of the Environment and the initiating department. Public reviews did not yet have a major role to play, and socioeconomic factors were not yet part of environmental impact assessments.

The enactment of EARP was significant to the development of Canadian resource and environmental policy in that it included a statutory basis for public participation and was a planning mechanism, occurring prior to a project rather than following it. Yet EARP was subjected to extensive criticism. Schrecker noted difficulties associated with 'its reliance on self-assessment of environmental impacts of specific projects by the department promoting them, without any external oversight.'[18] Criticism also focused on the facts that EARP rulings were non-binding, that federal and provincial processes conflicted with or overlapped each other, that citizen participation was limited and inadequate, and that many assessments were completed only *after* a project had finished, thus having, at best, a mitigative function.[19]

A lack of administrative and technical support further hampered the effectiveness of EARP. The decentralized and discretionary means of initiating assessments also led to questions about its procedural fairness and public access. While the initiative was presented by supporters as flexible and balanced, its lack of administrative support and its discretionary character undermined its utility and legitimacy.[20]

While these internal, bureaucratic, and technical factors influenced the formation of EARP, other factors were significant in its continuing evolution. Over the next two decades, periods of high unemployment and recession diminished the profile of environmental concerns, and while EARP was nominally geared to state-initiated projects, the trickle-down effect to the private sector assessing their environmental impacts was less than heartily received by the corporate sphere.

Nevertheless, during the 1980s, there was some increased momentum for strengthening EARP, but it was still limited by the factors mentioned above and the continuing low profile of the environment ministry within cabinet. When Charles Caccia became Liberal environment minister in 1983, only one year prior to an election, he urged the codification of the assessment process, which occurred in June 1984. In that year, EARP was modified by a 'guidelines' order to be 'a self assessment process under which the initiating department shall ... ensure that the environmental implications of all proposals for which it is the decision making authority are fully considered and where the implications are significant, refer the proposal to the Minister for public review by a Panel.'[21]

However, environmental assessment guidelines were still so flexible that projects could relatively easily escape the assessment process. Two specific cases dealing with large-scale water diversions in the prairie provinces drew public attention to the deficiencies in the existing process, especially to its discretionary nature. In 1989 and 1990, two Federal Court of Appeal rulings on the applicability of the EARP guidelines to the Rafferty-Alameda and the Oldman River dam projects strengthened the argument for replacing EARP by legislation.

In the case of the Rafferty-Alameda project, the Canadian Wildlife Federation challenged the federal licence for the construction of dams on Saskatchewan's Souris River on the ground that the licence had been issued without the government's compliance with EARP guidelines. While the construction of the dams was a provincial responsibility, the 1989 ruling[22] upheld the need for an environmental impact assessment due to the federal government's regulatory responsibility over water management. A licence granted to the Saskatchewan Water Corporation was quashed by the Federal Court of Appeal, which ordered the federal government to comply with the guidelines before issuing a new licence.[23]

In the Oldman River case, the Federal Court of Appeal quashed a construction licence for building a dam in Alberta because no environmental impact study had been done. In this case as well, the decision upheld the mandatory implementation of EARP. The ruling argued that the ministries involved in the construction of the Three Rivers Dam (Transport; Fisheries and Oceans) were bound by the EARP guidelines. In 1992, the Supreme Court narrowed these guidelines further but upheld their binding legal character.[24]

In both of these cases, the provinces' approval of continuing construction during the court process revealed the uncertainty governing the application of the federal assessment guidelines. These cases provided an impetus to the federal government to enact new legislation as a means of dealing with the vagueness and uncertainty of the situation. In due course, Bill C-78, the Canadian Environmental Assessment Act (CEAA), was introduced in Parliament on 8 June 1990.

The new legislation, the Canadian Environmental Assessment Act, SC 1992, c. 37 (CEAA), is stronger than the previous guidelines in some respects but weaker in many others.[25] Cotton and MacKinnon identify its principal features as

(1) increased accountability to the public for environmental assessments;
(2) improved public participation in environmental assessments;
(3) the establishment of procedural rules;
(4) the promotion of joint panels with provincial jurisdictions to avoid duplication;
(5) the introduction of mediation as an option where it is possible to dispense with a full public review panel;
(6) the establishment of follow-up and monitoring plans for major projects;
(7) the creation of a new agency (The Canadian Environmental Assessment Agency) ...
(8) allowance for special procedures for assessments in relation to such matters as native lands, international agreements and Crown corporations.[26]

The CEAA allows for a review process to determine the potential adverse environmental effects generated by a project. The projects requiring an environmental assessment are identified, including major federal projects such as the damming or diversion of rivers, the creation of reservoirs or lakes, offshore developments in aquatic environments, military bases, pulp and paper mills, asbestos mines, gas development, and hazardous waste facilities.[27] The process assesses the potential mitigation of adverse effects and rejects applications when adverse effects cannot be mitigated.

The CEAA reflects multiple impacts from development projects in that it recognizes that multiple interests can be affected by any major project and argues that the affected interests are entitled to participate in decision-making.[28] However, the scope and force of the federal role envisioned in the CEAA continued to be a source of concern to the provinces. While the act was passed in 1992, it was only proclaimed law in 1994 over continued provincial opposition with the addition of specific regulations limiting its jurisdiction and application.

A significant concession in the act allows the provinces to 'opt out' of many of its provisions if they adopt their own 'equivalent' standards and processes.[29] As Doern and Conway note, this concession is the manifestation of ongoing struggles being waged through the new CEAA legislation between the federal government and the provinces and between ENGOs and industry. The effectiveness of environmental assessments now rests with comparable provincial legislation being implemented.[30]

But not all provinces have been willing to do so. Some have created similar or even stronger rules. In Ontario, for instance, the Environmental Assessment Act[31] provides for the minister of the environment to assess the potential impact on the environment of proposed projects. The Environmental Assessment Board created under the act is an independent administrative tribunal that has the authority to hold hearings and make decisions regarding proposed projects. The funding panel may make awards for intervenor funding against project proponents, such as that of $27 million awarded to intervenors in the consideration of future electric power.[32]

However, other provinces, such as Alberta, have held out for a reduced federal presence in the assessment sphere.[33] At the Canadian Council of Ministers of the Environment (CCME) May 1995 meeting, federal Environment Minister Sheila Copps told provincial environment ministers that she would not weaken the CEAA: 'The central government opposes what it sees as a loss of national perspective on environmental issues ... We believe there's a role for the federal government to play in national environmental assessment and we're not prepared to put that on the table.'[34]

Nevertheless, by late 1995 there was serious discussion about the creation of a new set of Environmental Management Framework Agreements (EMFA) that would greatly reduce the federal role in environmental management. As Steven Kennett has argued,

Determining exactly what the post EMFA federal role will entail is not a simple matter. The statement of federal interests in the Framework Agreements refers to national and transboundary environmental measures, conducting Canada's international environmental relations, environmental matters relating to federal lands, works and undertaking, the special relationship with Aboriginal people, technical and scientific leadership, working with provinces to protect 'nationally significant ecosystems' [and] support provincial programs, resolution of interjurisdictional environmental matters, and public participation.[35]

The National Forest Sector Strategy

As the above discussion of environmental assessments has illustrated, two of the key problems in modern Canadian resource and environmental decision-making are the division of powers between federal and provincial governments and the fragmg entation of responsibilities at both levels. These problems reduce the potential for uniform treatment of environmental issues across the country and hinder efforts to develop comprehensive plans and procedures for dealing with resource and environmental issues and problems.

Different resource sectors reflect different institutional contexts, ranging from the federal mandate for the offshore fisheries to the provincial basis of forestry, so it is difficult to generalize from one industry to another. Yet discussion of the attempt to expand federal regulatory capacity into the forestry sector is useful as a means of understanding the range of constraints inhibiting shifts in this policy sector. As our examination of the 1987 National Forest Sector Strategy will show, the same forces that undermined national environmental assessment procedures have been at work in the resource sphere and have served to prevent the federal government from establishing a new regime of sustainable forestry in this country. Recent federal initiatives, like similar attempts made in 1949, 1966, and 1978, have foundered on the obstacles presented to any expanded federal role by constitutional authority over the forest resource vested in the provincial governments.

The Canadian forest products industry is one of Canada's largest manufacturing industries in terms of value-added in manufacturing, employment, and wages. Well over $60 billion in goods are shipped every year, representing about 15 per cent of total Canadian manufacturing shipments. The industry directly employs about 300,000 workers, approximately 80 per cent in manufacturing and 20 per cent in logging operations, and it generates a similar number of indirect jobs. Many plants are located in single-industry resource communities, of which about 300 are entirely dependent on the forest industry. The industry is a major source of foreign exchange earnings, with about one-half of production exported from the country and an annual positive net balance of trade of over $35 billion, or almost three-quarters of Canada's entire surplus on merchandise trade. Canada is the world's largest exporter of forest products, and Canadian exports account for about 20 percent of the world trade in forest products.[36]

In the mid-1970s, the federal government became concerned about the health of the forest sector as easily accessible resource supplies became exhausted and the cost structure of the industry increased dramatically. Some foreign firms began to vacate the country, and investment in new technology and equipment declined. While in opposition, Conservative MPs had long criticized the Liberal government's efforts to revitalize the sector,[37] and in the September 1984 federal election, the Conservatives made the reversal of the Liberal record a plank in their election platform. On obtaining office, the Mulroney government moved quickly to demonstrate its commitment to this promise.

The Conservatives formed a new Ministry of State for Forests and quadrupled planned federal expenditures in the forest sector from about $225 million to over $1 billion for the period 1985-90, signing a new series of Forest Resource Development Agreements (FRDAs) with each province under the Economic and Regional Development Agreement (ERDA) umbrella. In addition to the creation of a new ministry, the Conservatives moved to rationalize an array of over ninety ad hoc interdepartmental committees and task forces working on forest sector problems within the federal administration. They also combined two major private sector advisory groups to the minister of the environment and the minister of regional industrial expansion into a single Forest Sector Advisory Committee to the Minister of State for Forests. On the intergovernmental level, the government also supported the withdrawal of forest ministers from the Canadian Council of Resource and Environment Ministers (CCREM) and the formation of a separate Canadian Council of Forest Ministers.[38]

In addition, the government began a major process of policy development aimed at enunciating a new national forest policy to replace the Forest Sector Strategy for Canada adopted by the Liberals in September 1981.[39] The new Minister of State for Forests, Gerald Merrithew, placed the development of a new policy high on his agenda for the first term in office, and the federal government provided funding for a series of forestry forums held in various cities around the country in late 1985 and early 1986 leading up to the establishment of a National Forest Congress in Ottawa in April 1986. The forums were intended to bring together company officials, government personnel, labour representatives, academics, and other interested parties to discuss the future direction of forest policy in Canada. The recommendations of the forums[40] were then taken to the National Forest Congress for ratification.[41]

The first draft of the sectoral strategy presented at the 1986 congress contained many additional suggestions for federal action, including recommendations that exchange rate policy be clarified, that transportation deregulation be pursued, and that federal competition policy be altered to allow for specialization and export agreements between major firms. In addition, the congress proposals urged that the federal government ensure energy costs be kept in line with US trends, that the tax system be altered to replace ad hoc industrial subsidies with investment incentives, and that real estate taxes on production facilities be reduced. Finally, the congress proposals urged that the federal role in forest management funding be specified and acknowledged in legislation. All of these recommendations presaged an enlarged federal role in industrial development and forest management.

A significant change occurred, however, when the federal government attempted to obtain provincial support for the draft document. The document was referred to a committee of federal and provincial officials struck to set down the guidelines for a new national forest strategy. These guidelines were then referred to the Canadian Council of Forest Ministers at a final forestry forum at St. John, New Brunswick, in July 1987. In due course, the document *A National Forest Sector Strategy for Canada* appeared and was accepted by the government as representing federal forest policy.

The limited federal forestry role contained in the 1987 policy paper is remarkable given the much larger role envisioned in the first draft of the strategy that emerged from the forestry forums. Despite having begun a process of policy development aimed at increasing the federal role in forest policy, the government ended up with a document limiting the federal role to forest research, export enhancement, and, most important, continued funding for provincial forest management efforts, without any input into the establishment of those programs.[42]

Evaluating the Canadian Resource and Environmental Decision-Making Style

The case of the Canadian Environmental Assessment Act illustrated many of the key issues, both substantive and procedural, that are endemic to resource and environmental decision-making and that work against the introduction of anticipatory, rather than reactive, legislation on a national level. After a shaky start during their first term in office after 1984, the Conservatives attempted to collectively paint themselves as the 'friend of the environment' and took several important initiatives in the environmental arena after 1989.[43] These initiatives included the establishment of new bodies such as the National Round Table on the Environment and Economy[44] and the Winnipeg-based International Institute for Sustainable Development and the introduction of a highly visible 'Green Plan' aimed at consolidating the role of the Department of the Environment within the federal bureaucracy in the context of a national resource and environmental strategy.[45] These initiatives, which entailed major expenditures, ultimately had only symbolic value as successive budgets cut into planned allocations.[46]

Many of these efforts were largely symbolic attempts by the federal government to respond to global environmental initiatives,[47] but the two major pieces of legislation that the Conservatives enacted – the Canadian Environmental Protection Act (CEPA), and the Canadian Environmental Assessment Act (CEAA) – were intended to establish the basis for a 'second generation' of environmental regulation.[48] The fate of the CEAA illustrates several constraints to resource and environmental policy-making: the significance of the division of power between the federal and provincial governments; the problems caused by the role of the state as an agent of development; the problems that governments face in securing administrative and fiscal foundations for legislative support; the disjunction between Canadian models and examples generated by American policy; and the bureaucratic quagmire in which the political process of both framing and enacting legislation can get stuck.[49]

The record of federal efforts to influence national forest policy also shows that successive federal governments of differing political persuasions have been motivated by an impending production or financial crisis in resource industries to promote additional investment in resource exploration or the better utilization of existing resources. Each effort has involved the federal government in the provision of financial assistance to the industry either in infrastructural development or in subsidies for industry rationalization and modernization.

On each occasion, the federal government has attempted to move toward the implementation of a policy framework that would allow room for an ongoing federal presence in the regulation of resource activities. But while the government may have been successful in establishing a short-term presence in the sector, provincial opposition has resulted in the limitation of the federal role to providing funding for provincial programs and direct involvement in only a relatively minor range of areas, such as research and development, trade promotion, and public awareness.

Provincial resource rights have been exercised by bodies such as the Canadian Council of Resource and Environment Ministers and the Canadian Council of Forest Ministers, which had the final say in the outcome of both the 1987 Conservative policy initiatives and those of its 1980-1 Liberal predecessor. On each occasion, these groups blocked federal government efforts to expand its influence in this sector. Despite repeated federal efforts to circumvent the provinces through the establishment of 'national strategies' specifying a lead role for the federal government, it has been unable to force the provinces to accede to its proposals due to the constitutional entrenchment of provincial jurisdiction in the sector.

In Canada, the economic interests of the state as landlord and development proponent result in active state participation in resource and environmental policy subsystems. But decisionmakers in government face numerous constraints. Decisions are often constrained by information and time limitations,[50] by judicial oversight, and, as the two cases discussed above have amply illustrated, by the federal nature of the Canadian state, which divides jurisdiction between the federal and provincial governments and leads to ongoing conflicts between them in this sector, influencing the type of decision likely to be made.[51]

At the beginning of this chapter, we argued that two of the most significant aspects of the setting of a decision concern the extent to which government decisionmakers are dominated by, or embedded in, policy subsystems and the nature of the constraints that they face in exercising their will. Both factors affect the potential for autonomous state action required for major policy change.[52]

On the basis of the two dimensions of the state or societal dominance of the policy subsystem and the presence or absence of significant constraints under which decisionmakers operate, four typical decision-making styles can be identified. Governments firmly embedded in, and dominated by, other policy subsystem members, such as industry, are more likely to be involved in adjustment strategies than in comprehensive, 'rational' searches. Situations of high constraint, such as the prospect of generating substantial unemployment through the closure of mills unable to comply with regulatory standards, are likely to result in a bargaining approach to decision-making, rather than a rational, 'maximizing' strategy.

The interaction of the two variables result in four basic decision-making styles. *Incremental adjustments* are likely to occur when non-state policy subsystem members dominate and constraints on decisionmakers are many. In such situations, we would expect large-scale, high-risk decisions to be rare. In the opposite scenario, when the government is an equal or dominant player in a policy subsystem and constraints are few, more traditional *rational searches* for new and possibly major changes are possible. When a societally dominant subsystem exists and constraints are low, an adjustment strategy is likely, but one that may tend toward *satisfying* decisions. Finally, when constraints are high but governments are strong, *optimization* rather than 'maximization' decisions are likely.

How does this typology apply to Canadian environmental and natural resource decision-making? The discussion in Chapter 7 has already characterized the policy subsystem in this area as 'triadic,' meaning that a type of subsystem exists in which the government is a significant player. While environmental actors have emerged as players in the policy network, the process continues to foil their full participation. Productive interests, and especially business, are much more significant actors and can often block or parry government initiatives and intentions. In addition, as the discussion in earlier chapters has shown, state actors rely upon private industry for information and for job creation and investment. Hence, in terms of the first criterion, state actors in the resource and environmental subsystem are often dominated by production-based societal actors in the policy subsystem.

In terms of the second factor, this chapter has developed two case studies to shed light on the possible enabling and constraining factors in decision-making. These examples have explored various factors that have affected Canadian resource and environmental decision-making under several governments and have illustrated several serious constraints to contemporary government decision-making in Canada. While the government may have some autonomy given the triadic network in this sector, it is limited not only by its own direct and indirect economic interests in resource ventures but also by entrenched bureaucratic interests and, especially, by divisions of federal and provincial authority.

This combination of societal dominance by productive interests and high levels of institutional constraint suggests that decisions made in this sector are likely to be incremental adjustments. That is, these factors conspire against the development of new policies that differ substantially from the status quo. In the Canadian resource and environmental sector, the legacy of past decisions continues to direct decision-making along a traditional path. This is likely to remain the case until the constitutional constraints on government diminish or new sets of societal actors begin to offset the influence of productive interests in policy subsystems. At present, the continuing strength of producer interests within the context of divided federal and provincial jurisdiction continues to influence decision-making in a conservative and traditional manner.

9

Policy Implementation: The Administration of Canadian Resource and Environmental Policy

The implementation stage of the policy process translates policy decisions into action. While some decisions have been made on the general shape of a policy, still others are required for it to be set in motion. Funding must be allocated, personnel assigned, and rules of procedure developed. In Canada, 'most of the fundamental decisions concerning the quality of the Canadian environment are made in the administrative context.'[1] Resource and environmental legislation provides for the establishment of administrative bodies to develop and implement regulations, rules, standards, and policies. This process involves setting and applying rules and regulations, monitoring resource inventories, planning and evaluating projects, allocating permits, assessing compliance with regulations, administering funds, and a variety of related activities. Government employees from the municipal to the federal level are employed in putting policy in action.

The very concept of 'implementation,' often viewed as synonomous with 'administration,' contributes to the misunderstanding of this stage in the policy process. Administration encompasses numerous managerial functions, including planning, implementation, monitoring, and evaluation. Yet implementation is a more suitable term to capture the complexity of a process that involves not only the bureaucratic execution of political decisions but also the utilization of a gamut of governing tools or policy instruments in the effort to urge, bribe, coerce, or otherwise convince policy targets to adhere to the wishes of governments.

In Canada, for a variety of reasons discussed below, resource and environmental policy implementation has been closely associated with one particular tool of government: *regulation*. Regulation has been by far the most favoured government technique for controlling or restricting the activities of individuals and companies involved in various forms of resource harvesting, extraction, processing, and sales. Most legislative precepts, at both federal and provincial levels, have been directed toward 'regulatory' activity, especially in the area of toxic substance and pollution control.[2] Other aspects of environmental protection, such as wilderness preservation and species and habitat conservation, have been addressed in a similar fashion. As this chapter will show, the generally low-profile, complex, and closed nature of Canadian resource and environmental policy implementation has often served to obscure the significance of the decisions and the nature of the political processes at work in this stage of the policy cycle.

General Factors Affecting Policy Implementation

Translating policies into practice is not as simple as might first appear. For a host of reasons innate to the nature and circumstances of the issue or the organization of the administrative machinery in charge of the task, programs will be implemented in a variety of ways. Implementation is not always consistent, nor does it necessarily reflect the intent of policy, but these are the realities of policy implementation. It is important that we recognize these limitations if we are to understand the policy implementation stage of the policy cycle.

The nature of the problems affects the implementation of programs designed to address them. Policy decisions involve varying degrees of technical difficulty during implementation, some being more intractable than others.[3] Implementing some programs can be unproblematic, often because they are single decisions whose translation into practice is routine. The processing of regulatory permits to discharge pulp effluent, or the allocation of hunting and guiding licences, may well reflect the practices of past years unless legislation, production quotas, or administrators change. Yet increasingly, many environmental programs with complex aims encounter limitations of information, technology, or financial resources. New knowledge, information, or circumstances, such as the depletion of fish stocks, have significant ramifications for resource administration. Some problems are more difficult to tackle than others because of their complex, novel, or interdependent nature.

In addition to the nature of the problem being addressed by the policy, implementation is affected by social, economic, technological, and political contexts. Changes in *social conditions* may affect the interpretation of the problem and thus the manner in which the program is implemented. Thus, the increased demands and political presence of First Nations groups, for example, may affect the administration of land tenure, parks policies, and fishery quotas among other subjects. Changes in *economic conditions* can have a similar impact on policy implementation. For example, regulatory non-compliance may be interpreted differently for a single-industry community with no alternative employment options than for a more economically diversified area. Economic conditions vary by region, necessitating greater flexibility and discretion in implementation.[4] The availability of *new technology* can also cause changes in policy implementation. Policies of pollution control, for example, often change in the course of implementation after a more effective or cheaper abatement technology has been discovered. Variations in *political circumstances* have an impact on policy implementation as well. Changes of government may lead to changes in the way that policies are implemented without change in the policy itself. The appointment of new cabinet members and deputy ministers, for example, may reshape the administrative regime.

The organization of the bureaucratic apparatus in charge of implementing a policy is also a factor. Policy implementation is an inadvertent subject of the intra- and interorganizational conflicts endemic to the public policy process. Different bureaucracies within the government and at other levels of government (national, provincial, territorial, and local) are involved in implementing policy, each bureaucracy with its own interests, ambitions, and traditions that hamper the implementation process and shape its outcome.[5] For many agencies, implementation may simply be another opportunity for continuing struggles that they may have lost at earlier stages of the policy process.

The political and economic resources of target groups also affect the implementation of policies. Powerful groups affected by a policy can often condition the character of implementation by supporting or opposing it. It is therefore common for regulators to strike compromises with groups to make the task of implementation easier. Changing levels of public support for a policy can also affect implementation. Many policies witness a decline in support after the policy has been made, giving greater opportunity to administrators to vary the original intent. Of course, the implementers themselves may use surveys to argue that a program should be continued in the face of policymakers' or a group's demands to change the policy.[6]

Problems in the resource and environmental implementation process generally range from political and legislative concerns to technical, especially cost-related, issues.[7] Issues such as lack of funding, bureaucratic obstacles to communication, administrative redundancy or omission, and technical glitches tend to be addressed as if they were incrementally resolvable through adjustments to the regulatory process. The working relationship between the state and industry in the development of regulatory policy often becomes an exercise in legislative and economic pragmatism. Close contacts between regulators and regulated are viewed as necessary, in recognition of the expertise of the private sector as well as its key economic role. Legal, political, and technical reforms are then directed to the continuing rehabilitation and improvement of regulatory activity. There is little recognition that the underlying socioeconomic structure – the relationship between the state and economic forces, and the market-based model underlying many policy efforts – may exercise a significant constraint to the implementation of a regime of effective environmental protection or resource management.

Canadian Resource and Environmental Policy Instruments
In this section, prevalent resource and environmental policy instruments utilized in Canada will be discussed. They include laws and regulations and various kinds of administrative agencies, tribunals, and hearings.

Laws and Regulations
Following the passage and proclamation of resource and environmental laws in Canada, they are enforced by resource-related administrative actors and agencies at all levels of government. The considerable overlap between federal and provincial jurisdiction over environmental matters, and the historical pattern of development of resource and environmental legislation, have produced a complex and confusing context for the implementation of environmental protection. Furthermore, rules or policies controlling environmental quality are established not only by common law and legislative statute but also by regulations and guidelines drawn up by a variety of administrative agencies in different jurisdictions and resource sectors.

Several types of laws and regulations are relevant to Canadian resource and environmental policy-making. The *common law* refers to a body of rules that have been established over hundreds of years in the adjudication of disputes in Britain and that serve as precedents for the consideration of contemporary issues in Canada. New laws are passed by Parliament to replace or supplement the common law. These statutes, or *statutory laws*, take the form of acts, which list the powers to be exercised by the cabinet in making regulations; they create rules to follow as well as offences for non-compliance. For example, the Endangered Species Act states that it is within the cabinet's power to name species considered to be 'endangered' for the purpose of enforcing the act.[8]

In contrast to the more formal provisions of common and statutory law, the majority of resource and environmental 'rules' take the form of *regulations* prepared by civil servants, often in conjunction with industry.[9] While these regulations are legally binding and describe what constitute offences, they rarely require legislative oversight. Other government policies include standards, objectives, criteria, and guidelines, which, although unlegislated, provide the *de facto* source of direction and background to the administration of law. While these rules are not legally enforceable, they are used by the government as a basis for administering the law. They are also used as leverage, to influence industry practices, to test potential laws, to gain cooperation from industry, and to work out site-specific controls on a plant-by-plant basis.[10]

Standards establish general rules that usually take the form of *guidelines,* which specify, for example, that only a certain concentration of a contaminant may be emitted in a particular time period. These guidelines are the basis for licensing or approval processes that further establish conditions for setting more specific standards. The *licensing* of individual sources of pollution or other environmental degradation is based on modification of guidelines and general objectives to fit the circumstances of a specific operation – mill, plant, or factory – in a specific environment. Regulatory instruments include 'agreements' such as permits, licences, certificates of authorization, control orders, stop orders, or program approvals. These instruments are applied to local, individual circumstances of resource or environmental use, such as the pollution from a new mine or smelter. They include the licensing of approval resulting in permits specifying pollution limits, as well as environmental assessments, which are discussed below. Certificates of approval may specify how a plant should be constructed and operated. A timber licence could identify, among other things, areas of allowable cut, time periods allocated to cutting, and provisions for reforestation. Licensing, as well as the more general standard-setting process, is done through negotiations between industry or the licence applicant and the administrative agency. There is very little public access to this process.

Administrative Agencies, Tribunals, and Hearings
Although the responsibility for the implementation of resource and environmental policies ultimately rests with federal or provincial cabinet and with the executive committees or boards of control of municipal and other kinds of local councils, these groups are merely the top of the chain of command. The actual practice of administering policy is largely performed by the civil service operating in various administrative agencies and by members of appointed boards and tribunals. Civil servants 'draft the statutes and by-laws that the councils and legislatures pass; put together the regulations that give teeth and substance to the laws; and decide how and to whom the laws will be applied.'[11]

Resource policy in Canada has always been implemented by specific *administrative agencies* given the task of administering resources or resource lands. These agencies began as offices of the surveyor-general, became commissioners of Crown lands, and by the late nineteenth century had developed into embryonic government departments.[12] By the mid-twentieth century, all governments in Canada had a variety of specialized ministries dealing with resource and environmental issues. Not surprisingly, additional agencies take part in administering federal and provincial statutes and communicate with Ottawa concerning joint regulatory responsibilities. Joint federal-provincial committees have also been established to set standards, while the administration of legislation has been relegated to provincial environment departments.[13]

Tribunals are created by statute and perform many administrative functions, hearing appeals concerning licensing (e.g., of pesticides), certification (of personnel or programs), and permits (e.g., for disposal of effluents). Appointed by government, they usually represent, or purport to represent, some diversity of interests and expertise. Administrative tribunals are structured to enact policy, but their procedures and decisions reflect and inform the larger policy context. The administrative process is routinely initiated by a proponent's proposal or application for development.

Administrative hearings are conducted by tribunals in a quasijudicial fashion in order to aid the tribunals in their activities. Hearings are bound by rules of natural justice, and procedures may be dictated by statutory provisions (which may be general and discretionary). Decisions are designed to be binding on the ministry in question but may be subject to various political, administrative, and judicial appeals. *Public hearings* may be statutorily defined as a component of the administrative process. In the framework of administration, public hearings are directed toward securing regulatory compliance and the achievement of identified standards of environmental quality. They may act as a mechanism with which to appeal administrative decisions, as we discuss below. In most cases, however, hearings are held at the discretion of a decision-making authority and are often 'after the fact' public information sessions rather than true consultative devices.[14]

Issues in Canadian Resource and Environmental Regulation

While the administration of environmental policy has developed rapidly in recent decades, several issues still constrain the implementation of effective environmental protection. Andrew Thompson identified the lack of clearly stated goals and objectives (and of the will to attain those that are stated) as 'insufficient effort to provide regulators with the kind of practical information they require, inadequate funding and staffing, inconsistent enforcement policies and failure to inform and involve the public character of the Canadian regulatory system.'[15] Increased public recognition of environmental degradation, and the higher profile achieved by green politics in recent decades, implicitly serve as a critique of policy implementation in this sector. As Robert Paehlke has argued, while 'the administrative state has considered resource management to be a province of its own, ... the emergence of environmental politics in the latter part of this century ... is a token of (its) failings.'[16]

While the problems in administrative processes and structures are multiple and overlapping, we have condensed them into five major areas of discussion. They include (1) information and data limitations, (2) the normative nature of risk assessment and standard-setting, (3) the economic power of regulated groups, (4) the lack of public input into implementation, and (5) serious problems with enforcement mechanisms.[17]

Information and Data Limitations

As we have seen, typical regulatory processes include standard-setting, compliance, and enforcement. At the level of provincial jurisdiction, regulatory powers include setting environmental standards or objectives (based on the compilation of information and the consideration of future activities in the area); licensing industries or other proponents so as to comply with these standards; using negotiative arrangements, administrative orders, and a variety of other incentives in order to achieve compliance; and prosecuting infractions of regulations through the court system.[18]

The regulatory process is built around setting limits, or standards, for extraction, contamination, and degradation, and implementing these standards. There are a number of standards identified by regulations, including those placing limits on harvests and discharges, those governing the ambient level or effects of removals and discharges, and those pertaining to the design or operation of facilities. Most standards have set maximum concentration levels, or production ratios (pollution/waste to finished product), although increased understanding of the persistence and bioaccumulation of many substances has shifted standard-setting toward limits on total quantities of pollutants emitted annually.[19] The concept of 'zero tolerance' has also been introduced as a means of encouraging production without pollution. Different standards apply to new, as opposed to existing, pollution sources, with new plants (and their associated technology) being subjected to more stringent standards.

Historically, regulatory activity was developed to control industrial and economic resource activity and to mediate and mitigate environmental damage. Thus, standards have been set as a 'process of deciding how much pollution will be allowed to enter the environment each year. Thus it is through the standard-setting process that governments, and the larger society they represent, make the final trade-off between the goal of environmental protection and other, conflicting, economic and social objectives.'[20]

But standards are based on the adequacy of information available to administrative agencies. The information base necessary to set standards includes a description of the physical nature of the pollution or activity being regulated as well as the environmental, social, and economic impacts of potential regulation. Specific information on individual resource supplies, as well as more general information on the sources of pollutants and their environmental effects, are used in setting standards.

However, there have been problems associated with the accumulation and integration of requisite data. 'Baseline' data measuring the state of resource supplies have often been accumulated by industry in the form, for instance, of geological surveys of potential mining activity. These surveys have not always been integrated with one another or centrally organized on either a provincial or a federal basis. (Timber inventories conducted on a regional basis, for instance, with little provincial, centralized coordination of data have restricted knowledge of general and cumulative trends.)

The private and industrial basis of information generation has also meant that data collection has been geared to economic interests. Thus, recorded information may be specific instead of reflecting an array of ecosystemic values.[21] Because government agencies have not traditionally had extensive capabilities for generating this information, and because industry's data are economically driven, adequate consideration of a wide variety of indicators has not occurred. This limitation, in turn, hampers forecasting and planning. Moreover, because data have been primarily researched and produced by industry, they may be inaccessible to government agencies, let alone the general public.

Normative Nature of Risk Assessment and Standard-Setting

It is not just the quality, amount, and nature of the information available that comprise a problem in regulatory activity; the criteria by which standards are set may also be problematic. In theory, the establishment of emission standards, for instance, appears to be efficient, rational, and straightforward, including the following steps:

(1) establishment of objectives (including the definition of the relevant environment, its use, and what constitutes pollution; for instance, if water quality standards are being set, water should be clean enough for drinking, swimming, and/or boating);
(2) establishment of scientific criteria for meeting those objectives;
(3) setting of ambient concentration objectives;
(4) setting of emission standards, identifying all sources of pollution and the limits in terms of either concentration levels or total quantities;
(5) implementation of the standards.[22]

Of course, what is not visible in this description is the source of data, the process through which criteria, objectives, and standards are established, and the decisions that are made.

Numerous problems limit the utility of risk assessment and standards, based on the assumption of rational, objective, and replicable criteria. They generally reflect the advantaged position of the proponent or polluter in the regulatory process. The economic and social basis from which the use of the natural environment is derived (i.e., employment and profit) is a primary consideration guiding regulatory practice. The information base, as we have seen, is inadequate, changing, and largely supplied by industry or users. The identification of costs, benefits, and risks is also typically market driven. Macdonald has noted: 'The chief disadvantage with standards is that they tend to be set at a level that virtually all existing pollution sources can meet so as not to put anyone out of business. Consequently, it becomes almost the norm for everyone to pollute up to the maximum level permitted by the standard.'[23]

This situation poses problems for interests that are not based on standard economic values, such as aesthetic concerns. In addition, different interests may deter agreement as to the appropriate standards that should be established. Thus, the concept of regulation would appear to begin with the identification of the state of the environment and proceed to the determination of limits for pollution. In fact, the practice may work by 'starting with an examination of the polluting source and the economics of reducing pollution and then moving on to set emission standards without ever examining the receiving environment.'[24]

Economic Power of Regulated Groups

Unequal economic relations in the policy subsystem can also be a major problem at this stage of the policy process. Macdonald notes, for example, that the 'cost to the regulated industry and larger society is almost always a more important criterion in determining regulatory action than is the environmental damage caused by pollution.'[25]

Consider an example of the approval process provided by Macdonald. If a department or the Ministry of the Environment wants to reduce contamination by an industry, officials will discuss their objectives with industry or plant representatives. The ensuing 'abatement program' will consist of a formal, although not legally binding, program for pollution reduction, specifying desired levels of emissions and dates by which they will be put into effect.

This process of 'program approval' involves private negotiations between the polluter and officials (although in some jurisdictions, like Ontario, some public consultation sessions may have been added to the process). If the agency is not satisfied with the results, the program is incorporated into a legally binding 'control' order, which requires changes in industry procedures. If industry does not comply, a 'stop order' requires the industry to cease operation until the issue has been resolved. The regulated industry may appeal such orders through various environmental appeals boards.[26]

Perhaps the most central problems of regulation have been the negotiative relationship between the state and industry in setting standards and scheduling compliance and the corresponding lack of enforcement and prosecution. The involvement of the regulated group in the regulatory process counters the assumption of state impartiality. But there is a more general problem underlying industrial participation on the regulatory 'team.' It is the game itself, which appears to be more highly devoted to the maintenance of favourable economic conditions than to the issue of environmental or resource protection and management. The current economic infrastructure is assumed by both regulators and regulatees to be a primary and universal condition of regulation.

Economic concerns have become the primary rationale for regulation and the criteria on which it is evaluated. The underlying assumption is that industry is valuable as a source of profit and employment within society. 'Job blackmail,' the threat of large-scale industrial unemployment from plant closures, may be invoked to counter or postpone efforts at more stringent regulatory practices. Pollution abatement costs and profit losses are considered in the context of a cost-benefit analysis, whose parameters are secured by corporate accounting practices.[27] Concerns about industry's ability to implement pollution abatement technology have served as a rationale for extending compliance deadlines. As William Sinclair states, 'During lows in the business cycle, mill representatives merely have to claim economic hardship ... When economic conditions improve, mill representatives are in a position to claim any of a number of different reasons for avoiding controls.'[28] Resource shortages, competitiveness, and shifts in demand – reflecting the market character of capitalism – are all used by industry to resist regulatory change.

For the years between 1971 and 1985, for example, Sinclair reports that 'the total amount of capital investment on air and water pollution abatement as a percentage of total capital investment declined continuously.'[29] He further states, 'it is difficult to envision that the modest price increases which could be attributed to effluent controls would make any permanent difference to the international competitiveness of an individual mill or the industry.'[30]

Thus, the criticisms discussed above are directed not only to the issue of adequate pollution control but also to concerns about the nature and relations of the contemporary state and to the place of industry in the regulatory process. Perceptions of a pro-industry bias in pulp pollution regulations challenge assumptions of a fair and effective regulatory state. The shortcomings of the implementation process – a perceived structural alliance between the interests of industry and the state, a bureaucratic complexity that obscures and hinders the regulatory process, and an inaccessibility to the public that detracts from the accountability of the state and further enhances the position of industry – challenge mainstream assumptions of an impartial and effective implementation process.

Barriers to Public Participation

As was the case with various institutionalized commissions and inquiries discussed in Chapter 6 with respect to agenda-setting, the complexity of administrative agencies, tribunals, and their activities, as well as the lack of formal procedural access, also serve as barriers to public participation in the implementation process.

Consider the application of pesticides. They are approved at the federal level, with no public access to the process. Pesticide control branches of the provincial ministries of the environment usually administer licensing and certification programs, in addition to issuing permits for the application of pesticides. While certificates are required for pesticide vendors and applicators, licences are held by firms engaged in retail sales and pest control services. Hundreds of permits for pesticide use are issued every year. Different types of permits are required for different classes and uses of pesticides.

Some, although few, regulatory processes provide for public input, either as public hearings, required by environmental assessments, or as appeals to the permitting process discussed above. In the appeal process, citizens can appeal the decision of an administrator to approve a permit for a specified environmental use or decisions concerning licensing and certification. The appeal takes place before administrative tribunals established by the agency administering the appropriate legislation.

Administrative tribunals are established by statute and assume some of the functions of a court. Unlike courts, however, tribunals reflect 'considerable variation in procedural matters, such as the degree of formality, the admissibility of evidence, and the conduct of cross-examination.'[31] Tribunals hear appeals from decisions, approvals, actions, or orders of administrators of the agencies in which they are located. They offer the opportunity for public involvement at the administrative level. They are more informal, inexpensive, speedy, and flexible than courts.

While the administrative tribunal provides a means for public input to the regulatory process, and provides for a quick and specific response to relevant resource and to environmental issues, a number of problems still challenge its effectiveness, as we will discuss in Chapter 10. One problem is the lack of statutory provision for such tribunals in all provinces and in all sectors of resource and environmental use. While pesticide use may be appealed by the public in some provinces, there may be no similar provisions for the appeal of decisions about the allocation of fishing or timber licences, the issuing of park-use permits, or the licensing of guides and outfitters.

Although it is difficult to secure appropriate information if actors are external to administrative agencies or industry processes, as an appellant to an administrative decision, the public is typically required to assume the burden of proof. This role involves the presentation of material in such a way that it will contribute to a case for an 'unreasonable adverse effect.' Yet the lack of public access to scientific and program-specific information erects a substantial obstacle to such participation.

The reactive nature of the appeal process is another problem, because it directs public involvement to a responsive, rather than an anticipatory, position. With regard to herbicide or pesticide use, for instance, appeals may be directed only to an administrator's approval of a permit, not to the approval of the pesticide or the standard-setting process. Another problem is the composition of tribunals. Appointed by government, and ostensibly representing a diversity of interests, tribunal membership often reflects expertise that is influenced by alliance with, employment by, or past association with productive interests.

The discretionary nature of the proceedings of the tribunal has been another problem for appellants. For instance, tribunals may decide to accept 'public information' such as newspaper accounts while refusing letters of opinion from expert witnesses.[32] In addition, the lack of stated reasons for tribunal decisions, especially when tribunals uphold the licensing decisions made by administrators, makes it difficult for appellants to chart a strategy for appeal.

Lack of Effective Enforcement

In the past decade, public recognition of continuing regulatory noncompliance has led to many questions about the adequacy of regulatory enforcement. As Macdonald notes, the term 'enforcement,' 'with its connotations of rigorous action taken by the government to ensure that polluters obey the strict letter of the law, is relatively new.'[33] A tougher approach to regulatory enforcement reflects an increase in administrative capabilities in monitoring and enforcement.

Statutory provisions for enforcement include an array of investigative and information-gathering capabilities, as well as administrative orders for remedial action and the recovery of costs against those responsible for contamination or other damage. The complexity of these provisions mirrors that of other stages of standard-setting. At the federal level alone, by 1990 twenty-four departments had responsibilities relating to more than fifty federal statutes, and Environment Canada itself had responsibilities under thirty-six statutes relating to environmental issues alone.[34] Yet the enforcement of federal requirements has been, for the most part, delegated to the provinces.

Most offences are 'strict liability offenses, where the offense simply consists of doing the prohibited act, but where an accused may exculpate himself where he can prove, on a balance of probabilities, that he exercised all reasonable care or due diligence to avoid committing the offense.'[35] Typical offences include:

(1) causing environmental damage;
(2) failing to report a spill;
(3) failing to provide required information;
(4) providing false or misleading information;
(5) obstructing or failing to assist enforcement officers;
(6) failing to comply with requirements established by regulation;
(7) failing to obtain required permits or approvals before engaging in regulated activity;
(8) failing to comply with the terms of a permit or licence;
(9) failing to comply with an administrative order requiring remedial action.[36]

Enforcement officers carry out inspections to ensure compliance and to obtain evidence of non-compliance, and they call for remedial action if standards are not met. In cases of non-compliance, enforcement officers have the discretion to initiate or continue negotiations, working out arrangements by which the polluter may achieve compliance. However, the following formal responses may also be given: warnings, ministerial orders for remedial action, tickets, injunctions, prosecutions, penalties and court orders upon conviction, and civil suits to recover costs.[37]

A central issue in resource management and environmental protection is the method of securing compliance. Approaches to enforcement have been referred to as the use of 'the carrot' or 'the stick.' The carrot approach assumes that a greater degree of compliance will be secured by proponents' voluntary activity than through punitive action. In contrast, the stick approach involves the issuing of penalties through sanctions and is represented by the current tendency to toughen enforcement practices and penalties. While these are separate and contradictory models of enforcement, in practice they overlap and represent a continuum with various instruments having a greater emphasis on one or the other approach.[38]

A conciliatory style of regulatory enforcement, involving bargaining between government and industry, has traditionally characterized the Canadian approach to policy implementation. This approach, which has been characterized as 'relatively closed, consensual and consultative,'[39] has been favoured over the adversarial style characteristic of more punitive regimes. Non-compliance in this context leads to renewed negotiations and ongoing planning for the future 'harmonization' of regulatory goals and industrial practices rather than punishment. However, increased recognition of the large extent and ongoing character of non-compliance has led to pressure being placed upon governments to get tougher with enforcement and to move increasingly to judicial remedies.

The extent of non-compliance with regulatory standards has been, and continues to be, staggering. The Canadian Environmental Advisory Council, for example, observed a 'pattern of persistent, nation-wide non-compliance' with federal standards for liquid effluent from 1970 to 1977. More recent findings of industry's routine non-compliance with legislation has confirmed the inadequacy of current regulatory arrangements and appointments. A study of permit holders in two regions of the province between 1984 and 1986 found that over half of class 1 permittees (high priority and impact) were in violation of their permits on at least half of the times that compliance was monitored.[40] A study of other permit holders in two regions of the province also found a significant amount of regulatory non-compliance. Over half of class 1 permittees (high priority and impact) were in violation of their permits at least half of the times that compliance was monitored, and routine non-compliance was virtually never prosecuted by Waste Management Branch officials.[41]

Corporate bias is also reflected in the enforcement of regulations. Thus, in December 1989, an internal federal government document leaked to the public charged that the government grants large corporations 'immunity' from prosecution under the Fisheries Act. Large firms are not prosecuted, it was reported, because of a 'negotiate-and-compromise-at-all-costs philosophy,' while the 'little guy' is charged for minor offences. The author of the document, Otto Langer, a senior official with Fisheries and Oceans Canada, stated that 'We have been known for charging individuals for spills of deleterious substances (often accidental and less than a few gallons) and then [we] continually ignore the daily discharge of millions of gallons of toxic effluent from a mill next door.'[42] He further warned:

> We have determined that DFO [Department of Fisheries and Oceans]-friendly corporations or parties with provincial permits (as well as the BC agency issuing the permit that allowed the offense) will enjoy relative immunity from the Fisheries Act ... This is in addition to the years of

immunity we have given those mills that have been fortunate to have a continuous discharge and can negotiate and promise while they pollute ...

Failure to turn this matter around will result in a basket case enforcement program which has characterized the BC MOE [Ministry of the Environment] from the early 1980s to the present time. As you are aware, we have been critical of the nearly non-existent MOE habitat enforcement record. However, is it appreciated that we are slipping into the same rut?[43]

Langer's memo did not restrict its critique of regulatory enforcement to the efforts of industry. Langer also suggested that several prosecutions were never launched because either the provincial resource or environment ministries would have to be charged, and this would be 'political dynamite.'

More generally, Macdonald also describes a history of government inactivity and ineffectiveness regarding the enforcement of regulations, reflecting a 'pattern of government reluctance to enforce pollution reductions when economic interests were at stake.'[44] Although the lack of enforcement activity mirrors the privilege enjoyed by industry, additional explanations apply. One problem has been the lack of enforcement instruments and government personnel allotted to enforcement. Another has been the cost of compliance, which – to industry – may exceed the economic benefits, especially on a short-term basis, of remaining in business.

Increased public awareness of the extent of non-compliance has not only led to concerns over public health but has also increasingly brought into question the legitimacy of the state. In the mid-1980s, the enforcement of Canadian environmental law shifted to an expanded and tougher profile, with increased administrative provision for enforcement staff and tougher penalties. In 1985, for example, a major change in Ontario's enforcement policy to give greater emphasis to prosecution as an enforcement option, together with the creation of an Investigations and Enforcement Branch, staffed with professional investigators within the Ministry of the Environment, started a trend of increased enforcement activity in the province.[45] Between 1986 and 1988, the number of investigations in Ontario doubled, and by 1989 they had increased by 600 per cent from the beginning of the decade.[46]

The new 'get tough' policy was reflected by changes at the end of the decade in other provinces as well. In 1989, the BC government announced the creation of six regional environmental enforcement units to supplement the existing conservation officer service.[47] In Alberta, the reorganization of the Pollution Control Division of the provincial environment department also provided a greater enforcement emphasis.

Other changes have been the increased use of the judicial process to impose stiffer penalties and, in Ontario, the adoption of an environmental bill of rights to increase citizen participation in the enforcement process.[48] At the federal level, enforcement activity has also been increasing under the provisions of the Canadian Environmental Protection Act.

The Dynamics of Administrative Policy: The Case of Pulp Pollution

There have been a number of phases in the development of the administrative structure of Canadian resource and environmental policy implementation, and they come into sharper focus if we look at a specific case such as pulp pollution regulation.

While the state's involvement in the regulation of pulp pollution is not new, the character of its involvement has changed.[49] Prior to 1950, there was little legislation directly intended to protect the environment from industrial pollution. Rather, legislation addressed issues such as pollution control indirectly, within a larger statutory context of resource (e.g., fisheries) management or human health protection.[50] This legislation, while recognizing the potential harm inflicted by pollutants, was too general to be effective and was only sporadically enforced. Industrial pollution was considered to be the responsibility of the private sector, not only because scientific evidence of its consequences was limited; but because research was primarily initiated by and for industry. Because much industrial pollution was produced in hinterland areas, it was not considered to be deleterious to urban populations. Lack of recognition of both the extent and the negative consequences of pollution impeded the development of effective regulations.

However, in response to new technology, knowledge about the extent and consequences of pollution, and public pressure, a new era of state activity emerged between the late 1950s and early 1970s, and pollution control mechanisms were developed at both provincial and federal levels to integrate and strengthen regulatory approaches. A legislative and administrative framework for pollution regulation was established, and a 'permission to pollute' approach to regulation emerged at this time.

In British Columbia, for example, under the Pollution Control Act and its successor, the Waste Management Act (1982), regulations are issued on waste introduced into the environment, permits are issued to mills specifying pollution amounts, and schedules and penalties are provided for non-compliance with the acts. They establish a permit system by which wastes can be legally discharged according to pollution control guidelines. Managers use permits to set conditions such as special procedures, requirements for abatement technology, and site-specific criteria for effluents.

The BC government continued to expand the scope, force, and nature of its regulatory efforts in the early 1990s as concerns about the extent of regulatory non-compliance prompted tougher policies. The Waste

Management Amendment Act passed in 1989 increased the penalties provided in the act, and by November of that year, special environmental enforcement units had been established in each of the province's six administrative regions.[51] In December 1990, Cariboo Pulp and Paper was fined $275,000 for pollution offences, the largest fine levied against a BC pulp mill. Other businesses have been charged and convicted under the Waste Management Act in recent years.[52]

Furthermore, government reports now routinize and make publicly accessible industry's degree of compliance with regulatory standards, and this approach provides additional incentive to companies to improve performance. New standards have also been introduced. The province announced in 1989, for example, that, by the end of 1991, all mills were to have secondary treatment. New regulations issued under the Waste Management Act in December 1990 supplemented the existing permitting system by providing more extensive and routine control. The Pulp Mill and Paper Mill Liquid Effluent Control Regulation under the Waste Management Act requires all mills to 'install secondary effluent treatment works and meet specified limits for total suspended solids, biochemical oxygen demand, chlorinated organic compounds and toxicity by specified dates.'[53]

Thus, the first phase of implementation included the creation of new legislation and new agencies to deal with specific aspects of pollution. Existing authority for environmental protection was transferred from health departments to independent locations. The next step was the rationalization and integration of existing provisions for environmental protection in explicitly 'environmental' statutes and the creation of new legislation that would encompass and transcend 'pollution' activity.[54]

Other new directions in pulp pollution policy have emerged in the 1990s. In comparison to the *ex post* control approach characteristic of past efforts, the new emphasis is directed toward preventative approaches to pollution. The 'preventative and anticipatory' philosophy is based on 'recycling and reusing pollutants, on prohibiting or severely restricting discharges to prevent bioaccumulation or long-term environmental effects, and on forging more effective enforcement tools.'[55] In the July 1991 status report on pulp mill effluents, BC Environment Minister Dave Mercier announced that 'BC Environment's goal is to work with industry toward zero discharge of wastes.'[56]

The *precautionary principle*, which involves taking regulatory action to prevent contamination before there is absolute proof of harm, has been identified as an objective in many new standards. Furthermore, economic incentives have been discussed as a means of encouraging greater industry compliance with regulations. Subsidization of new environmentally friendly pollution abatement technology, creation of tax incentives, and establishment of pollution credits are among the instruments that have been suggested. Environmental assessment legislation, as well, is expected to reflect the continued evolution of the regulatory climate from mitigation to prevention.

This case shows how the creation and implementation of pollution control legislation has extended the role of the state in activities of resource management and environmental protection. The new era of pollution control legislation created in recent decades has altered the state's regulatory capabilities in several ways.

First, this new legislation involves the state in what had previously been the private affair of industry, as 'government must determine what are acceptable levels of pollutants, what abatement technologies are practicable, what industries can afford, and what the public will tolerate.'[57]

Second, the evolving regulatory regime is characterized by an increased administrative foundation for pollution control. This administrative development is directed toward the environmental consequences of pollution. The current development of omnibus environmental legislation reflects this tendency.

Third, the expansion of information concerning the regulatory process has been crucial in the creation of a new regulatory regime. There has been a significant increase in the information available on pollution sources and their environmental effects, although the process of data collection and analysis is by no means complete. Compliance reports integrating regulatory information are now made available to the public.

Fourth, a related change in regulatory policy involves the specification of more stringent standards and the introduction of a precautionary approach to environmental regulation.

Fifth, there has been an increase in the state's enforcement activities. Administrators can now request modifications to, and notifications of, impending pollution activities, close down existing mills, and require the implementation of monitoring equipment. There has been an increase in the functions and numbers of government environmental staff, and a new category of pollution inspectors has been created.

Sixth, there have been several new 'sustainable development' initiatives, which encompass a number of new implementation directions. Conceptually, regulation has evolved towards preventative strategies, which would sustain the long-term environmental viability of both industries and ecosystems. Alternative regulatory instruments such as economic incentives are also being introduced. In contrast to the 'behind closed doors' policy of state-industry negotiation, these incentives formally approve, for instance, the open trading of pollution permits to encourage industry's regulatory compliance.

Conclusion: The Style of Resource and Environmental Policy Implementation in Canada

In spite of the centrality and importance of administration to both resource management and environmental protection activities, implementation remains in many respects a 'missing link.'[58] Following the earlier visible and overtly political stages of the policy cycle, the implementation process is complex, internally orchestrated between bureaucrats and proponents, and usually much less accessible to public scrutiny.

Many noble efforts by governments and citizens to create a better and safer world have foundered at the implementation stage.[59] This has led not only to a greater appreciation of the difficulties encountered in policy implementation but also to the attempt to design policies in a manner that facilitates their implementation. While many government decisions continue to be made without adequate attention being paid to the difficulties of implementation, there is now a broad recognition of the need to take these concerns into account at earlier stages of the policy process. It is easier for policymakers to take the limitations into account and devise an appropriate response *ex ante* rather than *ex post*.[60]

The expansion of the activities and power of the administrative sphere as well as the increase in policy problems governments face, challenge many assumptions about policy implementation. Thompson has attempted to explain the Canadian propensity for regulation and a limited role for government in resource and environmental policy implementation by arguing that the traditional Canadian orientation toward resource protection has been fostered by 'the belief that publicly-owned resources *should* be free goods and that government's role *should* be restricted to that of regulator.'[61] Rather than understanding implementation as a simple 'follow-through' of policy measures by state agencies, we should view the discretionary character and bilateral basis of many administrative practices as revealing a much more politicized and potentially contentious policy process.

Assessing the reasons for instrument choice in any policy area, however, requires a multivariate explanation. In one of the most sophisticated works on the subject of policy implementation, Linder and Peters list a number of factors as playing a critical role in shaping patterns of policy instrument choice by governments.

First, the *features of the policy instruments* themselves are important for selection purposes, because some instruments are better suited for a task than are others.[62]

Second, they argue that *policy style and political culture,* and the depth of social cleavages, also have a critical bearing on the choice of an instrument. That is, each jurisdiction has its own pattern of social conflicts that predispose its decisionmakers to choose a particular instrument. Third, they argue that the choice of an instrument is circumscribed by the *organizational culture* of the agencies concerned and the nature of their links with clients and other agencies. And fourth, they argue that the *context of the problem situation*, its timing and the scope of actors that it includes, will also affect the choice of instrument.

This suggests that the choice of preferred policy instrument, such as regulation, is shaped by the characteristics of the instruments, the nature of the problem at hand, past experiences of governments in dealing with the same or a similar problem, the subjective preference of the decisionmakers, and the likely reaction to the choice by affected social groups. A preference for the use of particular instruments over a wide range of contexts, as is the case with the use of regulation in Canadian resource and environmental policy is explained by other factors as well.

Thompson and Chandler have suggested that the most significant factors are the preferences of state decisionmakers and the nature of the constraints within which they operate. Just as these two variables affect general decision-making styles, so they affect the general style of policy implementation. States must have a high level of administrative capacity in order to utilize market-based instruments and regulatory or direct provisional ones. When a state has few organizational, informational, or other resources, on the other hand, it will tend to utilize instruments such as incentives and propaganda or to rely on existing voluntary, community, or family-based instruments to achieve its ends.[63] The tendency to choose a particular instrument within these categories, however, is also affected by the level of state autonomy within a policy subsystem. Hence, a subsystem dominated by non-state actors will encourage the use of market, exhortative, or subsidy instruments, while, if the state enjoys a higher level of autonomy, it can attempt to use regulatory instruments or public enterprises to achieve its ends.

In Canada, as we have seen, the preferred instruments for resource and environmental policy implementation have been configured as bureaucratic rather than market based, but the context, style, and substance of the marketplace tend to infiltrate much of the regulatory process. Compliance has been approached in terms of market-based factors: profit margins and the economic viability of industry, employment patterns, and international competitiveness. Government subsidies to business underwrite compliance efforts, as in the case of subsidies for new technology that will enable industry to meet regulatory standards. The recent emphasis on market-based instruments, such as the issuing of pollution credits, confirms the tacit assumption of a market economy as the foundation of the policy process.

Nevertheless, administrative efforts are directly responsible for providing much of the activity of resource management and environmental protection, and their regulating efforts are an expanding locus of government activity. As we have seen, in contrast to the popular conception of governments regulating resource and environmental use independently of users, the implementation of Canadian policy in this sector operates largely as a bargaining relationship between government and industry. Historically, resource and environmental regulation was geared to business activity rather than to resource conservation or environmental protection. Industry, in pursuing its own productive interests, has supplied much of the baseline data, up-to-date technical information concerning abatement technology, and cost-benefit analyses concerning production, pollution, and abatement, from which regulatory standards have been set.

Because of the significance of resource-based industry to the Canadian economy, the historical dominance of single-industry production, the lack of broad-based economic competition, and the legacy of a staples economy, economic forces have provided the impetus for most existing regulation. Industry's role in developing regulations has been cost effective in the sense that governments have not been required to supply separate and potentially redundant information. But industry's regulatory role reaffirms the importance of private sector activity to the bilateral negotiative basis that characterize this as well as other stages of the policy process. The ability of industry to affect the regulatory process has contributed to the fact that environmental protection has usually occupied a back seat to resource exploitation throughout Canada's history.[64]

10

Policy Evaluation: The Political, Administrative, and Judicial Assessment of Canadian Resource and Environmental Policy

The model of the policy cycle used throughout this book is not only staged and sequential but also iterative and reflexive. That is, the model assumes from the outset that policy-making is a dynamic process in which policies are constantly in flux. Each stage not only reflects the larger socio-economic and political context but also refers back to the preceding stage(s), directing feedback that reinforms the direction and evolution of each stage of the policy process. A crucial stage in understanding these policy dynamics is policy evaluation. It is at this point that the results of the previous four stages of the cycle are examined along with the resulting policy itself and alterations to the policy made on the basis of those evaluations.[1] In this sense, evaluation provides a formal feedback loop, a means through which the entire process and the substance of the policy can be assessed and charted for ongoing revision.

Various actors play important roles in policy evaluation. Governments, for example, often initiate a process of assessing how a policy is working, while interested members of policy subsystems and the public are often also engaged in their own assessment of the workings and effects of the policy in order to express their support, opposition, or demand for changes to it. Thus, policy evaluation involves most of the key actors arrayed in policy subsystems in a variety of formal and informal means of assessment. It almost always involves bureaucrats and politicians in relevant policy networks, and it usually involves non-governmental members of policy networks and communities. It can also involve members of the public, who have an indirect say when they vote at elections.[2]

As we have seen, Canadian resource and environmental policy is evaluated in numerous ways throughout the policy cycle, as instruments and actors adapt to changing legislation, socioeconomic conditions, and ideological shifts. Evaluation ranges from ongoing informal assessment by the public to the scrutiny of specific instruments by technical staff in a program. Public protests by environmental groups represent an evaluation of existing policy, although this type of evaluation is *post hoc*, informal, and external to the policy 'loop.' Protests of predator control programs or seal hunts are in effect assessments of existing policy efforts and may contest specific arenas and decisions. Other evaluations may be reflected through procedural critiques, demands for more inclusive administrative organization, or access to information by the public.

Whether they realize it or not, subsystem members engaged in policy evaluation are often participating in a larger process of policy learning. There are several types of learning[3] that evaluations can engender. Some lessons are likely to concern practical suggestions about different aspects of the policy cycle as it has operated in the past. These include, for example, lessons about which policy instruments have succeeded in which circumstances and which have failed, or which issues have enjoyed public support in agenda-setting and which have not.[4] Other lessons are more about policy goals than means. This is a more fundamental type of learning, which is accompanied by changes in the thinking underlying a policy.[5]

While the concept of 'learning' may be generally associated with intentional, progressive, cognitive consequences of 'education,' policy learning has a broader meaning. That is, it refers to both intended and unintended consequences of activities as well as to both positive and negative implications. It refers to the immediate impacts of specific policies as well as to their long-term implications. Learning does not necessarily imply the conscious reinforcement or selection of alternative approaches, but it may include the modest adaptation of policy processes by a range of actors and relevant political and social institutions. Not all policy learning produces a visible response, which makes it difficult to assess the extent to which real change has been made.

As will be described below, subsystem members involved in evaluating Canadian resource and environmental policy-making do so in a variety of ways and in a number of important political, administrative, and judicial venues. Evaluation includes both informal and spontaneous responses to policy measures, as well as the formal adaptations emphasized in the policy framework. This chapter sets out the manner in which these evaluations have operated in the past and discusses the limited nature of policy learning that has resulted from these types of evaluations.

Definition of Policy Evaluation

For many observers, policy evaluation consists of assessing whether a public policy is achieving its stated objectives and, if not, what can be done to eliminate impediments to their attainment. Thus, David Nachmias defines policy evaluation as 'the objective, systematic, empirical examination of the effects ongoing policies and public programs have on their targets in terms of the goals they are meant to achieve.'[6]

This technocratic and 'rational' vision of policy evaluation, however, is seriously flawed, especially in its application. The goals in public policy are usually not stated clearly enough to find out to what extent they are being achieved, nor are they shared by all actors. Moreover, this type of analysis is also limited because of the difficulties involved in the attempt to develop objective standards by which to evaluate government success in dealing with subjective claims and socially constructed problems. Furthermore, the formal, overt goals stated by government typically gloss an array of 'latent objectives' that policy also serves. Thus, while governments may attempt to reduce industrial effluents through raising regulatory standards, they also have an interest in preserving conditions for employment and economic activity. Moreover, their presentation of their own efforts as equitable and independent is essential in maintaining public confidence and stability.

The notion of policy-making as rational rarely obscures its political and structural components. Policy evaluation, like activities that occur at the other stages of the policy cycle, is an inherently political activity. It is not always designed to reveal the effects of a policy. In fact, it is employed at times to disguise certain facts from being known, facts that are feared will show the government in poor light. It is also possible for governments to design the terms of evaluation in a way that leads to conclusions that would show a policy in a better light. Or, if government wants to change or scrap a policy, it can adjust the terms of the evaluation accordingly. Evaluation may thus serve as a key element in upholding the legitimacy of governments. Evaluation by those outside the government is similarly not always designed to improve a policy but often to criticize it in order to gain partisan political advantage or to pursue an ideological agenda.

Developing adequate and acceptable measures for policy evaluation, therefore, is a difficult and contentious task, as many authors have noted.[7] Analysts often resort to concepts such as 'success' or 'failure' to conclude an evaluation, but as Ingram and Mann caution,

> the phenomenon of policy failure is neither so simple nor certain as many contemporary critics of policy and politics would have us believe. Success and failure are slippery concepts, often highly subjective and reflective of an individual's goals, perception of need, and perhaps even psychological disposition toward life. The old story about asking two individuals how much milk is in the bottle and receiving two replies that appear to reflect their different approaches to life – one says half-full and the other half-empty – seems relevant.[8]

This is not to suggest that policy evaluation is an irrational process, devoid of genuine intentions to find out about the functioning of a policy and its effects. Rather, it is to caution against undue reliance on formal evaluation in drawing conclusions about a policy. Furthermore, our concerns are not simply to examine the polarities of success and failure but to assess the adaptability of the state and the potential of Canadian policy to change. To get the most out of policy evaluation, we must examine it from the perspectives we have adopted throughout this book. We need to look at the larger context of the policy process, not only the political aspects but also the social, economic, and ecological conditions to which policy responds. We also need to examine the interests of those who make and/or are affected by Canadian resource and environmental policy.

Mechanisms for the Evaluation of Canadian Resource and Environmental Policy

Several basic types of policy evaluation exist in the area of Canadian natural resource and environmental policy-making. While government decisions and actions in this area can be evaluated politically by voters and others at election times, the discussion in previous chapters has underlined the limited manner in which political parties and electoral processes turn on resource and environmental issues and concerns. Resource and environmental policies in Canada tend to be evaluated in administrative and judicial settings to a greater extent than in political forums.

This is not to say that some political evaluations are not significant. Legislative committees and task forces, for example, can and do evaluate resource and environmental policies and make recommendations for their alteration. However, such reviews are often ignored by governments that are not bound by their recommendations and that usually ask permanent officials for review of, and commentary on, a report, rather than respond directly to it. In this process, any original or radical recommendation is usually removed.[9]

Policies in this sector are evaluated in a variety of administrative and judicial settings by members of the relevant policy networks. Administrative arenas of government provide for both policy enactment and evaluation. While we focused in the preceding chapter on the implementation functions of administrative actions, their evaluative purpose is also significant.[10] Administrative evaluation provides a means through which the application of resource and environmental regulations may be assessed. Do they provide adequate incentives for compliance? What are the limitations of administrative decisions? Are sanctions appropriate to encourage compliance? Are enforcement measures adequate? Administrative appeals, tribunals, and other instruments provide a means for policy community members other than proponents to evaluate or challenge the ways in which policy has been implemented. For instance, members of environmental groups may launch an administrative appeal of an administrator's decision to approve an application for a timber licence or a pesticide permit.

As our discussion of the policy cycle indicates, administrative processes have traditionally been understood to be internal forms of government policy-making. Due to various procedural, legal, and financial constraints, members of policy communities are often excluded from these forums. As a result, these members may resort to judicial settings in their effort to include their concerns in policy evaluation.[11] Judicial evaluation provides one of the few means by which members of policy communities can challenge the activities of relatively closed policy networks. State actors also utilize the judicial evaluation process as a means of attaining and assessing regulatory compliance. The reasons for the success or failure of policy initiatives, and the potential of both the judicial and administrative evaluative process to inform and revise the policy cycle, will be addressed in the concluding section of this chapter.

The Administrative Evaluation of Canadian Resource and Environmental Policy

Administrative processes are usually assumed to function as relatively simple implementations of policies that have been honed through the complex machinations of the policy process. Yet they, too, may be imperfect – too costly, overly bureaucratic, inefficient, narrow, and unwieldy. Identifying and responding to these flaws is neither a well developed nor a routine feature of the policy process. Despite the possibility of including policy community members, the vast majority of administrative evaluation in Canada excludes non-network members of policy subsystems from participation. Furthermore, the information on which decisions are based, the reasons they are made, and the interests they serve are rarely, if ever, identified as issues in the administrative evaluation process.

In theory, as we have observed, public participation throughout the policy process serves an evaluative function by providing the opportunity to counter dominant economic interests and to monitor state-controlled processes. Even the stage of agenda-setting represents an implicit evaluation of past policies. Yet already limited opportunities for public involvement decline through the policy cycle, becoming progressively more limited. At the evaluative stage, members of policy communities have an infrequent opportunity to participate in a given process, as participatory 'rights' in administrative review tribunals and processes are often limited by statutory definition.[12] With the exception of EARP legislation and administrative appeals, the public has few rights to participate in evaluative processes. Schrecker, for example, notes the formal distinction in Environment Canada's internal public information and consultation policy between 'the "broad public commentary" solicited on proposed regulations and the "full consultation" with affected industries.'[13]

While principles of 'natural justice' inherent in the common law require that those affected by agency decisions be given adequate notice and a fair opportunity to be heard, administrative officials have often interpreted this requirement to mean that participants must have a direct economic interest in the issue under discussion.[14] Without personal economic (i.e., property) interests in an issue, there are no rights to participate in most agency decisions.[15] Thus, the issue of 'standing,' or the ability to participate in administrative deliberations and proceedings, continues to be problematic and favours existing policy network members.

Furthermore, just as the inclusion of the public at the administrative level is limited and discretionary, so also is the establishment of forums for the consideration of specific interests. The exclusion of the general public from many important resource and energy decisions in the areas of nuclear energy, air, and drinking water, as well as the more routine procedures of logging, fisheries, and pollution control, is a central limitation to administrative policy evaluation in Canada.

Criticisms of public participation in administrative evaluation processes echo and confirm those noted in Chapters 6 and 9. Procedures ostensibly designed to provide an evaluative role for the public, such as public hearings, display numerous procedural disadvantages that deter members of policy communities from competing adequately in the evaluation process with network members.

The funding of public participation in administrative tribunals or forums is restricted, although major gains in funding provisions have been made in the case of environmental assessments. The costs of participation are typically absorbed by members of the public. In the case of a BC Pesticide Control Appeal Board hearing concerning the application of herbicide 2,4-D, for example, a representative of the local South Okanagan Environmental Coalition, when cross-examined by the proponent's counsel, stated:

> You have to recognize that we are full-time in other professions in the Interior. We don't have staff members. We don't have access to libraries. It's very difficult to do a research project in this type of environment up here ... Whenever we had to do research, we've had to go to Vancouver. It takes a lot of effort, and time, and money, to get away from a job and go to Vancouver. To go to ... the Macmillan ... Library to find out that half the articles on 2,4-D are checked out and wondering who's got them out. So it's difficult to do that kind of work.[16]

Indeed, participants must sometimes assume the costs of the process if the tribunal decides against them. While this measure may be intended to discourage frivolous action by the public, it also provides a strong disincentive to legitimate participation. Effective public participation requires extensive financial resources to organize individuals, disseminate information, hire expert witnesses, conduct research, and prepare presentations. Furthermore, for the public, the benefits are typically collective and long term and fail to generate financial support or direct returns.

Public-based evaluation of policy is further limited by other procedural difficulties. The appeal process through which administrative hearings take place is directed to discrete levels of administrative action. For instance, the decision of the administrator of the appropriate agency regarding an activity such as pesticide applications may be appealed by the public. The appeal is therefore limited to the site-specific application of pesticides and cannot include criticisms of the registration and approval of the pesticide itself or of the overall application standards.

The inclusion of policy community members in the evaluative process challenges existing assumptions about the nature of the information on which decisions are based and the interests being served. The generation and communication of information, and the role of science in decision-making processes, are not easily reduced to standardized procedural matters. The difficulty in bringing members of the public 'up to speed' in the evaluative dialogue, as we have seen in discussions of previous stages of the policy cycle, has been exacerbated in part by the conjunction of dialogue between those 'in the know' – representatives of industry and, sometimes, government – and those lacking substantive or procedural expertise. The scientific nature of resource and environmental issues has thus been a rationale for upholding 'decision-making by experts' rather than making it a broadly based and publicly accessible process for evaluating and re-assessing existing policies.

The high costs associated with conducting research and generating information on new technology, pollution abatement, health consequences of pollution, and other issues have deterred governments and NGOs from taking on more extensive research. In contrast, it is in the interests of the private sector to carry out research that would promote productivity, a competitive position, and profits. Within the existing negotiative climate, it is to industry's advantage to secure information that would support its position in negotiations. Many evaluations of Canadian resource and environmental policy have been based on information supplied by regulated industries.[17] Industry reports of technological data and costs may overestimate or provide a version of the costs of cleanup or mitigation greatly different than that given by observers representing alternative interests.

Questions about the neutrality of scientific knowledge, and the context in which it is generated and applied, are also relevant to regulatory processes. Funding, facilities, and personnel required in the research process are fostered, if not always visibly, by political and economic forces. There have been numerous public health cases, such as those involving thalidomide, implants, and IUDs, in which testing was insufficient prior to the marketing and use of the product. The falsification of pesticide hazard data by the Industrial Bio Test Laboratories in the United States in the 1980s revealed the possibility that scientific information is not always reliable. An era of government downsizing has contributed to the privatization of laboratories in provinces such as British Columbia, a situation that has also raised questions about how to ensure the neutrality of testing.[18] In other incidents, such as the Grassy Narrows mercury poisoning of Native peoples, it is not the accuracy of knowledge but the lack of political willingness to implement that knowledge in the interests of protecting human lives that allows environmental degradation to occur.[19]

Furthermore, state-of-the-art knowledge is just that. Science is always in the process of being updated and refined, and our knowledge is contingent on data, context, and methodology. Most scientific methods assume that our understanding of natural environments is accurate and comprehensive. As we indicated in Chapter 9, there is little formal recognition of the gulfs and inaccuracies in what we now know of ecological systems and human health. The values manifested in much of the accumulation and dissemination of knowledge are not made explicit in the administrative evaluation process. The basis for regulatory guidelines is not simply the question of adverse harm; it is usually also defined within a cost-benefit framework. Costs and benefits of resource projects and environmental protection involve the consideration of both economic and social factors. They also involve the identification of all actors who may benefit from, or be harmed by, a project that will have an impact on the environment.

Yet the disaggregation of industrial interests (which represent both jobs and corporate profits) and public interests (which represent jobs, the ownership of public lands, and social and environmental health) makes the underlying cost-benefit equation complex and unequal. Furthermore, as noted above, costs and benefits may be presented differently by different interests. Sinclair, for example, challenges industry's assessment of costs and time guidelines for pulp regulation compliance by presenting alternative figures as well as alternative factors in the assessment:

Environmental authorities have failed to take into account adequately the enormous costs they may be imposing on present and future generations of Canadians as a result of concessions to pulp and paper manufacturers

... To the degree that government environmental enforcement procedures encourage marginal mills to continue to operate without improvements in production efficiency, they also are encouraging overutilization and waste of Canada's timber, water, and energy resources.[20]

The negotiative nature of administrative evaluation reflects the legal framework in which it is situated. Sometimes, as Schrecker points out, the preferred status of industry is entrenched in law, as in the case of legislative provisions that allow firms to initiate reviews or appeals that may stall their compliance with regulations.[21] While the enshrinement of resource management and environmental protection goals in legislation appears to be a formal, fixed process, the discretionary nature of most administrative activity is conducive to negotiating what this means in practice. As Thompson puts it: 'the reality is that the rules of environmental regulation are never clearly stated or certain, except in a purely symbolic sense. Instead the norms of conduct are the subject of negotiation and renegotiation between the regulator and the regulated right down to the moment of compliance or non-compliance.'[22]

As a negotiative style has developed to deal with the regulation of the private sector, the state has become dependent on industry participation in the process. To move toward greater government independence would involve increased costs, not only in generating information for setting standards but also in monitoring and enforcement. It is not feasible for government to 'crack down' on non-compliance by punitive measures alone, because the time, costs, and personnel associated with protracted litigation exceed most government budgets.[23]

The Evaluation of Non-Compliance

Administrative activities also provide a *de facto* form of policy evaluation through their treatment of regulatory violations. The severity of punishments, the ways in which they are administered, and the conditions under which sanctions are applied reflect the evaluation of policy. In this sense, administrators often evaluate policy in terms of its effectiveness, but their actions also evaluate individuals, corporations, and the public in terms of their compliance or non-compliance with regulatory standards. Administrative actors such as enforcement officers may prosecute individuals or corporations in violation of regulatory statutes. For instance, a company dumping toxic waste into the Fraser River and violating the BC Waste Management Act may be charged under the provisions of that act. This process is carried out in court. Amendments to the penalty provisions of many resource and environmental laws have extended the sentencing capabilities of the courts, both by raising the maximum level of fines and by providing for other penalties, such as the imprisonment of individuals, 'profit-stripping' fines, and the forfeit of property involved in the offence.[24]

Increased convictions and escalating fines provided by new statutes as well as by existing laws underline the emphasis on sanctions as key to regulatory compliance. The escalation of prosecutions and penalties at the beginning of the 1990s is striking. Lynne Huestis indicates that in Ontario from 1989 to 1990, for example, the number of persons and companies charged with offences increased by 30 per cent, the charges laid increased by 25 per cent, and the amount of fines imposed increased by 20 per cent. In 1991, Ontario courts convicted more than 240 companies, a 30 per cent jump over 1990.[25]

In British Columbia, comparisons between the 1989-90 fiscal year and that of 1990-1 reveal significant increases as well, with total charges made under all environmental legislation increasing by 10 per cent (with Waste Management Act charges expanding by 40 per cent) and total fines for all programs increasing by 171 per cent. In the period 1991-2, 154 businesses and individuals were convicted of pollution offences under the Waste Management Act.[26] Alberta witnessed a similar dramatic increase in enforcement activity, especially in charges laid against directors or officers of a corporation.

Significant monetary penalties in the early 1990s in Ontario included a fine for Bata Industries of $120,000, with two top executives each fined $12,000 for running an illegal waste dump, and a $300,000 fine against a battery plant, with a company executive fined $25,000 for dumping battery acid.[27] Fines of five and six figures have been imposed for environmental offences in dozens of cases.

Another means of securing compliance through punitive action is the extension of personal liability by many statutes, which may provide for a term of imprisonment. In 1990, an Ontario contractor became the first person sentenced to jail for conviction under an environmental statute.[28] In 1992, Severin Argenton, former president of Varnicolor Chemical Ltd., was sentenced to eight months in jail following a conviction of contaminating soil and groundwater on company property. At the federal level, CEPA provides for terms of imprisonment up to life for criminal negligence causing death or bodily harm.[29]

While fines are usually intended as deterrents or as punitive actions, the category of 'profit-stripping' fines recognizes the implicit economics of compliance and non-compliance. Economic incentives for non-compliance often exceed those of compliance. As Schrecker notes, 'the current command-penalty system of regulation generally allows penalties to be imposed on polluting firms only following prosecution and conviction.'[30] Given the historical lack of resources and government willingness to prosecute corporations for non-compliance, the economic incentive for delayed compliance remains significant. The costs of litigation may be less than those of a new technology required to meet current standards. Profit-stripping fines intend to eliminate the profit associated with the illegal activity. When an offender has been convicted under the Ontario Environmental Protection Act, for instance, the court may 'order the offender to pay a fine equal to the court's estimation of any monetary benefits that accrued to the offender as the result of the commission of the offense, in addition to any other fine that may have been imposed.'[31]

Sentencing orders are also contained in many resource and environmental statutes, and their use has also increased. CEPA contains an extensive range of sentencing options, including

> refraining from activity that may result in a repetition of the offense, remedying or avoiding harm to the environment, publishing the facts relating to the conviction, notifying persons affected of the offender's conduct ... posting a bond or security to ensure future compliance, submitting information to the Minister of the Environment with respect to the activities of the offender, compensating the Minister of [the] Environment for the cost of remedial or preventative action taken by the Minister regarding the offending conduct, performing community service, paying for research into the use and disposal of substances in respect of which the offense was committed, and other reasonable conditions to ensure the offender's good conduct.[32]

While actions initiated by administrative actors represent the majority of cases of environmental litigation, private prosecutions have also been utilized to enhance environmental protection. Common law actions, such as nuisance, riparian rights, and negligence, are useful when a person's property or economic interest is adversely affected by environmental contamination. These actions and their limitations are discussed in more detail in the following section.

There has also been a recent interest in using the Canadian Charter of Rights and Freedoms, as well as in articulating environmental bills of rights, which could provide members of the public with a venue for initiating environmental prosecutions.[33] Environmental bills of rights do not imply the rights of the *environment*, which is a question of standing, but designate the rights of *individuals* to enjoy natural environments. Bills of rights usually include provisions establishing each citizen's right to a healthy environment, acknowledging that the government has an obligation to protect the environment for future generations and giving citizens provisions for suits.[34] However, in practice, environmental bills of rights are subject to manipulation by the current government and provide less means for citizen action than many proponents allege since the steps required to bring a charge remain complex, expensive, and cumbersome.[35]

Judicial Evaluation of Canadian Resource and Environmental Policy

A second major forum for Canadian resource and environmental policy evaluation is the courts, primarily through the use of judicial reviews of administrative decision-making. Such reviews are directed to the failure of a government agency or actor to conduct itself properly given the extent of its existing regulatory powers. A successful action may result in a court requiring the administrative authority to perform its legal duty, or it may include an order striking down an unauthorized action (e.g., a licence approval that exceeds standards or an illegally issued permit).[36]

At least in theory, recourse to the courts to challenge administrative actions is open to a variety of affected interests. While the courts are generally used by 'losers' in the policy network to protest administrative actions and decisions, these forums can also be used, in specific circumstances, by policy community members attempting to alter the results of administrative proceedings from which they may have been excluded.

Both private prosecutions and administrative actions initiated by environmentalists are typically referred to as 'public interest' environmental lawsuits. While they do not represent every public interest, these legal actions are 'brought by persons with little or no economic or property interest in the outcome of a case – they are not bringing it for personal gain. The suit is being brought to protect an environmental interest shared by many members of the public, such as preventing pollution of a river or protecting a public forest from excessive logging.'[37]

In Canada, the proposal to enhance individual citizens' rights to use the courts to promote environmental values has been the subject of reform proposals since the early 1970s.[38] The concern here is with the issue of *standing*: who is capable of bringing an action before a court. This is a complex but significant issue for judicial evaluation.[39]

Standing is not an issue in criminal cases because Canada has always allowed individuals to lay criminal charges. The problem in regard to utilizing criminal actions in environmental matters is the burden of proof required for successful prosecution, especially the need to establish that the guilty party possessed a guilty mind, or *mens rea*, at the time of the crime.[40]

In civil law cases, two aspects of the question of standing in resource and environmental matters should be noted. One concerns standing with respect to private or personal grievances, the other with respect to public or collective matters. Various common law actions are available to private individuals to deal with private concerns, many of which can have an environmental impact. These include actions to correct a number of misdoings or torts respecting private property rights, such as nuisance, trespass, riparian rights, or negligence.[41] Canadian courts have historically preserved the right to initiate litigation (standing) in such matters solely to the individual aggrieved by one or more of these activities. What former Canadian Supreme Court justice William Estey noted in 1972 about private actions, however, remains true today: 'What is potentially more significant, of course, is standing in matters of the public interest as opposed to a purely private interest. In Canada, the rule has traditionally been that only the public attorney general may pursue cases pertaining to public grievances; either personally, or through the appointment of a private "relator."'[42]

In Canada, standing in public interest matters was extended slightly in the 1970s by the Supreme Court's ruling in the *Finlay* case.[43] However, the only area of Canadian law in which standing has been fully liberalized relates to constitutional cases pressed under the terms of the Canadian Charter of Rights and Freedoms. Until 1982, when the Charter was included in the Canadian constitution, constitutional cases remained the exclusive purview of federal and provincial attorney generals. Sections 24(1) and 52(1) of the Charter, however, allow citizens access to the courts to deal with infringements of their constitutional rights.

The impact of this change in rules of standing governing constitutional cases on resource and environmental litigation, however, has been negligible for several reasons. First, there is no direct link between the Charter and resource and environmental litigation. Although one of the Charter rights (Section 7) could be broadly interpreted as a right to a clean environment, it has not been thus construed by the courts, which have restricted its application to questions of the due process of law.[44] Second, and more generally, Canadian courts have ruled that the Charter applies only to relations between citizens and governments, therefore excluding matters dealing, for example, with relations between employees and employers or between citizens and polluting companies. And third, although Canadian courts have been quite liberal in relaxing standards of standing in constitutional cases, they have shown few signs of extending these principles to other types of public action.[45]

Thus, the effects of changes in standing on increasing the number of environmental cases appearing before Canadian courts have been slight. Data for Canada compiled from an examination of reported and unreported cases for the period 1980-9[46] reveal only 163 environmental cases dealt with at the superior court level (see Table 10.1).

By themselves, of course, these figures tell us little about whether or not the pattern of litigation in Canada is increasing, decreasing, or remaining stationary. However, ninety-two environmental cases were decided by Canadian superior courts over the first five years of the period 1980-9, while only seventy-one were decided in the second half of the decade, a decrease of 23 per cent. Moreover, as the data in Table 10.2 show, there was not a consistent upward trend in Canadian environmental litigations over the 1980s, although the number did increase substantially for several years after 1982.

Standing, of course, only deals with whether or not a case will actually be heard by a court and says nothing about the outcome of any case, although it is often incorrectly assumed that attaining standing equates with success. The true determinant of success is not the right to bring a grievance before the courts but the judicial recognition of the validity of a grievance and the application of a judicial remedy to it.

Canadian courts have a variety of legal remedies at their disposal in reviewing administrative actions.[47] The courts determine whether or not an administrative decision is valid or has legal effect on the basis of findings concerning errors in law.[48] This implies that, even if standing is

Table 10.1

Canadian superior court decisions on the environment by jurisdiction, 1980-9

Jurisdiction	Number of cases
Supreme Court of Canada	6
Federal Court of Canada	8
Newfoundland	2
Prince Edward Island	2
Nova Scotia	7
New Brunswick	2
Quebec	6
Ontario	44
Manitoba	5
Saskatchewan	8
Alberta	1
British Columbia	68
NWT	4
Yukon	0
Total	163

Source: M. Howlett, 'The Judicialization of Canadian Environmental Policy 1980-1989: A Test of the U.S.-Canada Convergence Hypothesis,' *Canadian Journal of Political Science* 27. 1 (1994): 99-125.

Table 10.2

**Environmental cases heard by Canadian
superior courts by year, 1980-9**

Year	Number of cases heard
1980	2
1981	5
1982	20
1983	27
1984	83
1985	13
1986	7
1987	17
1988	14
1989	20

Source: M. Howlett, 'The Judicialization of Canadian
Environmental Policy 1980-1989: A Test of the U.S.-Canada
Convergence Hypothesis,' *Canadian Journal of Political Science*
27.1 (1994): 99-125.

opened up in Canada (in itself an unlikely prospect), there is no guarantee that any resulting increase in litigation would actually lead to a different pattern of judicial decisions. Because Canadian courts do not attempt to review cases on the facts, as long as administrative agencies operate within their jurisdiction and according to the principles of fundamental justice and due process, their decisions are unlikely to be overturned. As Peter Hogg noted in his survey of administrative cases dealt with by the Canadian Supreme Court between 1949 and 1971:

By and large It seems to me the Supreme Court of Canada has been restrained in the exercise of its review function. The overall figures show that the agency wins more than half the time. And – more significantly – analysis shows that the cases in which the agency loses usually do have special features: either the agency is well outside its allotted power (this is rare), or the agency action is an unexpected use of its power, usually in conflict with a strong competing civil libertarian value.[49]

Has there been any movement in the resource and environmental area toward a more active judiciary in Canada? Once again, the answer appears to be no. Although changes at federal and provincial levels in the late 1960s and early 1970s appeared to presage a greater scope for judicial review, the courts themselves have proved very reluctant to alter their behaviour.[50] In fact, they have consistently deferred to legislators in policy matters, including those related to the environment.[51]

Close readings of those cases most often cited as evidence of a new standard of judicial review – the Oldman River case especially – reveal that they were decided on the basis of traditional and limited views of the scope of such reviews.[52] More quantifiably, Stewart Elgie has argued that public interest environmental litigation in Canada falls into two eras, the first from 1970 to 1986, and the second from 1987 to 1992.[53] During the first period, private environmental prosecutions, launched primarily through, or with the assistance of, the Canadian Environmental Law Association and the West Coast Environmental Law Association, were largely successful (twenty-one cases won out of twenty-eight contested). During the second period, they were not. Elgie notes a number of constraints on private environmental prosecutions that led to the reduced effectiveness of judicial review in the second period. They include the lack of citizen access to government-held information, the inadequacy of government monitoring and sampling, the lack of judicial recognition of the severity of environmental offences, and the added defence of reasonable care by the accused (which requires citizens to be capable of challenging industry's technological expertise).

Thus, in assessing the role of judicial evaluation of Canadian resource and environmental policy, several conclusions can be drawn. On the one hand, there has been some increase in recent years in the ability of affected parties to access the courts for reviews of administrative decisions and policy evaluations. New legislation in a number of substantive areas – including forests, parks, pesticides, endangered species, pollution, and environmental assessment – articulates more specific standards, erodes some of the past reliance on administrative discretion, and addresses new and emerging issues. More relaxed definitions of standing, environmental bills of rights, and greater provision for public interest access to judicial processes would suggest the expansion of judicial activity in dealing with environmental issues.

On the other hand, there continues to be a set of judicial practices in Canada that limits the scope of judicial review and prevents this forum from becoming an effective means by which citizens can challenge administrative actions. Observations of the differences between judicial style and content in Canada and the United States (where the courts do play a more substantial role in administrative evaluation) are appropriate in this context. Also, as Elgie comments, the

strength of U.S. environmental legislation [is that it] ... defines concrete enforceable obligations for officials in a number of areas including pollution control, environmental assessment, wildlife protection and public land management ... U.S. law also provides for citizen suits, which allow citizens to effectively enforce industry violations of environmental standards ... Canadian environmental legislation, by and large, is weaker than U.S. legislation, both in the scope of problems it addresses and in the discretion it confers on departmental decision-makers.[54]

Conclusion: Policy Evaluation and Learning in Canadian Resource and Environmental Policy-Making

As the discussion above has shown, due to the characteristics of the electoral, legislative, and judicial systems in Canada, policy evaluations in the resource and environmental sector are largely carried out in administrative forums that tend to favour the protection of the interests of established network members. How does this type of evaluative system contribute to the process of policy change and development?

As we discussed at the beginning of this chapter, policy actors and the organizations and institutions they represent can learn from the formal and informal evaluation of policies in which they are engaged. This knowledge can lead them to modify their positions to facilitate greater substantive or procedural policy change or to resist any alteration to the status quo.[55] Yet policy evaluations do not necessarily affect either the means or the goals of implementing the policy. In many cases, they can result in largely symbolic or cosmetic exercises in policy reflection. While evaluation implicitly offers a 'feedback loop' as an inherent part of the policy cycle, this loop is often not operationalized.

The capacity to absorb new information is one factor in any potential adaptation to, or learning from, the evaluative process. As Cohen and Levinthal have argued in the case of the private firm:

> The ability to evaluate and utilize outside knowledge is largely a function of the level of prior related knowledge. At the most elemental level, this prior knowledge includes basic skills or even a shared language but may also include knowledge of the most recent scientific or technological developments in a given field. Thus, prior related knowledge confers an ability to recognize the value of new information, assimilate it, and apply it to [commercial] ends. These abilities collectively constitute what we call [a firm's] 'absorptive capacity.'[56]

In a complex organization such as a firm or a government, this implies that learning is a cumulative process and that the existing store of knowledge largely determines what will be done with any new information that flows into the organization. In the case of resource and environmental policy-making, the two relevant variables affecting the potential for eval-uations to lead to institutional learning and hence to some form of policy change are (1) the organizational capacity of the state, including especial-ly its store of expertise in the subject area, and (2) the nature of the poli-cy subsystem and, especially, the links between administrators working in policy networks and larger policy communities, which must enable the dissemination of new information.

As Cohen and Levinthal suggest, only when state administrative capac-ity is high can we expect some kind of learning to occur. If a relatively closed network dominates the subsystem, however, this learning is likely to be restricted to drawing lessons about the effectiveness of existing arrangements. If the links between the network and the community are more open, we can expect social learning to occur as ideas and events in the larger policy community penetrate policy discussions. When state capacity is low, we can expect little learning to occur. If the policy subsys-tem in such circumstances is dominated by existing networks, formal types of evaluation with little substantive impact on policy instruments and goals are likely to occur. If the subsystem is more open to members of the policy community, a range of informal evaluations is also likely to occur, but we may still find little substantive impact on policy outcomes or processes.[57]

As the discussion in earlier chapters has demonstrated, in the context of Canadian resource and environmental policy-making, despite signifi-cant limitations caused by its federal structure, the state now has a large administrative capacity. Thus we would expect its personnel, organiza-tional, financial, and informational resources to promote some form of policy learning as a characteristic of policy evaluation in this sector. However, as we discussed in Chapter 7, the subsystem in this sector is dominated by a relatively closed, triadic policy network. Hence, it should come as no surprise that the policy learning that takes place in this sector largely consists of discussions surrounding the means to implement poli-cy – lesson-drawing – rather than the reconsideration of policy goals and activities.

The predominant form of policy evaluation found in Canadian resource and environmental policy-making is administrative. Such evaluations, vir-tually by definition, occur within the established institutions of govern-ment, involve established policy network members, and tend to consider only the efficiency and effectiveness of existing and alternative policy instruments rather than overall policy goals. The recent emphasis on mar-ket instruments as a means of encouraging regulatory compliance is an example. Rather than reconsidering the possible goals of policy – such as sustainable development and ecological preservation – the focus has been on evaluating alternative tools within the existing resource management framework.

Judicial and political evaluations, of course, include policy community members and hence are much more likely to reflect changes in social values and mores in their deliberations. While these latter two mechanisms are means by which the lessons of social learning can be brought into the sectoral policy process,[58] for the reasons discussed above, they play only a minor role in Canadian resource and environmental policy evaluation.

The administrative nature of the Canadian resource and environmental evaluative style results in a relatively restricted type of policy learning in which most efforts and results go into attempting to draw lessons about the relative merits of different means proposed to implement existing policies. Only rarely are the actual goals of resource and environmental policy-making considered in this process.

This is so because of the characteristics of the resource and environmental subsystem and its relationship to the evaluative process. Government and resource-industry interests arrayed in triadic policy networks dominate environmental groups and lead to relatively closed negotiations over most aspects of substantive policy and policy processes. From the setting of standards through to their approval, implementation, monitoring, and enforcement, industry participates in every moment of the policy cycle and plays a significant role in all its stages, including policy evaluation.

The bilateral, negotiative style of much Canadian resource and environmental policy-making is congruent with the discretionary character by which much resource and environmental legislation is formulated, implemented, and evaluated.[59] While the weight of industry participation may have been offset in recent decades by the increase in the scope and powers of government, and adversely affected by the entry of environmental groups into policy networks, the concept of a negotiative process between industry and government continues to fit the facts of Canadian resource and environmental policy-making.

The bargaining process is not industry-controlled but 'an uneven, ad hoc process with potentially inconsistent outcomes.'[60] For many observers, in fact, the relations between the regulatory state and the objects of regulation – primarily industry – comprise the key issue in, and constraint to, policy learning through the evaluative process in this sector. If evaluative design and processes incorporate the information and interests of industry, there is a question as to whether administrators can maintain a strong and independent course on behalf of other resource and environmental interests. The key issue around the evaluative process is the degree to which industry participation benefits or hampers resource management and environmental protection by restricting evaluation of alternative courses of action.

The result of the difficulties with political, administrative, and judicial evaluation cited above, in the context of the configuration of state absorptive capacity and network dominance of the policy subsystem, is that evaluations tend to be oriented toward a limited form of learning or lesson-drawing. This is certainly the case at present and appears to have been so for a considerable period of time in this sector. Thus, the lessons that need to be learned – how to encourage economic diversification, how to minimize environmental degradation in economic activity, how to provide for a more equitable distribution of wealth and well-being, how to implement measures for sustainability – are not usually dealt with in the formal evaluative process. Rather, only sporadic, external forces such as public protests tend to raise these issues, thereby challenging the legitimacy of administrative evaluations. The normal course of events finds policy evaluations perpetuating past practices and reinforcing the status quo rather than prescribing or demanding paradigmatic policy changes.

Part 5:
The Dynamics of Canadian Resource and Environmental Policy

This part provides a summary of the findings in this book. The actual and potential directions of Canadian resource and environmental policy are discussed using the framework set out in the text. In the final chapter, some of the emerging ideas affecting the evolution of this policy sector are raised, and their potential to alter the existing policy paradigm is assessed.

11
The Canadian Resource and Environmental Policy Style

Canadian texts in the resource and environmental area have tended to be written by economists, lawyers, and geographers and have said little about the policy process itself. It is frequently assumed that states simply make efficient decisions, but there is little consideration of why they would do so or of the constraints under which they operate.[1] Many legal analyses tend to deemphasize differences in the origins and power of competing interests in the policy process.[2] Some early works by political scientists and others shared the same flaw, tending to be descriptive, without raising analytical questions about the origins and objectives of policy processes.[3] As a result, to the present, it has been difficult to understand the reasons why Canadian resource and environmental policy outcomes have been the way they have or to comment with any certainty about the possible future directions of policy in this sector. The nature of Canadian policy and the potential for, and direction of, its evolution have been interpreted differently by different observers. This variation reflects those in the methods and the substantive and ideological interests of observers, the regional differences in resources and settlement patterns, and the historical changes in issues and political regimes that they have observed.

However, without an appropriate characterization of the social and economic context and the configuration of the Canadian resource and environmental policy process – its actors, their interests, and the institutions within which policies develop – it is virtually impossible to discern the contours of policy-making in this sector and the manner in which policy has evolved. And without an understanding of this evolution, it is difficult to place contemporary developments in their proper perspective.[4] Have there been significant changes in the character and capabilities of Canadian resource and environmental policy? Are the changes appearing in the existing policy style transitory or more permanent? Do they presage a major shift in policy paradigms, or are they merely intraparadigmatic developments?

This text has provided a framework within which to assess the nature of Canadian resource and environmental policy-making over time and the potential for policy change in this sector. The previous chapters established the key parameters and constraints under which Canadian resource and environmental policy has developed, the techniques used for its implementation, and the factors that have led to its development. Utilizing this information, we developed a model of the evolution of Canadian resource and environmental policy-making that identified the key actors in this process and described the ways in which their interests and ideas have come together through the institutions of Canadian governments to form current policy. In this chapter, we will review the principal characteristics of the Canadian resource and environmental policy style as it has evolved and assess the potential for major change to occur in this sector.

Key Variables Defining a Policy Style

Is it possible, then, to characterize Canadian resource and environmental policy as the reflection of a single policy style, or has this style evolved over time? The concept of policy style discussed in Chapter 5 is useful in that it conveys some idea of what constitutes 'normal' policy-making in a specific policy area or jurisdiction. It provides a needed contrast to a second, and more profound, pattern of policy change, one involving a 'paradigm shift,' or a significant revision of the revised or existing policy style to encompass new or different objectives through alternative processes. However, this contrast should not hide the fact that policy styles themselves are dynamic, reflecting changes in the socioeconomic, political, and ecological fabric of society. As we have seen, technological innovation, changes in government, ideological shifts, and social, cultural, economic, and demographic factors all contribute to the evolution of a style by introducing new issues, ideas, or actors into existing policy processes.

Most prominent studies to date have classified policy styles in terms of the twin dimensions of a government's typical problem-solving methodology and the pattern of its relationship with societal groups. Richardson, Gustafsson, and Jordan, for example, define a policy style as 'the interaction between (a) the government's approach to problem solving and (b) the relationship between government and other actors in the policy process.'[5] They mention 'anticipatory/active' and 'reactive' as the two general approaches to problem-solving. The relationships between state and societal actors are similarly divided into two categories: 'consensus,' and 'imposition'. These two factors generate four distinct types of policy-making styles, which the authors argue are characteristic of overall, national policy-making (see Figure 11.1).

Figure 11.1

An early model of national policy styles

Relationship between government and society	Dominant approach to problem-solving	
	Anticipatory	Reactive
Consensus	E.g., German, 'rationalist consensus' style	E.g., British 'negotiating' style
Imposition	E.g., French 'concertation' style	E.g., Dutch 'negotiation and conflict' style

Source: Adapted from Jeremy Richardson, Gunnel Gustafsson, and Grant Jordan, 'The Concept of Policy Style,' in J.J. Richardson, ed., *Policy Styles in Western Europe* (London: George Allen and Unwin 1982), 1-16.

These simple classifications do not, however, do justice to the complexity of the subject matter they are intended to describe. No government is entirely active or reactive; nor does any government always work through either consensus or imposition. A better way to conceptualize a government's approach to problem-solving is to conceive of it in terms of sector and of a set of patterns emerging across the stages of a sectoral policy cycle.[6]

As the discussion in Chapters 6 to 10 have shown, the nature of the policy subsystem is a crucial variable at all stages of the policy cycle. Societal and state actors are activated at the agenda-setting stage to identify and raise concerns. Societal groups represent a range of production-based and other interests, and as we have seen throughout this book, the conjuncture of these interests is significant in determining policy style. The degree of public access to, and membership in, the policy community is a basic consideration in assessing the character of the policy subsystem. However, it is not merely the composition of the policy community but also the frequency and the basis of the interaction within and between state and societal actors that are significant in determining the character of the subsystem. The role of policy subsystems is important in understanding policy formulation, because policy communities and networks play a major role in defining the options placed before decision-makers and articulating the potential direction and strategy of policy formulations.

At the decision-making stage, the complexity of the subsystem, that is, whether or not it is characterized by multiple membership, and the different pressures brought to bear on decision-makers, affects the capabilities of state actors. The constraints under which decisionmakers operate are important variables in explaining the typical pattern of decision-making found in government. At the stage of implementation, the administrative capacity of the state influences how and to what extent policy decisions are enacted. Internal relations between state actors, and the complexity and character of the policy subsystem, are crucial in understanding how implementation operates. Both variables also figure prominently in the discussion of policy evaluation. As we have seen, evaluation is an ongoing response to policy, ranging from informal public reactions to administrative adjustments to judicial processes. While more formal evaluation, such as a judicial decision, may result in visible 'learning' on the part of institutions and actors, the fluidity of much of the evaluative process brings into question the educational potential of existing policy processes.[7]

The extent of state autonomy, or its capacity to influence social actors and vice versa, also comprises a significant variable at each stage of the cycle. This was apparent in the agenda-setting stage, in which the ability or lack of ability of the public to drive state action was seen to be a crucial determinant of an agenda-setting style. It is true at the stage of policy formulation, in which the leadership or domination of state actors by societal ones, or vice versa, was seen to be a significant determinant of the nature of the policy network in a subsystem and hence of the likely type of policy solutions to be proffered by that subsystem. At the decision-making stage, the nature of the constraints placed on governments was seen to be a significant determinant of the type of decisions taken in a sector. At the stages of implementation and evaluation, the capacity of the state to learn and to implement its wishes is a crucial determinant of the types of action taken.

Hence, it should be apparent that the two most significant variables affecting a policy style are (1) the character of the relevant policy subsystem (including the range of actors, interests, and ideas within it, their relations to each other, and the extent to which networks enjoy or fail to enjoy policy community support), and (2) the powers of the state (including its administrative capacity and organization and the nature of the resource constraints under which it must operate).

The Contemporary Canadian Resource and Environmental Policy Style

The present Canadian resource and environmental policy style can be discerned from the choice of possibilities present at each stage of the policy cycle. As we discussed in Chapter 6, the agenda-setting stage of policy is the preliminary level, in which ideas and interests are politically defined and considered to be appropriate for policy discussion. In liberal democratic countries, self-identified and motivated interests lobby governments for the inclusion of their concerns in the consideration of any given matter. Governments are usually receptive, at least in theory, to a changing policy agenda, and the activities of lobbyists complement the accountability of the electoral system. Thus, as new information about environmental contaminants, for instance, is disseminated, it is usually assumed that interested groups – producers, labour, health representatives, consumers – will bring this knowledge to the attention of policy actors so that it can be included on the agenda. While other forces of mobilization, such as global pressure to conform to regulatory standards, may also introduce items to the agenda, the major emphasis at this stage is on the diffuse, informal, and public forms of organization that will bring issues to attention.

The increased visibility of environmental organizations in Canada, and the increased reference to 'multiple stakeholders,' support the notion of greater public involvement in agenda-setting in recent years. These organizations pressure governments in a variety of ways, such as direct lobbying, public education, protests, and media coverage, to include certain issues on the political agenda. The number and variety of organizations representing environmental interests have increased dramatically in recent decades. Their political sophistication and ability to lobby governments both directly and indirectly, through effective use of public education and the media, attest to their success in politicizing resource and environmental issues.

Nevertheless, these organizations remain limited in their success in setting the Canadian resource and environmental policy agenda. This limitation is due to a number of constraints. The informal and discretionary basis of issue identification does not ensure that the most serious issues get placed on the agenda, although media attention may help the most provocative to do so. This means that interests with money, power, political connections, or other backing are more likely to be addressed by governments, while other issues – often chronic, perhaps as yet unidentified, and serving no visible economic interest – tend to be ignored. Procedurally, there is no means to ensure that an item gets, and stays, on the agenda. While numerous initiatives have been devised to encourage public participation, they are typically issue specific and short lived. While this process may be financially efficient in terms of government costs, it assumes the existence of a large, easily mobilized environmental constituency that will continue to 'grease the wheels' on behalf of environmental issues, for example, when conditions for such mobilization may not exist. This assumption may produce a political placebo effect in two senses. First, if an issue appears to have penetrated the agenda, it is assumed that appropriate action, or at least consideration of action, will be forthcoming. Second, if there is no activism, it is assumed that there is no problem.

In Chapter 6, we considered three potential models of agenda-setting. *Outside initiation* represents the traditional model discussed above, which assumes the articulation and expansion of issues by non-governmental groups to reach the public and then the institutional agenda. The lack of formal provisions to generate public involvement in resource and environmental issues and the lack of incorporation of many issues on the formal, institutional agenda, thus deter the application of this model to agenda-setting in this sector. In comparison, the *mobilization* model assumes government initiation of agenda-setting, which has been represented in this sector by the development of venues such as round tables and consultative processes. The agenda-setting stage in Canadian resource and environmental policy-making is best interpreted as representing a form of *inside initiation*, in which specialized groups have priority access to the agenda.

The existing institutional ties and disproportionate clout of productive interests continue, in practice, to direct the agenda to their own ends in spite of pressure from emerging but disorganized and external non-productive interests. From a cost-benefit perspective, the costs and rewards that accrue to different interests from participation in this process are problematic. In contrast to actors whose interest is direct and financial, such as a mining corporation, the public interest is generated from non-material and indirect interests. Only a diffuse benefit – wild areas preserved for future generations, the decrease of exposure to health risks – is experienced by the public, while the direct costs of participation on individuals can be extensive. Industry practices have historically been created on the basis of existing knowledge and interests. Fishing licences have been allotted and regulatory standards adopted on this basis, because state agencies have adapted to an established process that responds to these interests. Yet while these interests profit from their activity, the onus remains largely on the public to mount any opposition to the status quo, despite the facts that the material base for public organization remains diffuse and that participation costs do not yield a surplus and are not recoverable.

Nevertheless, the success of the environmental movement and the range of emerging material interests that lend it support must be taken into account in assessing the contemporary Canadian resource and environmental policy style. Relevant policy issues have been successful in making it onto the institutional agenda, and environmental groups have become members of the policy community. While it may ebb and flow, there is an awareness of environmental issues that has become integral to Canadian politics. This awareness has contributed to the dissemination of an environmental ethic, which has begun to seep into the corridors of power. The ability of individuals to coalesce from a diffuse and large mass public into specific groups with identifiable interests and goals is a vindication of the democratic political system. Yet due to the constraints we have noted, agenda-setting often appears to be a symbolic exercise in public participation. The lack of assurance that a broader spectrum of resource and environmental issues will be included in policy deliberations, the decline in public involvement throughout the entire policy cycle, and the lack of formal recognition of this early involvement reinforce the marginality of the public, and the issues it represents, to the larger policy process.

The second step in the policy cycle, policy formulation, typically reflects the condensation of general actors and interests into specific groups and the articulation of potential policy options on the part of these groups. While agenda-setting is concerned with the potential organization of diffuse groups and individuals around both specific and general environmental interests, Chapter 7 showed that policy formulation begins with the identification of options by an already organized subsystem. At this stage, we are concerned not only about the composition of interest groups, in terms of the interests that they represent, but also about the relations between them and with government, as well as the benefits and constraints each has to the articulation of policy proposals. The principal actors included in the Canadian resource and environmental policy subsystem are state representatives and a variety of societal members (production-based business organizations, environmental groups, the media, political parties, and other interest groups).

We discussed the interests of the resource and environmental policy community, including government, business, labour and farm groups, environmental groups, First Nations organizations, and individuals involved in academic and consulting work. While these groups can be identified as a 'community' in that they are all involved to lesser or greater extents in the formulation of resource and environmental policy options, the bases that they represent and the perspectives that they hold are widely dissimilar. In this sense, Chapter 7 argued that policy formulation has involved a shift from a hegemonic policy community agreed on the basic elements of resource management to a larger and more fragmented one in which various policy goals now compete for attention.

The policy network refers not only to perceptions of involvement but also to the interaction between different organizations in the resource and environmental policy community. While there is strong evidence of the continuing negotiative character of the policy network, restricted primarily to state and industry members, environmental interests have nudged the existing bilateral network into an emerging triadic form. This is not to say that environmental groups have the same power and influence as productive and state interests in defining policy options. Rather, an emerging triadic network simply acknowledges the success of environmental groups in gaining access to the policy table. Groups such as the Canadian Environmental Law Association and the West Coast Environmental Law Association are now actively consulted by governments about a wide range of policy issues. The significance of this expansion of the policy network is not only that alternative and often conflicting perspectives are brought forward in formulating policy options; it is also that state actors have somewhat greater autonomy in distancing themselves from a purely bilateral position with industry. In theory, this may allow the state greater independence not only from productive interests but also from a legacy of positions accumulated through the historical evolution of policy to date.

The decision-making stage of the policy process, traditionally that receiving the greatest amount of attention, reinforces and extends the tendencies of the first two stages, as we discussed in Chapter 8. Decision-making refers to the production of decisions within the formal stages of the policy process, after positions and alternatives have already been articulated. However, as we indicated, such clarity and independence of decision-making rarely exist. Notions of an ideal, or rational, decision-making style assume a blank slate, the complete independence of governments, and only behind-the-scenes lobbying by a balanced coterie of interest groups. However, because of the legacy of institutional structures, the sedimentation of past decisions, and the privileged access of entrenched interests to the resource and environmental policy process, this rational form is rarely achieved. Swimming against the flow of a century, let alone a decade, of policy initiatives, and against the direct and indirect material interests of established actors, means that change is usually minimal. Decisions are made about issues that are not neutrally introduced into the policy cycle but are generally driven by productive as well as government interests, such as building a new gas or oil pipeline or a new dam.

The Canadian resource and environmental decision-making style reflects the traditional force of productive interests, but it appears to be softened by a more independent state buoyed by the emergence of new environmental interests in the policy network. This influence is felt in the toughening of environmental standards, such as those regarding industrial effluents and, more recently, auto emissions, even against the active efforts of industry to maintain a holding pattern of low standards. Of course, 'pro-environmental' decisions are not always associated exclusively with the interests of environmental groups. Productive interests as well may benefit from the regulation of standards on an industry- or sector-wide basis, while labour may also exert pressures to enhance workers' health and safety. Decisions are also made in order to bolster the image of the state as an independent and receptive force – in other words, to legitimate its existence.

The institutional structure and material interests of the policy subsystem deter the rationality of resource and environmental decision-making by restricting the autonomy and capacity of governments. As the case studies provided in Chapter 8 revealed, decision-making in Canadian resource and environmental policy takes place within a complex federal-provincial setting, with multiple actors vying for attention. As a result, relatively closed bargaining processes between powerful subsystem members continue to characterize decision-making in this sector.

While decision-making traditionally figures in many accounts as the most important stage of the policy cycle, we have demonstrated that the administration of policy is equally, if not more, significant in its effects. Administrative processes include most of the routine activities through which policy is executed: laws, rules, regulations, and standards, which effectively determine how policy is implemented by government agencies. As we described in Chapter 9, it is generally assumed that this phase of the policy cycle is the most formally defined, given its plethora of rules and regulations. In fact, the negotiative character of administrative practices, the discretionary basis and low profile of enforcement, combined with a lack of public involvement, limitations of data, increasing shortfalls in funding, and the normative character of risk assessment and standard-setting, reconfirm the prominent position occupied by regulated interests.

Chapter 9 argued that policy implementation has relied heavily on regulatory instruments. While traditionally there has been some consensus that the 'carrot' is a preferable mechanism to encourage compliance, the regulatory 'stick' has been wielding increased power, with increased fines and stronger enforcement protocols. This development also demonstrates the presence of emergent non-production based and production based interests, such as tourism in the policy process. Nonetheless, continuing reliance on regulatory efforts rather than on planning and other anticipatory and consultative modes of implementation reinforces the reactive character of most administrative actions and again emphasizes the strength of traditional actors in the policy subsystem. This is due in large part to the constraints under which the state operates. Although they have a relatively high capacity for administrative activity, including a well-organized and -staffed bureaucracy, in most cases Canadian governments face powerful actors engaged in a variety of resource-related activities, leading them to favour the use of regulatory and similar instruments to implement policy.

Resource and environmental policy does not end with its implementation. Regulating industrial effluents, legislating park use, and mitigating soil erosion are not final products but part of an ongoing policy process. Just as ecological systems are dynamic and continuous, this book describes how policy is also a never-ending story. Evaluation through political, administrative, and judicial means allows various actors to consider the success or failure of policy and may lead some to attempt to reshape policy so as to better serve their purpose. We refer to this stage as one dominated by administrative evaluation and its style as one usually involving only limited learning, because the majority of activity is undertaken by traditional state and industry actors in the policy network.

Chapter 10 noted that policy evaluation in this sector has relied to a large extent on formal administrative reviews. This means that established policy networks continue to exert traditional pressures and that the options considered for change tend to be pragmatic considerations about the merits of specific instruments for implementing policy rather than about generalized alternatives to them. Hence, the general policy framework tends not to be evaluated, and the momentum for any ideological or substantive shift must be generated at the front end of the policy cycle. This becomes a self-fulfilling prophecy whereby general options such as sustainable development or bio-regionalism, which could portend a major paradigm shift, evaporate in their transition through the policy cycle, as these ideas come in contact with more formal processes, entrenched networks, and established instruments. Judicial means of evaluation continue to be marginal, almost an afterthought within the resource and environmental policy context; the judiciary defers to political and administrative decisionmakers except in the most blatant instances of corruption, malfeasance, high-handedness, or incompetence. The effective closure of judicial avenues to public access through the narrow circumstances in which they are invoked means that they have not yet been fully utilized in the policy process, as has occurred in some other countries.

In terms of the larger context and complexity of policy development and implementation, we have argued that the policy process has expanded somewhat from a bilateral, bargaining style to a triadic one that encompasses a greater diversity of participation. The significant economic shifts we are experiencing, accompanied by increased ecological disorganization, portend a shift to a new policy paradigm. Yet it is not clear from this analysis that the institutional and procedural conditions of policy formation and implementation have shifted from their traditional constellations. That is, most elements of the Canadian policy style developed under the old resource management regime remain in place. The elements of the contemporary style are set out in Figure 11.2.

This general sectoral policy style will, of course, vary over particular issues and over time, but it is a relatively long-lasting characterization of the contemporary Canadian resource and environmental policy process. It exists, in large measure, due to the semipermanent characteristics of the

Figure 11.2

Components of the contemporary Canadian natural resource and environmental policy style

Stage of policy cycle	Style
Agenda-setting	Inside initiation
Policy formulation	
Type of policy community	Chaotic
Type of policy network	Emerging triadic
Decision-making	Optimizing adjustment
Policy implementation	
Instrument preferences	Regulatory
Policy evaluation	
Propensity for learning	Administrative lesson-drawing

Source: See Chapters 6 to 10.

political economic context, as well as to the more or less stable composition of the subsystem, which is involved at every stage of the policy process.

The policy subsystem in this sector is one in which there is a variety of interests and hence perspectives circulating in the policy community. Yet, the inner circle of the policy network is a more exclusive, triadic system, including close government-industry links and a weak set of environmental non-governmental organizations (ENGOs) with links primarily to government. This triadic network is able to effectively limit public participation in agenda-setting and policy formulation, thereby restricting the options placed before decisionmakers. It also affects the decisions that can be made, ensuring that they will emerge from bargaining between network members over the limited options set out in the predecisional stages. Finally, it ensures that administrative agencies will be charged with implementation and evaluation, again preventing meaningful new input or the articulation of a range of ideas and interests during these last two stages of the cycle.

The Process of Paradigmatic Policy Change

Canadian policy style thus continues to reflect a resource-based policy style predominantly reflecting the interests of 'productive' actors engaged in resource-based industrial activities. How can we assess the potential for changing Canadian policy from a resourcist to an environmental style? In Chapter 5, we discussed the utility of notions of policy paradigms and paradigmatic shifts as a basis for understanding large-scale policy change. Hall has argued that the typical process of paradigmatic policy change involves at least six stages. An entrenched paradigm usually has two stages:

one in which the paradigm is largely unchallenged, and one in which challenges begin to build up. The period of transition also involves two stages: one in which the challenges lead to some tentative or experimental changes, and one in which experts disagree openly with each other. And the period in which a new paradigm also exists has two stages: one in which the disagreements between experts go public and the relevant policy community is enlarged dramatically, and one in which the new paradigm is institutionalized.[8] The stages of this process are set out in Figure 11.3.

Has Canadian resource and environmental policy been proceeding through this pattern of change? Previous chapters have examined the transition of Canadian resource and environmental policy from that characterized by the simple private exploitation of public resources to that reflecting a bilateral negotiative approach to the management of environments, and further toward a more inclusive and pluralist environmental management style. On the basis of this discussion, we can discern a typical pattern of government attitudes and actions toward resources and the environment throughout the history of Canada. The progressive expansion of the role of the state, the transition from a closed to a more open negotiative process, and the extension of the terrain and substance of management have been significant features of this evolution.

Contemporary Environmental Initiatives

By the 1980s, the growing incidence of environmental conflict and litigation challenged the traditional framework of resource decision-making. The existing system of environmental policy-making layered on top of policies designed to maximize the financial returns from natural resources was increasingly regarded by many as inadequate. Increased concern for ecological integrity and the extent, rapidity, and consequences of environmental degradation was expressed in the media, in society, and among the ranks of scientists and administrators.

In the past decades, new initiatives at both federal and provincial levels of government were generated to enhance efforts at environmental protection. These efforts were triggered by both chronic and acute episodes of environmental degradation, as well as by increasing criticism concerning government (in)activity on behalf of the environment. Substantive changes, such as the introduction of the 'precautionary principle' in standard-setting, attempted to shift the tenor of regulatory reform from a reactive to a preventative approach. The introduction of broader policy instruments, such as land-use planning and growth management legislation, also reflected the emergence of an anticipatory focus on environmental stewardship. Proposals to fashion new methods of dispute reso-

Figure 11.3

A model of the process of policy paradigm change

Paradigm stability	in which the reigning orthodoxy is institutional-ized and policy adjustments are made largely by a closed group of experts and officials
Accumulation of anomalies	in which 'real-world' developments occur which are neither anticipated nor fully explicable in terms of the reigning orthodoxy
Experimentation	in which efforts are made to stretch the existing paradigm to account for the anomalies
Fragmentation of authority	in which experts and officials are discredited and new participants challenge the existing paradigm
Contestation	in which debate spills into the public arena and involves the larger political process, including electoral and partisan considerations
Institutionalization of a new paradigm	in which after a shorter or longer period of time the advocates of a new paradigm secure posi-tions of authority and alter existing organiza-tional and decision-making arrangements in order to institutionalize the new paradigm

---

Source: Adapted from Peter A. Hall, 'Policy Paradigms, Social Learning and the State: The Case of Economic Policy Making in Britain,' *Comparative Politics* 25.3 (1993): 275-96.

lution at the local level were developed. Techniques such as third-party conciliation, arbitration, and mediation joined traditional techniques of litigation and consultation in the effort to head off time-consuming and costly project halts and delays.[9]

As we have seen, at the federal level the 1980s witnessed the introduc-tion of a Green Plan and the revamping of existing environmental laws.[10] The establishment of a Sustainable Environment Fund, and of Environ-ment 2001, a Strategic Green Planning Initiative, represented a shift in pol-icy focus towards the explicitly environmental. Environmental legislative review projects and state-of-the-environment or sustainability reporting were other new activities that attempted to symbolize the government's commitment to environmental protection. At the provincial level, similar developments occurred.

Governments in Canada also continued to respond to international ini-tiatives throughout the 1980s and into the 1990s. Proposals were made to develop integrated 'environmental strategies,'[11] which were expected to replace the ad hoc and fragmented approach to environmental policy characteristic of the 1970s with a more coherent and consistent long-term plan – including new goals and decision-making processes. Much effort was put into plans to attain sustainable development, after the concept that was put forward by the UN-sponsored World Commission on Environment and Economy (the Brundtland Commission).[12]

Assessing the Contemporary Record

Despite all these developments in Canada in the contemporary era, forward-looking, comprehensive government action on long-term environmental protection has not been forthcoming. Although various strategies have been adopted in most Canadian jurisdictions over the past several years in order to pursue such a goal, institutional adaptation and implementation have been questionable. While the mid-1980s saw the development of major initiatives on resources and the environment at both federal and provincial levels, seemingly in accordance with similar initiatives taken in other countries and jurisdictions, the policy outcomes were limited in scope and were successively whittled down from their ambitious and innovative opening proposals.[13]

As the discussion in Chapter 8 has shown, this watering down is true of the development and entrenchment of the federal government's environmental assessment legislation.[14] Although ostensibly an effort to strengthen existing environmental assessment procedures, the final legislation, compared with initial expectations, reveals a process in which many major projects may receive ministerial exemptions. Various factors have also constrained the new Canadian Environmental Protection Act, with critics arguing that the new law actually weakens the previous protection regime.[15]

Despite lofty ambitions for institutional reforms such as the Round Table on Environment and Economy – expected by many to fundamentally alter government decision-making and facilitate long-term planning by harmonizing the interests of various groups with a 'stake' in the environment – these new bodies have been structured, staffed, and mandated in such a fashion as to prevent the accomplishment of these goals.[16] In the case of round tables, this failure led to charges that these bodies exist only as 'talking shops,' or delaying devices, designed to defuse the spirit of reform apparent in the mid- to late 1980s. Many of these structures have been downgraded in recent years and, in some cases, abolished.

Probably the most obvious failure, however, has been that of the establishment of a federal conservation strategy or 'Green Plan.'[17] Although expectations about the plan and the new priority to be given to environmental initiatives through the plan itself were high, the lengthy process of plan approval resulted in a final document that was greatly restricted in its application and coverage. In addition, actual expenditure plans remained vague, and subsequent developments saw even the general budgetary

goals quickly cut back. Even sympathizers now argue that the plan is largely symbolic in nature.[18]

The decline in federal efforts in the environmental arena after the failure of these initiatives can be easily discerned from an inspection of the
record of the Liberal government after 1994. In Chapter 4 of their 1993
election manifesto, *Creating Opportunity*, the Liberals argued that business
and environmental issues had become closely intertwined as industry
leaders saw 'waste reduction, recycling and efficient use of energy and raw
resources as ways to reduce production and waste disposal costs, lower liability and regulatory uncertainty, and improve overall efficiency.'[19] While
'green' industries were highlighted for potential growth by this document,
environmental regulations and the uncertainty they caused investors were
also singled out as having a major debilitating effect on growth in the
Canadian economy. Figure 11.4 provides an overview of the twelve major
promises on the environment made by the Liberals.

By the end of their first term in office, however, the government had only
followed through on the promises to survey existing regulations, create
Agenda 21, and aid municipal sewer construction. Most of the remaining
promises have been delayed by provincial opposition or cuts in renewed
efforts to balance the budget.[20]

Among environmentalists and others, this record of unfulfilled expectations has resulted in serious discontent with the policy status quo. This
'green dilemma' originates in the perception that a major and long-term
social, political, and economic problem – environmental degradation – is
failing to receive adequate treatment by government. As a study prepared
for the Canadian Environmental Assessment Research Council in 1990
noted:

[Canadian government] strategy is essentially reactive and aims at ame-
liorating the effects of industrial activity without necessarily changing it.
While it has been successful at mitigating certain instances of environmental degradation, such as urban air pollution, it has not prevented
environmental deterioration in the form of acid rain, the spread of toxic
chemicals, the degradation of agricultural soils, the destruction of wildlife
habitat, the depletion of the ozone layer and climatic change. These are
all examples of environmental problems which have worsened in the last
two decades, notwithstanding the application of mitigative strategies.[21]

Canadian resource and environmental policy has not yet made the transition to a new paradigm, that would address these issues in terms of new
policy goals and ideas. General paradigmatic stability is reflected in the
continued institutional viability of policy formation and implementation

Figure 11.4

Liberal Red Book Promises on the Environment

1 Conduct a comprehensive baseline study of federal taxes, grants, and subsidies in order to identify barriers and disincentives to sound environmental practices.
2 Appoint a federal environmental auditor general reporting directly to Parliament with powers of investigation similar to the financial auditor-general.
3 Amend the Canadian Environmental Assessment Act to shift decision-making to an independent Canadian Environmental Assessment Agency.
4 Set timetables for the phasing out of the most persistent toxic substances.
5 Assist provincial, regional, and municipal governments to improve sewage and water treatment facilities.
6 Make environmental technologies and services a major component of Canada's strategy for economic growth, and commit 25 per cent of new federal research and development funding to technologies that 'substantially reduce the harmful effects of industrial activity on the environment.'
7 Review the Canadian Environmental Protection Act to 'make pollution prevention a national goal and to strengthen the enforcement of federal pollution standards.' The government also promised to use the review to examine the possibility of giving members of the public access to the courts to press environmental claims.
8 Develop a value-added industrial policy, i.e., one that would 'foster increased employment without over-exploitation of resources.'
9 Work with the provinces to cut carbon dioxide emissions by 20 per cent from 1988 levels.
10 Complete the country's system of national parks and reserves to ensure that a sample of each natural region is protected and that the total protected area amounts to at least 12 per cent of Canada.
11 Create Action 21, an independent national campaign similar to the health-oriented Participaction campaign. The program would build public awareness of the Rio Agenda 21 issues.
12 Make sustainable development a cornerstone of Canadian foreign policy; support the leadership of the International Joint Commission to reduce pollution in the Great Lakes.

Source: Liberal Party of Canada, *Creating Opportunity* (Toronto: Liberal Party of Canada 1993), Chapter 4.

consistent with the old paradigm of resource management. Yet the 'accumulation of anomalies' ranging from resource scarcity to pollution to unemployment continues to challenge the effectiveness of existing policies and associated institutions. In response, governments have begun to innovate by creating new instruments and actors, from environmental assessment reviews to royal commissions of inquiry, from task forces on the environment to round tables on the environment and economy. Authority is fragmented not only by the emergence of new actors, such as environmental groups, but also by the 'interference' of actors from other subsystems – for example, health departments and agencies or competing industries such as tourism. This contestation is augmented by the media as well as through public education campaigns and protests sponsored by groups such as Greenpeace. However, the full transition to a new paradigm of 'ecological management' or ecologically sustainable development has not occurred and continues to be resisted by existing actors in the policy process.[22]

Nevertheless, it is important to recall that the existing policy style has not always been in place and that it does show some signs of wear. This is especially apparent at the stages of policy formulation and evaluation. As we discussed in Chapter 7, the fragmented or 'chaotic' policy community has come about only as environmental groups have mobilized and contested the commodity-oriented resource management ideas associated with the old resource paradigm, breaking down a more or less hegemonic policy community in so doing. These groups have made some inroads into the policy network and have altered its structure from a bilateral one to the present triadic form. As Chapter 10 noted, these groups have also had an effect on policy evaluation, using formal judicial reviews to challenge the results of closed administrative hearings and inquiries. Due to the self-imposed limits on judicial behaviour set out by Canadian courts, however, this activity has not yet been able to substantially alter the dominant administrative mode of evaluation. As well, at the other stages of agenda-setting, decision-making, and implementation, the changes in policy subsystem membership have not yet had a sizeable impact.

This means that, although changes have been occurring in Canadian resource and environmental policy-making, they have affected only certain aspects of some stages of the policy cycle and have only succeeded in modestly altering some aspects of the predominant policy style. In terms of Hall's model of paradigmatic policy change, in spite of occasional sparks pointing to the need to resolve or prevent an 'environmental crisis,' this sector remains very much within the transitionary phase, with fragmentation of authority and experimentation in the forefront of policy development.

Yet the sector is not static. Rather, as this book has shown, the sectoral policy paradigm has moved well beyond the second stage of accumulation of anomalies, for significant gaps have appeared between the dominant set of commodity-based ideas and the realities of resource depletion and environmental damage. Present Canadian resource and environmental policies have failed to deal effectively with many concerns about resource scarcity, including ozone depletion, declines in biodiversity, pollution, toxic wastes, and nuclear hazards, and these concerns have led to some movements toward experimentation with different forms of policy delivery.

Conclusion: The General Nature of Canadian Resource and Environmental Policy

Over a long period, Canadian policy can be understood to have shifted from a system of laissez-faire resource exploitation to a system in which governments are heavily involved in a complex regime of resource management and environmental protection.

This shift encompasses several features. Canada's history as a staples economy has encouraged resource extraction, traditionally driven by private interests. The growth of government's role in resource extraction parallels the general expansion of the Keynesian welfare state, increased public knowledge about the potential adverse effects of resource degradation, and increased competition and conflict over access to resources.

Increasing demands from other interests and conflicts among stakeholders have accompanied the increase in government activitiy and pressured the state to become more accessible and accountable to the public.[23] Additional knowledge about ecological complexity and greater understanding of the extent of human dependence on natural ecosystems have contributed to the emergence of a more environmentally friendly resource policy. In the current regime, resource extraction is only one aspect of an economic process that has widespread implications for social and ecological processes.

Canadian resource and environmental policy has shifted from its early support of private resource extraction in a staples context and continues to evolve in a rapidly changing socioeconomic and ecological context. Despite the changing representation of interests in the policy network, however, and the continuing evolution of administrative arrangements, this policy area continues to exhibit a distinct policy style reflecting the continuing dominance of an old paradigm of resource management.

Policy styles are dynamic and mirror changing socioeconomic conditions and new ideological patterns, as we have discussed throughout this text. Although elements of the sectoral policy style have changed in reaction to the factors set out above, and while some elements of a new style may exist in the resource and environmental sector, these developments are congruent with expectations of normal, intraparadigmatic policy change within the policy process. Whereas the nature of the policy subsystem has changed somewhat from earlier epochs, the development of a triadic subsystem has so far had little impact on the basic set of institutions, processes, and ideas that comprise the old paradigm. The presence of new groups, emerging interests, and different ideas in the policy subsystem, however, signals entrance of the old paradigm into the stages of fragmentation of authority and contestation as new voices work toward the articulation of a new policy paradigm.

12
Conclusion: The Future of the Canadian Resource and Environmental Policy Paradigm

This book has described the prevailing Canadian resource and environmental paradigm as one of resource management. The restricted network dominated by state and business interests helps to explain not only why this kind of policy exists in this sector but also why it is relatively long-lasting. This type of subsystem has proven highly resistant to change and remains capable of restricting the range of ideas and interests that enter into policy deliberations. This situation might not be problematic if there were ongoing and unquestioning public support for dominant institutions, or if an era of economic stability and ecological sustainability existed, but neither is the case in contemporary Canada.

In very general terms, the Canadian resource and environmental policy style appears to have evolved in recent years from a closed, bargaining model toward a more open model and from a resource to an environmentally oriented regime. Yet through the analysis of the mechanics of the policy cycle presented in Chapters 6 through 10, it has become clear that many elements of this transition may be more symbolic than real. While increasing numbers and types of actors have been included in the process, their 'participation' remains largely restricted to the primary stages of the policy process, and their influence on the process remains much less significant than that of traditional economic interests.[1]

This is not to say, however, that policy-making in this sector is static or that there have been no signs of change in the existing resource and environmental policy paradigm. Emerging economic interests from tourism and aquaculture to wildflower and mushroom harvesting are increasingly competing with traditional extractive interests. A new set of ideas and concerns about the nature of the environment and the relations between the social and natural worlds is now circulating in the policy community, although it has so far had a limited impact on existing policy networks. The potential for these ideas, and the actors and interests that generate them, to continue to challenge the existing paradigm is discussed below.

The Potential Sources of Paradigmatic Policy Change

We have attempted to combine two perspectives in order to analyze resource and environmental policy in Canada. The discussion presented in Chapters 1 to 11 combines a political economic analysis with a policy process approach. As we have argued, this combination complements both traditional policy studies and political economic analyses by adding several explanatory dimensions to each. Policy analyses have tended to suspend their economic underpinnings and to search for additional explanations of actions solely within the dynamics of institutional and organizational climates and actors. Adding a political economic dimension to the analysis means that, rather than perceiving economic activities as structurally independent from the body politic, the economic foundations of a society are seen as a primary force in the articulation of public policy.[2] Material interests and motivations and their bases of power are understood to influence social institutions and their decisions. Ideological shifts are perceived to arise not from isolated events and personalities but in the context of evolving material interests.

But adding a policy process dimension to political economic models also helps to resolve several concerns often raised about traditional political economic analyses of governments and state decision-making. While its economic foundations ensure a 'grounded' approach to environmental questions, political economy usually restricts the analysis of ideological factors in government actions by severely curtailing the degree of autonomy that those factors are assumed to have from material practices. Other social variables – such as age, ethnicity, and gender – are also often reduced to their economic aspects rather than considered as independent factors influencing government actions.

As the discussion in this book has shown, however, the contradictions between different economic interests, and the continuing evolution of the politics of resource and environmental issues in Canada, deter a simplistic and unicausal explanation of policy development. Understanding the contradictions inherent in the contemporary Canadian economy and their impact on policy-making requires a more sophisticated analysis incorporating not only political and economic variables but also ideological, sociological, and institutional ones.[3]

We have used a political economic approach as the base for our analysis, arguing that Canadian government actions reflect the larger socio-economic context in which they are located. This approach is especially relevant because of several features of contemporary Canadian society. They include its erratic but progressive evolution from a staples to a more diversified economy and the social and ecological consequences of this change, such as a social legacy of evolving resource communities, regional inequalities, resource shortages, and continuing concerns about the distribution of wealth and income. Also relevant are the ideological shifts and developments in policy discourse that are shaped by, and in turn shape, this social and economic transition, as we will discuss in this chapter.

This analysis has focused on several aspects of the existing policy process. First, the public has tended to be very limited in its involvement in resource and environmental policy-making, taking a backseat to government policy initiation. Second, relatively closed policy networks have played a major role in restricting the flow of information and ideas into policy debates in government. Third, the manner in which policy decisions are actually undertaken in governments has resulted in decision-making according to bargaining, or 'satisfycing,' rather than optimizing criteria. Fourth, administrators translate the expressions of politicians into government action through the use of top-down, regulatory processes rather than bottom-up, participatory ones. And, fifth, the evaluation of existing policies is usually limited and means-oriented rather than including the assessment of both policy measures and policy goals.[4] How likely is it that any of these fundamental characteristics of the existing Canadian resource and environmental policy process will change?

Numerous emerging issues appear especially conducive to the reformation of Canadian resource and environmental policy. The political economic approach adopted in this text argues that economic, especially production-based forces, are central to policy-making. Change in the material conditions of production, then, would be one major source of policy change. Conflict between forestry and tourism over resource use, for example, may promote greater environmental protection. While competition with international producers may lead resource companies to excessive harvesting or inadequate regeneration of renewable resources, it can also force industry's compliance with tighter pollution standards. The addition of value-added components to the production cycle could accommodate decreased resource exploitation while providing additional jobs. These and other economic changes are conducive to policy change in the direction of a more diverse environmental policy style by altering the capacity of business to resist state efforts in this direction.

Under way are significant changes in the basic structure of the Canadian economy. Among them, a continuing pattern of economic diversification and restructuring toward a more service-oriented workforce, the impact of free trade and globalization, and escalating resource scarcity are key issues. Often, the very identification and understanding of ecological issues only becomes a concern when current production activities are threatened through resource scarcity. Understanding of the interdependencies of the economy and the environment is becoming increasingly evident. 'It is estimated that, directly and indirectly, humanity consumes up to 40 percent of the net primary productivity of all terrestrial ecosystems, ... and the demand is growing. To satisfy this demand, more and more of the global ecosystem is coming under human management, and virtually every segment of the planet is being changed in one way or another.'[5]

The policy process approach adopted in this book helps us understand how this set of factors influences policy-making and can lead to significant policy change. The development of a range of new ideas about the relations between humans and the environment – in economic, aesthetic, spiritual, and health contexts – has contributed to a new type of policy discourse. This new discourse is generated by increased understanding of ecological systems and by the emergence of alternative theoretical perspectives, including ecofeminism, deep ecology, bioregionalism, and sustainable development. While this discourse currently exists in the policy community outside the triadic network, its inclusion in policy network deliberations would certainly alter the policy options put forward in this sector. New techniques such as ecological economics and improved environmental impact assessments can also lead to change in institutional patterns that tend to perpetuate existing policy processes and outcomes.

What is the potential for these alterations in institutional and economic practices and emergent ideological perspectives to be reflected in Canadian policy? What are the constraints? Will these issues consolidate and perpetuate existing trends or counter them? At what stage of the policy cycle and under which conditions will the influence of these issues be reflected? This chapter will explore these emerging issues.

Changing Economic Conditions: Tertiarization, Liberalization, Globalization, and Ecological Change

Canadian resource and environmental policy has been shaped by the uneven and incomplete transition of Canada from a staples economy, dependent on resource extraction and trade, to a more diversified 'post-staples' economy. In so doing, new interests arise and old ones change. This process in turn affects subsystem composition and membership and the range of ideas and actors present in the policy process. In Canada, the growth of an urban-based tertiary sector has created a foundation for the emergence of alternative policy styles that are based on employment less directly dependent on resource extraction, and policy networks that are more open and varied in membership. Among the key components of this economic transition in the Canadian context are economic diversification and tertiarization, free trade agreements and trade liberalization, globalization, and ecological change.

Tertiarization: Economic Restructuring toward a Poststaples Economy

The continuing development of the Canadian economy reflects an uneven process of economic diversification, which implies a decreased reliance on the primary sector and the increased importance of secondary and tertiary sectors. Relative to that in other industrialized countries, Canada's development of manufacturing has traditionally been light and uneven, and the contemporary focus is on expansion of the tertiary or service sector.

While each province reflects unique circumstances of resource availability, historical settlement patterns, and governance, Quebec and Ontario have experienced the greatest industrialization, becoming the core of the Canadian economy. Resource extraction continues to play a significant role even at the centre, and megaprojects of recent decades – such as the James Bay hydroelectric project in Quebec – reflect a continuing if shifting base of resource extraction. Peripheral provinces once completely dependent on resource extraction face significant problems. The Maritime provinces and Newfoundland have been especially hard hit by the rapid decline of the fishery and the 1993 closure of the cod fishery, and state-induced efforts at mandatory economic diversification have been less than successful. British Columbia, too, is projecting rapid declines in the timber industry and the fishery.

The progression of much of Canada toward a poststaples economy both supports and contradicts key suppositions of the traditional staples analysis of Canada's future economic development. From the latter perspective, hinterland areas supply resource commodities to the more industrialized and urban core areas, limiting their own development. Yet while this portrayal may be true for some regions and provinces, the departure of other regions and provinces from this traditional picture has implications for resource policy. As Thomas Hutton has observed, 'mature, advanced' staple economies share many of the following features:

(1) substantial depletion of resource endowments;
(2) well-established export markets for principal staple commodities;
(3) increasingly capital- and technology-intensive resource extraction processes;
(4) increasing competition from lower-cost staple regions;
(5) evolution of development from 'pure' extraction to increased refining and secondary processing of resource commodities;
(6) increasing diversification of the industrial structure, with manufacturing, tourism, and local administration and services;
(7) evolution of settlements both within and outside the metropolis;
(8) increasing pressure from environmental groups to inhibit traditional modes of resource extraction and stimulate development alternatives.[6]

Thus, while many provinces may still be characterized as 'resource dependent,' the character and degree of resource dependence are in transition. In the forest industry, for example, there has been increased exploitation of second- and third-growth timber and increased reliance on less accessible forest resources. Much of the conflict in recent years has been triggered by the efforts of lumber companies to cut the few remaining old-growth forests or those previously inaccessible and uneconomical to harvest. Increasing pressures on resource stocks, often from multiple users, intensifies resource demand and threatens long-term employment in traditional industries.

Although the transition to a more diversified economy may not be smooth nor inevitable, there are a number of structural shifts that may be identified with this momentum toward a poststaples economy:

(1) severe pressures on the province's critical resource sector;
(2) the prospect of even more substantial contractions in resource industries over the 1990s and beyond, reflecting structural supply and demand conditions as well as increasing public concerns about resource depletion and environmental degradation;
(3) rapid sectoral shifts in the economy, including:
   (a) a shift to services in the provincial economy;
   (b) rapid tertiarization;
   (c) significant industrial expansion in regional centres;
(4) an *internal* 'reconfiguration' of growth and development, with a significant increase in metropolitan shares of population and employment, the emergence of regional economic centres, but the decline of smaller resource-dependent communities;
(5) an *external* reorientation of key international relationships, characterized not merely by increasing trade and global markets but also by a rapid integration within new markets, networks, and societies.[7]

Economic restructuring has most often been associated with changes in developed economies, particularly in the secondary and tertiary sectors. These changes have been associated throughout the country with the movement of capital offshore, global competition, and technological innovation, and these factors have resulted in the downsizing of the workforce and extensive job loss. These shifts in the labour force have a number of implications for resource policy. The loss of existing jobs and the inadequate creation of new jobs are increasingly problematic.[8] Job shortages result in additional pressure for resource extraction and the continuation of policy favouring staples export.

While the need for increased diversification and especially the growth of the tertiary sector imply the creation of more jobs with proportionally less direct resource reliance and negative environmental impacts, the creation of alternative employment has been slow and itself subject to global competition. Restraint in state programs has also accompanied restructuring in many provinces. Funding for government programs has decreased in many sectors, and 'restraint' policies presage a continuing climate unsupportive of enhanced government expenditures.[9] Decreased state budgets directly and indirectly affect policy initiatives: they restrict the design of new programs, the enforcement of existing regulations, and the emergence of alternative instruments. By doing so, they also reinforce corporate policy measures and detract from the implementation of any new policy paradigm.

Yet a more optimistic economic scenario incorporates the potential results of stronger environmental policies, which may also directly or indirectly foster the growth of emerging service- and production-based industries. The following industries, identified by Hutton, could then be represented along with existing actors (possibly having different or evolving interests) in policy subsystems:

(1) environmental industries and services (environmental protection industries, or EPIs, include production and service sector firms that develop and apply new technologies, materials, and innovations in systems and processes);
(2) resource restoration and recycling (fisheries enhancement, reforestation);
(3) value-added resource industries and products (custom wood products, furniture);
(4) new products from industrial residues (fibreboard plants);
(5) alternative energy sources (fuel cells for public transit);
(6) tourism and convention industry.[10]

Liberalization: The Free Trade Agreements

The North American Free Trade Agreement (NAFTA), signed under the Mulroney government in 1993, has paved the way for the acceleration of many existing economic trends and initiated others. It is still relatively early to assess the cumulative effect of NAFTA on the Canadian environment and economy, but there has been lengthy and contentious discussion of potential issues.

While NAFTA formally provides only a continental link between trading partners, it symbolically represents the increased global pressures of an increasingly competitive advanced capitalism. NAFTA proponents have emphasized its potential encouragement of trade through the elimination of tariffs. The classical economic foundations of NAFTA assume a continental economy in which the benefits of an increased market will flow equally to all producers as the competitive play of economies of scale in the North American market will stimulate higher productivity at cheaper costs to consumers. The expansion of trade, from this perspective, is conducive to increasing specialization and rising productivity, thereby bringing lower consumer prices and higher wages. Furthermore, the increasingly competitive global context provides an incentive for Canada to be inside the loop of any future moves toward continental protectionism.

Critics, however, have identified several potential problems with free trade for the Canadian economy, its resources, and the environment. The classic concept of 'free trade' assumes a neutral market and ignores the historical, structural, demographic, and biophysical factors that have been identified by staples and dependency schools as restricting economic development. From a critical perspective, the imperfect competition that has traditionally characterized the Canadian economy – a staples economy, with extensive foreign (primarily US) ownership – is intensified by NAFTA, rather than neutralized, in spite of the concept of competitive fairness. Free trade is viewed by many to be responsible for the 'deindustrialization of Canada,' as manufacturing jobs are exported and as job creation lags behind job loss.[11] While Canada's harsh climate and diffuse population contribute to higher energy and transportation costs, which in turn restrict our competitive capabilities, these factors are obscured by the image of a 'level playing field' of competition. Moreover, the potential erosion of social programs such as medicare, unemployment insurance, provincial equalization, and minimum wage rates through increasingly competitive practices has also been a key source of concern.

NAFTA has implications for resource and environmental policy as well. Canada's involvement in the continental economy, it is argued, will be at a cost not only to social programs but also to ecological integrity. The 'harmonization' of Canadian regulations with the often lower standards in other countries, for instance, means for critics that the lowest common denominator – those standards cheapest to implement – will prevail. It is argued that NAFTA will intensify the corporate dominance of agriculture and deliver the final blows to the already struggling family farm or ranch. Food produced under weaker standards in other countries (use of unregulated pesticides, irradiation) will be sold to Canadian consumers and further erode efforts for food self-sufficiency and health protection.

Among the other environmental concerns about NAFTA are the exploitation and depletion of Canadian energy reserves. The differential position of Canada and Mexico as net energy exporters, in contrast to the position of the United States as an energy importer, is seen to benefit the United States. Potential problems for Canada's energy resources include the following:

(1) The United States is guaranteed a proportional share of Canada's energy resources, even in times of shortage.

(2) Canada's National Energy Board is rendered powerless to regulate exports.
(3) High exports will deplete our reserves of oil and gas.
(4) With the depletion of conventional reserves, energy costs will escalate dramatically.
(5) Tapping into alternative energy reserves requires more megaprojects such as the Arctic Gas Project, which threatens wildlife in the north.
(6) Governments cannot apply environmental standards outside their own jurisdictions; hence, Canadian policy is not binding for energy use in the United States or Mexico.
(7) By selling oil and gas without factoring in replacement costs, consumption is intensified, greenhouse gases are released, and global climate change is enhanced. Measures toward energy efficiency are also uneconomical in this context.[12]

For resource and environmental policy, NAFTA has two primary consequences. First, it shapes and intensifies the competitive context in which resource extraction and production are undertaken. Within the framework of increased competition in a market model, the costs of protecting ecological systems as well as human labour are excluded. Increased pressure on resources means additional pressure for more intensive harvesting. Continuing corporate concentration and foreign ownership are not conducive to the creation of value-added but can reinforce existing trends of staples dependency.

Second, the regulatory climate is challenged by NAFTA. The harmonization of Canadian regulations with lower standards in the United States and Mexico is one such aspect. In the preliminary discussions surrounding NAFTA, many argued that this harmonization would benefit the global environment, because lower standards, such as those found in Mexico, would be upscaled. Yet within the context of a free market, the quest for the bottom line prevails. Canadian regulations on pollution levels, environmental protection, and worker safety may be jeopardized. Furthermore, the explicit and implicit market orientation of the agreement undermines existing standards. Decreased levels of environmental protection, coupled with an emphasis on 'bottom-line' competition and a decline in state enforcement capabilities, produce ecological 'additions,' such as pollution, that are increasingly harmful. In a context of increased resource scarcity but equal access to resources, Canada stands to lose control over its resources and, ultimately, the resources themselves.

Thus, for many, NAFTA signifies an erosion of the democratic process that is the foundation for resource and environmental policy. 'Canadians will be unable to determine their own trade-related laws and standards because continental trade regulations will override the legislative powers of local, provincial, state, and even federal governments.'[13] Furthermore, dispute settlement panels created under NAFTA provisions have the power to make decisions that may contravene existing regulations. The panels are composed of experts from the field of trade law, but there is no provision for representation from labour, environmental groups, and other groups. NAFTA may well have the effect of not just narrowing the policy network but also overriding its powers.

Globalization

While NAFTA is identified as a formal, continental manifestation of globalization, the increased power and conditions of the international marketplace that it represents are also being felt throughout the world.[14] Corporate concentration, while not a recent phenomenon, is increasing at a rapid rate. It has been estimated that, by the year 2000, 'a few hundred multinational corporations will account for more than half the value of goods and services produced in the entire world.'[15]

One interpretation of the roots of globalization emphasizes the expansion of the marketplace, with greater opportunities for production and trade in new locations. Yet because globalization takes place within an existing history and pattern of commerce, it is more likely that existing trends will continue to be exacerbated. It is likely that globalization will consolidate Canada's semiperipheral position. While some diversification has taken place, there are many factors that restrict our competitive potential, including high labour costs, expensive social programs, the lack of economies of scale, and a high degree of foreign investment. While the availability of resources in Canada will continue to attract investment, this will only reinforce elements of the existing staples economy.

Furthermore, increased globalization, as we mentioned above, detracts from the potential for innovative public policy-making. The growing hegemony of a global marketplace further reduces the capacity of the Canadian state to act in opposition to productive interests. While this is congruent with Canada's historical position of dependence, the global parameters of contemporary transnational corporations exceed the territory and power of their predecessors. Globalization has also reconfigured the relations between the north and south in terms of the distribution of wealth and the processes of production. Policy initiatives, while geared today primarily to domestic repercussions, will also increasingly take into account their international consequences.

Economic Growth and Ecological Change

The global economy has expanded fivefold since mid-century. As Sandra Postel has noted: 'As much was produced in two-and-a-half months of 1990 as in the entire year of 1950. World trade, moreover, grew even faster:

exports of primary commodities and manufactured products rose eleven-fold.'[16] Yet this economic prosperity has come at a price, both socially and ecologically. While contributing to greater affluence, it has also resulted in the concentration and increased polarization of wealth within and between nations. Ecologically, increases in productivity, technological change, and the global restructuring of economic activity are responsible for international declines in biodiversity and carrying capacity, the ability to support future generations on the basis of existing biophysical resources.

Industrial societies introduce 'destructive additions' such as pollution, toxic wastes, and greenhouse gases to the ecosphere, while they extract ever-increasing amounts of natural resources. As Schnaiberg and Gould argue, 'The technological capacity emerging from the technological revolution to create greater levels of more pernicious additions and greater levels of more pernicious resource extraction for exponentially expanding populations has meant that industrial societies can and do exceed ecological limits in ways that were and are impossible for pre- or non-industrial societies.'[17]

The integrity of ecological systems has been affected by the escalation and scale of economic activity in Canada. The rapid increase of human populations within a relatively short time span, and projections of even more dramatic demographic acceleration, have accompanied economic growth. In many parts of Canada, 'economic expansion ... was largely driven by an unsustainable drawing down of the ... natural resource base, including a tripling of forest fibre consumption over three decades, a serious depletion of marine and other wildlife stocks, massive extraction of largely non-renewable mineral reserves, and a general degradation of soil quality.'[18] Economic development within the context of a staples economy undergoing tertiarization and accelerated growth is also ecologically significant in terms of the loss of biodiversity, resource scarcity, and environmental pollution. The rapid declines in the east coast, and increasingly the west coast, fisheries, the deterioration of urban air and water quality, and the scarcity of old-growth forests are just a few of the negative ecological impacts.

As the treadmill of production and consumption accelerates, increased demands on ecosystems are made, for raw materials and for sources of energy. In addition, advanced technology and capital investment contribute to the 'restructuring' of ecological systems. Monoculture plantations of timber stock, fruits, grains, and fish are designed for cheap maintenance and increased productivity, and they are consistent with industrial clearcutting and other large-scale and capital-intensive forms of resource extraction.[19]

Resource scarcity has conflicting implications for development and for policy. On the one hand, given inadequate infrastructure and development incentives, it may signal the demise of human communities as well as those of other species. Declines in habitat and species have already been noted as a result of the expansion of human settlements and the unsustainable extraction of raw materials.[20] Policy measures may reflect increasing pressure on the corporate side to continue 'business as usual' by ignoring the enforcement of compliance regulations or by extending the harvesting of endangered resource stocks. On the other hand, resource scarcity provides incentives for economic diversification as a basis for community survival.

New Actors and Ideas in the Policy Process

Economic diversification has increased the number of stakeholders and diffused their interests. Some new economic interests have emerged, such as tourism (especially ecotourism), but these actors are easily able to fit into and contest existing policy processes and institutions.[21] As policy networks expand to include a broader representation of interests, certain groups are notable for their traditional exclusion from, or continued underrepresentation in, the policy process. Women and First Nations, for example, have vested interests in environmental policy but continue to be underrepresented in existing processes.

Women contribute to environmental impacts in many ways not rendered visible by formal policy processes. Although they make up half the population, they remain underrepresented in the resource and environmental policy subsystem, and their participation in the decision-making, administration, and implementation stages of policy remains inadequate. This situation, however, parallels women's marginal economic status in resource communities, their lower participation rate in resource extraction, especially its technically driven aspects, and their underrepresentation in organized labour movements related to resource production.[22]

While women are underrepresented in the primary sector, this does not mean that their work is environmentally insignificant or that they should be restricted from the policy process. In an environmental context, women's work in the household and the labour force involves the conversion of natural resources into products and processes utilized by humans. In household work, women convert natural resources – agricultural products, fish, timber – into products that can be used or consumed by family members. Women's work not only brings natural environments into the household and converts them for household use; it also insulates households from the environment by providing their members with shelter and clothing, protecting them from the elements. In health care and family roles, women increasingly mediate the social effects of pollution and the increasing damage to the environment caused by efficient and cheap industrial production processes.

Women's experience of environments, their relation to the production process, and their access to decision-making reflect differences of class, race, and age. In Canada, women in aboriginal groups are more likely than other women to live in poverty; they also experience the results of resource degradation directly as the loss of both a culture and a living. Rural women, especially farmers, experience natural environments as residence, work site, and source of revenue, while pesticides, physical isolation, and poverty have varying but direct effects on these women's lives. An understanding of women's relations to resources and environments contributes to a more complete understanding of the significance and potentially broader boundaries of policy. Women may increase their representation in the policy process as more women enter the workforce and the political arena, but also with the expansion of the environmental component of the policy process itself.

As the discussions in Chapters 3 and 7 have shown, First Nations have been active in the policy subsystem, but their representation to date remains issue and region specific. Nevertheless, the rationale for the participation of non-urban aboriginal populations in resource and environmental policy-making has been strengthened due to (1) their claim to prior ownership and use of resources; (2) their expertise in aspects of resource use, especially related to hunting, trapping, and fishing; and (3) the impacts of resource policy on their lives, because of their historical hinterland settlement patterns and their lack of control over the secondary effects of resource extraction, such as pollution and habitat destruction.

Despite their dominance in areas such as hunting, trapping, and freshwater fishing, First Nations participation in the resource policy subsystem is sporadic and sector specific. Justice Thomas Berger's Royal Commission of Inquiry into the Mackenzie Valley Pipeline in the mid-1970s represented a novel departure for resource policy, with an explicit focus on aboriginal concerns. Within certain policy processes, First Nations can play a primary role. The concept of 'comanagement' increasingly invoked in fishery and parks management, for example, reflects the dual management of resources by aboriginal and state governments.[23] In both the sport and the commercial fishery, aboriginal peoples are primary actors. With regard to other resources, the participation of indigenous peoples is more discretionary and largely restricted to policy formation rather than to implementation.

The increasing profile of First Nations, the land claims issue, and the trend toward self-government all suggest that their involvement in policy processes is likely to increase. The traditional marginal representation of indigenous peoples in the policy process could be further challenged by a scenario of indigenous ownership. If, for instance, land claims are settled so as to restore indigenous control over vast areas, and if the move toward increasing self-government continues, the origins and control of the policy process in some sectors would probably shift increasingly to aboriginal hands. Furthermore, the alliance of Native and environmental interests that surfaces in many resource disputes, especially the protection of land, reflects particular strategies and configurations of interests and may be expected to shift in response to external and internal pressures.

The entry of environmental groups into policy subsystems and the continued efforts of women, First Nations, and others to gain entry into resource and environmental policy communities and networks have generated new ideas and policy discourses that are challenging the traditional resource management paradigm.

These new ideas and discourses challenge, although in different ways, the perspective from which contemporary Canadian policy in the sector has been formed and implemented and through which most resource management practices have evolved. These alternative perspectives fall along a broad spectrum from 'biocentric' philosophies that challenge what are thought to be the 'anthropocentric' fallacies of resource management to the antipatriarchal concerns of ecofeminism. In between falls the less radical vision of a reformation of contemporary society in ways that allow for the sustainability of both the human and the natural worlds.

Deep Ecology and Bioregionalism

'Deep ecology' is a critique of the anthropocentric perspective that permeates resource policy, our institutions, and our society.[24] Rather than perceiving human activity as the major and sometimes the only activity on earth, deep ecologists emphasize our dependence and impact on other species.[25] This perspective was inspired by a number of cross-currents: rapid declines in wilderness, open spaces, and resources in many countries; dramatic increases in human population; and recognition of the limitations of technological development, science, and rationalism. Deep ecologists argue that we, as human beings, must recognize our connections to natural systems rather than understand the natural environment as simply a resource for, and backdrop to, the project of human history.

Deep ecology also supports a shift in resource policy from a 'conservationist' to a 'preservationist' approach.[26] Resource conservation is directed primarily to human needs (hunting, ranching, forestry) rather than to the processes of ecological systems (habitat protection, oxygenation, water filtration). Under the conservationist approach, the natural environment remains a resource to be used by human beings, with its value primarily derived from the marketplace. Deer and elk are thus valued in terms of revenues from game licences, while forests are managed in terms of stumpage rates and the revenues from annual allowable cuts. The interdependence of all organisms and their additional values remain hidden or secondary concerns.

Resource preservation, on the other hand, reflects a non-consumptive approach to resource management, one that would maintain natural systems for purposes additional to extraction, production, and consumption. Within a preservationist model, values other than human benefit and, especially, economic gain, are formally attributed to nature. Reasons for protecting wilderness, thus, include not only the economic value associated with tourism but also a range of values such as recreation, aesthetics, habitat preservation, or biodiversity.

Several discussions central to deep ecology deal with the relations of human beings to other species and the complexity of ecological explanation, themes appropriate to policy analysis but usually overlooked in the assumption of manifest (i.e., human) destiny. For instance, if we adopt a perspective of 'biospheric egalitarianism,'[27] all forms of life have intrinsic value, and humans are of neither greater nor lesser value than other species, a view that seriously challenges the traditional human-centred premise of resource use. The deep ecology position questions the primacy of human actions and interests, a primacy often taken for granted, and challenges the basis and process of resource policy in its present form. A deep ecologist understands the consequences of forestry practices as including not only economic gain but also soil erosion and habitat decline for spotted owls and salmon, among other species.

The deep ecology approach is compatible with a number of alternative strategies for supporting human life that respect ecological integrity and are relevant to policy formulation and implementation. One theme is an emphasis on *decentralization*, in which local forms of organization and control of technology are considered more appropriate to environmental protection than current large-scale bureaucratic enterprise, because they are more responsive and adaptable to local requirements. Another theme is a preference for *appropriate technology*, typically low in ecological impact and oriented to specific and local needs, rather than large-scale use.[28] In contrast to megaprojects such as hydroelectric generation sites (James Bay, the Columbia River, the Peace River) or nuclear power plants, small-scale and 'soft,' non-fossil fuel projects are preferred. The use of solar energy, wind generators, and thermal energy, with smaller impacts and costs, are promoted.[29]

Bioregionalism is another aspect of deep ecological thinking; it integrates an ecological perspective with a rationale for decentralization and provides an alternative basis for ecological governance.[30] Bioregionalists argue that present institutions, especially our political systems, are based on bureaucratic, rather than ecological or even human, needs. The key elements and the boundaries of ecosystems, they argue, are not reflected by these institutions, and this means that political and economic decisions do not reflect the unique characteristics of an area. A political constituency, for example, may include portions of the coastal rainforest as well as an interior arid zone, and the forestry and agricultural policies developed for one may be inappropriate for the other. Bioregionalists argue that decisions regarding mineral licences, the siting of industrial mills and factories, and the zoning of land would more adequately support and protect the needs of local citizens and the environment if they were made by residents of the area rather than by shareholders of a corporation or by remote political representatives.[31]

Deep ecology challenges the apparent neutrality of contemporary resource and environmental policy by recognizing its anthropocentrism, not only in its substantive interests but also in its processes. This view has helped to shift policy discourse from a narrow resourcist point of view to more ecologically conscious perspectives. The process of economic development and the movement from staples dependency to an urban and more diverse economic base have provided a basis from which this perspective can now be articulated. As people enter into more diverse relations with natural environments, similar policy ideas will continue to develop.

Ecofeminism

Ecofeminists focus on the common experiences and interests of women and nature. They endorse two basic principles: the affinity of women to the natural environment due to their common productive and reproductive functions, and their mutual subordination and control by patriarchal systems of power.[32] Parallel contributions are made by women and nature to the support of social and ecological systems. Women perform both reproductive and other labour: they give birth to and nurse their young, they socialize and care for children, they support and nurture family members, and they perform the majority of domestic work. The caretaking work that women do, and their responsibility for the mechanics of daily subsistence, mean that they are more likely to be aware of, and be directly dependent on, ecological systems, especially women in non-urban environments. Other species also reproduce and care for their young, thereby providing the infrastructure – oxygenation, water purification, soil enrichment – through which human and other forms of life are made possible. This engagement in the maintenance of life-support systems provides the work performed by women with a link to nature.

While radical ecofeminism celebrates the contributions of women and nature to survival, it also recognizes their joint oppression by patriarchy. The control of women's reproductive rights by the church and the state, and the low wages and poor working conditions experienced by women, it is argued, reflect their oppression by the interests of men. In the view of many ecofeminists, the management of nature in practices ranging from hydroelectric megaprojects to trapping and hunting reflects the parallel patriarchal exploitation and devaluation of earth/household work.[33]

Yet a potential 'essentialism' – the biological association of women with reproductive and domestic responsibility – is problematic for many other feminists who understand women's gendered roles as produced by social organization and socialization. A more critical ecofeminist position argues that women's roles are limited by the larger context of class and gender inequality. The dual subordination of women and nature reflects the combined power exerted by patriarchy and capitalism. Male elites and corporations benefit from the activities of natural ecosystems, which include not only the provision of raw materials but also the maintenance of an environment – air, water, soil – on which all human life is based. In a global extension of this perspective, development processes are viewed as especially injurious to women, because male ownership of increasingly privatized land and transitions to market-based agriculture have further eroded women's status in many developing countries. Moreover, the exploitation of women and nature is linked through the global expansion of development, which has 'destroyed women's productivity both by removing land, water and forests from their management and control, as well as by the ecological destruction of soil, water, and vegetation systems so that nature's productivity and renewability have been impaired.'[34]

Women's underrepresentation in policy arenas, as discussed above, thus reflects more than oversight and institutional lag. Rather, it reflects an ongoing lack of recognition of the systemic ways in which women's relations to the environment are invisible and devalued. The additional representation of women as actors in the policy process begins to address ecofeminist concerns, yet the ecofeminist perspective would also extend the boundaries and content of resource and environmental policy to include a broader array of ideas.

Sustainability and Ecological Economics

As we have seen, the accelerating scope and pace of change in economic development have brought about increased wealth, but they have also brought about ecological disorganization and increasing social polarization. The term 'sustainability' implies the possibility of reintegrating economic, social, and environmental considerations, although there is much disagreement about both these objectives and the strategies for achieving them.

The mainstream version of sustainability is based on a neoclassical economic model that emphasizes individual choice and the market regulation of goods and services. The harnessing of development to an environmentally enlightened market promises to provide new business opportunities, thereby fostering greater potential for the trickling down of wealth (through all social and ecological layers) through increased and appropriate employment and investment. New 'green' products and technologies, propelled by a market demand, are viewed as compatible with the protection of environmental quality.[35]

Neoclassical models assume that the primary issues on the sustainability agenda – environmental degradation and socioeconomic inequality – can be addressed and corrected by market forces and government remedies.[36] But as we have noted, neoclassical economics avoids the long-term consequences of environmental degradation – the diminishing vitality of the resource base, the extinction of species, and the social consequences of excessive pollution – such as increased costs to human health.[37]

For many observers, however, the sustainability of ecological systems and the redistribution of wealth are antagonistic to growth and the continuing privatization of profit. While neoclassical economics understands the economy as separate from the environment, an ecological perspective views economics as integrated with, and dependent on, the ecosphere. *Ecological economics* encompasses a spectrum of approaches that range from the incorporation of environmental factors into mainstream equations to a critique of mainstream market approaches to natural environments.[38]

In this perspective, resources are perceived as a form of 'ecological capital,' and economic growth may be understood as the transformation of ecological to economic capital through the process of resource extraction. International trade can be viewed as the 'expropriation of carrying capacity.'[39] Free trade, in turn, becomes an oxymoron, because resource extraction, while counted as income, becomes a debit to species survival. The long-term and side-effects of industrial production are considered externalities and displaced to other budgets in standard corporate accounting practices. The costs of mitigating these environmental externalities – such as pollution, the deterioration of air, water, and soil, and the extinction of species – are passed on to, and absorbed by, the general public, other budgets, and other species.

While standard economic models and accounting systems have traditionally failed to take into account ecological values, ecological economics 'internalizes' them. In an ecological economic approach, the regenerative costs of ecological maintenance, the remediation of degraded land, and the mitigation of toxic pollutants are included in economic costs. This approach reshapes the economics of the environment by reducing the traditional profit margin, extending pricing, and 'diversifying' the accounting system to grasp a much wider environmental context of economic transactions.

The concept of sustainability represents an ideological shift within the ranks of economists and many government officials that begins to integrate ecological and social concerns in policy recommendations and evaluations. Sustainability explores the implications of contemporary socioeconomic patterns for long-term human and ecological survival. The ecological economic framework offers a vision of a transition to a sustainable future that is acknowledged to be difficult but possible for Canada to forge. Sustainable development is expected to 'meet the needs of the present without compromising the ability of future generations.'[40]

The transition to a sustainable future requires a departure from a tradition of market-driven economics to one increasingly concerned with maintaining the viability of social and ecological systems. This transition will require a number of shifts identified in this chapter, especially the continuing diversification of the economy, the recognition and empowerment of additional actors, and the incorporation of an ecological economics, and indeed an ecological approach, into all stages of the policy process.

As Hutton states, we face 'a massive "sustainability deficit," i.e., a legacy of costs and resource depletion which must now be seriously addressed, and which includes badly eroded stocks of natural capital, and widespread environmental degradation, as well as major social, economic, and fiscal deficits.'[41] This situation is true throughout Canada. Timber and fish stocks especially have been depleted, while consumption patterns have increased. Resources have been exploited at levels exceeding their replacement, and replenishment of this stock of natural capital will require new investments that may be increasingly difficult to secure in an era of diminishing capital. As Hawkens has put it, 'At some time in the relatively near future we will achieve a "balance" between what we are consuming and the capacity of the earth's ecosystems to provide those needs, although under existing models of production and consumption, it is likely to be far different and cause far more suffering than we are presently willing to admit ... A restorative economy means thinking big and long into the future.'[42]

Future Scenarios for Canadian Resource and Environmental Policy

Resource and environmental policy has been only one aspect of the Canadian state's role in economic development. While the material and ideological changes we have been discussing set the context for possible changes in policy paradigms, significant reforms to existing institutional arrangements are required if effective alternatives are to be developed. We have already discussed the role of, and potential for, modifications to environmental assessment processes to alter policy-making. While this legislation, as we discussed in earlier chapters, has been difficult to implement, it requires the consideration of potential impacts prior to, rather than after, an activity. This appears to be a logical version of the precautionary principle, of considering the ecological implications of an activity prior to its initiation. Integrated demographic and ecological data for all species, regions, and conditions also needs to be developed not only to record historical changes in ecological conditions but also to make projections of social and economic adjustments to ensure future ecological integrity. While technological innovations such as Geographical Information Systems facilitate the production of a contemporary database, the complexity of ecological systems, the lack of historical baseline studies, inadequate government coordination, and funding shortfalls all continue to impede this process.

While development has been primarily driven by corporate interests, government and public sector agencies have supported infrastructure investments, resource megaprojects, and continuing efforts to promote economic diversification. The building of roads, extensions of investment in national rail systems, developments of ports, and continuing investment in forestry and mining industries have supported economic development and impacted resources in their own right.

As such, Canadian resource and environmental policy has helped to shape the economic transition that we are experiencing on both a national and a global scale. While resource extraction has been the basis of communities and the backbone of provincial economies, impending and actual resource scarcity now points to the necessity for a diversified and more sustainable economic base and enhanced measures for environmental protection. While policy in the past has benefited the short-term interests of specific industries, the subsequent lack of conservation of resources is now pivotal. With economic diversification, the emergence of multiple stakeholders representing a variety of economic interests holds the potential for transition in the existing policy paradigm toward the development of new policy regime.

The changes to productive processes and economic structures discussed above have a number of implications, sometimes contradictory, for resource and environmental policy-making. On the one hand, increased competition, a continued, if more indirect, dependence on resource extraction, and resource scarcity place additional demands on resources.

This situation is conducive to the maintenance of a negotiative policy style with accelerated demands from industry to increase fishery and timber yields and annual allowable cuts. We could envision a worst-case scenario, assuming multiple stakeholders representing only extractive interests, from which the policy climate would be predisposed to ecological strip-mining, but by a variety rather than a monopoly of interests. The lack of structural incentives for sustainability within the existing market context of multinational firms thriving from short-term profits is a significant hurdle for the transition from a reactive extraction-based resource and environmental policy to a planned, ecologically benign one.

Yet an increasingly diverse economy holds the potential for the continuing emergence of more diverse stakeholders and policy ideas. The complexity of the policy subsystem could in theory produce a more effective set of checks and balances against continued unabated consumption. As employment shifts to sectors that are less directly resource dependent, alternative interests are more likely to be represented in the policy process. For existing resource industries, the increased environmental character of policy, as reflected in higher production standards and enforced regulatory compliance, requires a short-term adjustment but may enable long-term benefits by enhancing market acceptance and prolonging resource capabilities. New industries will be generated through value-added processes and other emerging fields, such as resource restoration and recycling, as well as through the production of new products. In these ways, changing policy subsystems have the potential to reshape the dominant Canadian resource and environmental policy style toward a more open process, one that would be more susceptible to the range of new actors and ideas currently circulating in the policy community.

Conclusion: Toward a New Paradigm?

At present, resource and environmental policy in Canada remains significant both symbolically and substantively. In an era in which the increased power and scope of transnational corporations threaten to exceed the power of nations, the capabilities of the Canadian state in implementing policy directives are increasingly at risk. The existing Canadian resource and environmental policy style and paradigm provide inadequate stewardship and not only erode our source of sustenance and environmental well-being but also limit our opportunities to exercise leadership on a global scale.

Nevertheless, Canadian resource and environmental policy is in the midst of a process that may result in paradigmatic change. Driven by new ideas in the policy community and by changing interests in the policy network, this policy area has modified some elements of its old style but has not yet completed a transition from the old paradigm of resource management.[43]

There is no guarantee, of course, that the sector will develop a new paradigm.[44] In fact, at present the contours of the new paradigm are by no means clear, and the contest between new and old members of the policy subsystem is bitter and rivalrous. This discontent ensures that policy community members will not give up their efforts to develop resource and environmental policies more to their liking. These efforts, in turn, ensure that Canadian resource and environmental policy will remain unstable and the subject of much controversy, at least until a new paradigm emerges to replace the old one.

Notes

Chapter 1: Canadian Natural Resource and Environmental Policy

1 Lester R. Brown, Janet Abramovitz, Chris Bright, Christopher Flavin, Gary Gardner, Hal Kane, Anne Platt, Sandra Postel, David Roodman, Aaron Sachs, and Linda Starke, *State of the World 1996: A Worldwatch Institute Report on Progress toward a Sustainable Society* (New York: Norton 1996), 4.

2 Robert D. Kaplan, 'The Coming Anarchy,' *Atlantic Monthly* (February 1994), 58. See also Robert D. Kaplan, *The Ends of the Earth: A Journey to the Frontiers of Anarchy* (New York: Random House [Vintage Departures] 1996).

3 Peter Morton, 'Canadians Second-Richest, Report Says,' *Financial Post* (16 September 1995), 3.

4 Ibid.; and Julian Beltrame, 'World Bank Predicts Rosy Future for Canada,' *Vancouver Sun* (18 September 1995), A7.

5 Fifty per cent of Crown lands are in provincial or territorial jurisdiction, while 40.3 per cent are located in federal parks and under federal jurisdiction in the Yukon and the Northwest Territories. This does not take into account lands disputed by, or currently under, First Nations control. Statistics Canada, *Human Activity and the Environment 1994*, Catalogue 11-509E (Ottawa: Statistics Canada 1994), 219.

6 See, for example, Patricia Marchak, 'What Happens When Common Property Becomes Uncommon?' *BC Studies* 80 (1988-9): 3-23; and Patricia Marchak, 'Uncommon Property,' in P. Marchak, N. Guppy, and J. McMullan, eds., *Uncommon Property: The Fishing and Fish-Processing Industries in British Columbia* (Vancouver: University of British Columbia Press 1989), 3-33. More generally, see Elinor Ostrom, Roy Gardner, and James Walker, *Rules, Games, and Common-Pool Resources* (Ann Arbor: University of Michigan Press 1994), and Elinor Ostrom, *Governing the Commons: The Evolution of Institutions for Collective Action* (New York: Cambridge University Press 1990).

7 See John A. Altman and Ed Petkus Jr., 'Towards a Stakeholder-Based Policy Process: An Application of the Social Marketing Perspective to Environmental Policy Development,' *Policy Sciences* 27 (1994): 37-51.

8 Norman Wengert, *Natural Resources and the Political Struggle* (Garden City, NY: Random House 1955).

9 See Robert Paehlke, 'Democracy, Bureaucracy, and Environmentalism,' *Environmental Ethics* 10.4 (1989): 291-328; Robyn Eckersley, 'Liberal Democracy and the Rights of Nature: The Struggle for Inclusion,' *Environmental Politics* 4.4 (1995): 169-98; and, more generally, Jurgen Habermas, *Legitimation Crisis* (Boston: Beacon Press 1975).

10 Statistics Canada, *Human Activity,* 44.

11 Ibid., 55.

12 Ibid., 44.

13 Ibid., 1.

14 On the most publicized of these, see Leslie Harris, 'The East Coast Fisheries,' in B. Mitchell, ed., *Resource and Environmental Management in Canada: Addressing Conflict and Uncertainty* (Toronto: Oxford University Press 1995), 130-50.
15 Statistics Canada, *Human Activity,* 218.
16 On the outbreak of mercury-related Minimata disease in Canada, see Warner Troyer, *No Safe Place* (Toronto: Clarke, Irwin 1977).
17 See Donald A. Chant, 'A Decade of Environmental Concern: Retrospect and Prospect,' *Alternatives* 10 (1981): 3-6; J.D. Priscoli and P. Homenuck, 'Consulting the Publics,' in R. Lang, ed., *Integrated Approaches to Resource Planning and Management* (Calgary: University of Calgary Press 1986), 67-79; A.P. Grima, 'Participatory Rites: Integrating Public Involvement in Environmental Impact Assessment,' in J.B.R. Whitney and V.W. Maclaren, eds., *Environmental Impact Assessment: The Canadian Experience* (Toronto: University of Toronto Institute for Environmental Studies 1985), 33-51; and Law Reform Commission of Canada, *Policy Implementation, Compliance and Administrative Law* (Ottawa: Law Reform Commission of Canada 1986).
18 Frank R. Baumgartner and Bryan D. Jones, 'Agenda Dynamics and Policy Subsystems,' *Journal of Politics* 53.4 (1991): 1047-74.
19 Anthony Scott, *Natural Resources: The Economics of Conservation* (Toronto: University of Toronto Press 1955).
20 Herman E. Daly and Kenneth N. Townsend, eds., *Valuing the Earth: Economics, Ecology, Ethics* (Cambridge, MA: MIT Press 1993); Maarten A. Hajer, *The Politics of Environmental Discourse: Ecological Modernization and the Policy Process* (Oxford: Clarendon 1995).
21 Herman E. Daly and John B. Cobb, Jr., *For the Common Good: Redirecting the Economy toward Community, the Environment, and a Sustainable Future* (Boston: Beacon Press 1994).
22 T.F. Schrecker, *Political Economy of Environmental Hazards* (Ottawa: Law Reform Commission of Canada 1984).
23 Statistics Canada, *Human Activity,* 15.
24 Northrop Frye, *The Bush Garden: Essays on the Canadian Imagination* (Toronto: Anansi 1971); Margaret Atwood, *Survival: A Thematic Guide to Canadian Literature* (Toronto: Anansi 1972). See also Rebecca Raglon, 'Women and the Great Canadian Wilderness: Reconsidering the Wild,' *Women's Studies* 25 (1996): 513-31.
25 Richard Kazis and Richard L. Grossman, *Fear at Work: Job Blackmail, Labor, and the Environment* (New York: Pilgrim Press 1982).
26 See Duncan M. Taylor, *Off Course: Restoring the Balance between Canadian Society and the Environment* (Ottawa: International Development Research Centre 1994).
27 Douglas Torgerson, 'Between Knowledge and Politics: Three Faces of Policy Analysis,' *Policy Sciences* 19.1 (1986): 33-59.
28 On this methodology, see M. Howlett and M. Ramesh, *Studying Public Policy: Policy Cycles and Policy Subsystems* (Toronto: Oxford University Press 1995).
29 Peter A. Victor, 'Economics and the Challenge of Environmental Issues,' in W. Leiss, ed., *Ecology versus Politics in Canada* (Toronto: University of Toronto Press 1979), 34-56.
30 Nancy D. Olewiler, *The Regulation of Natural Resources in Canada: Theory and Practice* (Ottawa: Economic Council of Canada 1981).
31 Hugh Heclo, 'Issue Networks and the Executive Establishment,' in A. King, ed., *The New American Political System* (Washington, DC: American Enterprise Institute for Public Policy Research 1978), 87-124.
32 Cf. Douglas Torgerson, 'Power and Insight in Policy Discourse: Post-Positivism and Problem Definition,' in L. Dobuzinskis, M. Howlett, and D. Laycock, eds., *Policy Studies in Canada: The State of the Art* (Toronto: University of Toronto Press 1996), 266-98.
33 John A. Livingston, *The Fallacy of Wildlife Conservation* (Toronto: McClelland and Stewart 1981).
34 Neil Evernden, *The Natural Alien: Humankind and Environment* (Toronto: University of Toronto Press 1993).
35 George Hoberg, 'Sleeping with an Elephant: The American Influence on Canadian Environmental Regulation,' *Journal of Public Policy* 11.1 (1991): 107-31.
36 Canada, *The State of Canada's Environment* (Ottawa: Supply and Services 1991), 1-5.

37 Ibid., 1-7.
38 Ibid., 1-8.
39 See Garrett Hardin, 'The Tragedy of the Commons,' Science 162 (1968): 1243-8. Concerning forest tenure, see Anthony Scott, John Robinson, and David Cohen, eds., *Managing Natural Resources in British Columbia: Markets, Regulations, and Sustainable Development* (Vancouver: UBC Press 1995); Ken Drushka, Bob Nixon, and Roy Travers, eds., *Touch Wood: B.C. Forests at the Crossroads* (Madeira Park: Harbour Publishing 1993).
40 R. Lang, ed., *Integrated Approaches to Resource Planning and Management* (Calgary: University of Calgary Press 1986).
41 Max Oehlschlaeger, *The Idea of Wilderness* (New Haven, CT: Yale University Press 1991), 286-7. See also Neil Evernden, *Natural Alien;* and Neil Evernden, *The Social Creation of Nature* (Baltimore: Johns Hopkins University Press 1992).
42 Oehlschlaeger, *Idea*, 286-7.
43 On sustainable development, see the UN-sponsored Brundtland Report: World Commission on Environment and Development, *Our Common Future* (Oxford: Oxford University Press 1987). On deep ecology, see Bill Devall, *Simple in Means, Rich in Ends: Practicing Deep Ecology* (Salt Lake City: Peregrine Smith Books 1988); and Arne Naess, *Ecology, Community, and Lifestyle: Outline of an Ecosophy* (Cambridge, UK: Cambridge University Press 1989).

Chapter 2: The Socioeconomic Context

1 H.A. Innis, *The Fur Trade in Canada* (Toronto: University of Toronto Press 1930); H.A. Innis, *Problems of Staple Production in Canada* (Toronto: Ryerson Press 1933).
2 M.H. Watkins, 'A Staple Theory of Economic Growth,' *Canadian Journal of Economics and Political Science* 29.2 (1963): 141-58; M.H. Watkins, 'The Staple Theory Revisited,' *Journal of Canadian Studies* 12.5 (1977): 83-95.
3 Michael Howlett and M. Ramesh, *The Political Economy of Canada: An Introduction* (Toronto: McClelland and Stewart 1992).
4 W.W. Rostow, *The Stages of Economic Growth: A Non-Communist Manifesto* (Cambridge, UK: Cambridge University Press 1960).
5 See Margaret Fagan and Donald Lloyd, *Dynamic Canada: The Environment and the Economy* (Toronto: McGraw-Hill Ryerson 1991), 297.
6 On the origins and development of the concept of economic sectors, see Allan G.B. Fisher, *The Clash of Progress and Security* (New York: A.M. Kelley 1966); and Joachim Singelmann, *From Agriculture to Services: The Transformation of Industrial Employment* (Beverly Hills: Sage Publications 1978).
7 Simon S. Kuznets, *Modern Economic Growth: Rate, Structure and Spread* (New Haven: Yale University Press 1966); Herbert G. Grubel, ed., *Conceptual Issues in Service Sector Research: A Symposium* (Vancouver: Fraser Institute 1987); Richard B. McKenzie, 'The Emergence of the "Service Economy": Fact or Artifact?' in Grubel, ed., *Conceptual Issues,* 73-97.
8 On the methods used to calculate indirect multipliers, see Canada, Department of Regional Economic Expansion, *Single-Sector Communities* (Ottawa: Department of Regional Economic Expansion 1977).
9 Dependency theory in the 1960s and 1970s identified continuing patterns of underdevelopment in Third World nations, but it is also applicable in some ways to Canada. The dependency model explains the economic inequality between nations as beneficial to the developed countries at the helm of the capitalist enterprise. Poor countries (and poor regions within countries) form the hinterland for the urban and industrialized centre of capitalism, the metropolis. The metropolis, represented by countries such as Great Britain, Japan, and the United States, dominates other regions economically by extracting economic surplus through ownership of multinational corporations located in the hinterland. The hinterland remains a source of cheap labour and cheap raw materials. André Gunder Frank, *On Capitalist Underdevelopment* (Bombay: Oxford University Press 1975).
10 John Whalley, ed., *Canada's Resource Industries and Water Export Policy* (Toronto: University of Toronto Press 1986); Terry Bennett and David L. Anderson, *An Inter-Sectoral Study of*

Canada's Resource Industries, Technical Paper No. 8 (Kingston: Queen's University Centre for Resource Studies 1988).

11 David R. Cameron, 'The Growth of Government Spending: The Canadian Experience in Comparative Perspective,' in K. Banting, ed., *State and Society* (Toronto: University of Toronto Press 1986), 21-52.

12 On the general environmental impact of colonialism, see Alfred W. Crosby, *Ecological Imperialism: The Biological Expansion of Europe 900-1900* (Cambridge, UK: University of Cambridge Press 1992).

13 Canada, Department of External Affairs, *A Review of Canadian Trade Policy: A Background Document to Canadian Trade Policy for the 1980s* (Ottawa: Supply and Services 1983).

14 G.E. Salembier, A.R. Moore, and F. Stone, *The Canadian Import File: Trade, Protection and Adjustment* (Montreal: Institute for Research on Public Policy 1987); Frank Stone, *Canada, the GATT and the International Trade System* (Montreal: Institute for Research on Public Policy 1984).

15 Although Canada has traditionally maintained a trade surplus on merchandise account (i.e., it has exported more goods than it has imported), this surplus pays for the even larger deficits that Canada tends to run on its non-merchandise account, including trade in services and transfer of profits by subsidiaries of foreign firms. Canada, Department of Finance, *The Canada-U.S. Free Trade Agreement: An Economic Assessment* (Ottawa: Supply and Services 1988).

16 Michael E. Porter, *Canada at the Crossroads: The Reality of a New Competitive Environment* (Ottawa: Business Council on National Issues/Supply and Services 1991); Jorge Niosi, *Technology and National Competitiveness* (Montreal: McGill-Queen's University Press 1991).

17 Glen Williams, *Not for Export: Toward a Political Economy of Canada's Arrested Industrialization* (Toronto: McClelland and Stewart 1983).

18 Rodney de C. Grey, *United States Trade Policy Legislation: A Canadian View* (Montreal: Institute for Research on Public Policy 1982).

19 See Charles Brian Cadsby and Kenneth Woodside, 'The Effects of the North American Free Trade Agreement on the Canada-United States Trade Relationship,' *Canadian Public Policy* 19.4 (1993): 450-62; Duncan Cameron, *The Free Trade Deal* (Toronto: James Lorimer 1988); and Ricardo Grinspun and Maxwell A. Cameron, eds., *The Political Economy of North American Free Trade* (Kingston: McGill-Queen's University Press 1993). See also Economic Council of Canada, *Venturing Forth: An Assessment of the Canada-U.S. Trade Agreement* (Ottawa: Economic Council of Canada 1988), 3.

20 See, for example, M.C. Webb and M.W. Zacher, *Canada and International Mineral Markets: Dependence, Instability and Foreign Policy* (Kingston: Queen's University Centre for Resource Studies 1988).

21 Irene Ip, 'An Overview of Provincial Government Finance,' in M. McMillan, ed., *Provincial Public Finances* (Toronto: Canadian Tax Foundations 1991); Isabella D. Horry and Michael A. Walker, *Government Spending Facts* (Vancouver: Fraser Institute 1991).

22 Robert J. Brym, ed., *Regionalism in Canada* (Toronto: Irwin 1986), 8.

23 Harry Hiller, *Canadian Society: A Macro Analysis* (Scarborough: Prentice-Hall 1991), 156.

24 Morley Gunderson, *Economics of Poverty and Income Distribution* (Toronto: Butterworths 1983); Morley Gunderson, Leon Muszynski, and Jennifer Keck, *Women and Labour Market Poverty* (Ottawa: Canadian Advisory Council on the Status of Women 1990).

25 B. Carniol, 'Resisting Cuts to Social Programs,' *Canadian Review of Social Policy* 31 (1993): 105.

26 Rex A. Lucas, *Minetown, Milltown, Railtown: Life in Canadian Communities of Single Industry* (Toronto: University of Toronto Press 1971).

27 Harry Hiller, *Canadian Society: A Macro Analysis* (Scarborough: Prentice-Hall 1991), 156, 93.

28 Sylvia Hale, *Controversies in Sociology: A Canadian Introduction* (Toronto: Copp Clark Pitman 1990), 429.

29 Evelyn Pinkerton, ed., *Co-operative Management of Local Fisheries: New Directions for Improved Management and Community Development* (Vancouver: University of British Columbia Press 1989).

30 Punam Khosla, *Review of the Situation of Women in Canada* (Toronto: National Action Committee on the Status of Women 1994).

31 Ibid., 8.

32 Pat Armstrong and Hugh Armstrong, *The Double Ghetto* (Toronto: McClelland and Stewart 1994), 25. See also Diane Alfred, *Women in the B.C. Labour Market* (Vancouver: Economic Services Branch, Employment and Immigration Canada 1989).

33 Martha Macdonald, 'Becoming Visible: Women and the Economy,' in Geraldine Finn, ed., *Limited Edition* (Halifax: Fernwood Books 1994), 167.

34 Doris Anderson, *The Unfinished Revolution: The Status of Women in Twelve Countries* (Toronto: Doubleday Canada 1991), 219.

35 James O'Connor, 'Capitalism, Nature, Socialism: A Theoretical Introduction,' *Capitalism, Nature, Socialism* 1.1 (1988): 11-38; Peter A. Victor, 'Economics and the Challenge of Environmental Issues,' in W. Leiss, ed., *Ecology versus Politics in Canada* (Toronto: University of Toronto Press 1979), 34-56.

36 See Canada, *The State of Canada's Environment* (Ottawa: Supply and Services 1991), 1-9.

37 Ibid., 1-12.

38 D. Alexander, 'Bioregionalism: Science or Sensibility?' *Environmental Ethics* 12.2 (1990): 161-71; Christopher Plant and Judith Plant, eds., *Turtle Talk: Voices for a Sustainable Future* (Philadelphia: New Society Publishers 1990).

39 See, for instance, S.D. Clark, *The New Urban Poor* (Toronto: McGraw-Hill Ryerson 1978); and Anthony Cohen, *The Management of Myths* (St. John's: Institute for Social and Economic Research 1975).

40 Lawrence Felt, 'Regional Disparity, Resource Development, and Unequal Accumulation,' in P.S. Li and B.S. Bolaria, eds., *Contemporary Sociology: Critical Perspectives* (Toronto: Copp Clark Pitman 1993), 252.

41 Ibid., 254.

Chapter 3: The Institutional Context

1 For greater discussion of the concept of 'relative autonomy,' see N. Poulantzas, *State, Power, Socialism* (London: Verso 1978); F. Block, 'Beyond Relative Autonomy: State Managers as Historical Subjects,' *Socialist Register* (1980): 227-42. In the Canadian context, see the essays contained in Leo Panitch, ed., *The Canadian State: Political Economy and Political Power* (Toronto: University of Toronto Press 1977).

2 Albert Szymanski, *The Capitalist State and the Politics of Class* (Cambridge, UK: Winthrop Publishers 1978), Chapter 4.

3 See W. Easterbrook and Hugh G.J. Aitken, *Canadian Economic History* (Toronto: Macmillan 1956); Robert Greenhalgh Albion, *Forests and Sea Power: The Timber Problems of the Royal Navy 1652-1862* (Hamden: Archon Books 1965).

4 Graeme Wynn, 'Administration in Adversity: The Deputy Surveyors and Control of the New Brunswick Crown Forest before 1844,' *Acadiensis* 7.1 (1977): 51-62; J. Howard Richards, 'Lands and Policies: Attitudes and Controls in the Alienation of Lands in Ontario during the First Century of Settlement,' *Ontario History* 50.4 (1958): 193-209.

5 Robert E. Cail, *Land, Man, and the Law: The Disposal of Crown Lands in British Columbia 1871-1913* (Vancouver: University of British Columbia Press 1972); Richard S. Lambert and Paul Pross, *Renewing Nature's Wealth: A Centennial History of the Public Management of Lands, Forests, and Wildlife in Ontario 1763-1967* (Toronto: Department of Lands and Forests 1967); J.E. Hodgetts, *Pioneer Public Service* (Toronto: University of Toronto Press 1957).

6 Judson F. Clark, 'Forest Revenues and Forest Conservation,' *Forest Conservation* 3.1 (1907): 19-30; British Columbia, *Crown Charges for Early Timber Rights ...* (Vancouver: Ministry of Lands, Forests and Water Resources 1974); British Columbia, *Timber Appraisal: Policies and Procedures for Evaluating Crown Timber in British Columbia ...* (Vancouver: Ministry of Lands, Forests and Water Resources 1974).

7 Harold A. Innis, *The Fur Trade in Canada: An Introduction to Canadian Economic History* (New Haven, CT: Yale University Press 1930); Harold A. Innis, *Problems of Staple Production in Canada* (Toronto: Ryerson Press 1933); Arthur R.M. Lower, *The North American Assault*

on the Canadian Forest: A History of the Lumber Trade between Canada and the United States (Toronto: Ryerson Press 1938); A.R.M. Lower and H.A. Innis, *Settlement and the Forest Frontier in Eastern Canada* (Toronto: Macmillan 1936).

8 H.V. Nelles, *The Politics of Development: Forests, Mines, and Hydro-Electric Power in Ontario 1849-1941* (Toronto: Macmillan 1974).

9 Christopher Armstrong, *The Politics of Federalism: Ontario's Relations with the Federal Government, 1867-1942* (Toronto: University of Toronto Press 1981); Gerard V. La Forest, *Disallowance and Reservation of Provincial Legislation* (Ottawa: Department of Justice 1955); J.C. Morrison, 'Oliver Mowat and the Development of Provincial Rights in Ontario: A Study in Dominion-Provincial Relations 1867-1896,' in Department of Public Records and Archives, ed., *Three History Theses* (Toronto: Department of Public Records and Archives 1961); Nelles, *Politics of Development.* The most significant case was *Smylie* v. *Queen*, OAR 27 1900, which upheld Ontario's manufacturing condition on pulpwood exports against the federal trade and commerce power.

10 See Thomas L. Burton, *Natural Resource Policy in Canada* (Toronto: McClelland and Stewart 1974). For the American antecedents of this movement, see Samuel Hays, *Conservation and the Gospel of Efficiency: The Progressive Movement in Conservation 1890-1920* (New York: Atheneum Press 1969).

11 See J.G. Nelson, 'Canada's National Parks: Past, Present and Future,' in J. Marsh and G. Wall, eds., *Recreational Land Use: Perspectives on Its Evolution in Canada* (Ottawa: Carleton University Press 1982); J.H. White, *Forestry on Dominion Lands* (Ottawa: Commission of Conservation 1915); and Roderick Nash, *Wilderness and the American Mind* (New Haven, CT: Yale University Press 1967).

12 R. Peter Gillis and Thomas R. Roach, *Lost Initiatives: Canada's Forest Industries, Forest Policy, and Forest Conservation* (New York: Greenwood Press 1986); Alan F.J. Artibise and Gilbert A. Stelter, 'Conservation Planning and Urban Planning: The Canadian Commission of Conservation in Historical Perspective,' in R. Kain, ed., *Planning for Conservation* (New York: St. Martin's Press 1981); C.R. Smith and D.R. Witty, 'Conservation of Resources and Environment: An Exposition and Critical Evaluation of the Commission of Conservation, Canada,' *Plan Canada* 11.1 (1970): 55-71; C.R. Smith and D.R. Witty, 'Conservation of Resources and Environment: An Exposition and Critical Evaluation of the Commission of Conservation, Canada,' *Plan Canada* 11.3 (1972): 199-216.

13 Murray Rankin, 'Environmental Regulation and the Changing Canadian Constitutional Landscape,' in G. Thompson, M.L. McConnell, and L.B. Huestis, eds., *Environmental Law and Business in Canada* (Aurora, ON: Canada Law Books 1993), 53.

14 Doug Macdonald, *The Politics of Pollution: Why Canadians Are Failing Their Environment* (Toronto: McClelland and Stewart 1991), 135.

15 'An Act Respecting Forest Conservation,' 13 Geo. VI c. 8 1949. Although ostensibly an act to promote and aid provincial forest conservation efforts, the 1949 Canada Forest Act was utilized by the federal government to promote forest resource development and the expansion of the Canadian forest industry. Almost $24 million of the $63.8 million spent by the federal government under the terms of the act between 1951 and 1967 was allocated for forest access road construction. Thorne, Stevenson, and Kellogg, *Funding Mechanisms for Forest Management* (Toronto: Canadian Council of Resource and Environment Ministers 1981).

16 Royal Commission on Canada's Economic Prospects, *Final Report of the Royal Commission on Canada's Economic Prospects* (Ottawa: Queen's Printer 1957); J.E. Hodgetts, *The Canadian Public Service* (Toronto: University of Toronto Press 1974).

17 Price Waterhouse Associates, *A Study of Taxation Practices Related to the Pulp and Paper Industry: Part II Phase II – Other Fiscal Measures* (Ottawa: Government of Canada 1973).

18 Marilyn Dubasak, *Wilderness Preservation: A Cross-Cultural Comparison of Canada and the United States* (New York: Garland 1990).

19 See O. Dwivedi, 'The Canadian Government Response to Environmental Concern,' *International Journal* 28 (1972-3): 134-52.

20 Peter N. Nemetz, 'Federal Environmental Regulation in Canada,' *Natural Resources Journal* 26 (1986): 551-608; Peter N. Nemetz, 'The Fisheries Act and Federal-Provincial Environmental Regulation: Duplication or Complementarity?' *Canadian Public Administration* 29 (1986): 401-24; MacDonald, *Politics of Pollution*, 135; James W. Parlour, 'The Politics of Water Pollution Control: A Case Study of the Canadian Fisheries Act Amendments and the Pulp and Paper Effluent Regulations 1970,' *Journal of Environmental Management* 13 (1981): 127-49.

21 G.B. Doern and Thomas Conway, *The Greening of Canada: Federal Institutions and Decisions* (Toronto: University of Toronto Press 1994).

22 M. Paul Brown, 'Organizational Design as Policy Instrument: Environment Canada in the Canadian Bureaucracy,' in R. Boardman, ed., *Canadian Environmental Policy: Ecosystems, Politics, and Process* (Toronto: Oxford University Press 1992), 25.

23 Among the functions appropriated from other ministries by Environment Canada were environmental quality activities such as the Water Sector, Atmospheric Environment Service, Air Pollution Control and Public Health Engineering, the Canada Land Inventory, and the Canadian Wildlife Service. Alain F. Desfosses, *Environmental Quality Strategic Review: A Follow-On Report of the Task Force on Program Review* (Ottawa: Supply and Services 1986), 28-9.

24 Desfosses notes, for instance, that responsibility for pollution was maintained by a number of agencies, including External Affairs's responsibility for water pollution under the International Joint Commission (IJC); Indian and Northern Affairs's responsibility for water pollution in the North and for national parks; National Health and Welfare's responsibility for the effects of pollution on humans; and the Department of Transport's responsibility for water, air, and noise pollution from appropriate transportation sources and routes. Ibid.

25 Macdonald, *Politics of Pollution*, 141.

26 Michael Atkinson, ed., *Governing Canada* (Toronto: Harcourt Brace 1994); James G. March and Johan Olsen, *Rediscovering Institutions: The Organizational Basis of Politics* (New York: Free Press 1989).

27 Stephen D. Krasner, ed., *International Regimes* (Ithaca, NY: Cornell University Press 1983); Volker Rittberger and Peter Mayer, eds., *Regime Theory and International Relations* (Oxford: Clarendon Press 1993).

28 Peter M. Haas, Robert O. Keohane, and Marc A. Levy, eds., *Institutions for the Earth: Sources of Effective International Environmental Protection* (Boston: MIT Press 1993).

29 John Stewart, *The Canadian House of Commons* (Montreal and Kingston: McGill-Queen's University Press 1977).

30 R. Kent Weaver and Bert A. Rockman, 'Assessing the Effects of Institutions,' in R.K. Weaver and B.A. Rockman, eds., *Do Institutions Matter? Government Capabilities in the United States and Abroad* (Washington, DC: Brookings Institute 1993), 1-41.

31 Kenneth Wheare, *Federal Government* (Oxford: Oxford University Press 1964).

32 Bruce Mitchell, 'The Provincial Domain in Environmental Management and Resource Development,' in O. Dwivedi, ed., *Resources and the Environment: Policy Perspectives for Canada* (Toronto: McClelland and Stewart 1980), 49-76; Peter N. Nemetz, 'Federal Environmental Regulation in Canada,' *Natural Resources Journal* 26 (1986): 551-608.

33 Canada, Department of Justice, *A Consolidation of the Constitution Acts 1867 to 1982* (Ottawa: Supply and Services 1983).

34 Roger Cotton and Kelley M. MacKinnon, 'An Overview of Environmental Law in Canada,' in G. Thompson, M.L. McConnell, and L.B. Huestis, eds., *Environmental Law and Business in Canada* (Aurora, ON: Canada Law Books 1993), 1-30.

35 Gerard V. La Forest, *Natural Resources and Public Property under the Canadian Constitution* (Toronto: University of Toronto Press 1969), 3-47, 164-95.

36 A. Scott and A. Neher, eds., *The Public Regulation of Commercial Fisheries in Canada* (Ottawa: Supply and Services 1981).

37 This was also true of a small portion of British Columbia originally transferred to the federal government for railway construction purposes in the terms of Confederation of that province in 1871; see Chester Martin, *'Dominion Lands' Policy* (Toronto: Macmillan 1938).

38 Ronald M. Burns, *Conflict and Its Resolution in the Administration of Mineral Resources in Canada* (Kingston: Queen's University Centre for Resource Studies 1976).
39 Cf. W.R. Lederman, 'The Offshore Reference,' in William R. Lederman, *The Courts and the Canadian Constitution: A Selection of Essays* (Toronto: McClelland and Stewart 1964).
40 Dale Gibson, 'Constitutional Jurisdiction over Environmental Management in Canada,' *University of Toronto Law Journal* 23 (1973): 54-87.
41 S.I. Bushnell, 'Constitutional Law – Proprietary Rights and the Control of Natural Resources,' *Canadian Bar Review* 58 (1980): 157-69.
42 Gerard V. La Forest, *The Allocation of Taxing Power under the Canadian Constitution* (Toronto: Canadian Tax Foundation 1981).
43 Michael Howlett, 'Forest Policy in Canada: Resource Constraints and Political Interests in the Canadian Forest Sector,' doctoral dissertation, Queen's University, 1988; A.R. Thompson and H.R. Eddy, 'Jurisdictional Problems in Natural Resource Management in Canada,' in W.D. Bennett et al., eds., *Essays on Aspects of Resource Policy* (Ottawa: Science Council of Canada 1973), 67-96.
44 See Michael Whittington, *CCREM: An Experiment in Interjurisdictional Co-Ordination* (Ottawa: Science Council of Canada 1978).
45 On the doctrine of paramountcy in Canadian constitutional interpretation, see Eric Colvin, 'Legal Theory and the Paramountcy Rule,' *McGill Law Journal* 25.1 (1979-80): 82-98; and W.R. Lederman, 'The Concurrent Operation of Federal and Provincial Laws in Canada,' *McGill Law Journal* 9.3 (1962-3): 185-99.
46 J. Peter Meekison, Roy J. Romanow, William D. Moull, *Origins and Meaning of Section 92A: The 1982 Constitutional Amendment on Resources* (Montreal: Institute for Research on Public Policy 1985).
47 Marsha A. Chandler, 'Constitutional Change and Public Policy: The Impact of the Resource Amendment (Section 92A),' *Canadian Journal of Political Science* 19.1 (1986): 103-26.
48 On the negotiations and conditions that led to the enactment of Section 92A, see Michael Howlett, 'The Politics of Constitutional Change in a Federal System: Institutional Arrangements and Political Interests in the Negotiation of Section 92A of the Canadian Constitution Act (1982),' *Publius: The Journal of Federalism* 21.1 (1991): 121-42.
49 K. Swinton, *Competing Constitutional Visions: The Meech Lake Accord* (Toronto: Carswell 1988); K. McRoberts and P. Monahan, eds., *The Charlottetown Accord, the Referendum and the Future of Canada* (Toronto: University of Toronto Press 1993).
50 Peter N. Nemetz, 'The Fisheries Act and Federal-Provincial Environmental Regulation: Duplication or Complementarity?' *Canadian Public Administration* 29 (1986): 401-24. See also Alastair R. Lucas, 'Natural Resources and the Environment: A Jurisdictional Primer,' in D. Tingley, ed., *Environmental Protection and the Canadian Constitution* (Edmonton: Environmental Law Centre 1987). These attacks continue: see Paul Waldie, 'Strike Down Green Law, IPSCO Asks: Steelmakers Want Supreme Court to Rule CEPA Unconstitutional,' *Globe and Mail* (2 April 1996): B8; and Steven A. Kennett, 'Nova Pipeline Jurisdiction: Federal or Provincial?' *Resources* 54 (1996): 1-6.
51 This was the case with the acknowledgment of federal powers under the 'Peace, Order and Good Government' clause of the Constitution by the Supreme Court of Canada in the *Crown Zellerbach* case; see *R. v. Crown Zellerbach, National Reporter* 84 (1988): 1-68; and J.B. Hanebury, 'Environmental Impact Assessment in the Canadian Federal System,' *McGill Law Journal* 36 (1991): 962-1005.
52 For a partial list of Canadian environmental statutes in areas including land, water, air, hazardous wastes, noise, solid wastes, energy, wildlife, fish, and forests, as well as general laws relating to environmental protection, see Statistics Canada, *Human Activity and the Environment* (Ottawa: Ministry of Industry, Science and Technology 1991), 34-6.
53 Murray Rankin, 'Environmental Regulation and the Changing Canadian Constitutional Landscape,' in Thompson, McConnell, and Huestis, eds., 31-51; David Vanderzwaag and Linda Duncan, 'Canada and Environmental Protection: Confident Political Faces, Uncertain Legal Hands,' in R. Boardman, ed., *Canadian Environmental Policy: Ecosystems, Politics and Process* (Toronto: Oxford University Press 1992), 3-23.

54 On aboriginal rights and title, see Peter Cumming and N.H. Mickenberg, eds., *Native Rights in Canada* (Toronto: General Publishing 1972); P.J. Usher, F.J. Tough, and R.M. Galois, 'Reclaiming the Land: Aboriginal Title, Treaty Rights and Land Claims in Canada,' *Applied Geography* 12 (1992): 109-32; and D. Raunet, *Without Surrender, Without Consent: A History of the Nishga Land Claims* (Vancouver: Douglas and McIntyre 1984).

55 On the history of the treaties, see L. Upton, 'The Origins of Canadian Indian Policy,' *Journal of Canadian Studies* 8 (1973): 51-61; E. Titley, *A Narrow Vision: Duncan Campbell Scott and the Administration of Indian Affairs in Canada* (Vancouver: University of British Columbia Press 1986); W.E. Daugherty and D. Madill, *Indian Government under Indian Act Legislation, 1868-1951* (Ottawa: Indian Affairs and Northern Development 1980); and E. Patterson, 'A Decade of Change: Origins of the Nishga and Tsimshian Land Protests in the 1880s,' *Journal of Canadian Studies* 18 (1983): 40-54.

56 On the 1982 changes, see B. Slattery, 'The Constitutional Guarantee of Aboriginal and Treaty Rights,' *Queen's Law Journal* 8 (1983): 232-73. On the earlier constitutional status of Native rights, see N. Bankes, 'Indian Resource Rights and Constitutional Enactments in Western Canada, 1871-1930,' in L. Knafla, ed., *Law and Justice in a New Land: Essays in Western Canadian Legal History* (Toronto: Carswell 1986), 129-64.

57 A.M. Ervin, 'Contrasts between the Resolution of Native Land Claims in the United States and Canada Based on Observations of the Alaska Native Land Claims Movement,' *Canadian Journal of Native Studies* 1 (1981): 123-40.

58 J.A. Long, 'Political Revitalization in Canadian Native Indian Society,' *Canadian Journal of Political Science* 23 (1990): 751-74; P. Tennant, *Aboriginal Peoples and Politics: The Indian Land Question in British Columbia 1849-1989* (Vancouver: UBC Press 1990).

59 B. Slattery, 'The Hidden Constitution: Aboriginal Rights in Canada,' *American Journal of Comparative Law* 32 (1984): 361-92 ; B.H. Wildsmith, *Aboriginal People and Section 25 of the Canadian Charter of Rights and Freedoms* (Saskatoon: University of Saskatchewan Native Law Centre 1988).

60 K.L. Brock, 'The Politics of Aboriginal Self-Government: A Canadian Paradox,' *Canadian Public Administration* 34 (1991): 272-86; D.E. Sanders, 'An Uncertain Path: The Aboriginal Constitutional Conferences,' in J.M. Weiler and R.M. Elliot, eds., *Litigating the Values of a Nation* (Toronto: Carswell 1986), 63-77; D.E. Sanders, 'The Indian Lobby,' in R. Simeon and K. Banting, eds., *And No One Cheered: Federalism, Democracy and the Constitution Act* (Toronto: Methuen 1983), 301-32.

61 K. Lysyk, 'The Indian Title Question in Canada: An Appraisal in the Light of Calder,' *Canadian Bar Review* 51 (1973): 450-80; W.H. McConnell, 'The Calder Case in Historical Perspective,' *Saskatchewan Law Review* 38 (1974): 88-122; D. Sanders, 'The Nishga Case,' *BC Studies* 19 (1973): 3-20.

62 T. Morantz, 'Aboriginal Land Claims in Quebec,' in K. Coates, ed., *Aboriginal Land Claims in Canada* (Toronto: Copp Clark Pitman 1992), 101-30; J. O'Reilly, 'The Courts and Community Values: Litigation Involving Native Peoples and Resource Development,' *Alternatives* 15 (1988): 40-48.

63 On their negotiation, see T. Berger, 'Native History, Native Claims and Self-Determination,' *BC Studies* 57 (1983): 10-23; F. Cassidy, ed., *Reaching Just Settlements: Land Claims in British Columbia* (Vancouver: Oolichan Books/Institute for Research on Public Policy 1991); H.A. Feit, 'Negotiating Recognition of Aboriginal Rights: History, Strategies and Reactions to the James Bay and Northern Quebec Agreement,' *Canadian Journal of Anthropology* 1 (1980): 159-70.

64 Canada, *Northeastern Quebec Agreement* (Ottawa: Information Canada 1978); Canada, *Sechelt Indian Band Self-Government Act* (Ottawa: Queen's Printer 1986); Canada, *The Western Arctic Claim: The Inuvialuit Final Agreement* (Ottawa: Indian and Northern Affairs Canada 1984); Canada, *Comprehensive Land Claim Umbrella Final Agreement between the Government of Canada, the Council for Yukon Indians and the Government of the Yukon* (Ottawa: Indian and Northern Affairs Canada 1990); Canada, *Gwich'in Comprehensive Land Claim Agreement* (Ottawa: Indian and Northern Affairs Canada 1992); Canada, *Agreement in Principle for the Nunavut Settlement Area* (Ottawa: Indian and Northern Affairs Canada

1992); Quebec, *The James Bay and Northern Quebec Agreement* ... (Québec: Editeur Officiel du Québec 1976).

65 Coates, ed., *Aboriginal Land Claims*.

66 D. Sanders, 'The Supreme Court of Canada and the "Legal and Political Struggle" over Indigenous Rights,' *Canadian Ethnic Studies* 22 (1990): 122-9; M. Asch and P. Macklem, 'Aboriginal Rights and Canadian Sovereignty: An Essay on *R.V. Sparrow*,' *Alberta Law Review* 29 (1991): 498-517. See also F. Cassidy, ed., *Aboriginal Title in British Columbia: Delgamuukw v. the Queen* (Vancouver: Oolichan Books/Institute for Research on Public Policy 1992).

67 M. M'Gonigle, 'Developing Sustainability: A Native/Environmentalist Prescription for Third-Level Government,' *BC Studies* 84 (1989): 65-99; M. Boldt and J.A. Long, 'Native Indian Self-Government: Instrument of Autonomy or Assimilation?' in J.A. Long and M. Boldt, eds., *Governments in Conflict* (Toronto: University of Toronto Press 1988), 38-56; P. Macklem, 'First Nations Self-Government and the Borders of the Canadian Legal Imagination,' *McGill Law Journal* 36.2 (1991): 382-486.

68 Mary Ellen Turpel, 'The Charlottetown Discord and Aboriginal Peoples' Struggle for Fundamental Political Change,' in K. McRoberts and P. Monahan, eds., *The Charlottetown Accord, the Referendum, and the Future of Canada* (Toronto: University of Toronto Press 1993), 117-51.

69 See P. Usher, 'Some Implications of the Sparrow Judgement for Resource Conservation and Management,' *Alternatives* 18 (1991): 20-2. See also *R.V. Van der Peet*, SCC File No. 23803 (22 August 1996).

70 K. Lysyk, 'Approaches to Settlement of Indian Title Claims: The Alaska Model,' *UBC Law Review* 8 (1973): 321-42; C. Hunt, 'Approaches to Native Land Settlements and Implications for Northern Land Use and Resource Management Policies,' in R.F. Keith and J.B. Wright, eds., *Northern Transitions* (Ottawa: Canadian Arctic Resources Committee 1978), 5-41.

71 M.W. Wagner, 'Footsteps along the Road: Indian Land Claims and Access to Natural Resources,' *Alternatives* 18 (1991): 22-8. On water rights in general, also a major issue on the Prairies, see Claudia Notzke, *Aboriginal Peoples and Natural Resources in Canada* (Toronto: Centre for Aboriginal Management, Education and Training 1994).

72 Notzke, *Aboriginal Peoples*.

73 J. Keeping, *The Inuvialuit Final Agreement* (Calgary: Canadian Institute of Resources Law 1989); L. MacLachlan, 'The Gwich'in Final Agreement,' *Resources* 36 (1991): 6-11; E.J. Peters, *Existing Aboriginal Self-Government Arrangements in Canada: An Overview* (Kingston: Queen's University Institute of Intergovernmental Relations 1987).

74 Co-management of resources between aboriginal and non-aboriginal governments appears to be the order of the day. See Evelyn Pinkerton, ed., *Cooperative Management of Local Fisheries: New Directions for Improved Management and Community Development* (Vancouver: University of British Columbia Press 1989). More generally, see F. Cassidy and N. Dale, *After Native Claims? The Implications of Comprehensive Claims Settlements for Natural Resources in British Columbia* (Montreal: Institute for Research on Public Policy 1988).

75 Andrew Roman and Kelly Hooey, 'The Regulatory Framework,' in Thompson, McConnell, and Huestis, eds., 53-70.

76 G.B. Doern and Thomas Conway, *The Greening of Canada: Federal Institutions and Decisions* (Toronto: University of Toronto Press 1994).

77 All of these agencies have gone through a number of organizational and name changes over the years. For a survey up to the mid-1970s, see J.E. Hodgetts, *The Canadian Public Service: A Physiology of Government 1867-1970* (Toronto: University of Toronto Press 1973).

78 D. Macdonald, *The Politics of Pollution* (Toronto: McClelland and Stewart 1991), 143.

79 Roman and Hooey, 'Regulatory Framework,' 53-70.

80 Gabriel A. Almond, 'The International-National Connection,' *British Journal of Political Science* 19.2 (1989): 237-59; Peter Gourevitch, 'The Second Image Reversed: The International Sources of Domestic Politics,' *International Organization* 32 (1978): 881-912.

81   See Robert O. Keohane and Helen V. Milner, eds., *Internationalization and Domestic Politics* (Cambridge, UK: Cambridge University Press 1996); Miles Kahler, *International Institutions and the Political Economy of Integration* (Washington, DC: Brookings Institute 1995); and Martin List and Volker Rittberger, 'International Environmental Management,' in A. Hurrell and B. Kingsbury, eds., *The International Politics of the Environment: Actors, Interests and Institutions* (Oxford: Clarendon Press 1992), 85-109.

82   Oran Young, *International Environmental Regimes* (Ithaca, NY: Cornell University Press 1989); Oran Young, 'The Politics of International Regime Formation: Managing Natural Resources and the Environment,' *International Organization* 43.3 (1989): 349-76.

83   W.T. Easterbrook and Hugh G.J. Aitken, *Canadian Economic History* (Toronto: Gage 1980).

84   M. Howlett and M. Ramesh, *The Political Economy of Canada: An Introduction* (Toronto: McClelland and Stewart 1992).

85   J.L. Granatstein, 'Free Trade between Canada and the United States: The Issue That Will Not Go Away,' in D. Stairs and G. Winham, eds., *The Politics of Canada's Economic Relationship with the United States* (Toronto: University of Toronto Press 1985), 1-51.

86   GATT, *Basic Instruments and Selected Documents* (Geneva: GATT 1969).

87   In 1947, GATT was signed by twenty-three nations, including Canada, at the American initiative. Since then, the number of nations acceding to it expanded to eighty-nine, with another thirty maintaining de facto application of its rules. The original provisions of the agreement have remained essentially intact, even though many rules have been modified to strengthen, extend, or clarify these provisions through the adoption of a number of supplementary codes and agreements over the years. See Robert O. Keohane, 'Multilateralism: An Agenda for Research,' *International Journal* 45 (1990): 731-64.

88   Howlett and Ramesh, *Political Economy*.

89   Canada, Department of Finance, *The Canada-U.S. Free Trade Agreement: An Economic Assessment* (Ottawa: Supply and Services 1988).

90   Steven Globerman, ed., *Continental Accord: North American Economic Integration* (Vancouver: Fraser Institute 1991).

91   Rod Dobell and Michael Neufeld, eds., *Beyond NAFTA: The Western Hemisphere Interface* (Lantzville, BC: Oolichan Books 1993).

92   Robert J. Gale, 'NAFTA and Its Implications for Resource and Environmental Management,' in B. Mitchell, ed., *Resource and Environmental Management in Canada: Addressing Conflict and Uncertainty* (Toronto: Oxford University Press 1995), 99-129.

93   Economic Council of Canada, *Venturing Forth: An Assessment of the Canada-U.S. Trade Agreement* (Ottawa: Economic Council of Canada 1988), 11-12.

94   See S. Shrybman, 'International Trade and the Environment: An Environmental Assessment of Present GATT Negotiations,' *Alternatives* 17 (1990): 20-9; John Whalley, 'Regional Trade Arrangements in North America: CUSTA and NAFTA,' in J. de Melo and A. Panagariya, eds., *New Dimensions in Regional Integration* (Cambridge, UK: Cambridge University Press 1993), 352-89; and J. Kirton and S. Richardson, eds., *Trade, Environment, and Competitiveness: Sustaining Canada's Prosperity* (Ottawa: National Round Table on Environment and Economy 1992).

95   See especially Pierre Marc Johnson and André Beaulieu, *The Environment and NAFTA: Understanding and Implementing the New Continental Law* (Washington, DC: Island Press 1996); also Annette Baker Fox, 'Environment and Trade: The NAFTA Case,' *Political Science Quarterly* 110.1 (1995): 49-68; C. Thomas and G.A. Tereposky, 'The NAFTA and the Side Agreement on Environmental Co-Operation,' *Journal of World Trade* 27.6 (1993): 5-34.

96   Peter S. Thacher, 'The Role of the United Nations,' in A. Hurrell and B. Kingsbury, eds., *The International Politics of the Environment* (Oxford: Clarendon Press 1992), 183-211; Hayward R. Alker and Peter M. Haas, 'The Rise of Global Ecopolitics,' in N. Choucri, ed., *Global Accord: Environmental Challenges and International Responses* (Boston: MIT Press 1993), 205-54.

97   Tony Brenton, *The Greening of Machiavelli: The Evolution of International Environmental Politics* (London: Royal Institute of International Affairs 1994); Peter Bartelmus, *Environment, Growth and Development: The Concepts and Strategies of Sustainability* (London: Routledge 1994). Some major international environmental organizations are

based in Canada. Montreal, for example, is home to the NAFTA Environmental Commission on Environmental Cooperation, as well as to the permanent secretariat to the UN Convention on Biological Diversity.
98 Kenneth Piddington, 'The Role of the World Bank,' in Hurrell and Kingsbury, eds., 212-27.
99 Statistics Canada, *Human Activity*.
100 Richard Benedick, *Ozone Diplomacy* (Cambridge, MA: Harvard University Press 1991); Michael Grubb, *The Earth Summit Agreements: A Guide and Assessment* (London: RIIA/Earthscan 1993).
101 Linda C. Reif, 'International Environmental Law,' in Thompson, McConnell, and Huestis, eds., 71-103.
102 For alternative perspectives on the effectiveness of these standards, see Daniel C. Esty, *Greening the GATT: Trade, Environment and the Future* (Washington, DC: Institute of International Economics 1994); and C. Fred Runge, *Freer Trade, Protected Environment: Balancing Trade Liberalization and Environmental Institutions* (Washington, DC: Council on Foreign Relations 1994).
103 The constitutional constraint on policymakers, however, is two-edged: that is, because the Constitution does not clearly demarcate jurisdictional boundaries in this area of social and economic life, some duplication and overlap in services, regulation, and monitoring are inevitable. While those concerned with efficient administration and accountable expenditures may decry this situation, there are some advantages, from an environmental perspective, to restricting the freedom of individual jurisdictions to do as they wish with their resources and environments. That is, as Peter Nemetz has pointed out, duplication in oversight ensures that no jurisdiction is able to 'opt out' of environmental protection and simply 'high grade' or stripmine its resources. Nemetz, 'Fisheries Act.'

Chapter 4: Policy Actors
1 Grant Jordan has discussed the many images and metaphors used to describe policy subsystems. See Grant Jordan, 'Iron Triangles, Woolly Corporatism and Elastic Nets: Images of the Policy Process,' *Journal of Public Policy* 1 (1981): 95-123; Grant Jordan, 'Sub-Governments, Policy Communities and Networks: Refilling the Old Bottles?' *Journal of Theoretical Politics* 2 (1990): 319-38.
2 Bryan D. Jones, *Reconceiving Decision-Making in Democratic Politics: Attention, Choice and Public Policy* (Chicago: University of Chicago Press 1994).
3 Lance deHaven-Smith and Carl E. Van Horn, 'Subgovernment Conflict in Public Policy,' *Policy Studies Journal* 12 (1984): 627-42.
4 Douglas Cater, *Power in Washington: A Critical Look at Today's Struggle in the Nation's Capital* (New York: Random House 1964).
5 Marver H. Bernstein, *Regulating Business by Independent Commission* (Princeton, NJ: Princeton University Press 1955); Samuel Huntington, 'The Marasmus of the ICC: The Commissions, the Railroads and the Public Interest,' *Yale Law Review* 61.4 (1952): 467-509; Theodore Lowi, *The End of Liberalism: Ideology, Policy and the Crisis of Public Authority* (New York: Norton 1969).
6 Michael T. Hayes, 'The Semi-Sovereign Pressure Groups: A Critique of Current Theory and an Alternative Typology,' *Journal of Politics* 40 (1978): 134-61; Randall B. Ripley and Grace A. Franklin, *Congress, the Bureaucracy, and Public Policy* (Homewood, IL: Dorsey Press 1980).
7 Hugh Heclo, 'Issue Networks and the Executive Establishment,' in Anthony King, ed., *The New American Political System* (Washington, DC: American Enterprise Institute for Public Policy Research 1978), 87-124.
8 Hugh Heclo, *Modern Social Politics in Britain and Sweden: From Relief to Income Maintenance* (New Haven, CT: Yale University Press 1974), 308-10.
9 Hugh Heclo, 'Issue Networks,' 88.
10 Ibid., 102.
11 Building on Heclo's insights, Paul Sabatier and his colleagues developed a complex scheme for conceptualizing the activities of policy actors in policy subsystems. They coined the term 'advocacy coalition' to refer to a specific type of policy subsystem characterized by agreement between subsystem members as to the basic direction of specific

sets of public policies. See Paul A. Sabatier and Hank C. Jenkins-Smith, 'The Advocacy Coalition Framework: Assessment, Revisions, and Implications for Scholars and Practitioners,' in P.A. Sabatier and H.C. Jenkins-Smith, eds., *Policy Change and Learning: An Advocacy Coalition Approach* (Boulder: Westview 1993).

12 Paul Sabatier, 'Knowledge, Policy-Oriented Learning, and Policy Change,' *Knowledge: Creation, Diffusion, Utilization* 8 (1987): 664.

13 Peter J. Katzenstein, 'Conclusion: Domestic Structures and Strategies of Foreign Economic Policy,' *International Organization* 31 (1977): 879-920. See also H. Brinton Milward and Gary L. Walmsley, 'Policy Subsystems, Networks and the Tools of Public Management,' in Robert Eyestone, ed., *Public Policy Formation* (Greenwich: JAI Press 1984), 3-25.

14 R.A.W. Rhodes, 'Power-Dependence, Policy Communities and Intergovernmental Networks,' *Public Administration Bulletin* 49 (1984): 4-31.

15 Ibid., 14-15.

16 Keith E. Hamm, 'Patterns of Influence among Committees, Agencies, and Interest Groups,' *Legislative Studies Quarterly* 8 (1983): 415.

17 Stephen Wilks and Maurice Wright, 'Conclusion: Comparing Government-Industry Relations: States, Sectors, and Networks,' in S. Wilks and M. Wright, eds., *Comparative Government-Industry Relations: Western Europe, the United States, and Japan* (Oxford: Clarendon Press 1987), 298.

18 L.J. Sharpe, 'Central Coordination and the Policy Network,' *Political Studies* 33 (1985): 361-81.

19 Jack L. Walker, 'The Diffusion of Knowledge and Policy Change: Toward a Theory of Agenda-Setting,' paper presented at the Annual Meeting of the American Political Science Association, Chicago, 1974.

20 A similar conception of a policy community has emerged in the international relations literature in which loose groups of knowledge actors – epistemic communities – are said to underlie many international institutions and regimes. See Peter M. Haas, 'Introduction: Epistemic Communities and International Policy Coordination,' *International Organization* 46 (1992): 3.

21 David Lowenthal, 'Awareness of Human Impacts: Changing Attitudes and Emphases,' in B.L. Turner II, ed., *The Earth as Transformed by Human Action* (Cambridge, UK: Cambridge University Press 1993), 126.

22 N. Malcolm, 'Green Thoughts in a Blue Shade,' *Spectator* 6 (1989): 7, as cited in Lowenthal, 'Awareness,' 127.

23 Robert Gibson, 'Out of Control and Beyond Understanding: Acid Rain as a Political Dilemma,' in R. Paehlke and D. Torgerson, eds., *Environmental Politics and the Administrative State* (Peterborough: Broadview Press 1990), 248.

24 Murray J. Edelman, *Constructing the Political Spectacle* (Chicago: University of Chicago Press 1988); Christopher J. Bosso, 'Setting the Agenda: Mass Media and the Discovery of Famine in Ethiopia,' in M. Margolis and G.A. Mauser, eds., *Manipulating Public Opinion: Essays on Public Opinion as a Dependent Variable* (Pacific Grove: Brooks/Cole 1989), 153-74; F.L. Cook, T.R. Tyler, E.G. Goetz, M.T. Gordon, D. Protess, D.R. Leff, and H.L. Molotch, 'Media and Agenda Setting: Effects on the Public, Interest Group Leaders, Policy Makers, and Policy,' *Public Opinion Quarterly* 47.1 (1983): 16-35.

25 Frederick J. Fletcher and Lori Stahlbrand, 'Mirror or Participant? The News Media and Environmental Policy,' in R. Boardman, ed., *Canadian Environmental Policy: Ecosystems, Politics, and Process* (Toronto: Oxford University Press 1992), 196.

26 Michael Howlett, 'Issue-Attention Cycles Reconsidered: Preliminary Empirical Findings on the Dynamics of Agenda-Setting in Canada,' paper presented at the Annual Meeting of the Canadian Political Science Association, Montreal, 1995.

27 Kathryn Harrison and George Hoberg, 'Setting the Environmental Agenda in Canada and the United States: The Cases of Dioxin and Radon,' *Canadian Journal of Political Science* 24.1 (1991): 3-27.

28 Vaughan Lyon, 'Green Politics: Political Parties, Elections, and Environmental Policy,' in Boardman, ed., 127.

29 Jeremy Wilson, 'Green Lobbies: Pressure Groups and Environmental Policy,' in Boardman, ed., 109-25.

30 Maurice Herbert Dobb, *Theories of Value and Distribution since Adam Smith: Ideology and Economic Theory* (Cambridge, UK: Cambridge University Press 1973); Joseph S. Keiper, Ernest Kurnow, Clifford D. Clark, and Harry H. Segal, *Theory and Measurement of Rent* (Philadelphia: Chilton 1961); Piero Sraffa, ed., *The Works and Correspondence of David Ricardo* (Cambridge, UK: Cambridge University Press 1951).

31 However, each collective interest may be pursued by a number of political actors, and conflicts may occur between actors pursuing similar fundamental interests. Albert M. Church, *Conflicts over Resource Ownership: The Use of Public Policy by Private Interests* (Lexington, KY: Lexington Books 1982). Similarly, alliances between actors may occur in the pursuit of political advantage. Hence, natural resource politics should be conceived as involving a shifting system of alliances within an overall context of conflicting political interests stemming from the economics of natural resource production.

32 A peculiar characteristic of the Canadian case that elevates governments to the status of chief 'landlord' is the extensive public ownership of land and resources. This pattern of public ownership originated for a variety of historical reasons having to do with British practices of Crown ownership and legislative control exchanged for guarantees of support for government expenses, that is, the guarantee of the 'civil list' in the pre-Confederation period. See Gerard V. La Forest, *Natural Resources and Public Property under the Canadian Constitution* (Toronto: University of Toronto Press 1969).

33 Charles Lindblom, *Politics and Markets: The World's Political Economic Systems* (New York: Basic Books 1977).

34 Jaime de Melo and Arvind Panagariya, eds., *New Dimensions in Regional Integration* (Cambridge, UK: Cambridge University Press 1993); R.J. Barry Jones, *Globalisation and Interdependence in the International Political Economy* (London: Pinter 1995); Miles Kahler, *International Institutions and the Political Economy of Integration* (Washington, DC: Brookings Institute 1995).

35 Katzenstein, 'Conclusion.'

36 Andrew J. Taylor, *Trade Unions and Politics* (Basingstoke: Macmillan 1989), 1.

37 See Edward O. Laumann and David Knoke, *The Organizational State: Social Choice in National Policy Domains* (Madison: University of Wisconsin Press 1987); and David Knoke, *Political Networks: The Structural Perspective* (Cambridge, UK: Cambridge University Press 1987).

38 Stephen Breyer, *Regulation and Its Reform* (Cambridge, MA: Harvard University Press 1982); Alan Cairns, 'The Past and Future of the Canadian Administrative State,' *University of Toronto Law Journal* 40 (1990): 319-61; Richard A. Posner, 'Theories of Economic Regulation,' *Bell Journal of Economics and Management Science* 5 (1974): 335-58; Margot Priest and Aron Wohl, 'The Growth of Federal and Provincial Regulation of Economic Activity 1867-1978,' in W.T. Stanbury, ed., *Government Regulation: Scope, Growth, Process* (Montreal: Institute for Research on Public Policy 1980), 69-150.

39 John Markoff, 'Governmental Bureaucratization: General Processes and an Anomalous Case,' *Comparative Studies in Society and History* 17 (1975): 479-503; Edward C. Page, *Political Authority and Bureaucratic Power: A Comparative Analysis* (Brighton: Wheatsheaf 1985).

40 Graham T. Allison and Morton H. Halperin, 'Bureaucratic Politics: A Paradigm and Some Policy Implications,' *World Politics* 24 [Supplement] (1972): 40-79.

41 Larry B. Hill, Introduction, in Larry B. Hill, ed., *The State of Public Bureaucracy* (Armonk, NY: M.E. Sharpe 1992), 1-11.

42 Sharon L. Sutherland, 'The Public Service and Policy Development,' in M. Michael Atkinson, ed., *Governing Canada: Institutions and Public Policy* (Toronto: Harcourt Brace Jovanovich 1993).

43 Daniel McCool, 'Subgovernments and the Impact of Policy Fragmentation and Accommodation,' *Policy Studies Review* 8 (1989): 264-87. Atkinson and Coleman developed a scheme, similar to that presented here, based on the organization of state and society and the links between the two. In their view, the two critical questions are

whether societal interests are centrally organized and whether the state has the capacity to develop policies independently of them – in other words, its level of autonomy from societal actors. See Michael Atkinson and William Coleman, 'Strong States and Weak States: Sectoral Policy Networks in Advanced Capitalist Economies,' *British Journal of Political Science* 19 (1989): 54. Other efforts resulted in more complex and, ultimately, confusing taxonomies. Thus, for example, Franz Van Waarden argued that networks vary according to seven criteria: number and type of actors, function of networks, structure, institutionalization, rules of conduct, power relations, and actor strategies. See Franz Van Waarden, 'Dimensions and Types of Policy Networks,' *European Journal of Political Research* 21 (1992): 29-52.

44 Jane Jenson, 'Paradigms and Political Discourse: Protective Legislation in France and the United States before 1914,' *Canadian Journal of Political Science* 22 (1989): 235-58. For an application of the concept of a policy paradigm, see Peter A. Hall, 'Policy Paradigms, Experts, and the State: The Case of Macroeconomic Policy-Making in Britain,' in S. Brooks and A.-G. Gagnon, eds., *Social Scientists, Policy, and the State* (New York: Praeger 1990); and Michael Howlett, 'Policy Paradigms and Policy Change: Lessons from the Old and New Canadian Policies towards Aboriginal Peoples,' *Policy Studies Journal* 22.4 (1994): 631-51.

Chapter 5: The Resource and Environmental Policy Process

1 See Wallace Clement, 'Debates and Directions: A Political Economy of Resources,' in W. Clement and G. Williams, eds., *The New Canadian Political Economy* (Kingston: McGill-Queen's University Press 1989), 36-53. Original works by staples theorists dealing with specific resources include A.R.M. Lower and H.A. Innis, *Settlement and the Forest Frontier in Eastern Canada* (Toronto: Macmillan 1936); W.A. Mackintosh, *Prairie Settlement: The Geographical Setting* (Toronto: Macmillan 1934); Chester Martin, *'Dominion Lands' Policy* (Toronto: Macmillan 1938); Harold Adams Innis, *The Fur Trade in Canada: An Introduction to Canadian Economic History* (New Haven, CT: Yale University Press 1930); Harold A. Innis, *Problems of Staple Production in Canada* (Toronto: Ryerson Press 1933); and Arthur R.M. Lower, *The North American Assault on the Canadian Forest: A History of the Lumber Trade between Canada and the United States* (Toronto: Ryerson 1938).

2 Ray Schmidt, 'Canadian Political Economy: A Critique,' *Studies in Political Economy* 6 (1981): 65-92; Wallace Clement and Daniel Drache, *The New Practical Guide to Canadian Political Economy* (Toronto: Lorimer 1985); Patricia Marchak, 'Canadian Political Economy,' *Canadian Review of Sociology and Anthropology* 22 (1985): 673-709.

3 Good reviews of individual sectors include Edward A. Carmichael and C.M. Herrera, *Canada's Energy Policy: 1985 and Beyond* (Toronto: C.D. Howe Institute 1984); P. Marchak, N. Guppy, and J. McMullen, eds., *Uncommon Property: The Fishing and Fish-Processing Industries in British Columbia* (Toronto: Methuen 1987); Patricia M. Marchak, *Green Gold: The Forest Industry in British Columbia* (Vancouver: University of British Columbia Press 1983); E. Weeks and L. Mazany, *The Future of the Atlantic Fisheries* (Montreal: Institute for Research on Public Policy 1983); David Yudelman, *Canadian Mineral Policy Past and Present: The Ambiguous Legacy* (Kingston: Queen's University Centre for Resource Studies 1985); Richard C. Zuker, *Blue Gold: Hydro-Electric Rent in Canada* (Ottawa: Supply and Services 1984); R. Peter Gillis and Thomas R. Roach, *Lost Initiatives: Canada's Forest Industries, Forest Policy, and Forest Conservation* (New York: Greenwood Press 1986); and Donald MacKay, *Heritage Lost: The Crisis in Canada's Forests* (Toronto: Macmillan 1985).

4 Comparative cross-national studies are especially poor at present. Some comparative studies of the performance of specific natural resource industries in Canada and elsewhere exist, as do some comparisons of Canadian government policies with those in other countries. Few studies, however, attempt to compare industrial performance within the same jurisdiction or the policies of different Canadian jurisdictions toward the same industry. Exceptions include H.V. Nelles, *The Politics of Development: Forests, Mines, and Hydro-Electric Power in Ontario 1849-1941* (Toronto: Macmillan 1974); and Bruce W. Wilkinson, 'Canada's Resource Industries: A Survey,' in J. Whalley, ed., *Canada's Resource Industries and Water Export Policy* (Toronto: University of Toronto Press 1986), 1-159.

5   Examples of the work of economists include F.J. Anderson, *Natural Resources in Canada: Economic Theory and Policy* (Toronto: Methuen 1985); and Barry C. Field and Nancy D. Olewiler, *Environmental Economics* (Toronto: McGraw-Hill Ryerson 1995). For examples of legal analyses, see S.I. Bushnell, 'Constitutional Law – Proprietary Rights and the Control of Natural Resources,' *Canadian Bar Review* 58 (1980): 157-69; John D. Whyte, *The Constitution and Natural Resource Revenues* (Kingston: Queen's University Institute of Intergovernmental Relations 1982); Nigel Bankes and J.O. Saunders, eds., *Public Disposition of Natural Resources: Essays from the First Banff Conference on Natural Resources Law, Banff, Alberta, April 12-15 1983* (Calgary: Canadian Institute of Resources Law 1984); J. Cohen and M. Krashinsky, 'Capturing the Rents on Resource Land for the Public Landowner: The Case for a Crown Corporation,' *Canadian Public Policy* 2.3 (1976): 411-23; and Michael Crommelin and Andrew Thompson, eds., *Mineral Leasing as an Instrument of Public Policy* (Vancouver: University of British Columbia Press 1977).
6   Mark Sproule-Jones, 'Public Choice Theory and Natural Resources: Methodological Explication and Critique,' *American Political Science Review* 76 (1982): 790-804.
7   G. Bruce Doern and Glen Toner, *The Politics of Energy: The Development and Implementation of the National Energy Program* (Toronto: Methuen 1985).
8   On public choice theory generally, see Dennis C. Mueller, *Public Choice II* (Cambridge, UK: Cambridge University Press 1989); and Iain McLean, *Public Choice: An Introduction* (Oxford: Basil Blackwell 1987).
9   For the most part, 'interests' are defined in subjective terms, that is, in terms of the definition of the policy 'actors' themselves. Doern and Toner, *Politics of Energy,* for example, argue that 'interests are those economic and political actors that have the capability to exercise power' (12). This, of course, leads to another ad hoc categorization of interests to include various governments and corporations active in the area. Toner notes the key role played by political conflict in the policy process, but he does not systematically analyze it, instead relying on another classification of 'inter-relationships of power' that allows him to define intergovernmental, government-industry, interregional, Canada-US, and partisan relationships as key to determining relevant policy actors. See Glen Toner, 'The Politics of Energy and the National Energy Program: A Framework and Analysis,' doctoral dissertation, Carleton University 1984, 42-62. As a result, political interests are made synonymous with political actors in a somewhat tautological manner, and the difficult question of the relationship between interest and actor is explained away.
10 William N. Dunn, 'Methods of the Second Type: Coping with the Wilderness of Conventional Policy Analysis,' *Policy Studies Review* 7 (1988): 720-37.
11 For an example of its utilization in the United States, see James Lester, ed., *Environmental Politics and Policy: Theories and Evidence* (Durham, NC: Duke University Press 1989).
12 Charles O. Jones, *An Introduction to the Study of Public Policy* (Monterey, CA: Brooks/Cole 1984). For a critique of this model, see Hank C. Jenkins-Smith and Paul A. Sabatier, 'The Study of Public Policy Processes,' in P.A. Sabatier and H.C. Jenkins-Smith, eds., *Policy Change and Learning: An Advocacy Coalition Approach* (Boulder, CO: Westview 1993).
13 Harold D. Lasswell, *The Decision Process: Seven Categories of Functional Analysis* (College Park: University of Maryland 1956). See also Harold D. Lasswell, *A Pre-View of Policy Sciences* (New York: Elsevier 1971).
14 Garry D. Brewer, 'The Policy Sciences Emerge: To Nurture and Structure a Discipline,' *Policy Sciences* 5.3 (1974): 239-44. See also Garry Brewer and Peter deLeon, *The Foundations of Policy Analysis* (Homewood, IL: Dorsey Press 1983).
15 James E. Anderson, *Public Policymaking* (New York: Praeger 1975).
16 Deborah A. Stone, *Policy Paradox and Political Reason* (Glenview, IL: Scott, Foresman 1988); Laurence H. Tribe, 'Policy Science: Analysis or Ideology?' *Philosophy and Public Affairs* 2.1 (1972): 66-110; James G. March and Johan Olsen, 'Organizational Choice under Ambiguity,' in J.G. March and J. Olsen, eds., *Ambiguity and Choice in Organizations* (Bergen: Universitetsforlaget 1979).
17 Paul A. Sabatier, 'Toward Better Theories of the Policy Process,' *PS: Political Science and Politics* 24.2 (1991): 144-56.

18 Margaret Weir, 'Ideas and the Politics of Bounded Innovation,' in S. Steinmo, K. Thelen, and F. Longstreth, eds., *Structuring Politics: Historical Institutionalism in Comparative Analysis* (Cambridge, UK: Cambridge University Press 1992), 188-216.

19 Jenny Stewart, 'Corporatism, Pluralism and Political Learning: A Systems Approach,' *Journal of Public Policy* 12.3 (1992): 243-56.

20 M. Howlett and M. Ramesh, *Studying Public Policy: Policy Cycles and Policy Subsystems* (Toronto: Oxford University Press 1995).

21 What are often portrayed as 'new' industrial and environmental policy initiatives, for example, offer extra subsidies to industries or tighten the regulation of polluting activities. Nelson W. Polsby, *Political Innovation in America: The Politics of Policy Initiation* (New Haven, CT: Yale University Press 1984).

22 Charles E. Lindblom, 'The Science of Muddling Through,' *Public Administration Review* 19 (1959): 79-88; Charles E. Lindblom, 'Still Muddling, Not Yet Through,' *Public Administration Review* 39 (1979): 517-26; Michael T. Hayes, *Incrementalism and Public Policy* (New York: Longmans 1992).

23 Frank R. Baumgartner and Bryan D. Jones, *Agendas and Instability in American Politics* (Chicago: University of Chicago Press 1993). See also Frank R. Baumgartner and Bryan D. Jones, 'Agenda Dynamics and Policy Subsystems,' *Journal of Politics* 53 (1991): 1044-74; Patrick Kenis, 'The Pre-Conditions for Policy Networks: Some Findings from a Three Country Study on Industrial Re-Structuring,' in B. Marin and R. Mayntz, eds., *Policy Networks: Empirical Evidence and Theoretical Considerations* (Boulder, CO: Westview Press 1991), 297-330.

24 In the first uses of the term, it was usually argued that each country or jurisdiction had a peculiar pattern of policy-making. However, it was soon pointed out that the concept is more appropriately focused at the sectoral level because distinctive patterns of policy-making were found at that level rather than at the national one. Gary Freeman, 'National Styles and Policy Sectors: Explaining Structured Variation,' *Journal of Public Policy* 5 (1985): 467-96; William D. Coleman, 'Policy Convergence in Banking: A Comparative Study,' *Political Studies* 42 (1994): 274-92.

25 Carolyn Tuohy, *Policy and Politics in Canada: Institutionalized Ambivalence* (Philadelphia: Temple University Press 1992); David Vogel, *National Styles of Regulation: Environment Policy in Great Britain and the United States* (Ithaca, NY: Cornell University Press 1986).

26 Vogel, *National Styles.*

27 This process of policy change has been likened by some authors to the general process of change in scientific communities, a phenomenon associated for decades with major shifts in scientific paradigms. In this sense, the concept of a paradigm owes its modern origin to Thomas Kuhn's work on the nature of scientific learning and the development of scientific theories. In Kuhn's original formulation, the exact contours of a paradigm are unclear, extending from the limited sense of a specific scientific theory about a phenomenon to the more general sense of a prescientific inquisitive *weltanschauung,* or worldview, that allows science to be carried out at all. Margaret Masterman, 'The Nature of a Paradigm,' in I. Lakatos and A. Musgrave, eds., *Criticism and the Growth of Knowledge* (London: Cambridge University Press 1970). In his later works, Kuhn was more specific, arguing that a paradigm is synonymous with the notion of a 'disciplinary matrix.' It is 'what the members of a scientific community, and they alone, share.' Thomas S. Kuhn, 'Second Thoughts on Paradigms,' in Frederick Suppe, ed., *The Structure of Scientific Theories* (Chicago: University of Chicago Press 1974), 463.

28 Peter A. Hall, 'Policy Paradigms, Experts, and the State: The Case of Macroeconomic Policy-Making in Britain,' in S. Brooks and A.-G. Gagnon, eds., *Social Scientists, Policy, and the State* (New York: Praeger 1990), 59.

29 Hank C. Jenkins-Smith, Gilbert K. St. Clair, and Brian Woods, 'Explaining Change in Policy Subsystems: Analysis of Coalition Stability and Defection over Time,' *American Journal of Political Science* 35 (1991): 851-80; Baumgartner and Jones, 'Agenda Dynamics.'

30 The pattern of change associated with shifts in paradigms has elsewhere been termed a 'punctuated equilibrium' model. In this pattern of development, policy change alternates between long periods of stability involving incremental adaptations and brief periods of

revolutionary upheaval. See Gudmund Hernes, 'Structural Change in Social Processes,' *American Journal of Sociology* 82 (1976): 513-47; Connie J.G. Gersick, 'Revolutionary Change Theories: A Multilevel Exploration of the Punctuated Equilibrium Paradigm,' *Academy of Management Review* 16 (1991): 10-36; Jane Jenson, 'Paradigms and Political Discourse: Protective Legislation in France and the United States before 1914,' *Canadian Journal of Political Science* 22 (1989): 235-58.

Chapter 6: Agenda-Setting

1 On the general issues involved in agenda-setting in Canada, see Michael Howlett, 'Issue-Attention and Punctuated Equilibria Models Reconsidered: An Empirical Examination of the Dynamics of Agenda-Setting in Canada,' *Canadian Journal of Political Science* forthcoming 30.1 (1997). See also Stephen Hilgartner and Charles L. Bosk, 'The Rise and Fall of Social Problems: A Public Arenas Model,' *American Journal of Sociology* 94 (1981): 53-78; Joseph W. Schneider, 'Social Problems Theory: The Constructionist View,' *Annual Review of Sociology* 11 (1985): 209-29.

2 Roger W. Cobb and Charles D. Elder, *Participation in American Politics: The Dynamics of Agenda-Building* (Boston: Allyn and Bacon 1972), 12.

3 On the role of royal commissions and inquiries, see the essays contained in A. Paul Pross, Innis Christie, and John A. Yogis, eds., *Commissions of Inquiry* (Toronto: Carswell 1990).

4 On the cyclical nature of some environmental issues, see Anthony Downs, 'Up and Down with Ecology – The "Issue-Attention Cycle,"' *Public Interest* 28 (1972): 38-50.

5 Alan Cawson, 'Pluralism, Corporatism and the Role of the State,' *Government and Opposition* 13.2 (1978): 178-98; William E. Connolly, 'The Challenge to Pluralist Theory,' in W.E. Connolly, ed., *The Bias of Pluralism* (New York: Atherton Press 1969), 3-34; Martin J. Smith, 'Pluralism, Reformed Pluralism and Neopluralism: The Role of Pressure Groups in Policy-Making,' *Political Studies* 38 (1990): 302-22.

6 R. Cobb, J.K. Ross, and M.H. Ross, 'Agenda Building as a Comparative Political Process,' *American Political Science Review* 70 (1976): 126.

7 Carole Pateman, *Participation and Democratic Theory* (Cambridge, UK: Cambridge University Press 1970).

8 See, for example, J.A. Schumpeter, *Capitalism, Socialism, and Democracy* (New York: Harper and Row 1942).

9 R.A. Dahl, *A Preface to Democratic Theory* (Chicago: University of Chicago Press 1956).

10 Phillip Green, *Retrieving Democracy: In Search of Civic Equality* (Totowa, NJ: Rowman and Allanheld 1985); John C. Pierce, Nicholas Lovrich Jr., and Masahiko Matsuoka, 'Support for Citizen Participation: A Comparison of American and Japanese Citizens, Activists and Elites,' *Western Political Quarterly* 43.1 (1990): 39-59.

11 Robert Paehlke, *Environmentalism and the Future of Progressive Politics* (New Haven, CT: Yale University Press 1989).

12 See Kathryn Harrison and George Hoberg, 'Setting the Environmental Agenda in Canada and the United States: The Cases of Dioxin and Radon,' *Canadian Journal of Political Science* 24.1 (1991): 3-27; and Howlett, 'Issue-Attention.'

13 John W. Kingdon, *Agendas, Alternatives and Public Policies* (Boston: Little, Brown 1984), 3-4.

14 Riley E. Dunlap and Kent D. Van Liere, 'Commitment to the Dominant Social Paradigm and Concern for Environmental Quality,' *Social Science Quarterly* 66 (1984): 1013-27.

15 George Altmeyer, 'Three Ideas of Nature in Canada, 1893-1914,' *Journal of Canadian Studies* 11 (1976): 21-36; R.C. Brown, 'The Doctrine of Usefulness: Natural Resource and Natural Park Policy in Canada, 1867-1914,' in J.G. Nelson, ed., *Canadian Parks in Perspective* (Montreal: Harvest House 1970), 46-62; see also the essays contained in M.L. McAllister, ed., *Changing Political Agendas* (Kingston: Queen's University Centre for Resource Studies 1992).

16 John Stewart, *The Canadian House of Commons* (Montreal: McGill-Queen's University Press 1974).

17 J.E. Hodgetts, *The Canadian Public Service: A Physiology of Government 1867-1970* (Toronto: University of Toronto Press 1973).

18 I.D. Thompson, 'The Myth of Integrated Wildlife/Forestry Management,' *Queen's Quarterly* 94 (1987): 609-21.

19 See A. Paul Pross, *Group Politics and Public Policy* (Toronto: Oxford University Press 1992).

20 Maureen A. Molot, 'Public Resource Corporations: Impetus and Evolution,' in N. Bankes and J.O. Saunders, eds., *Public Disposition of Natural Resources* (Calgary: Canadian Institute of Resources Law 1984), 285-305.

21 See, for example, Canadian Pulp and Paper Association, *Response to Challenges and Choices: The Interim Report of the Royal Commission on the Economic Union and Developmental Prospects for Canada* (Montreal: Canadian Pulp and Paper Association 1984), 8. The positions contained in this document parallel those outlined by industry representatives in an extensive questionnaire survey carried out by the Pulp and Paper Research Institute of Canada in the early 1970s. See K.M. Jegr and K.M. Thompson, *The Canadian Pulp and Paper Industry: Threats and Opportunities 1980-1990* (Montreal: Pulp and Paper Research Institute of Canada 1975). More generally, see William D. Coleman, 'Analyzing the Associative Action of Business: Policy Advocacy and Policy Participation,' *Canadian Public Administration* 28 (1985): 413-33; William D. Coleman, *The Emergence of Business Interest Associations in Canada: An Historical Overview* (Montreal: Canadian Political Science Association 1985); William D. Coleman, 'Canadian Business and the State,' in K. Banting, ed., *The State and Economic Interests* (Toronto: University of Toronto Press 1986), 245-89; and William D. Coleman and H.J. Jacek, 'The Roles and Activities of Business Interest Associations in Canada,' *Canadian Journal of Political Science* 16 (1983): 257-80.

22 Martin Robin, *Radical Politics and Canadian Labour 1880-1930* (Kingston: Queen's University Industrial Relations Centre 1968); Charles Lipton, *The Trade Union Movement of Canada 1827-1959* (Montreal: Canadian Social Publications 1967); Irving M. Abella, *Nationalism, Communism, and Canadian Labour: The CIO, the Communist Party and the Canadian Congress of Labour 1935-1956* (Toronto: University of Toronto Press 1973).

23 Wallace Clement, *Hardrock Mining: Industrial Relations and Technological Changes at Inco* (Toronto: McClelland and Stewart 1981); Wallace Clement, *The Struggle to Organize: Resistance in Canada's Fishery* (Toronto: McClelland and Stewart 1986); Wallace Clement, 'Labour in Exposed Sectors: Canada's Resource Economy,' in W. Clement, ed., *The Challenge of Class Analysis* (Ottawa: Carleton University Press 1988), 89-103.

24 Canada, *Directory of Labour Organizations in Canada, 1985* (Ottawa: Department of Labour 1985), 48, 78, 159, 189; and Canada, *Directory of Labour Organizations in Canada 1992/1993* (Ottawa: Supply and Services 1985), 25, 47, 73, 107, 131.

25 Canada, *Directory 1985*, 62-3, 78-9, 182, 222-24. Despite this fragmentation, by 1985 the individual membership figures for the CPU and IWA mean that together they would have comprised the seventh largest union in the country and the third largest industrial union, following only the three large public service unions, the Canadian Union of Public Employees (CUPE), the National Union of Provincial Government Employees (NUPGE), and the Public Service Alliance (PSA); the service-oriented United Food and Commercial Workers International Union; and the Industrial United Steelworkers of America and United Auto Workers (UAW) – now Canadian Auto Workers (CAW). Canada, *Directory 1985*, xxii-iii.

26 Douglas A. Hibbs Jr., 'On the Political Economy of Long-Run Trends in Strike Activity,' *British Journal of Political Science* 8 (1978): 153-75; R. Lacroix, 'Strike Activity in Canada,' in W.C. Riddell, ed., *Canadian Labour Relations* (Toronto: University of Toronto Press 1986).

27 Smith, 'Pluralism'; Connolly, 'Challenge.'

28 H. Chapin and D. Deneau, *Access and the Policy-Making Process* (Ottawa: Canadian Council on Social Development 1978). The degree of public participation has been widely debated. Barry Sadler, 'Basic Issues in Public Participation: A Background Perspective,' in B. Sadler, ed., *Involvement and Environment: Proceedings of the Canadian Conference on Public Participation* (Edmonton: Environment Council of Alberta, 1978).

29 World Commission on Environment and Economy, *Our Common Future* (Oxford: Oxford University Press 1987).

30 The construction of this particular 'policy image,' or the perception of a policy problem, is significant because of the way that it interacts with membership in relevant policy subsystems. As Baumgartner and Jones argue, 'When they are portrayed as technical problems rather than as social questions, experts can dominate the decision-making process. When the ethical, social, or political implications of such policies assume center stage, a much broader range of participants can suddenly become involved.' Frank R. Baumgartner and Bryan D. Jones, 'Agenda Dynamics and Policy Subsystems,' *Journal of Politics* 53 (1991): 1047.

31 Ronald Inglehart, *The Silent Revolution* (Princeton, NJ: Princeton University Press 1977); Ronald Inglehart, 'Post-Materialism in an Environment of Insecurity,' *American Political Science Review* 75 (1981): 880-900; Ronald Inglehart, *Culture Shift in Advanced Industrial Society* (Princeton, NJ: Princeton University Press 1990).

32 Stephen F. Cotgrove, *Catastrophe or Cornucopia: The Environment, Politics, and the Future* (Chichester, UK: John Wiley & Sons 1982); R.E. Dunlap and K.D. Van Liere, 'The New Environmental Paradigm: A Proposed Measuring Instrument and Preliminary Results,' *Journal of Environmental Education* 9 (1978): 10-19.

33 H. Bakvis and N. Nevitte, 'The Greening of the Canadian Electorate: Environmentalism, Ideology and Partisanship,' in R. Boardman, ed., *Canadian Environmental Policy: Ecosystems, Politics and Process* (Toronto: Oxford University Press 1992), 144-63; Paehlke, *Environmentalism*.

34 F.H. Buttel, 'New Directions in Environmental Sociology,' *Annual Review of Sociology* 13 (1987): 465-88.

35 R. Jones and R.E. Dunlap, 'The Social Bases of Environmental Concern: Have They Changed over Time?' *Rural Sociology* 57.1 (1992): 28-47.

36 Bakvis and Nevitte, 'Greening.' This decline was not replicated in all jurisdictions, however. See Donald E. Blake, Neil Guppy, and Peter Urmetzer, 'Being Green in B.C.: Public Attitudes towards Environmental Issues,' working paper, Fraser Basin Eco-Research Study, University of British Columbia, Vancouver, January 1996.

37 R. Peter Gillis and Thomas R. Roach, *Lost Initiatives: Canada's Forest Industries, Forest Policy, and Forest Conservation* (New York: Greenwood Press 1986); B.W. Hodgins, J. Benidickson, and P. Gillis, 'The Ontario and Quebec Experiments in Forest Reserves,' *Journal of Forest History* 26 (1982): 20-33; M.W. Bucovetsky, 'The Mining Industry and the Great Tax Reform Debate,' in A. Pross, ed., *Pressure Group Behavior in Canadian Politics* (Toronto: McGraw-Hill Ryerson 1975).

38 Doug Macdonald, *The Politics of Pollution: Why Canadians Are Failing Their Environment* (Toronto: McClelland and Stewart 1991), 31-2.

39 Cf. Lorna Stefanick, 'The Green Wave: Canada's Environmental Lobby,' paper presented at the Canadian Political Science Association meeting, Calgary, 1994; and Laurie Adkin, 'Counter-Hegemony and Environmental Politics in Canada,' in W.K. Carroll, ed., *Organizing Dissent: Contemporary Social Movements in Theory and Practice* (Toronto: Garamond 1992), 135-56.

40 Frederick H. Buttel, 'Social Science and the Environment: Competing Theories,' *Social Science Quarterly* 57 (1976): 307-23; Johan Galtung, 'The Green Movement: A Socio-Historical Exploration,' *International Sociology* 1 (1986): 75-90; Philip Lowe and Jane Goyder, *Environmental Groups in Politics* (London: Allen and Unwin 1983); Claus Offe, 'Challenging the Boundaries of Institutional Politics: Social Movements since the 1960s,' in C.S. Maier, ed., *Changing Boundaries of the Political: Essays on the Evolving Balance between the State and Society, Public and Private in Europe* (Cambridge, UK: Cambridge University Press 1987), 63-105; F. Sandbach, 'A Further Look at the Environment as a Political Issue,' *International Journal of Environmental Studies* 12.2 (1978): 99-110; Allan Schnaiberg, *The Environment: From Surplus to Scarcity* (New York: Oxford University Press 1980). See also Lester W. Milbrath, 'Environmental Beliefs and Values,' in M.G. Hermann, ed., *Political Psychology* (San Francisco: Jossey-Bass 1986), 97-138.

41 Leslie Pal, *Interests of State* (Montreal: McGill-Queen's University Press 1994).

42 See Lorna Stefanick, 'From Protest to Participation: A Comparison of Environmental Activism in B.C. and Ontario,' paper presented at the Annual Meeting of the Canadian Political Science Association, Montreal, 1995.
43 Blake, Guppy, and Urmetzer, 'Being Green.'
44 Bakvis and Nevitte, 'Greening,' 163.
45 Jeremy Wilson, 'Green Lobbies: Pressure Groups and Environmental Policy,' in R. Boardman, ed., *Canadian Environmental Policy: Ecosystems, Politics, and Process* (Toronto: Oxford University Press 1992), 110-11.
46 Ibid., 116.
47 Ibid., 109.
48 Liora Salter, Debra Slaco, and Karin Konstantynowicz, *Public Inquiries in Canada* (Ottawa: Science Council of Canada 1981).
49 Thomas Berger, *Northern Frontier, Northern Homeland: The Report of the Mackenzie Valley Pipeline Inquiry*, Vol. 1 (Ottawa: Supply and Services 1977).
50 Sadler, 'Basic Issues,' 8.
51 British Columbia, Commission on Resources and Environment, *Annual Report to British Columbia Legislative Assembly* (Victoria: Commission on Resources and Environment 1993), 8.
52 Ibid.
53 Michael Howlett, 'The Round Table Experience: Representation and Legitimacy in Canadian Environmental Policy Making,' *Queen's Quarterly* 97 (1990): 580-601.
54 At least two distinct methods of selection were utilized in creating Canadian round tables. One method was completely closed to public input. The other method was fairly open and involved some effort at public involvement. Although the actual selection of nominees was always a closed process involving only senior government ministers and officials, in several instances direct public involvement in the nomination process was pursued. In several cases, public consultation on round table structure was also solicited through the use of task forces on environment and economy.
55 Bruce Mitchell and Richard Turkheim, 'Environmental Impact Assessments: Principles, Practices and Canadian Experiences,' in R.R. Kreuger and B. Mitchell, eds., *Managing Canada's Renewable Resources* (Toronto: Methuen 1977).
56 Pross, Christie, and Yogis, eds., *Commissions*.
57 Alistair Lucas, 'Fundamental Prerequisites for Citizen Participation,' in B. Sadler, ed., *Involvement and Environment* (Edmonton: Environment Council of Alberta 1978), 43-57.
58 Natalie Minunzie, 'The Chain-Saw Revolution: Environmental Activism in British Columbia,' MA thesis, Simon Fraser University, 1993.
59 Kenneth Engelhart and Michael Trebilcock, *Public Participation in the Regulatory Process: The Issue of Funding*, Working Paper No. 17 (Ottawa: Economic Council of Canada 1981).
60 Terry M. Moe, *The Organization of Interests: Incentives and the Internal Dynamics of Political Interest Groups* (Chicago: University of Chicago Press 1980); Mancur Olson, *The Logic of Collective Action: Public Goods and the Theory of Groups* (Cambridge, MA: Harvard University Press 1965); Mancur Olson, 'A Theory of the Incentives Facing Political Organizations: Neo-Corporatism and the Hegemonic State,' *International Political Science Review* 7.2 (1986): 165-89.
61 Engelhart and Trebilcock, *Public Participation*.
62 Lucas, 'Fundamental Prerequisites.'
63 Engelhart and Trebilcock, *Public Participation*.
64 Melody Hessing, 'Production of the Public Voice: Public Participation in the Hearing Process as Contemporary Democracy,' doctoral dissertation, University of British Columbia, 1984, 166.
65 British Columbia, *Royal Commission of Inquiry into Uranium Mining, Proceedings*, Vol. 4, (Victoria: Queen's Printer 1979), 422-3.
66 Roger W. Cobb and Charles D. Elder, *Participation in American Politics: The Dynamics of Agenda-Building* (Boston: Allyn and Bacon 1972), 85.
67 Cobb, Ross, and Ross, 'Agenda Building,' 127.
68 Ibid., 132.

69 Ibid.
70 Ibid., 135.
71 Ibid., 136.
72 Later analyses have shown that a fourth model of agenda-setting also exists, one in which governments may simply act on high levels of public concern, without the need for such concern to be formally articulated by groups through an outside initiation process. This fourth model of agenda-setting has been termed a *consolidation* pattern. M. Howlett and M. Ramesh, *Studying Public Policy: Policy Cycles and Policy Subsystems* (Toronto: Oxford University Press 1995). Given an acute environmental event, such as the Exxon Valdez spill, we would expect a direct response from government to deal with the crisis and to prevent further episodes, reflecting its ability to simply consolidate public sentiment in special cases.
73 For examples of the application of this model to resource and environmental issues in Canada and elsewhere, see Duncan K. MacLellan, 'The Domestic Politics of the Federal-Provincial Eastern Canada Acid Rain Control Programme: A Case Study of Agenda-Building,' paper presented at the Annual Meeting of the Canadian Political Science Association, Calgary, 1994; and Leslie R. Alm and Charles Davis, 'Agenda-Setting and Acid Precipitation in the United States,' *Environmental Management* 17 (1992): 807-16.
74 Peter J. May, 'Reconsidering Policy Design: Policies and Publics,' *Journal of Public Policy* 11.2 (1991): 187-206.
75 Frank R. Baumgartner and Bryan D. Jones, 'Agenda Dynamics and Policy Subsystems,' *Journal of Politics* 53 (1991): 1044-74; Frank R. Baumgartner and Bryan D. Jones, *Agendas and Instability in American Politics* (Chicago: University of Chicago Press 1993); Frank R. Baumgartner and Bryan D. Jones, 'Attention, Boundary Effects, and Large-Scale Policy Change in Air Transportation Policy,' in D.A. Rochefort and R.W. Cobb, eds., *The Politics of Problem Definition: Shaping the Policy Agenda* (Lawrence: University of Kansas Press 1994).
76 Paehlke, *Environmentalism;* Robert Paehlke, 'Democracy and Environmentalism: Opening a Door to the Administrative State,' in Paehlke and Torgerson, eds., *Managing Leviathan.*
77 C.G. Morley, *The Legal Framework for Public Participation in Canadian Water Management* (Burlington, ON: Inland Waters Directorate, Ontario Region, Water Planning and Management Branch 1975), 73.

Chapter 7: Policy Formulation
1 Although most use of the concept of a policy subsystem is of recent origin, the term itself dates to the mid-1950s. See, for example, J. Leiper Freeman, *The Political Process: Executive Bureau-Legislative Committee Relations* (New York: Random House 1955).
2 Nikolas Zahariadis and Christopher S. Allen, 'Ideas, Networks and Policy Streams: Privatization in Britain and Germany,' *Policy Studies Review* 14.1-2 (1995): 71-98.
3 Charles O. Jones, *An Introduction to the Study of Public Policy* (Monterey, CA: Brooks/Cole 1984), 78.
4 Ralph K. Huitt, 'Political Feasibility,' in Austin Rannay, ed., *Political Science and Public Policy* (Chicago: Markham Publishing 1968).
5 British Columbia, Commission on Resources and Environment, *Annual Report to the British Columbia Legislative Assembly* (Victoria: Commission on Resources and Environment 1993), 11.
6 The rationale of public involvement is extended by some political theorists beyond an instrumental approach – geared to producing better decisions – to include civic and community benefits. As an educational tool, more direct and decentralized forms of decision-making would contribute to community cohesion, produce a well-informed electorate, and foster an environmentally informed citizenry. Participation in arenas such as consultative tribunals would not only educate citizens in the substantive areas of concern, such as pesticide hearings, but also teach them about the functions and processes of state agencies and environmental law. The expressive effects of participation further contribute to the development of individuals' capabilities of self-expression. See also Dorothy Nelkin, *Controversy: Politics of Technical Decisions* (Beverly Hills: Sage 1979).

7 David M. Lenny, 'The Case for Funding Citizen Participation in the Administrative Process,' *Administrative Law Review* 28 (1978): 491.
8 J.W. Parlour and S. Schatzow, 'The Mass Media and Public Concern for Environmental Problems in Canada 1960-72,' *International Journal of Environmental Studies* 13 (1978): 14.
9 Kathyrn Harrison, 'Environmental Protection in British Columbia: Postmaterial Values, Organized Interests and Party Politics,' in R.K. Carty, ed., *Politics, Policy and Government in British Columbia* (Vancouver: University of British Columbia Press 1996), 290-309.
10 Vaughan Lyon, 'The Reluctant Party: Ideology versus Organization in Canada's Green Movement,' *Alternatives* 12 (1985-6): 3-9.
11 Vaughan Lyon, 'Green Politics: Political Parties, Elections, and Environmental Policy,' in Boardman, ed., *Canadian Environmental Policy*.
12 By the 1980s, the CPPA represented the interests of sixty-four companies in the Canadian pulp and paper industry. Canadian Pulp and Paper Association, *Reference Tables* (Montreal: Canadian Pulp and Paper Association, various years).
13 See William D. Coleman, 'The Emergence of Business Interest Association in Canada: An Historical Overview,' paper presented at the Canadian Political Science Association, Montreal, 1985; and William D. Coleman, *Business and Politics: A Study of Collective Action* (Montreal: McGill-Queen's Press 1988), 144-71.
14 The first national association, the Canadian Forest Industries Council, was formed in 1983 as a federation of provincial associations to oppose threatened US countervailing tariffs against Canadian softwood lumber imports. For a list of the member associations at the time of its formation, see Canadian Forest Industries Council, *Canadian Forest Industries 1986 Data Book* (Ottawa: Canadian Forest Industries Council 1986), I.
15 In the mid-1980s, provincial associations included the New Brunswick Forest Products Association, the Nova Scotia Forest Products Association, the Quebec Forest Industries Association, the Quebec Lumber Manufacturers Association, the Ontario Lumber Manufacturers Association, the Ontario Forest Industries Association, the Alberta Forest Products Association, the Interior (BC) Lumber Manufacturers Association, the Cariboo Lumber Manufacturers Association (BC), the Council of Forest Industries of British Columbia – Northern Interior Lumber Section, and the Council of Forest Industries of British Columbia. Manufacturers of various wood products have also formed associations in several provinces, as have truck loggers and businesses involved in retail and wholesale lumber operations.
16 P. Kumar, 'Union Growth in Canada: Retrospect and Prospect,' in W.C. Riddell, ed., *Canadian Labour Relations* (Toronto: University of Toronto Press 1986), 95-160.
17 R.D. Brown, 'The Fight over Resource Profits,' *Canadian Tax Journal* 22 (1974): 315-37.
18 L. Copithorne, 'Natural Resources and Regional Disparities: A Skeptical View,' *Canadian Public Policy* 5.2 (1979): 181-94.
19 See David M. Olson and Michael L. Mezey, 'Parliaments and Public Policy,' in D.M. Olson and M.L. Mezey, eds., *Legislatures in the Policy Process: The Dilemmas of Economic Policy* (Cambridge, UK: Cambridge University Press 1991), 1-24.
20 C.E.S. Franks, *The Parliament of Canada* (Toronto: University of Toronto Press 1987). For an example of the problems parliamentary committees contend with in attempting to influence government policies, see Robert Matas, 'Environment Must Come First, Caccia Insists: Committees' Proposals for Protection Viewed by Some as Threat to Investment Climate,' *Globe and Mail* (19 October 1995): A17; and Robert Matas, 'Bureaucrats Pan MPs' Environmental Law Proposals: Committee's Recommendations Are Bad Science Potentially Costly to Business and Government, Officials Say,' *Globe and Mail* (16 October 1995): A7.
21 Leslie Pal, *Interests of State* (Montreal: McGill-Queen's University Press 1994); Sandra Burt, 'Canadian Women's Groups in the 1980s: Organizational Development and Policy Influence,' *Canadian Public Policy* 16.1 (1990): 17-28 .
22 Herman Bakvis and David MacDonald, 'The Canadian Cabinet: Organization, Decision-Rules, and Policy Impact,' in M. Michael Atkinson, ed., *Governing Canada: Institutions and Public Policy* (Toronto: Harcourt Brace Jovanovich 1993).

23 Calvin Sandborn and Bill Andrews, 'Pulp Mill Decision Is a Disaster,' *Vancouver Sun* (20 December 1990): A11, as cited in West Coast Environmental Law Research Foundation, Newsletter (21 January 1991): 3.
24 Ibid.
25 R.F. Adie and G. Thomas, *Canadian Public Administration: Problematical Perspectives* (Scarborough, ON: Prentice-Hall 1987); K. Kernaghan, 'Power, Parliament and Public Servants in Canada: Ministerial Responsibility Reexamined,' *Canadian Public Policy* 5 (1979): 383-96; K. Kernaghan, 'The Public and Public Servant in Canada,' in K. Kernaghan, ed., *Public Administration in Canada: Selected Readings* (Toronto: Methuen 1985), 323-30.
26 See A. Pross, 'Canadian Pressure Groups in the 1970s: Their Role and Their Relations with the Public Service,' *Canadian Public Administration* 18 (1975): 121-35.
27 O. Dwivedi, ed., *The Administrative State in Canada* (Toronto: University of Toronto Press 1982).
28 On the perceptions of government officials, see Scott Bennett and Margaret McPhail, 'Policy Process Perceptions of Senior Canadian Federal Civil Servants: A View of the State and Its Environment,' *Canadian Public Administration* 35 (1992): 299-316.
29 Questionnaires were sent to 129 environmental groups, 131 corporations, 220 labour unions, and seventy-seven Native groups selected on the basis of their size and stability to ensure coverage of the largest and most long-standing members of this community. To qualify for the survey, environmental groups had to have more than five members and a permanent mailing address over the past year. All Canadian publicly held corporations that had over $30 million in profits were polled, as were Canadian labour unions with over 2,500 members. The seventy-seven long-established aboriginal tribal councils located across the country were used to gauge Native concerns. By 1 January 1991, 238 responses – providing a 44 per cent response rate – had been received. The surveys elicited responses in a number of areas, including general information about the group – its location, resources, structure, and so forth; its views on the principle of sustainable development; and its general conception of the environmental problems that society faces. See Jim Bruton and Michael Howlett, 'Differences of Opinion: Round Tables, Policy Networks and the Failure of Canadian Environmental Strategy,' *Alternatives* 19 (1992): 25.
30 Andrew S. McFarland, 'Interest Groups and Theories of Power in America,' *British Journal of Political Science* 17.2 (1987): 129-47.
31 The divisions within the environmental movement in terms of overall goals have often been commented upon. The most significant divisions correspond to conflicts between conservationists and preservationists, anthropocentric and biocentric worldviews, deep and shallow ecologists, and materialists and postmaterialists. Other divisions, of course, exist between feminist and socialist environmentalism and ecologism. See Volkmar Lauber, 'Ecology, Politics and Liberal Democracy,' *Government and Opposition* 13.2 (1978): 199-217; Tim Luke, 'The Dreams of Deep Ecology,' *Telos* 76 (1988): 65-92; H.M. Enzensberger, 'A Critique of Political Ecology,' *New Left Review* 84 (1974): 3-31; Ronald Inglehart, *The Silent Revolution* (Princeton, NJ: Princeton University Press 1977); Ronald Inglehart, 'Post-Materialism in an Environment of Insecurity,' *American Political Science Review* 75 (1981): 880-900; N. Watts and G. Wandesforde-Smith, 'Postmaterial Values and Environmental Policy Change,' in D.E. Mann, ed., *Environmental Policy Formation* (Lexington, MA: Lexington Books 1981), 29-42.
32 Jeremy Wilson, 'Wilderness Politics in B.C.,' in W.D. Coleman and G. Skogstad, eds., *Policy Communities and Public Policy in Canada: A Structural Approach* (Mississauga, ON: Copp Clark Pitman 1990), 143.
33 Peter H. Pearse, 'Reconciling Competing Demands on Resources,' in N. Bankes and J.O. Saunders, eds., *Public Disposition of Natural Resources* (Calgary: Canadian Institute of Resources Law 1984), 343-54.
34 Richard England and Barry Bluestone, 'Ecology and Social Conflict,' in H.E. Daly, ed., *Toward a Steady-State Economy* (San Francisco: W.H. Freeman 1973), 190-214; N. Wengert, 'Citizen Participation: Practice in Search of a Theory,' in A.E. Utton, ed., *Natural Resources for a Democratic Society: Public Participation in Decision-Making* (Boulder, CO: Westview Press

1976), 23-40; Norman I. Wengert, *Natural Resources and the Political Struggle* (New York: Random House 1955).

35 H.G. Thorburn, *Planning and the Economy: Building Federal-Provincial Consensus* (Toronto: Lorimer 1984).

36 Philipe C. Schmitter, 'Interest Intermediation and Regime Governability in Western Europe and North America,' in S. Berger, ed., *Organizing Interests in Western Europe* (Cambridge, UK: Cambridge University Press 1983), 287-330.

37 Paul A. Sabatier, 'Knowledge, Policy-Oriented Learning, and Policy Change,' *Knowledge: Creation, Diffusion, Utilization* 8 (1987): 649-92; Paul A. Sabatier, 'An Advocacy Coalition Framework of Policy Change and the Role of Policy-Oriented Learning Therein,' *Policy Sciences* 21.2-3 (1988): 129-68.

38 Peter M. Haas, 'Introduction: Epistemic Communities and International Policy Coordination,' *International Organization* 46 (1992): 1-36.

39 Coleman and Skogstad, eds., *Policy Communities;* Bernd Marin and Renate Mayntz, eds., *Policy Networks: Empirical Evidence and Theoretical Considerations* (Boulder, CO: Westview Press 1991); A. Paul Pross, *Group Politics and Public Policy* (Toronto: Oxford University Press 1992).

40 Timothy J. Farnham and Paul Mohai, 'A Shift in Values: Non-Commodity Resource Management and the Forest Service,' *Policy Studies Journal* 23 (1995): 268-80.

41 On the notion of a policy paradigm or typical pattern of policy discourse, see Jane Jenson, 'Paradigms and Political Discourse: Protective Legislation in France and the United States before 1914,' *Canadian Journal of Political Science* 22 (1989): 235-58; Peter A. Hall, 'Policy Paradigms, Experts, and the State: The Case of Macroeconomic Policy-Making in Britain,' in S. Brooks and A.G. Gagnon, eds., *Social Scientists, Policy, and the State* (New York: Praeger 1990), 53-78.

42 Robert G. Healy and William Ascher, 'Knowledge in the Policy Process: Incorporating Environmental Information in the Natural Resources Policy Making,' *Policy Sciences* 28 (1995): 1-19.

Chapter 8: Decision-Making

1 Garry Brewer and Peter DeLeon, *The Foundations of Policy Analysis* (Homewood, IL: Dorsey Press 1983), 179.

2 Margaret Weir, 'Ideas and the Politics of Bounded Innovation,' in S. Steinmo, K. Thelen, and F. Longstreth, eds., *Structuring Politics: Historical Institutionalism in Comparative Analysis* (Cambridge, UK: Cambridge University Press 1992), 188-216.

3 Elizabeth May, 'Political Realities,' in Monte Hummel, ed., *Endangered Spaces: The Future for Canada's Wilderness* (Toronto: Key Porter Books 1989), 84.

4 Anthony Cahill and E. Sam Overman, 'The Evolution of Rationality in Policy Analysis,' in Stuart S. Nagel, ed., *Policy Theory and Policy Evaluation* (New York: Greenwood Press 1990), 11-28; Herbert A. Simon, 'Proverbs of Administration,' *Public Administration Review* 6 (1946): 53-67; Herbert A. Simon, 'A Behavioral Model of Rational Choice,' *Quarterly Journal of Economics* 69 (1955): 99-118; Herbert A. Simon, *Administrative Behavior: A Study of Decision-Making Processes in Administrative Organization* (New York: Macmillan 1957); Herbert A. Simon, *Models of Man, Social and Rational: Mathematical Essays on Rational Human Behavior in a Social Setting* (New York: Wiley 1957).

5 The rational model argues that decisions are based on objective assessments of alternative options and that the most efficient, predictable, and scientifically based option is selected. The incremental model recognizes that policy options reflect pragmatic factors, which include organizational, ideological, and practical constraints, as well as actors' past experiences. Decisions would thus be expected to reflect prior knowledge or experience and to be subject to identified organizational constraints. An incremental model would tend to follow past experience. David Braybrooke and Charles Lindblom, *A Strategy of Decision: Policy Evaluation as a Social Process* (New York: Free Press of Glencoe 1963); Charles E. Lindblom, 'The Science of Muddling Through,' *Public Administration Review* 19 (1959): 79-88. The mainstream position in public administration was that, while the

rational model was preferable in theory, the incremental model best described the actual practice of decision-making in governments.

6 Gilbert Smith and David May, 'The Artificial Debate between Rationalist and Incrementalist Models of Decision-Making,' *Policy and Politics* 8 (1980): 147-61; Yehezkel Dror, *Public Policymaking Re-Examined* (San Francisco: Chandler 1968); Amitai Etzioni, 'Mixed-Scanning: A "Third" Approach to Decision-Making,' *Public Administration Review* 27 (1967): 385-92.

7 See, for example, the 'irrational' model proposed by March and Olsen and others. M. Cohen, J. March, and J. Olsen, 'A Garbage Can Model of Organizational Choice,' *Administrative Science Quarterly* 17.1 (1972): 1-25.

8 John Forester, 'Bounded Rationality and the Politics of Muddling Through,' *Public Administration Review* 44 (1984): 23-31; John Forester, *Planning in the Face of Power* (Berkeley: University of California Press 1989).

9 Forester, 'Bounded Rationality,' 23.

10 Ibid., 25.

11 Ibid.

12 Notable exceptions include M.W. Bucovetsky, 'The Mining Industry and the Great Tax Reform Debate,' in A. Pross, ed., *Pressure Group Behavior in Canadian Politics* (Toronto: McGraw-Hill Ryerson 1975), 89-114; Bruce W. Hodgins and Jamie Benidickson, *The Temagami Experience: Recreation, Resources and Aboriginal Rights in the Northern Ontario Wilderness* (Toronto: University of Toronto Press 1989); Elizabeth E. May, *Paradise Won: The Struggle for South Moresby* (Toronto: McClelland and Stewart 1990); Ian Urquhart and Larry Pratt, *The Last Great Forest* (Edmonton: NeWest Press 1994); and Larry Pratt, *The Tar Sands* (Edmonton: Hurtig 1973).

13 Albeit with the majority of this period (1984-93) under Conservative rule. While the prior Liberal administration (1968-79; 1980-4) promised a variety of environmental actions, as Doern and Conway note, 'Trudeau's legacy on the environment could be viewed as initial support followed in short order by retrenchment and lack of interest in the face of economic and constitutional concerns.' G. Bruce Doern and Thomas Conway, *The Greening of Canada: Federal Institutions and Decisions* (Toronto: University of Toronto Press 1994), 201.

14 Ibid., 191.

15 Ibid., 192. See also Donald J. Savoie, *Regional Economic Development: Canada's Search for Solutions* (Toronto: University of Toronto Press 1986).

16 George Hoberg, 'Sleeping with an Elephant: The American Influence on Canadian Environmental Regulation,' *Journal of Public Policy* 11 (1991): 107-31; George Hoberg, 'Environmental Policy: Alternative Styles,' in M.M. Atkinson, ed., *Governing Canada: Institutions and Public Policy* (Toronto: Harcourt Brace Jovanovich 1993), 307-42.

17 The power of initiative for conducting assessments was allocated to sectoral departments rather than centralized under Environment Canada, and this allocation perpetuated the fragmentation of environmental protection and deterred agreement on legal provisions for assessment. Thomas Meredith, 'Assessing Environmental Impacts in Canada,' in Bruce Mitchell, ed., *Resource and Environmental Management in Canada: Addressing Conflict and Uncertainty* (Toronto: Oxford University Press 1995), 335-59.

18 Ted Schrecker, 'The Canadian Environmental Assessment Act: Tremulous Step Forward, or Retreat into Smoke and Mirrors?' *Canadian Environmental Law Reports* 5 (1991): 192-246.

19 Ted Schrecker, 'Of Invisible Beasts and the Public Interest: Environmental Cases and the Judicial System,' in R. Boardman, ed., *Canadian Environmental Policy: Ecosystems, Politics and Process* (Toronto: Oxford University Press 1992), 83-105.

20 Peter Jacobs, Peter Mulvihill, and Barry Sadler, 'Environmental Assessment: Current Challenges and Future Prospects,' in S.A. Kennett, ed., *Law and Process in Environmental Management* (Calgary: Canadian Institute for Resources Law 1993), 13-27.

21 *Environmental Assessment and Review Process Guidelines Order*, SOR/84/867 (21 June 1984), s. 3.

22 *Canada Wildlife Federation Inc.* v. *Minister of the Environment*, 287 CELR 3 1989.

23 Roger Cotton and Kelley M. MacKinnon, 'An Overview of Environmental Law in Canada,' in G. Thompson, M.L. McConnell, and L.B. Huestis, eds., *Environmental Law and Business in Canada* (Aurora, ON: Canada Law Books 1993), 1-30.

24 *Friends of the Oldman River Society* v. *The Queen in Right of Alberta et al.*, 1 DLR 88 1992.

25 See Schrecker, 'Canadian Environmental Assessment Act,' 192. See also Joseph de Pencier, 'The Federal Environmental Assessment Process: A Practical Comparison of the EARP Guidelines Order and the Canadian Environmental Assessment Act,' *Journal of Environmental Law and Practice* 3 (1993): 329-43.

26 Cotton and MacKinnon, 'Overview,' 16.

27 Canada, Federal Environmental Assessment Review Office, 'List of Major Projects Requiring a Comprehensive Study,' discussion draft, June 1991.

28 Robert Bartlett, 'Ecological Reason in Administration: Environmental Impact Assessment and Administrative Theory,' in R. Paehlke and D. Torgerson, eds., *Managing Leviathan: Environmental Politics and the Administrative State* (Peterborough: Broadview Press 1990), 81-96.

29 Alistair R. Lucas, 'Jurisdictional Disputes: Is "Equivalency" a Workable Solution?' in D. Tingley, ed., *Into the Future: Environmental Law and Policy for the 1990s* (Edmonton: Environmental Law Centre 1990), 25-36.

30 See Steven Kennett, 'Inter-Jurisdictional Harmonization of Environmental Assessment in Canada,' in Kennett, ed., *Law and Process*, 277-318; Steven A. Kennett, 'Hard Law, Soft Law and Diplomacy: The Emerging Paradigm for Intergovernmental Co-Operation in Environmental Assessment,' *Alberta Law Review* 31 (1993): 644-61; and Kathyrn Harrison, 'Prospects for Intergovernmental Harmonization in Environmental Policy,' in D. Brown and J. Hiebert, eds., *Canada: The State of the Federation 1994* (Kingston: Queen's University Institute of Intergovernmental Relations 1995), 179-99.

31 *Environmental Assessment Act,* RSO (1990): c.e. 18.

32 Cotton and MacKinnon, 'Overview.'

33 Alberta energy projects are exempt from the provisions of the Alberta Environmental Protection and Enhancement Act, and the act gives considerable discretion to provincial administrators regarding assessment procedures. See Steven A. Kennett, 'Environmental Assessment in Alberta Meets the Rule of Law,' *Resources* 52 (1995): 5-8.

34 West Coast Environmental Law Research Foundation, Newsletter (9 June 1995): 4.

35 Steven A. Kennett, 'The Environmental Management Framework Agreement: Reforming Federalism in Post-Referendum Canada,' *Resources* 52 (1995): 1-5.

36 While the sector is composed of a variety of industries, it is overwhelmingly dominated by three multi-billion-dollar-a-year industries. The softwood lumber industry produces a variety of products, but its main commodity is dimension lumber destined for North American residential construction. The market pulp industry provides a variety of specialized chemical and mechanical pulps for paper and paperboard manufacture. The largest single subsector, and the most export reliant, is the Canadian newsprint industry, which ships the bulk of its production to markets in the United States. Canadian Forest Industries Council, *Canadian Forest Industries Data Book* (Ottawa: Canadian Forest Industries Council, various years); Canadian Pulp and Paper Association, *Reference Tables* (Montreal: Canadian Pulp and Paper Association, various years); Donald J. Savoie, *Regional Economic Development: Canada's Search for Solutions* (Toronto: University of Toronto Press 1986); United Nations Food and Agricultural Organization, *Yearbook of Forest Products* (Rome: United Nations Food and Agricultural Organization, various years).

37 Frank Oberle and Warren Everson, *The Green Ghetto: Can We Save Canadian Forestry?* (Ottawa: Mimeo 1983).

38 Michael Howlett, 'The 1987 National Forest Sector Strategy and the Search for a Federal Role in Canadian Forest Policy,' *Canadian Public Administration* 32.4 (1989): 545-63.

39 See Canada, *A Forest Sector Strategy for Canada* (Ottawa: Ministry of the Environment, 1981).

40 Canadian Council of Forest Ministers, *Report on the Canadian Forestry Forums, 1985-1986* (Ottawa: Canadian Council of Forest Ministers 1986).

41 Howlett, 'National Forest Sector Strategy.'

42 This fate was similar to that of earlier federal efforts, notably the 1981 Liberal plan. See Ibid.

43 Doern and Conway, *Greening of Canada*; G. Bruce Doern, 'Getting It Green: Canadian Environmental Policy in the 1990s,' in G.B. Doern, ed., *The Environmental Imperative: Market Approaches to the Greening of Canada* (Toronto: C.D. Howe Institute 1990), 1-18; G. Bruce Doern, *Getting It Green: Case Studies in Canadian Environmental Regulation* (Toronto: C.D. Howe Institute 1990); G. Bruce Doern, 'Johnny-Green-Latelies: The Mulroney Environmental Record,' in F. Abele, ed., *How Ottawa Spends 1992-93: The Politics of Competitiveness* (Ottawa: Carleton University Press 1992), 353-76.

44 As part of a federal-provincial effort at environmental coordination, the federal government created the round table to usher in a new process of multistakeholder consultation. Canadian Council of Resource and Environment Ministers, *Report of the National Task Force on Environment and Economy* (Ottawa: Supply and Services 1987); National Task Force on Environment and Economy, *Progress Report of the National Task Force on Environment and Economy* (Toronto: Canadian Council of Resource and Environment Ministers 1988).

45 The Green Plan process was a major policy planning exercise that included multiple public consultations and other mechanisms for public input. See Canada, *Canada's Green Plan for a Healthy Environment* (Ottawa: Supply and Services 1990).

46 Glen Toner, 'The Green Plan: From Great Expectations to Eco-Backtracking ... to Revitalization?' in S.D. Phillips, ed., *How Ottawa Spends 1994-95: Making Change* (Ottawa: Carleton University Press 1994), 229-60.

47 George Hoberg and Kathyrn Harrison, 'It's Not Easy Being Green: The Politics of Canada's Green Plan,' *Canadian Public Policy* 20.2 (1994): 119-37; Michael Howlett, 'The Round Table Experience: Representation and Legitimacy in Canadian Environmental Policy Making,' *Queen's Quarterly* 97 (1990): 580-601. On the international initiatives, see Peter Jacobs and D.A. Munro, eds., *Conservation with Equity: Strategies for Sustainable Development* (Cambridge, UK: International Union for the Conservation of Nature and Natural Resources 1987); and World Commission on Environment and Development, *Our Common Future* (Oxford: Oxford University Press 1987).

48 On the first generation, see Doug Macdonald, *The Politics of Pollution: Why Canadians Are Failing Their Environment* (Toronto: McClelland and Stewart 1991); and John Swaigen, 'Environmental Law 1975-1980,' *Ottawa Law Review* 12 (1980): 439-88.

49 At the federal level, see Doern and Conway, *Greening of Canada*, 209. The significance of these constraints has also been noted at the provincial level. See Mark S. Winfield, 'The Ultimate Horizontal Issue: The Environmental Policy Experience of Alberta and Ontario 1971-1993,' *Canadian Journal of Political Science* 27.1 (1994): 129-52.

50 On these constraints, see Evert A. Lindquist, 'What do Decision Models Tell Us about Information Use?' *Knowledge in Society* 1.2 (1988): 86-111; David A. Rochefort and Roger W. Cobb, 'Problem Definition, Agenda Access, and Policy Choice,' *Policy Studies Journal* 21 (1993): 56-71; David J. Webber, 'The Distribution and Use of Policy Knowledge in the Policy Process,' in W.N. Dunn and R.M. Kelly, eds., *Advances in Policy Studies since 1950* (New Brunswick, NJ: Transaction Publishers 1992).

51 Grace Skogstad and Paul Kopas, 'Environmental Policy in a Federal System: Ottawa and the Provinces,' in Boardman, ed., *Canadian Environmental Policy*, 43-59. See also O. Dwivedi and R.B. Woodrow, 'Environmental Policy-Making and Administration in a Federal State: The Impact of Overlapping Jurisdictions in Canada,' in W.M. Chandler and C.W. Zollner, eds., *Challenges to Federalism* (Kingston: Queen's University Institute of Intergovernmental Relations 1989), 265-89.

52 Philip H. Pollock III, Stuart A. Lilie, and M. Elliot Vittes, 'Hard Issues, Core Values and Vertical Constraint: The Case of Nuclear Power,' *British Journal of Political Science* 23.1 (1993): 29-50.

Chapter 9: Policy Implementation
1 Canadian Bar Association, ed., *Sustainable Development in Canada: Options for Law Reform* (Ottawa: Canadian Bar Association 1990), 9.

2 Kathryn Harrison and George Hoberg, *Risk, Science and Politics: Regulating Toxic Substances in Canada and the United States* (Montreal: McGill-Queen's University Press 1994). This despite much lip service paid to the 'advantages' of market-based instruments. See Arthur Donner and Fred Lazar, 'The Economic Effects of an Environmental Tax,' in Allan M. Maslove, ed., *Taxes as Instruments of Public Policy* (Toronto: University of Toronto Press 1994), 93-166.

3 Daniel A. Mazmanian and Paul A. Sabatier, *Implementation and Public Policy* (Glenview, IL: Scott, Foresman 1983), 21-25.

4 Ibid., 31.

5 See Eugene Bardach, *The Implementation Game* (Cambridge, MA: MIT Press 1977); and Richard F. Elmore, 'Organizational Models of Social Program Implementation,' *Public Policy* 26.2 (1978): 185-228.

6 Christopher Hood, 'Using Bureaucracy Sparingly,' *Public Administration* 61.2 (1983): 197-208; Christopher Hood, *The Tools of Government* (Chatham: Chatham House 1986).

7 Allan Schnaiberg, *The Environment: From Surplus to Scarcity* (New York: Oxford University Press 1980).

8 David Estrin and John Swaigen, *Environment on Trial: A Handbook of Ontario Environmental Law* (Toronto: Canadian Environmental Law Research Foundation 1978).

9 Kernaghan Webb, 'Between the Rocks and Hard Places: Bureaucrats, the Law and Pollution Control' *Alternatives* 14 (1987): 4-13; Kernaghan Webb and John C. Clifford, *Pollution Control in Canada: The Regulatory Approach in the 1980s* (Ottawa: Law Reform Commission of Canada 1988).

10 Estrin and Swaigen, *Environment on Trial,* 10.

11 Ibid.

12 J.E. Hodgetts, *Pioneer Public Service* (Toronto: University of Toronto Press 1957); J.E. Hodgetts, *The Canadian Public Service: A Physiology of Government 1867-1970* (Toronto: University of Toronto Press 1973); Richard S. Lambert and Paul Pross, *Renewing Nature's Wealth: A Centennial History of the Public Management of Lands, Forests, and Wildlife in Ontario 1763-1967* (Toronto: Department of Lands and Forests 1967).

13 Kathryn Harrison, *Passing the Buck: Federalism and Canadian Environmental Policy* (Vancouver: UBC Press 1996).

14 A. Grima, 'Participatory Rites: Integrating Public Involvement in Environmental Impact Assessment,' in J.B.R. Whitney and V.W. Maclaren, eds., *Environmental Impact Assessment: The Canadian Experience* (Toronto: University of Toronto Institute for Environmental Studies 1985), 33-51.

15 Andrew R. Thompson, *Environmental Regulation in Canada* (Vancouver: Westwater Research Institute 1980), 5.

16 Robert Paehlke, 'Democracy and Environmentalism: Opening a Door to the Administrative State,' in R. Paehlke and D. Torgerson, eds., *Managing Leviathan: Environmental Politics and the Administrative State* (Peterborough: Broadview Press 1990), 35-55.

17 Sheila Jasonoff, 'Procedural Choices in Regulatory Science,' *Technology and Society* 17 (1995): 279-93.

18 Doug Macdonald, *The Politics of Pollution: Why Canadians Are Failing Their Environment* (Toronto: McClelland and Stewart 1991), 137.

19 Ibid., 161.

20 Ibid., 159.

21 The very term 'baseline data' is inappropriate to descriptions of natural environments in which centuries of resource extraction have already taken place. Furthermore, inventories reflect the development of methodologies and data collection strategies that may not yet be capable of identifying, much less measuring, species and substances. As Macdonald notes, 'The physical data and socio-economic information on which regulation is based are limited and to some degree uncertain and ambiguous, with interpretation inevitably being influenced by the assumptions and interests of the different parties ... At present there are very few neutral sources of information on either the physical or economic aspects of pollution.' Ibid.

22 Andrew J. Roman and Kelly Hooey, 'The Regulatory Framework,' in G. Thompson, M.L. McConnell, and L.B. Huestis, eds., *Environmental Law and Business in Canada* (Aurora, ON: Canada Law Books 1993), 55.

23 Doug Macdonald, *The Politics of Pollution*, 162-63.

24 Ibid., 165.

25 Ibid., 157.

26 Ibid., 172-73.

27 The scheduling of compliance is predicated on the perceived financial ability of industry to implement new technology. Parlour and others have noted that, when the regulations of the Fisheries Act were drawn up in 1971, the marginal economic position of the industry was used as a rationale for a two-tiered system of regulations, because it was assumed that current mills were unable to pay for the changes necessary to meet compliance. Chris Rolfe, 'Federal Regulation of Systemic Pollution from the Pulp and Paper Industry in British Columbia: Barriers to Enforcement and Proposals for Reform' (Victoria: University of Victoria 1989), 22.

28 William Sinclair, 'Controlling Effluent Discharges from Canadian Pulp and Paper Manufacturers,' *Canadian Public Policy* 17.1 (1991): 99.

29 Sinclair, 'Controlling Effluent Discharges,' 99, 97.

30 Ibid., 99, 96.

31 Tim Roberts, *Pesticides: The Legal Questions* (Vancouver: Legal Services Society 1981), 37.

32 Ibid., 37.

33 Macdonald, *Politics of Pollution*, 180.

34 Lynne Huestis, 'Enforcement of Environmental Law in Canada,' in Thompson, McConnell, and Huestis, eds., *Environmental Law*, 246.

35 Ibid., 244-5.

36 Ibid.

37 Ibid., 245.

38 Robert Paehlke, 'Regulatory and Non-Regulatory Approaches to Environmental Protection,' *Canadian Public Administration* 33.1 (1990): 17-36.

39 Peter N. Nemetz, 'The Fisheries Act and Federal-Provincial Environmental Regulation: Duplication or Complementarity?' *Canadian Public Administration* 29 (1986): 401-24.

40 Richard Brown and Murray Rankin, 'Persuasion, Penalties and Prosecution: Administrative v. Criminal Sanctions,' in M. Friedland, ed., *Securing Compliance: Seven Case Studies* (Toronto: University of Toronto Press 1990), 334.

41 Ibid.

42 *Vancouver Sun* (1 December 1989): A1.

43 Ibid.

44 Macdonald, *Politics of Pollution*, 180.

45 Huestis, 'Enforcement,' 250.

46 Ibid., 251.

47 Ibid., 271.

48 Mark S. Winfield, 'Achieving the Holy Grail? A Legal and Political Analysis of Ontario's Environmental Bill of Rights,' paper presented at the Annual Meeting of the Canadian Political Science Association, Montreal, 1995.

49 See, especially, James W. Parlour, 'The Politics of Water Pollution Control: A Case Study of the Canadian Fisheries Act Amendments and the Pulp and Paper Effluent Regulations 1970,' *Journal of Environmental Management* 13 (1981): 127-49; Peter Victor and Terrence Burrell, *Environmental Protection Regulation: Water Pollution and the Pulp and Paper Industry,* Technical Report No. 14 (Ottawa: Economic Council of Canada 1981); A. Lucas, 'Water Pollution Control Law in British Columbia,' *University of British Columbia Law Review* 4 (1969): 56.

50 Webb and Clifford, *Pollution Control;* Macdonald, *Politics of Pollution,* 135.

51 Calvin Sandborn, William J. Andrews, and Brad Wylynko, *Preventing Toxic Pollution: Towards a British Columbia Strategy* (Vancouver: West Coast Environmental Law Research Foundation 1991), 49.

52 From the periods 1988-9 and 1990-1, the number of charges laid under the Waste Management Act rose from approximately forty-six to 220. Fines rose by a factor of almost ten, from $90,025 to $884,031 over the same period. Ibid.

53 David Vander Zwaag and Brenda McLuhan, 'Pulp and Paper Pollution: Shifting Legal Approaches and the Search for Sustainable Industries,' in Thompson, McConnell, and Huestis, eds., *Environmental Law,* 479-522.

54 Roman and Hooey make a distinction between the types of environmental damage to which regulation may be directed. *Contamination* refers to the discharge or spill of a substance into the air, soil, or water and may include noise, vibration, or radiation. *Degradation,* on the other hand, does not necessarily involve discharging materials but may include clearcutting or decreasing the viability of species through habitat loss. Roman and Hooey, 'Regulatory Framework,' 53-69.

55 Vander Zwaag and McLuhan, 'Pulp and Paper Pollution,' 480.

56 West Coast Environmental Law Research Foundation, Newsletter 15.10 (1991): 2.

57 Webb and Clifford, *Pollution Control,* 14.

58 Erwin C. Hargrove, *The Missing Link: The Study of the Implementation of Social Policy* (Washington, DC: The Urban Institute 1975), 1.

59 On policy failures, see David Dery, *Problem Definition in Policy Analysis* (Lawrence: University of Kansas Press 1984); Murray J. Edelman, *Constructing the Political Spectacle* (Chicago: University of Chicago Press 1988); and Helen M. Ingram and Dean E. Mann, 'Policy Failure: An Issue Deserving Analysis,' in H.M. Ingram and D.E. Mann, eds., *Why Policies Succeed or Fail* (Beverly Hills: Sage Publications 1980), 11-32. Larson lists four reasons for failure, two extra-governmental and two intra-governmental. They are (1) poor implementation procedures, (2) intergovernmental complexity, (3) vague and unrealistic goals, and (4) changes in the economic environment. See James S. Larson, *Why Government Programs Fail: Improving Policy Implementations* (New York: Praeger 1980).

60 See Stephen H. Linder and B. Guy Peters, 'From Social Theory to Policy Design,' *Journal of Public Policy* 4 (1984): 237-59; Stephen H. Linder and B. Guy Peters, 'The Analysis of Design or the Design of Analysis?' *Policy Studies Review* 7 (1988): 738-50.

61 Thompson, *Environmental Regulation,* 17. In her analysis of the development of provincial Crown corporations in the resource field, Chandler also pointed a finger at ideology, noting the tendency of governments with either a strong provincialist or a nationalist orientation to go beyond regulation to the use of public enterprises in resource development. Marsha A. Chandler, 'The Politics of Public Enterprise,' in J.R.S. Pritchard, ed., *Crown Corporations in Canada: The Calculus of Instrument Choice* (Toronto: Butterworths 1983), 185-218.

62 Linder and Peters argue that instruments vary according to four general categories of features: (1) *resource intensiveness,* including administrative cost and operational simplicity; (2) *targeting,* including precision and selectivity; (3) *political risk,* including the nature of support and opposition, public visibility, and chances of failure; and (4) *constraints on state activity,* including difficulties with coerciveness and ideological principles limiting government activity. Stephen H. Linder and B. Guy Peters, 'Instruments of Government: Perceptions and Contexts,' *Journal of Public Policy* 9 (1989): 47.

63 M. Howlett and M. Ramesh, *Studying Public Policy* (Toronto: Oxford University Press 1995).

64 For a rare cross-national empirical study attempting to assess the effectiveness of this Canadian negotiative approach to implementation, see Kathryn Harrison, 'Is Co-operation the Answer? Canadian Environmental Enforcement in Comparative Context,' *Journal of Policy Analysis and Management* 14 (1995): 221-44.

Chapter 10: Policy Evaluation

1 After the completion of policy evaluation, the problem and solutions may be reconceptualized completely, in which case the cycle will swing back to agenda-setting or some other stage of the cycle, or the status quo may be maintained. The reconceptualization may consist of minor changes or fundamental reformulation of the problem, including

terminating the policy altogether. Peter deLeon, 'Policy Evaluation and Program Termination,' *Policy Studies Review* 2 (1983): 631-47.

2 Garry Brewer and Peter DeLeon, *The Foundations of Policy Analysis* (Homewood, IL: Dorsey Press 1983), 319-26.

3 Colin Bennett and Michael Howlett, 'The Lessons of Learning: Reconciling Theories of Policy Learning and Policy Change,' *Policy Sciences* 25 (1991): 275-94.

4 The first type is endogenous learning, which, following Rose, can be referred to as 'lesson drawing.' This type of learning originates within the formal policy process and affects the choice of means or technique employed by policymakers in their efforts to achieve their goals. Richard Rose, 'Comparative Policy Analysis: The Program Approach,' in M. Dogan, ed., *Comparing Pluralist Democracies: Strains on Legitimacy* (Boulder, CO: Westview Press 1988), 219-41; Richard Rose, 'What Is Lesson-Drawing?' *Journal of Public Policy* 11 (1991): 3-30.

5 Following Hall, this second type of learning is exogenous and can be referred to as 'social learning.' It originates outside the policy process and affects the constraints or capacities of policymakers to alter society. Peter A. Hall, 'Policy Paradigms, Social Learning and the State: The Case of Economic Policy Making in Britain,' *Comparative Politics* 25 (1993): 275-96. The move toward privatization and the consideration of inflation as a more serious problem than unemployment in many countries in the 1980s are instances of this second type of learning. See M. Howlett and M. Ramesh, 'Patterns of Policy Instrument Choice, Policy Styles, Policy Learning and the Privatization Experience,' *Policy Studies Review* 12.1 (1993): 3-24.

6 David Nachmias, *Public Policy Evaluation* (New York: St. Martin's Press 1979), 4.

7 Charles W. Anderson, 'The Place of Principles in Policy Analysis,' *American Political Science Review* 73 (1979): 711-23; Donna H. Kerr, 'The Logic of "Policy" and Successful Policies,' *Policy Sciences* 7 (1976): 351-63. See, especially, Ronald Manzer, 'Policy Rationality and Policy Analysis: The Problem of the Choice of Criteria for Decision-Making,' in O. Dwivedi, ed., *Public Policy and Administrative Studies* (Guelph: University of Guelph 1984), 27-40.

8 Helen M. Ingram and Dean E. Mann, 'Policy Failure: An Issue Deserving Analysis,' in H.M. Ingram and D.E. Mann, eds., *Why Policies Succeed or Fail* (Beverly Hills: Sage 1980), 852.

9 An excellent case in point concerns the mandated five-year review of the Canadian Environmental Protection Act (CEPA) by the House of Commons Standing Committee on Environment and Sustainable Development. After a lengthy hearing process, in 1995 the committee concluded that CEPA was flawed in many aspects and made numerous suggestions for its revision. Negative official reviews of the report, however, seriously blunted its impact. For the CEPA report itself, see House of Commons Standing Committee on Environment and Sustainable Development, *Its about Our Health*, electronic document available at <http://www.web.apc.org/cepa911/recoms.toc.html>. For the government's response to the report, see Environment Canada, *Environmental Protection Legislation Designed for the Future ...*, electronic document available at <http://www.doe.ca/cepa/govtresp/efront.html>. On the reaction to the review, see Robert Matas, 'Environment Must Come First, Caccia Insists: Committee's Proposals for Protection Viewed by Some as Threat to Investment Climate,' *Globe and Mail* (19 October 1995): A17; and Robert Matas, 'Bureaucrats Pan MPs' Environmental Law Proposals: Committee's Recommendations Are Bad Science Potentially Costly to Business and Government, Officials Say,' *Globe and Mail* (16 October 1995): A7.

10 In the United States, where over 80 per cent of regulations developed by the Environmental Protections Agency (EPA) are challenged in the courts, more time and attention have been paid to alternative regulatory approaches than in many other countries. See 'Rethinking Regulation: Negotiation as an Alternative to Traditional Rulemaking,' *Harvard Law Review* 94.8 (1981): 1871-91; Philip J. Harter, 'Negotiating Regulations: A Cure for the Malaise?' *Environmental Impact Assessment Review* 3.1 (1982): 75-91; and Gerard McMahon, *Regulatory Negotiation: A Response to the Crisis of Regulatory Legitimacy* (Cambridge, MA: Harvard University Program of Negotiation 1985).

11 Frank R. Baumgartner and Bryan D. Jones, *Agendas and Instability in American Politics* (Chicago: University of Chicago Press 1993).
12 Alistair Lucas, 'Fundamental Prerequisites for Citizen Participation,' in B. Sadler, ed., *Involvement and Environment* (Edmonton: Environment Council of Alberta 1978), 43-57.
13 Ted Schrecker, 'Resisting Regulation: Environmental Policy and Corporate Power,' *Alternatives* 13 (1985): 10.
14 Lucas, 'Fundamental Prerequisites,' 48.
15 Alistair Lucas, 'Legal Foundations for Public Participation in Environmental Decision-Making,' *Natural Resources Journal* 16 (1976): 73-102.
16 Melody Hessing, 'Production of the Public Voice: Public Participation in the Hearing Process as Contemporary Democracy,' doctoral dissertation, University of British Columbia, Vancouver, 1984, 142.
17 James W. Parlour, 'The Politics of Water Pollution Control: A Case Study of the Canadian Fisheries Act Amendments and the Pulp and Paper Effluent Regulations 1970,' *Journal of Environmental Management* 13 (1981): 127-49; William Sinclair, *Controlling Pollution from Canadian Pulp and Paper Manufacturers: A Federal Perspective* (Ottawa: Environment Canada 1991); Ted Schrecker, 'Environmental Hazards: A Critical Approach to Policy Analysis,' in O. Dwivedi and R.B. Woodrow, eds., *Public Policy and Administrative Studies* (Guelph: University of Guelph Department of Political Studies 1985), 143-54.
18 Kathryn Harrison and W.T. Stanbury, 'Privatization in British Columbia: Lessons from the Sale of Government Laboratories,' *Canadian Public Administration* 33 (1990): 165-97.
19 Warner Troyer, *No Safe Place* (Toronto: Clarke, Irwin 1977).
20 William Sinclair, 'Controlling Effluent Discharges from Canadian Pulp and Paper Manufacturers,' *Canadian Public Policy* 17.1 (1991): 102.
21 Schrecker, 'Resisting Regulation,' 19.
22 Andrew R. Thompson, *Energy Project Approval in British Columbia* (Vancouver: Westwater Research Centre, University of British Columbia 1981), 33.
23 Schrecker, 'Resisting Regulation,' 11.
24 Lynne Huestis, 'Enforcement of Environmental Law in Canada,' in G. Thompson, M.L. McConnell, and L.B. Huestis, eds., *Environmental Law and Business in Canada* (Toronto: Canada Law Books 1993), 252.
25 Ibid., 259.
26 *Vancouver Sun* (11 September 1992): A11.
27 Ibid.
28 Huestis, 'Enforcement,' 253.
29 Ibid., 252.
30 Schrecker, 'Resisting Regulation,' 11.
31 Huestis, 'Enforcement,' 252.
32 Ibid., 252-3.
33 In Canada, environmental bill of rights legislation was passed in the Northwest Territories and Yukon in 1991 and in Ontario in 1994. S. Elgie, 'Environmental Groups and the Courts: 1970-1992,' in Thompson, McConnell, and Huestis, eds., *Environmental Law*. The first environmental bill of rights in North America was passed in Michigan in 1970. See Joseph L. Sax, 'The Public Trust Doctrine in Natural Resource Law: Effective Judicial Intervention,' *Michigan Law Review* 68 (1969-70): 473-566.
34 Environmental bills of rights have been identified as a means of expanding public access to judicial processes concerning environmental protection. In the United States, laws for citizen suits entitle the public to enforce environmental legislation through civil rather than criminal proceedings, and environmental bills of rights legislation in Canada could provide a similar option. Citizen suits allow individuals to bring civil as opposed to criminal actions against the violation of an environmental statute or permit and sometimes more generally against the impairment of the natural environment. Joseph L. Sax, *Defending the Environment: A Strategy for Citizen Action* (New York: Alfred A. Knopf 1971).
35 On Ontario's recent Environmental Bill of Rights and its limitations, see Mark S. Winfield, 'Achieving the Holy Grail? A Legal and Political Analysis of Ontario's Environmental Bill of Rights,' paper presented at the Annual Meeting of the Canadian

Political Science Association, Montreal, 1995; and 'Cost-Cutting Ontario Revokes Portion of Environmental Bill,' *Vancouver Sun* (18 January 1996): A6.
36 Louis L. Jaffe, *English and American Judges as Lawmakers* (Oxford: Clarendon 1969); Louis L. Jaffe, *Judicial Control of Administrative Action* (Boston: Little, Brown 1965); Albert S. Abel, 'Appeals against Administrative Decisions III: In Search of a Basic Policy,' *Canadian Public Administration* 5 (1962): 65-75; William H. Angus, 'Judicial Review: Do We Need It?' in D.J. Baum, ed., *The Individual and the Bureaucracy* (Toronto: York University 1975), 101-35.
37 Elgie, 'Environmental Groups,' 189.
38 Peter Z.R. Finkle and Alastair R. Lucas, eds., *Environmental Law in the 1980s: A New Beginning* (Calgary: Faculty of Law, University of Calgary 1981); R.T. Franson and T. Burns, 'Environmental Rights for the Canadian Citizen: A Prescription for Reform,' *Alberta Law Review* 12.2 (1974): 153-71.
39 Andrew J. Roman, '*Locus Standi*: A Cure in Search of a Disease?' in J. Swaigen, ed., *Environmental Rights in Canada* (Toronto: Butterworths 1981), 11-59.
40 Kernaghan Webb, 'On the Periphery: The Limited Role for Criminal Offenses in Environmental Protection,' in Tingley, ed., *Into the Future*, 58-69.
41 S. Elder, 'Environmental Protection through the Common Law,' *Western Ontario Law Review* 12 (1973): 107-71; M.I. Jeffery, 'Environmental Enforcement and Regulation in the 1980s: *Regina* v. *Sault Ste. Marie* Revisited,' *Queen's Law Journal* 10.1 (1984): 43-70.
42 Willard Estey, 'Public Nuisance and Standing to Sue,' *Osgoode Hall Law Journal* 10 (1972): 563-82. In the United States, the situation is quite different. The courts have allowed notions of a 'public trust,' that is, of common resources such as air or the seashore controlled by neither public nor private authorities, that citizens may protect through recourse to the courts. Sax, 'Public Trust Doctrine.' While a 1972 US Supreme Court decision rejected the argument that natural objects such as trees and streams should have standing in their own right, it did accept that recreational users such as hikers would experience significant potential injury from a development of the area in which they would be entitled to 'standing.' As Justice William O. Douglas stated in his decision, 'before these priceless bits of Americana (such as a valley, an alpine meadow, a river or a lake) are forever lost or are so transformed as to be reduced to the eventual rubble of our urban environment, the voice of the existing beneficiaries of these environmental wonders should be heard. Perhaps they will not win. Perhaps the bulldozers of "progress" will plow under all the aesthetic wonders of this beautiful land ... But those people who have so frequented the place as to know its values and wonders will be able to speak for the entire ecological community.' As cited in Elgie, 'Environmental Groups,' 197-8.
43 1 SCR 1975, 138. In 1976, the Supreme Court ruled in *McNeil* v. *Nova Scotia Board of Censors* (2 SCR 1976, 265) that a part of its earlier ruling in *Thorson*, distinguishing between regulatory and legislative pronouncements in granting increased standing, was unworkable. In 1981, it ruled in *Borowski* v. *Minister of Justice of Canada* (2 SCR 1981, 575) that constitutionality extended to violations of the (then) non-constitutionally entrenched Canadian Bill of Rights. Thomas A. Cromwell, *Locus Standi: A Commentary on the Law of Standing in Canada* (Toronto: Carswell 1986).
44 Franklin Gertler, Paul Muldoon, and Marcia Valiante, 'Public Access to Environmental Justice,' in Canadian Bar Association, ed., *Sustainable Development*, 79-97.
45 Ontario Law Reform Commission, *Report on the Law of Standing* (Toronto: Ministry of the Attorney General 1989).
46 These included the Dominion Law Reports, Dominion Reporter Service, Supreme Court Reporter, Canadian Environmental Law Reporter, Western Canada Environmental Law Reports, reporters for each of Canada's ten provinces, as well as the WWR, MPLR, MR, FTR, and SCCD. These sources were checked manually and by computerized database searches for any cases dealing with significant keywords, such as 'environment,' 'pollution,' et cetera, that occurred in the decade 1980-9.
47 Kenneth Kernaghan, 'Judicial Review of Administration Action,' in K. Kernaghan, ed., *Public Administration in Canada: Selected Readings* (Toronto: Methuen 1985), 358-73.

48 H.W.R. Wade, 'Anglo-American Administrative Law: Some Reflections,' *Law Quarterly Review* 81 (1965): 357-79; H.W.R. Wade, 'Anglo-American Administrative Law: More Reflections,' *Law Quarterly Review* 82 (1966): 226-52. In the US, a different rule for judicial review has developed, and it encompasses review on both points of law and points of fact. This is due to the willingness of US courts to set aside administrative decisions not only on questions of jurisdiction and natural justice but also if the decision is found to lack 'substantial evidence' in its support. Jaffe, *Judicial Control*.

49 P. Hogg, 'The Supreme Court of Canada and Administrative Law 1949-1971,' *Osgoode Hall Law Journal* 11 (1973): 187-223.

50 Abel, 'Appeals'; Angus, 'Judicial Review'; H.J. Lawford, 'Appeals against Administrative Decisions I: The Function of Judicial Review,' *Canadian Public Administration* 5 (1962): 46-54.

51 R. Dussault and L. Borgeat, *Administrative Law: A Treatise* (Toronto: Carswell 1990); Neil Finkelstein and Brian M. Rogers, eds., *Recent Developments in Administrative Law* (Agincourt, ON: Carswell 1987).

52 J. de Pencier, 'Oldman River Dam and Federal Environmental Assessment Now and in the Future,' *Journal of Environmental Law and Protection* 2 (1992): 293-315; Alastair R. Lucas, 'Judicial Review of the Environmental Assessment Process: Has Federal Environmental Assessment Been Judicialized?' paper presented at the 6th CIRL Conference on Natural Resources Law, Ottawa, 1993.

53 Elgie, 'Environmental Groups.' See also M. Howlett, 'The Judicialization of Canadian Environmental Policy 1980-1989: A Test of the U.S.-Canada Convergence Hypothesis,' *Canadian Journal of Political Science* 27.1 (1994): 99-125.

54 Elgie, 'Environmental Groups,' 210.

55 See Giandomenico Majone, *Evidence, Argument, and Persuasion in the Policy Process* (New Haven, CT: Yale University Press 1989).

56 Wesley M. Cohen and Daniel A. Levinthal, 'Absorptive Capacity: A New Perspective on Learning and Innovation,' *Administrative Science Quarterly* 35 (1990): 128-52.

57 M. Howlett and M. Ramesh, *Studying Public Policy: Policy Cycles and Policy Subsystems* (Toronto: Oxford University Press 1995).

58 Bennett and Howlett, 'Lessons of Learning.'

59 Thompson, *Energy Project Approval*, 34.

60 Schrecker, 'Resisting Regulation,' 11; Andrew J. Roman and Kelly Hooey, 'The Regulatory Framework,' in Thompson, McConnell, and Huestis, eds., *Environmental Law*, 58.

Chapter 11: The Canadian Resource and Environmental Policy Style

1 F.J. Anderson, *Natural Resources in Canada: Economic Theory and Policy* (Toronto: Methuen 1985); Bruce Mitchell, *Geography and Resource Analysis* (New York: Wiley 1989).

2 Law Reform Commission of Canada, *Policy Implementation, Compliance and Administrative Law* (Ottawa: Law Reform Commission of Canada 1986); Kernaghan Webb and John C. Clifford, *Pollution Control in Canada: The Regulatory Approach in the 1980s* (Ottawa: Law Reform Commission of Canada 1988).

3 O. Dwivedi, *Protecting the Environment: Issues and Choices, Canadian Perspectives* (Vancouver: Copp Clark Publishing 1974). While most existing Canadian analyses assume an active state, they are less concerned with the state's relations with other forces, ranging from corporate to global influences. The nature of societal actors involved in the Canadian environmental policy process is also little developed. See Ted Schrecker, 'The Mobilization of Bias in Closed Systems: Environmental Regulation in Canada,' *Journal of Business Administration* 15.1-2 (1984-5): 43-63.

4 Terrence J. Downey, 'Understanding Policy-Making: A Necessary First Step for Environmentalists,' *Alternatives* 14 (1987): 30-4.

5 Jeremy Richardson, Gunnel Gustafsson, and Grant Jordan, 'The Concept of Policy Style,' in J.J. Richardson, ed., *Policy Styles in Western Europe* (London: George Allen and Unwin 1982), 13.

6 Gary Freeman, 'National Styles and Policy Sectors: Explaining Structured Variation,' *Journal of Public Policy* 5 (1985): 467-96.

7 M. Howlett and M. Ramesh, *Studying Public Policy: Policy Cycles and Policy Subsystems* (Toronto: Oxford University Press 1995).

8 A much-cited example of change in policy paradigms pertains to economic policy in the years following World War II, when Keynesianism emerged as the dominant paradigm. Unlike the previous era, in which the state was seen as having little direct role in determining the level of economic activity, Keynesianism (the term refers to Keynes's ideas in practice) promoted an active government role in the management of the economy. Peter A. Hall, Introduction, in P.A. Hall, ed., *The Political Power of Economic Ideas: Keynesianism across Nations* (Princeton, NJ: Princeton University Press 1989), 3-26.

9 On alternative dispute resolution in Canada, see A.H.J. Dorcey and C.L. Riek, 'Negotiation-Based Approaches to the Settlement of Environmental Disputes in Canada,' in B. Sadler, ed., *The Place of Negotiation in Environmental Assessment* (Ottawa: Canadian Environmental Assessment Research Council 1989), 7-36; Steven Shrybman, *Environmental Mediation: From Theory to Practice* (Ottawa: Environment Canada, Environmental Protection Service 1989). More generally, see Gail Bingham, *Resolving Environmental Disputes: A Decade of Experience* (Washington, DC: Conservation Foundation 1986); Laura M. Lake, *Environmental Mediation, the Search for Consensus* (Boulder, CO: Westview Press 1980); Ann Painter, 'The Future of Environmental Dispute Resolution,' *Natural Resources Journal* 28 (1988): 145-70; and Robert B. Goldmann, ed., *Roundtable Justice: Case Studies in Conflict Resolution: Reports to the Ford Foundation* (Boulder, CO: Westview Press 1980).

10 Jamie Benidickson, 'Environmental Law Survey: Part I,' *University of Ottawa Law Review* 24 (1992): 734-811; Jamie Benidickson, 'Environmental Law Survey: Part II,' *University of Ottawa Law Review* 25 (1993): 123-54.

11 E.W. Manning, 'Conservation Strategies: Providing the Vision for Sustainable Development,' *Alternatives* 16 (1990): 24-29. These were first suggested by the World Conservation Strategy, developed in 1980 by the Swiss-based International Union for the Conservation of Nature and Natural Resources (IUCN). Although the IUCN process was still active in the mid-1980s, the call for conservation strategies was co-opted by the Brundtland Commission's own appeal for the use of similar strategies to promote sustainable development, a fact recognized and accepted by IUCN. IUCN, *World Conservation Strategy* (Gland, Switz.: IUCN 1980); IUCN, *From Strategy to Action: How to Implement the Report of the World Commission on Environment and Development* (Gland, Switz.: IUCN 1988); Peter Jacobs and D.A. Munro, eds., *Conservation with Equity: Strategies for Sustainable Development* (Cambridge, UK: IUCN 1987). For an example of these plans, see Canada, *Canadian Arctic Marine Conservation Strategy: Discussion Paper* (Ottawa: Department of Fisheries and Oceans 1987).

12 Ignacy Sachs, 'The Strategies of Ecodevelopment ... ,' *Ceres* 17.4 (1984): 17-21; World Commission on Environment and Development, *Our Common Future* (Oxford: Oxford University Press 1987). Some of these efforts were rudimentary, others more sophisticated. The federal-provincial approval accorded the Brundtland Commission's recommendations was reflected by the establishment of a National Task Force on Environment and Economy in 1987. Canadian Council of Resource and Environment Ministers, *Report of the National Task Force on Environment and Economy* (Ottawa: Supply and Services 1987).

13 Canadian Bar Association, ed., *Sustainable Development in Canada: Options for Law Reform* (Ottawa: Canadian Bar Association 1990); Douglas A. Smith, 'Defining the Agenda for Environmental Protection,' in K.A. Graham, ed., *How Ottawa Spends 1990-91: Tracking the Second Agenda* (Ottawa: Carleton University Press 1990), 113-36.

14 T. Fenge and L.G. Smith, 'Reforming the Federal Environmental Assessment and Review Process,' *Canadian Public Policy* 12 (1986): 596-605.

15 Canadian Environmental Advisory Council, *Review of the Proposed Environmental Protection Act* (Ottawa: Supply and Services 1987); Ted Schrecker, 'The Canadian Environmental Assessment Act: Tremulous Step Forward or Retreat into Smoke and Mirrors?' *Canadian Environmental Law Reports* 5 (1991): 192-246.

16 Jim Bruton and Michael Howlett, 'Differences of Opinion: Round Tables, Policy Networks and the Failure of Canadian Environmental Strategy,' *Alternatives* 19 (1992): 25; Howlett, 'Round Table Experience.'
17 G. Bruce Doern, 'The Federal Green Plan: Assessing the "Prequel,"' *Commentary* 17 (1990): 1-8; G. Bruce Doern, 'Shades of Green: Gauging Canada's Green Plan,' *Commentary* 29 (1991): 1-12; Canada, *Canada's Green Plan for a Healthy Environment* (Ottawa: Supply and Services 1990).
18 George Hoberg and Kathyrn Harrison, 'It's Not Easy Being Green: The Politics of Canada's Green Plan,' *Canadian Public Policy* 20 (1994): 119-37.
19 Liberal Party of Canada, *Creating Opportunity* (Toronto: Liberal Party of Canada 1993).
20 In September 1994, the government launched a Canadian Environmental Industries initiative to assist small and medium-sized businesses in developing new environmental technologies. However, in the 1993 announcement of the Liberal's 'New Economic Policy,' the emphasis was on a neo-Schumpeterian growth strategy based on technological innovation and productivity increases, not on environmental issues or concerns for the sustainability of any such development. In fact, the only time 'environment' appears in the document is in terms of creating a better 'environment' for investment. The Liberal's first term in office coincided with a period of respite at the international level following the 'failure' of the Rio conference in 1992 to establish a clear international environmental agenda. In this circumstance, it should not be surprising that virtually every aspect of Liberal environmental policy-making has been driven by domestic concerns such as the state of federal-provincial relations and the electoral salience of the deficit issue. See Susan D. Phillips, 'Making Change: The Potential for Innovation under the Liberals,' in S.D. Phillips, ed., *How Ottawa Spends 1994-95: Making Change* (Ottawa: Carleton University Press 1994); and Michael Howlett, 'Sustainable Development: Environmental Policy,' in A. Johnson and A. Stritch, eds., *Canadian Public Policy: Globalization and Political Parties* (Toronto: Copp Clark Longman 1996).
21 François Bregha, et al., *The Integration of Environmental Considerations into Government Policy* (Ottawa: Canadian Environmental Assessment Research Council 1990).
22 Laurie Adkin, 'Labour, Ecology and the Politics of Convergence,' in F. Cunningham et al., eds., *Social Movements/Social Change: The Politics and Practice of Organizing* (Toronto: Between the Lines 1989), 48-73.
23 See Mary Louise McAllister, 'Administrative Reform and "Shared Decision-Making": Prospects for the Mining Sector,' in E.R. Black, M. Howlett, and P.J. Smith, eds., *Proceedings of the First Annual Meeting* (Vancouver: BC Political Studies Association 1996), 159-76.

Chapter 12: Conclusion
1 This is a feature of environmental policy processes in other countries as well. See Mario Diani, *Green Networks: A Structural Analysis of the Italian Environmental Movement* (Edinburgh: University of Edinburgh Press 1995).
2 While the political economic framework utilized here is critical of the workings of the economic system, it shares with its more liberal counterparts a concern with the distributive characteristics of modern societies. The liberal economic model, however, generally fails to question the material consumption of goods itself as problematic and to explore the ecological consequences of consumeristic production processes. James O'Connor, 'Capitalism, Nature, Socialism: A Theoretical Introduction,' *Capitalism, Nature, Socialism* 1.1 (1988): 11-38; Peter A. Victor, 'Economics and the Challenge of Environmental Issues,' in W. Leiss, ed., *Ecology versus Politics in Canada* (Toronto: University of Toronto Press 1979), 34-56.
3 Glenn Williams, 'Greening the New Canadian Political Economy,' *Studies in Political Economy* 37 (1992): 5-30; Laurie Adkin, 'Environmental Politics, Political Economy, and Social Democracy in Canada,' *Studies in Political Economy* 45 (1994): 130-69.
4 These problems are not limited to the resource and environmental sector, of course, or to Canada. See Donna H. Kerr, 'The Logic of "Policy" and Successful Policies,' *Policy Sciences* 7 (1976): 351-63; Dean E. Mann, ed., *Environmental Policy Implementation: Planning and Management Options and Their Consequences* (Lexington: Lexington Books 1982); Dean E.

Mann and Helen M. Ingram, 'Policy Issues in the Natural Environment,' in H.M. Ingram and R.K. Godwin, eds., *Public Policy and the Natural Environment* (Greenwich: JAI Press 1985), 15-45; Alfred A. Marcus, *Promise and Performance: Choosing and Implementing an Environmental Policy* (Westport, CT: Greenwood 1980).

5 Canada, *The State of Canada's Environment, 1991* (Ottawa: Supply and Services 1991), 27-34.

6 Thomas A. Hutton, *Visions of a 'Post-Staples' Economy: Structural Change and Adjustment Issues in British Columbia,* PI No. 3 (Vancouver: Centre for Human Settlements 1994), 4-5.

7 Adapted from ibid., 1-2.

8 See Craig Heron and Robert Storey, *On the Job: Confronting the Labour Process in Canada* (Montreal: McGill-Queen's University Press 1986); and Stephen McBride, *Not Working: State, Unemployment, and Neo-Conservatism in Canada* (Toronto: University of Toronto Press 1992).

9 The 1995 announcement of a three-year 30 per cent cutback in Environment Canada's budget, and cuts to federal transfer payments, have been diluted by the emphasis on decentralization and euphemistic descriptions of reorganization. Environment Canada, *Program Review and Environment Canada* (Ottawa: Environment Canada 1995).

10 Adapted from Thomas A. Hutton, *Economic Implications of Environmental Enhancement: A Review and Interpretation of the Contemporary Literature,* prepared for Ministry of the Environment, Lands and Parks, Government of British Columbia (Vancouver: University of British Columbia, Centre for Human Settlements 1995), 25-28.

11 Mel Hurtig, *The Betrayal of Canada* (Toronto: Stoddart 1991); Ricardo Grinspun and Maxwell A. Cameron, eds., *The Political Economy of North American Free Trade* (Kingston: McGill-Queen's University Press 1993).

12 Canadian Environmental Law Association, *NAFTA Facts: A Series of Information Sheets about the Effects of NAFTA: NAFTA and Energy* (Toronto: Canadian Environmental Law Association, n.d.).

13 Ibid.

14 Paul Hirst and Grahame Thompson, 'The Problems of "Globalization": International Relations, National Economic Management and the Formation of Trading Blocs,' *Economy and Society* 21 (1992): 357-96.

15 Richard T. Schaefer, *Sociology* (New York: McGraw-Hill 1989), 421.

16 Sandra Postel, 'Carrying Capacity: Earth's Bottom Line,' in L. Brown et al., eds., *State of the World 1994: A Worldwatch Institute Report on Progess towards a Sustainable Society* (New York: Norton 1994), 6.

17 Allan Schnaiberg and Kenneth Alan Gould, *Environment and Society: The Enduring Conflict* (New York: St. Martin's Press 1994), 26.

18 Hutton, *Economic Implications,* 33-4.

19 While biodiversity has declined in the North, it is now increasingly threatened in the South, the site of economic expansion and the recipient of development incentives and trade enhancements. Two-thirds of all species (3.3 million) live in the tropics. Edward C. Wolf, *On the Brink of Extinction: Conserving the Diversity of Life,* Worldwatch Paper 78 (Washington, DC: Worldwatch Institute 1987), 10. At the rate at which tropical forests are being cleared, it has been estimated that one-third to one-half of them will have lost their capacity to support their existing biodiversity. From two-thirds to three-quarters of a million species are at risk in tropical forests alone.

20 Jutta Brunnee, 'Beyond Rio? The Evolution of International Environmental Law,' *Alternatives* 20 (1993): 16-25.

21 Tourism represents traditional economic, or 'productive,' interests, but it does so from a non-consumptive position. Tourism, of course, may undermine environmental values, such as when too many boats descend on herds of whales or too many recreational vehicles invade parks and demand increasingly higher levels of non-wilderness amenities. But tourism is allied with environmental interests in terms of many of its perspectives, such as wilderness preservation and critiques of clearcut logging, while its economic position legitimates environmental perspectives in market terms. See P.W. Williams, 'Tourism and

the Environment: No Place to Hide,' *World Leisure and Recreation* 34.2 (1992): 1-9; and P.W. Williams, 'Ecotourism: An Emerging Tourism Product with Emerging Management Challenges,' *Texas Tourism Trends* 5.3 (1993): 1-5.

22 See Cathy Nesmith and Pamela Wright, 'Gender, Resources and Environmental Management,' in B. Mitchell, ed., *Resource and Environmental Management in Canada: Addressing Conflict and Uncertainty* (Toronto: Oxford University Press 1995), 80-98.

23 Evelyn Pinkerton, ed., *Cooperative Management of Local Fisheries: New Directions for Improved Management and Community Development* (Vancouver: University of British Columbia Press 1989).

24 George Sessions, 'Ecological Consciousness and Paradigm Change,' in M. Tobias, ed., *Deep Ecology* (San Marcos, CA: Avant Books 1988).

25 Arne Naess, 'Deep Ecology and Ultimate Premises,' *Ecologist* 18.4-5 (1980): 128-35.

26 Max Oehlschlager, *The Idea of Wilderness: From Prehistory to the Age of Ecology* (New Haven, CT: Yale University Press 1991).

27 Martin Lewis, *Green Delusions: An Environmentalist Critique of Radical Environmentalism* (Durham, NC: Duke University Press 1994).

28 David Orton, 'Opposing Forest Spraying,' *Capitalism, Nature, Socialism* 2.1 (1991): 109-23.

29 E.G. Shumacher, *Small Is Beautiful: Economics as if People Mattered* (New York: Harper and Row 1973).

30 Stephanie Mills, 'The Bio-Regionalists – Who Are They and What Do They Do?' *E – The Environmental Magazine* 2.5 (1991): 40-2. For a sympathetic treatment, see Christopher Plant and Judith Plant, eds., *Turtle Talk: Voices for a Sustainable Future* (Philadelphia: New Society Publishers 1990); Kirkpatrick Sale, *Dwellers in the Land* (San Francisco: Sierra Club 1985); Van Andruss et al., eds., *Home! A BioRegional Reader* (Gabriola, BC: New Society Publishers 1990). More critical reviews include Donald Alexander, 'Bioregionalism: Science or Sensibility?' *Environmental Ethics* 12 (1990): 161-73; and Alan B. Nichols, 'Bioregionalism: Pragmatic or Idealistic?' *Water Environment and Technology* 3.3 (1991): 57-71.

31 Charles H. Foster, *Experiment in Bioregionalism: The New England River Basin Story* (Hanover: University Press of New England 1984); Anna Maria Gillis, 'The New Forestry: An Eco-System Approach to Land Management,' *Bioscience* 40 (1990): 558-62; R. Edward Grumbine, 'Ecosystem Management for Native Diversity: How to Save Our National Parks and Forests,' *Forest Watch* 9.6 (1988): 21-7.

32 Melody Hessing, 'Making the Connections: Ecofeminist Perspectives on Women and Environment,' *Alternatives* 19 (1993): 14-21.

33 Carolyn Merchant, *The Death of Nature: Women, Ecology and the Scientific Revolution* (San Francisco: Harper and Row 1983); Vandana Shiva, *Staying Alive: Women, Ecology and Development* (London: Zed Books 1989).

34 Vandana Shiva, 'Development as a New Project of Western Patriarchy,' in I. Diamond and G.F. Orenstein, eds., *Reweaving the World: The Emergence of Ecofeminism* (San Francisco: Sierra Club Books 1991).

35 Michael Howlett and Rebecca Raglon, 'Constructing the Environmental Spectacle: Green Ads and the Corporate Image 1910-1990,' *Environmental History Review* (US) 16.4 (1992): 53-73.

36 Robert Paehlke, 'Regulatory and Non-Regulatory Approaches to Environmental Protection,' *Canadian Public Administration* 33.1 (1990): 17-36. See also G. Bruce Doern, ed., *The Environmental Imperative: Market Approaches to the Greening of Canada* (Toronto: C.D. Howe Institute 1990); and Walter E. Block, ed., *Economics and the Environment: A Reconciliation* (Vancouver: Fraser Institute 1990).

37 Herman E. Daly and John B. Cobb Jr., *For the Common Good: Redirecting the Economy toward Community, the Environment, and a Sustainable Future* (Boston: Beacon Press 1994).

38 Herman E. Daly and Kenneth N. Townsend, eds., *Valuing the Earth: Economics, Ecology, Ethics* (Cambridge, MA: MIT Press 1993); Robert Costanza, ed., *Ecological Economics: The Science and Management of Sustainability* (New York: Columbia University Press 1991).

39 William Rees, 'Ecological Footprints and Appropriated Carrying Capacity: What Urban Economics Leaves Out,' paper presented at Globe '92, Vancouver, 16-20 March 1992.

40 Commission on Environment and Development, *Our Common Future* (New York: Oxford University Press 1987), 9.
41 Hutton, *Visions*, 16.
42 Paul Hawkens, *The Ecology of Commerce* (New York: Harper Business 1993), 212.
43 Janel M. Curry-Roper and Steven McGuire, 'The Individualist Imagination and Natural Resource Policy,' *Society and Natural Resources* 6 (1993): 259-72.
44 Leslie Pal, 'Competing Paradigms in Policy Discourses: The Case of International Human Rights,' *Policy Sciences* 28 (1995): 185-207; Christopher McGrory Klycza and Eric Mlyn, 'Privileged Ideas and State Interests: Bombs, Trees and State Autonomy,' *Policy Studies Journal* 23 (1995): 203-17.

Bibliography

Adie, R.F., and P.G. Thomas. *Canadian Public Administration: Problematical Perspectives.* Scarborough: Prentice Hall 1987

Adkin, Laurie. 'Labour, Ecology and the Politics of Convergence.' In *Social Movements/Social Change: The Politics and Practice of Organizing,* ed. Frank Cunningham, Sue Findlay, Marlene Kadar, Alan Lennon, and Ed Silva, 48-73. Toronto: Between the Lines 1989

–. 'Counter-Hegemony and Environmental Politics in Canada.' In *Organizing Dissent: Contemporary Social Movements in Theory and Practice,* ed. W.K. Carroll, 135-56. Toronto: Garamond 1992

–. 'Environmental Politics, Political Economy, and Social Democracy in Canada.' *Studies in Political Economy* 45 (1994): 130-69

Albion, Robert Greenhalgh. *Forests and Sea Power: The Timber Problems of the Royal Navy 1652-1862.* Hamden: Archon Books 1965

Alexander, D. 'Bioregionalism: Science or Sensibility?' *Environmental Ethics* 12.2 (1990): 161-71

Alker, Hayward R., and Peter M. Haas. 'The Rise of Global Ecopolitics.' In *Global Accord: Environmental Challenges and International Responses,* ed. N. Choucri, 205-54. Boston: MIT Press 1993

Allison, Graham T., and Morton H. Halperin. 'Bureaucratic Politics: A Paradigm and Some Policy Implications.' *World Politics* (Supplement) 24 (1972): 40-79

Alm, Leslie R., and Charles Davis. 'Agenda-Setting and Acid Precipitation in the United States.' *Environmental Management* 17.6 (1992): 807-16

Almond, Gabriel A. 'Review Article: The International-National Connection.' *British Journal of Political Science* 19.2 (1989): 237-59

Altman, John A., and Ed Petkus, Jr. 'Towards a Stakeholder-Based Policy Process: An Application of the Social Marketing Perspective to Environmental Policy Development.' *Policy Sciences* 27 (1994): 37-51

Altmeyer, George. 'Three Ideas of Nature in Canada, 1893-1914.' *Journal of Canadian Studies* 11 (1976): 21-36

Anderson, Charles W. 'The Place of Principles in Policy Analysis.' *American Political Science Review* 73 (1979): 711-23

Anderson, Doris. *The Unfinished Revolution: The Status of Women in Twelve Countries.* Toronto: Doubleday 1991

Anderson, F.J. *Natural Resources in Canada: Economic Theory and Policy.* Toronto: Methuen 1985

Anderson, James E. *Public Policymaking.* New York: Praeger 1975

Andruss, Van Christopher Plant, Judith Plant, and Eleanor Wright, eds. *Home! A BioRegional Reader.* Gabriola: New Society Publishers 1990

Armstrong, Christopher. *The Politics of Federalism: Ontario's Relations with the Federal Government, 1867-1942.* Toronto: University of Toronto Press 1981

Armstrong, Pat, and Hugh Armstrong. *The Double Ghetto.* Toronto: McClelland and Stewart 1994

Artibise, Alan F.J., and Gilbert A. Stelter. 'Conservation Planning and Urban Planning: The Canadian Commission of Conservation in Historical Perspective.' In *Planning for Conservation*, ed. R. Kain. New York: St. Martins 1981

Asch, M., and Macklem, P. 'Aboriginal Rights and Canadian Sovereignty: An Essay on *R. v. Sparrow.*' *Alberta Law Review* 29 (1991): 498-517

Atkinson Michael, ed. *Governing Canada* Toronto: Harcourt Brace 1994

Atkinson Michael, and William Coleman, 'Strong States and Weak States: Sectoral Policy Networks in Advanced Capitalist Economies.' *British Journal of Political Science* 19 (1989): 54

Atkinson, Michael M., and William D. Coleman. 'Policy Networks, Policy Communities and the Problems of Governance.' *Governance* 5.2 (1992): 154-80

Atwood, Margaret. *Survival: A Thematic Guide to Canadian Literature.* Toronto: Anansi 1972

Bakvis, Herman, and David MacDonald. 'The Canadian Cabinet: Organization, Decision-Rules, and Policy Impact.' In *Governing Canada: Institutions and Public Policy*, ed. M. Michael Atkinson. Toronto: Harcourt Brace Jovanovich 1993

Bakvis, Herman, and Neil Nevitte. 'The Greening of the Canadian Electorate: Environmentalism, Ideology and Partisanship.' In *Canadian Environmental Policy: Ecosystems, Politics and Process*, ed. R. Boardman, 144-63. Toronto: Oxford University Press 1992

Bankes, N. 'Indian Resource Rights and Constitutional Enactments in Western Canada, 1871-1930.' In *Law and Justice in a New Land: Essays in Western Canadian Legal History*, ed. L. Knafla, 129-64. Toronto: Carswell 1986

Bankes, Nigel, and J.O. Saunders, eds. *Public Disposition of Natural Resources: Essays from the First Banff Conference on Natural Resources Law, Banff, Alberta, April 12-15, 1983.* Calgary: Canadian Institute of Resources Law 1984

Bardach, Eugene. *The Implementation Game.* Cambridge: MIT Press 1977

Bartelmus, Peter. *Environment, Growth and Development: The Concepts and Strategies of Sustainability.* London: Routledge 1994

Baumgartner, Frank R., and Bryan D. Jones. 'Agenda Dynamics and Policy Subsystems.' *Journal of Politics* 53.4 (1991): 1044-74

–. *Agendas and Instability in American Politics.* Chicago: University of Chicago Press 1993

–. 'Attention, Boundary Effects, and Large-Scale Policy Change in Air Transportation Policy.' In *The Politics of Problem Definition: Shaping the Policy Agenda*, ed. D.A. Rochefort and R.W. Cobb, 50-66. Lawrence: University of Kansas Press 1994

Benedick, Richard. *Ozone Diplomacy.* Cambridge: Harvard University Press 1991

Benidickson, Jamie. 'Environmental Law Survey: Part I.' *University of Ottawa Law Review* 24.3 (1992): 734-811

–. 'Environmental Law Survey: Part II.' *University of Ottawa Law Review* 25.1 (1993): 123-54

Bennett, Colin, and Michael Howlett, 'The Lessons of Learning: Reconciling Theories of Policy Learning and Policy Change.' *Policy Sciences* 25.3 (1991): 275-94

Bennett, Scott, and Margaret McPhail. 'Policy Process Perceptions of Senior Canadian Federal Civil Servants: A View of the State and Its Environment.' *Canadian Public Administration* 35.3 (Autumn 1992): 299-316

Bennett, Terry, and David L. Anderson. *An Inter-Sectoral Study of Canada's Resource Industries.* Technical Paper No. 8. Kingston: Queen's University Centre for Resource Studies 1988

Berger, Thomas. *Northern Frontier, Northern Homeland: The Report of the Mackenzie Valley Pipeline Inquiry*, Vol. 1. Ottawa: Ministry of Supply and Services 1977

Bernstein, Marver H. *Regulating Business by Independent Commission.* Princeton: Princeton University Press 1955

Bingham, Gail. *Resolving Environmental Disputes: A Decade of Experience.* Washington, DC: Conservation Foundation 1986

Blake, Donald E., Neil Guppy, and Peter Urmetzer. *Being Green in B.C.: Public Attitudes towards Environmental Issues.* Vancouver: Fraser Basin Eco-Research Study 1996

Block, Walter E., ed. *Economics and the Environment: A Reconciliation*. Vancouver: Fraser Institute 1990

Boldt, M., and J.A. Long. 'Native Indian Self-Government: Instrument of Autonomy or Assimilation?' In *Governments in Conflict*, ed. J.A. Long and M. Boldt, 38-56. Toronto: University of Toronto Press 1988

Bosso, Christopher J. 'Setting the Agenda: Mass Media and the Discovery of Famine in Ethiopia.' In *Manipulating Public Opinion: Essays on Public Opinion as a Dependent Variable*, ed. M. Margolis and G.A. Mauser, 153-74. Pacific Grove: Brooks/Cole 1989

Braybrooke, David, and Charles Lindblom. *A Strategy of Decision: Policy Evaluation as a Social Process*. New York: Free Press of Glencoe 1963

Bregha, François, Jamie Benidickson, Don Gamble, Tom Shillington, and Ed Weick. *The Integration of Environmental Considerations into Government Policy*. Ottawa: Canadian Environmental Assessment Research Council 1990

Brenton, Tony. *The Greening of Machiavelli: The Evolution of International Environmental Politics*. London: Royal Institute of International Affairs 1994

Brewer, Garry D. 'The Policy Sciences Emerge: To Nurture and Structure a Discipline.' *Policy Sciences* 5.3 (1974): 239-44

Brewer, Garry, and Peter deLeon. *The Foundations of Policy Analysis*. Homewood: Dorsey 1983

Breyer, Stephen. *Regulation and Its Reform*. Cambridge: Harvard University Press 1982

British Columbia. *Crown Charges for Early Timber Rights: Royalties and Other Levies for Harvesting Rights on Timber Leases, Licences and Berths in British Columbia - First Report of the Task Force on Crown Timber Disposal, February 1974*, Vancouver: Ministry of Lands, Forests and Water Resources 1974

–. *Timber Appraisal: Policies and Procedures for Evaluating Crown Timber in British Columbia – Second Report of the Task Force on Crown Timber Disposal July 1974*. Vancouver: Ministry of Lands, Forests and Water Resources 1974

British Columbia Commission on Resources and Environment. *Annual Report to British Columbia Legislative Assembly, Commission on Resources and Environment*. Victoria: Commission on Resources and Environment 1993

British Columbia Round Table on the Environment and the Economy, Core Economy Group. 'An Economic Framework for Sustainability: A Draft Discussion Paper for the Citizens of British Columbia.' Victoria: British Columbia Round Table on the Environment and the Economy 1993

Brock, K.L. 'The Politics of Aboriginal Self-Government: A Canadian Paradox.' *Canadian Public Administration* 34 (1991): 272-86

Brown, M. Paul. 'Organizational Design as Policy Instrument: Environment Canada in the Canadian Bureaucracy.' In *Canadian Environmental Policy: Ecosystems, Politics, and Process*, ed. R. Boardman, 24-42. Toronto: Oxford University Press 1992

Brown, Lester R., Janet Abramovitz, Chris Bright, Christopher Flavin, Gary Gardner, Hal Kane, Anne Platt, Sandra Postel, David Roodman, Aaron Sachs, and Linda Starke. *State of the World 1996: A Worldwatch Institute Report on Progress toward a Sustainable Society*. New York: W.W. Norton 1996

Brown, R.C. 'The Doctrine of Usefulness: Natural Resource and Natural Park Policy in Canada, 1867-1914.' In *Canadian Parks in Perspective*, ed. J.G. Nelson, 46-62. Montreal: Harvest House 1970

Brown, R.D. 'The Fight Over Resource Profits.' *Canadian Tax Journal* 22.4 (1974): 315-37

Brown, Richard, and Murray Rankin. 'Persuasion, Penalties and Prosecution: Administrative v. Criminal Sanctions.' In *Securing Compliance: Seven Case Studies*, ed. M. Friedland, 325-50. Toronto: University of Toronto Press 1990

Brunnee, Jutta. 'Beyond Rio? The Evolution of International Environmental Law.' *Alternatives* 20.1 (1993): 16-25

Bruton, Jim, and Michael Howlett. 'Differences of Opinion: Round Tables, Policy Networks and the Failure of Canadian Environmental Strategy.' *Alternatives* 19.1 (1992): 25

Brym, Robert J., ed. *Regionalism in Canada*. Toronto: Irwin 1986

Buchanon, James, Robert Tollison, and Gordon Tullock, eds. *Towards a Theory of the Rent-Seeking Society*. College Station, TX: Texas A & M Press 1980

Bucovetsky, M.W. 'The Mining Industry and the Great Tax Reform Debate.' In *Pressure Group Behavior in Canadian Politics*, ed. A.P. Pross, 89-114. Toronto: McGraw-Hill Ryerson 1975

Burns, Ronald M. *Conflict and Its Resolution in the Administration of Mineral Resources in Canada*. Kingston: Centre for Resource Studies, Queens University 1976

Burt, Sandra. 'Canadian Women's Groups in the 1980s: Organizational Development and Policy Influence.' *Canadian Public Policy* 16.1 (1990): 17-28

Burton, Thomas L. *Natural Resource Policy in Canada*. Toronto: McClelland and Stewart 1974

Bushnell, S.I. 'Constitutional Law – Proprietary Rights and the Control of Natural Resources.' *Canadian Bar Review* 58 (1980): 157-69

–. 'The Control of Natural Resources through the Trade and Commerce Power and Proprietary Rights.' *Canadian Public Policy* 6.2 (1980): 313-24

Buttel, F.H. 'New Directions in Environmental Sociology.' *Annual Review of Sociology* 13 (1987): 465-88

Buttel, Frederick H. 'Social Science and the Environment: Competing Theories.' *Social Science Quarterly* 57.2 (1976): 307-23

Cadsby, Charles Brian, and Kenneth Woodside. 'The Effects of the North American Free Trade Agreement on the Canada-United States Trade Relationship.' *Canadian Public Policy* 19.4 (1993): 450-62

Cail, Robert E. *Land, Man, and the Law: The Disposal of Crown Lands in British Columbia 1871-1913*. Vancouver: UBC Press 1972

Cairns, Alan. 'The Past and Future of the Canadian Administrative State.' *University of Toronto Law Journal* 40 (1990): 319-61

Cameron, David R. 'The Growth of Government Spending: The Canadian Experience in Comparative Perspective.' In *State and Society*, ed. K. Banting, 21-52. Toronto: University of Toronto Press 1986

Cameron, Duncan. *The Free Trade Deal*. Toronto: James Lorimer 1988

Cammack, Paul. 'Bringing the State Back In?' *British Journal of Political Science* 19.2 (1989): 261-90

–. 'The New Institutionalism: Predatory Rule, Institutional Persistence, and Macro-Social Change.' *Economy and Society* 21.4 (1992): 397-429

Canada. *Canadian Arctic Marine Conservation Strategy: Discussion Paper*. Ottawa: Department of Fisheries and Oceans 1987

–. *Northeastern Quebec Agreement*. Ottawa: Information Canada 1978

–. *The Western Arctic Claim: The Inuvialuit Final Agreement*. Ottawa: Indian and Northern Affairs Canada 1984

–. *Sechelt Indian Band Self-Government Act*. Ottawa: Queen's Printer 1986

–. *Canada's Green Plan: Canada's Green Plan for a Healthy Environment*. Ottawa: Ministry of Supply and Services 1990

–. *Comprehensive Land Claim Umbrella Final Agreement between the Government of Canada, the Council for Yukon Indians and the Government of the Yukon*. Ottawa: Indian and Northern Affairs 1990

–. *The State of Canada's Environment*. Ottawa: Ministry of Supply and Services Canada 1991

–. *Agreement in Principle for the Nunavut Settlement Area*. Ottawa: Indian and Northern Affairs 1992

–. *Gwich'in Comprehensive Land Claim Agreement*. Ottawa: Indian and Northern Affairs 1992

Canada, Department of External Affairs. *A Review of Canadian Trade Policy: A Background Document to Canadian Trade Policy for the 1980s*. Ottawa: Ministry of Supply and Services 1983

Canada, Department of Finance. *The Canada-U.S. Free Trade Agreement: An Economic Assessment*. Ottawa: Ministry of Supply and Services 1988

Canada, Department of Justice. *A Consolidation of the Constitution Acts 1867 to 1982*. Ottawa: Ministry of Supply and Services 1983

Canada, Department of Regional Economic Expansion. *Single-Sector Communities*. Ottawa: Department of Regional Economic Expansion 1977

Canadian Bar Association, ed. *Sustainable Development in Canada: Options for Law Reform*. Ottawa: Canadian Bar Association 1990

Canadian Council of Resource and Environment Ministers. *Report of the National Task Force on Environment and Economy*. Ottawa: Ministry of Supply and Services 1987

Canadian Environmental Advisory Council. *Review of the Proposed Environmental Protection Act*. Ottawa: Ministry of Supply and Services 1987

Canadian Environmental Law Association. *NAFTA Facts: A Series of Information Sheets about the Effects of NAFTA: NAFTA and Energy*. Toronto: Canadian Environmental Law Association, n.d.

Canadian Pulp and Paper Association. *Response to Challenges and Choices: The Interim Report of the Royal Commission on the Economic Union and Developmental Prospects for Canada*. Montreal: Canadian Pulp and Paper Association 1984

Carmichael, Edward A., and C.M. Herrera. *Canada's Energy Policy: 1985 and Beyond*. Toronto: C.D. Howe Institute 1984

Cassidy, F., ed. *Aboriginal Title in British Columbia: Delgamuukw v. The Queen*. Vancouver: Oolichan Books/Institute for Research on Public Policy 1992

Cassidy, Frank, and Norman Dale. *After Native Claims? The Implications of Comprehensive Claims Settlements for Natural Resources in British Columbia*. Halifax: Institute for Research on Public Policy 1988

Castles, Francis G. 'The Impact of Parties on Public Expenditure.' In *The Impact of Parties: Politics and Policies in Democratic Capitalist States*, ed. F.G. Castles. London: Sage Publications 1982

Castles, Frank, and Robert D. McKinlay. 'Does Politics Matter: An Analysis of the Public Welfare Commitment in Advanced Democratic States.' *European Journal of Political Research* 7.2 (1979): 169-86

Chandler, Marsha A. 'The Politics of Public Enterprise.' In *Crown Corporations in Canada: The Calculus of Instrument Choice*, ed. J.R.S. Pritchard, 185-218. Toronto: Butterworths 1983

-. 'Constitutional Change and Public Policy: The Impact of the Resource Amendment (Section 92A).' *Canadian Journal of Political Science* 19.1 (1986): 103-26

Chant, Donald A. 'A Decade of Environmental Concern: Retrospect and Prospect.' *Alternatives* 10.1 (1981): 3-6

Chapin, H., and D. Deneau. *Access and the Policy-Making Process*. Ottawa: Canadian Council on Social Development 1978

Church, Albert M. *Conflicts over Resource Ownership: The Use of Public Policy by Private Interests*. Lexington: Lexington Books 1982

Claff, Cindy, John Douglas, Karl Keller, and John Moore. 'Federal Environmental Litigation in 1977: National Environmental Policy Act.' *Harvard Environmental Law Review* 2 (1977): 199-240

Clark, Judson F. 'Forest Revenues and Forest Conservation.' *Forest Conservation* 3.1 (1907): 19-30

Clark, S.D. *The New Urban Poor*. Toronto: McGraw-Hill Ryerson 1978

Clement, Wallace. *Hardrock Mining: Industrial Relations and Technological Changes at Inco*. Toronto: McClelland and Stewart 1981

-. *The Struggle to Organize: Resistance in Canada's Fishery*. Toronto: McClelland and Stewart 1986

-. 'Labour in Exposed Sectors: Canada's Resource Economy.' In *The Challenge of Class Analysis*, ed. W. Clement, 89-103. Ottawa: Carleton University Press 1988

-. 'Debates and Directions: A Political Economy of Resources.' In *The New Canadian Political Economy*, ed. W. Clement and G. Williams, 36-53. Montreal and Kingston: McGill-Queen's University Press 1989

Clement, Wallace, and Daniel Drache. *The New Practical Guide to Canadian Political Economy*. Toronto: James Lorimer 1985

Coates, K., ed. *Aboriginal Land Claims in Canada: A Regional Perspective*. Toronto: Copp Clark Pitman 1992

Cobb, R., J.K. Ross, and M.H. Ross, 'Agenda Building as a Comparative Political Process.' *American Political Science Review* 70 (1976): 132

Cobb, Roger W., and Charles D. Elder. *Participation in American Politics: The Dynamics of Agenda-Building*. Boston: Allyn and Bacon 1972

Cohen, J., and M. Krashinsky. 'Capturing the Rents on Resource Land for the Public Landowner: The Case for a Crown Corporation.' *Canadian Public Policy* 2.3 (1976): 411-23

Cohen, M., J. March, and J. Olsen. 'A Garbage Can Model of Organizational Choice.' *Administrative Science Quarterly* 17.1 (1972): 1-25

Cohen, Wesley M., and Daniel A. Levinthal. 'Absorptive Capacity: A New Perspective on Learning and Innovation.' *Administrative Science Quarterly* 35 (1990): 128-52

Coleman, William D. 'Analyzing the Associative Action of Business: Policy Advocacy and Policy Participation.' *Canadian Public Administration* 28.3 (1985): 413-33

-. 'The Emergence of Business Interest Association in Canada: An Historical Overview.' Paper presented to the Canadian Political Science Association, Montreal, 1985

-. 'Canadian Business and the State.' In *The State and Economic Interests*, ed. K. Banting, 245-89. Toronto: University of Toronto Press 1986

-. *Business and Politics: A Study of Collective Action*. Montreal and Kingston: McGill-Queen's Press 1988

-. 'Policy Convergence in Banking: A Comparative Study.' *Political Studies* 42 (1994): 274-92

Coleman, William D., and H.J. Jacek. 'The Roles and Activities of Business Interest Associations in Canada.' *Canadian Journal of Political Science* 16.2 (1983): 257-80

Coleman, William D., and Grace Skogstad, eds. *Policy Communities and Public Policy in Canada: A Structural Approach*. Toronto: Copp Clark Pitman 1990

Colvin, Eric. 'Legal Theory and the Paramountcy Rule.' *McGill Law Journal* 25.1 (1979-1980): 82-98

Connolly, William E. 'The Challenge to Pluralist Theory.' In *The Bias of Pluralism*, ed. W.E. Connolly, 3-34. New York: Atherton Press 1969

Cook, F.L., T.R. Tyler, E.G. Goetz, M.T. Gordon, D. Protess, D.R. Leff, and H.L. Molotch. 'Media and Agenda Setting: Effects on the Public, Interest Group Leaders, Policy Makers, and Policy.' *Public Opinion Quarterly* 47.1 (1983): 16-35

Copithorne, L. 'Natural Resources and Regional Disparities: A Skeptical View.' *Canadian Public Policy* 5.2 (1979): 181-94

Costanza, Robert, ed. *Ecological Economics: The Science and Management of Sustainability*. New York: Columbia University Press 1991

Cotgrove, Stephen F. *Catastrophe or Cornucopia: The Environment, Politics, and the Future*. Chichester, UK: John Wiley and Sons 1982

Cotton, Roger, and Kelley M. MacKinnon. 'An Overview of Environmental Law in Canada.' In *Environmental Law and Business in Canada*, ed. G. Thompson, M.L. McConnell, and L.B. Huestis, 1-30. Aurora: Canada Law Book 1993

Council of Forest Industries of British Columbia. *Native Land Claims in British Columbia: A Background Paper*. Vancouver: COFI 1986

Crommelin, Michael, and Andrew Thompson, eds. *Mineral Leasing as an Instrument of Public Policy*. Vancouver: UBC Press 1977

Cromwell, Thomas A. *Locus Standi: A Commentary on the Law of Standing in Canada*. Toronto: Carswell 1986

Crosby, Alfred W. *Ecological Imperialism: The Biological Expansion of Europe 900-1900*. Cambridge: Cambridge University Press 1992

Cumming, Peter, and N.H. Mickenberg, eds. *Native Rights in Canada*. Toronto: General Publishing 1972

Curry-Roper, Janel M., and Steven McGuire, 'The Individualist Imagination and Natural Resource Policy.' *Society and Natural Resources* 6 (1993): 259-72

Daly, Herman E., and John B. Cobb, Jr. *For the Common Good: Redirecting the Economy toward Community, the Environment, and a Sustainable Future*. Boston: Beacon Press 1994

Daly, Herman E., and Kenneth N. Townsend, eds. *Valuing the Earth: Economics, Ecology, Ethics.* Cambridge, MA: MIT Press 1993

Daugherty, W.E., and D. Madill. *Indian Government under Indian Act Legislation, 1868-1951.* Ottawa: Indian Affairs and Northern Development 1980

Deardon, Philip, and Rick Rollins, eds. *Parks and Protected Areas in Canada.* Toronto: Oxford University Press 1993

deHaven-Smith, Lance, and Carl E. Van Horn, 'Subgovernment Conflict in Public Policy.' *Policy Studies Journal* 12 (1984): 627-42

deLeon, Peter. 'Policy Evaluation and Program Termination.' *Policy Studies Review* 2.4 (1983): 631-47

de Pencier, J. 'Oldman River Dam and Federal Environmental Assessment Now and in the Future.' *Journal of Environmental Law and Practice* 2.3 (1992): 292-312

de Pencier, Joseph. 'The Federal Environmental Assessment Process: A Practical Comparison of the EARP Guidelines Order and the Canadian Environmental Assessment Act.' *Journal of Environmental Law and Practice* 3.3 (1993): 329-43

Dery, David. *Problem Definition in Policy Analysis.* Lawrence: University of Kansas Press 1984

Desfosses, Alain F. *Environmental Quality Strategic Review: A Follow-on Report of the Task Force on Program Review.* Ottawa: Ministry of Supply and Services 1986

Devall, Bill. *Simple in Means, Rich in Ends: Practicing Deep Ecology.* Salt Lake City: Peregrine Smith 1988

Diani, Mario. *Green Networks: A Structural Analysis of the Italian Environmental Movement.* Edinburgh: University of Edinburgh Press 1995

Dobb, Maurice Herbert. *Theories of Value and Distribution Since Adam Smith: Ideology and Economic Theory.* Cambridge: Cambridge University Press 1973

Dobell, Rod, and Michael Neufeld, eds. *Beyond NAFTA: The Western Hemisphere Interface.* Lantzville: Oolichan Books 1993

Doern, G. Bruce. 'Getting It Green: Canadian Environmental Policy in the 1990s.' In *The Environmental Imperative: Market Approaches to the Greening of Canada*, ed. G.B. Doern, 1-18. Toronto: C.D. Howe Institute 1990

–, ed. *The Environmental Imperative: Market Approaches to the Greening of Canada.* Toronto: C.D. Howe Institute 1990

–. 'The Federal Green Plan: Assessing the "Prequel."' *Commentary* 17 (1990): 1-8

–. *Getting It Green: Case Studies in Canadian Environmental Regulation.* Toronto: C.D. Howe Institute 1990

–. 'Shades of Green: Gauging Canada's Green Plan.' *Commentary* 29 (1991): 1-12

–. 'Johnny-Green-Latelies: The Mulroney Environmental Record.' In *How Ottawa Spends 1992-93: The Politics of Competitiveness*, ed. F. Abele, 353-76. Ottawa: Carleton University Press 1992

Doern, G.B., and Thomas Conway. *The Greening of Canada: Federal Institutions and Decisions.* Toronto: University of Toronto Press 1994

Doern, G. Bruce, and Glen Toner. *The Politics of Energy: The Development and Implementation of the National Energy Program.* Toronto: Methuen 1985

Donner, Arthur, and Fred Lazar. 'The Economic Effects of an Environmental Tax.' In *Taxes as Instruments of Public Policy*, ed. Allan M. Maslove, 93-166. Toronto: University of Toronto Press 1994

Dorcey, A.H.J., and C.L. Riek. 'Negotiation-Based Approaches to the Settlement of Environmental Disputes in Canada.' In *The Place of Negotiation in Environmental Assessment*, ed. B. Sadler, 7-36. Ottawa: Canadian Environmental Assessment Research Council 1989

Downey, Terrence J. 'Understanding Policy-Making a Necessary First Step for Environmentalists.' *Alternatives* 14.2 (1987): 30-4

Drushka, Ken, Bob Nixon, and Ray Travers. *Touch Wood: B.C. Forests at the Crossroads.* Madeira Park: Harbour Publishing 1993

Dubasak, Marilyn. *Wilderness Preservation: A Cross-Cultural Comparison of Canada and the United States.* New York: Garland 1990

Duncan, Linda F., ed. *Environmental Enforcement: Proceedings of the National Conference on the Enforcement of Environmental Law.* Edmonton: Environmental Law Centre 1985

Dunlap, R.E., and K.D. Van Liere. 'The New Environmental Paradigm: A Proposed Measuring Instrument and Preliminary Results.' *Journal of Environmental Education* 9 (1978): 10-19

Dunn, William N. 'Methods of the Second Type: Coping with the Wilderness of Conventional Policy Analysis.' *Policy Studies Review* 7.4 (1988): 720-37

Dussault, R., and L. Borgeat. *Administrative Law: A Treatise.* Toronto: Carswell 1990

Dwivedi, O.P. 'The Canadian Government Response to Environmental Concern.' *International Journal* 28 (1972-73): 134-52

–. *Protecting the Environment: Issues and Choices, Canadian Perspectives.* Toronto: Copp Clark Pitman 1974

–, ed. *The Administrative State in Canada.* Toronto: University of Toronto Press 1982

Dwivedi, O.P., and R.B. Woodrow, 'Environmental Policy-Making and Administration in a Federal State: The Impact of Overlapping Jurisdictions in Canada.' In *Challenges to Federalism*, ed. W.M. Chandler and C.W. Zollner. Kingston: Queen's University Institute of Intergovernmental Relations 1989

Dye, Thomas R. *Understanding Public Policy.* Englewood Cliffs, NJ: Prentice-Hall 1972

Easterbrook, W., and Hugh G.J. Aitken. *Canadian Economic History.* Toronto: Macmillan 1956

Eckersley, Robin. 'Liberal Democracy and the Rights of Nature: The Struggle for Inclusion.' *Environmental Politics* 4.4 (1995): 169-98

Economic Council of Canada. *Venturing Forth: An Assessment of the Canada-U.S. Trade Agreement.* Ottawa: Economic Council of Canada 1988

Edelman, Murray J. *Constructing the Political Spectacle.* Chicago: University of Chicago Press 1988

Elder, P.S. 'Environmental Protection through the Common Law.' *Western Ontario Law Review* 12 (1973): 107-71

Elgie, S. 'Environmental Groups and the Courts: 1970-1992.' In *Environmental Law and Business in Canada*, ed. G. Thompson, M. McConnell, and L. Huestis. Toronto: Canada Law Books 1993

Elmore, Richard F. 'Organizational Models of Social Program Implementation.' *Public Policy* 26.2 (1978): 185-228

Engelhart, Kenneth, and Michael Trebilcock. *Public Participation in the Regulatory Process: The Issue of Funding.* Working Paper No. 17. Ottawa: Economic Council of Canada 1981

England, Richard, and Barry Bluestone. 'Ecology and Social Conflict.' In *Toward a Steady-State Economy*, ed. H.E. Daly, 190-214. San Francisco: W.H. Freeman 1973

Enloe, Cynthia H. *The Politics of Pollution in a Comparative Perspective: Ecology and Power in Four Nations.* New York: McKay 1975

Environment Canada. *Program Review and Environment Canada.* Ottawa: Environment Canada 1995

–. *Environmental Protection Legislation Designed for the Future – A Renewed CEPA.* Electronic Document Available at <http://www.doe.ca/cepa/govtresp/efront.html>

Enzensberger, H.M. 'A Critique of Political Ecology.' *New Left Review* 84 (1974): 3-31

Erbring, Lutz, and Edie N. Goldenberg. 'Front Page News and Real World Cues: A New Look at Agenda-Setting by the Media.' *American Journal of Political Science* 24.1 (1980): 16-49

Ervin, A.M. 'Contrasts between the Resolution of Native Land Claims in the United States and Canada Based on Observations of the Alaska Native Land Claims Movement.' *Canadian Journal of Native Studies* 1 (1981): 123-40

Estey, Willard. 'Public Nuisance and Standing to Sue.' *Osgoode Hall Law Journal* 10 (1972): 563-82

Estrin, David, and John Swaigen. *Environment on Trial: A Handbook of Ontario Environmental Law.* Toronto: Canadian Environmental Law Research Foundation 1978

–, eds. *Environment on Trial: A Guide to Ontario Environmental Law and Policy.* Toronto: Institute for Environmental Law and Policy 1993

Esty, Daniel C. *Greening the GATT: Trade, Environment and the Future*. Washington DC: Institute of International Economics 1994

Evans, Peter B. 'Transnational Linkages and the Economic Role of the State: An Analysis of Developing and Industrialized Nations in the Post-World War II Period.' In *Bringing the State Back In*, ed. D.R. Peter Evans and Theda Skocpol, 192-226. Cambridge: Cambridge University Press 1985

Evernden, Neil. *The Social Creation of Nature*. Baltimore: Johns Hopkins University Press 1992

–. *The Natural Alien: Humankind and Environment*. Toronto: University of Toronto Press 1993

Fagan, Margaret, and Donald Lloyd. *Dynamic Canada: The Environment and the Economy*. Toronto: McGraw-Hill Ryerson 1991

Farnham, Timothy J., and Paul Mohai. 'A Shift in Values: Non-commodity Resource Management and the Forest Service.' *Policy Studies Journal* 23.2 (1995): 268-80

Felt, Lawrence. 'Regional Disparity, Resource Development, and Unequal Accumulation.' In *Contemporary Sociology: Critical Perspectives*, ed. Peter S. Li and B. Singh Bolaria, 243-61. Toronto: Copp Clark Pitman

Fenge, T., and L.G. Smith. 'Reforming the Federal Environmental Assessment and Review Process.' *Canadian Public Policy* 12.4 (1986): 596-605

Field, Barry C., and Nancy D. Olewiler. *Environmental Economics*. Toronto: McGraw-Hill Ryerson 1995

Finkelstein, Neil, and Brian M. Rogers, eds. *Recent Developments in Administrative Law*. Agincourt, ON: Carswell 1987

Finkle, Peter Z.R., and Alastair R. Lucas, eds. *Environmental Law in the 1980s: A New Beginning*. Calgary: Faculty of Law, University of Calgary 1981

Fisher, Allan G.B. *The Clash of Progress and Security*. New York: A.M. Kelley 1966

Fletcher, Frederick J., and Lori Stahlbrand. 'Mirror or Participant? The News Media and Environmental Policy.' In *Canadian Environmental Policy*, ed. Robert Boardman, 144-63. Toronto: Oxford University Press 1992

Forester, John. 'Bounded Rationality and the Politics of Muddling Through.' *Public Administration Review* 44 (1984): 23-31

–. *Planning in the Face of Power*. Berkeley: University of California Press 1989

Foster, Charles H. *Experiment in Bioregionalism: The New England River Basin Story*. Hanover: University Press of New England 1984

Fox, Annette Baker. 'Environment and Trade: The NAFTA Case.' *Political Science Quarterly* 110.1 (1995): 49-68

Frank, Andre Gunder. *On Capitalist Underdevelopment*. Bombay: Oxford University Press 1975

Franks, C.E.S. *The Parliament of Canada*. Toronto: University of Toronto Press 1987

Franson, R.T., and P.T. Burns. 'Environmental Rights for the Canadian Citizen: A Prescription for Reform.' *Alberta Law Review* 12.2 (1974): 153-71

Freeman, Gary P. 'National Styles and Policy Sectors: Explaining Structured Variation.' *Journal of Public Policy* 5 (1985): 467-96

Gaffield, Chad, and Pam Gaffield, eds. *Consuming Canada: Readings in Environmental History*. Toronto: Copp Clark Pitman 1995

Galanter, Marc. 'Reading the Landscape of Disputes: What We Know and Don't Know (And Think We Know) about Our Allegedly Contentious and Litigious Society.' *UCLA Law Review* 31 (1983): 4-71

Gale, Robert J.P. 'NAFTA and Its Implications for Resource and Environmental Management.' In *Resource and Environmental Management in Canada: Addressing Conflict and Uncertainty*, ed. Bruce Mitchell, 99-129. Toronto: Oxford University Press 1995

Galtung, Johan. 'The Green Movement: A Socio-Historical Exploration.' *International Sociology* 1.1 (1986): 75-90

GATT. *Basic Instruments and Selected Documents*. Geneva: GATT 1969

Gersick, Connie J.G. 'Revolutionary Change Theories: A Multilevel Exploration of the Punctuated Equilibrium Paradigm.' *Academy of Management Review* 16.1 (1991): 10-36

Gertler, Franklin, Paul Muldoon, and Marcia Valiante. 'Public Access to Environmental Justice.' In *Sustainable Development in Canada: Options for Law Reform*, ed. Canadian Bar Association Committee on Sustainable Development in Canada, 79-97. Ottawa: Canadian Bar Association 1990

Gibson, Dale. 'Constitutional Jurisdiction Over Environmental Management in Canada.' *University of Toronto Law Journal* 23 (1973): 54-87

Gibson, Robert. 'Out of Control and Beyond Understanding: Acid Rain as a Political Dilemma.' In *Managing Leviathan: Environmental Politics and the Administrative State*, ed. Robert Paehlke and Douglas Torgerson, 243-82. London: Belhaven Press 1990

Gillis, Anna Maria. 'The New Forestry: An Eco-System Approach to Land Management.' *Bioscience* 40.8 (1990): 558-62

Gillis, R. Peter, and Thomas R. Roach. *Lost Initiatives: Canada's Forest Industries, Forest Policy, and Forest Conservation*. New York: Greenwood Press 1986

Gillroy, John Martin, and Maurice Wade, eds. *The Moral Dimensions of Public Policy Choice: Beyond the Market Paradigm*. Pittsburgh: University of Pittsburgh Press 1992

Giroux, Lorne. *Enforcement Practices of Environment Canada*. Ottawa: Canadian Environmental Advisory Council 1985

Globerman, Steven, ed. *Continental Accord: North American Economic Integration*. Vancouver: Fraser Institute 1991

Goldmann, Robert B., ed. *Roundtable Justice: Case Studies in Conflict Resolution: Reports to the Ford Foundation*. Boulder, CO: Westview Press 1980

Gourevitch, Peter. 'The Second Image Reversed: The International Sources of Domestic Politics.' *International Organization* 32 (1978): 881-912

Granatstein, J.L. 'Free Trade between Canada and the United States: The Issue That Will Not Go Away.' In *The Politics of Canada's Economic Relationship with the United States*, ed. D. Stairs and G. Winham, 1-51. Toronto: University of Toronto Press 1985

Grey, Rodney de C. *United States Trade Policy Legislation: A Canadian View*. Montreal: Institute for Research on Public Policy 1982

Grima, A.P. 'Participatory Rites: Integrating Public Involvement in Environmental Impact Assessment.' In *Environmental Impact Assessment: The Canadian Experience*, ed. J.B.R. Whitney and V.W. Maclaren, 33-51. Toronto: University of Toronto Institute for Environmental Studies 1985

Grinspun, Ricardo, and Maxwell A. Cameron, eds. *The Political Economy of North American Free Trade*. Montreal and Kingston: McGill-Queens University Press 1993

Grubb, Michael. *The Earth Summit Agreements: A Guide and Assessment*. London: RIIA/Earthscan 1993

Grubel, Herbert G., ed. *Conceptual Issues in Service Sector Research: A Symposium*. Vancouver: Fraser Institute 1987

Grumbine, R. Edward. 'Ecosystem Management for Native Diversity: How to Save Our National Parks and Forests.' *Forest Watch* 9.6 (1988): 21-7

Gunderson, Morley. *Economics of Poverty and Income Distribution*. Toronto: Butterworths 1983

Gunderson, Morley, Leon Muszynski, and Jennifer Keck. *Women and Labour Market Poverty*. Ottawa: Canadian Advisory Council on the Status of Women 1990

Haas, Ernst B. 'Is There a Hole in the Whole? Knowledge, Technology, Interdependence, and the Construction of International Regimes.' *International Organization* 29 (1975): 827-76

–. 'Why Collaborate? Issue-Linkage and International Regimes.' *World Politics* 32.3 (1980): 357-405

Haas, Peter M. 'Introduction: Epistemic Communities and International Policy Coordination.' *International Organization* 46 (1992): 3

Haas, Peter M., Robert O. Keohane, and Marc A. Levy, eds. *Institutions for the Earth: Sources of Effective International Environmental Protection*. Boston: MIT Press 1993

Habermas, Jurgen. *Legitimation Crisis*. Boston: Beacon Press 1975

Haggard, Stephen, and Beth A. Simmons. 'Theories of International Regimes.' *International Organization* 41.3 (1987): 491-517

Hajer, Maarten A. *The Politics of Environmental Discourse: Ecological Modernization and the Policy Process.* Oxford: Clarendon 1995

Hale, Sylvia. *Controversies in Sociology: A Canadian Introduction.* Toronto: Copp Clark Pitman 1995

Hall, Peter A. 'Introduction.' In *The Political Power of Economic Ideas: Keynesianism across Nations,* ed. Peter A. Hall, 3-26. Princeton: Princeton University Press 1989

–. 'Policy Paradigms, Experts, and the State: The Case of Macroeconomic Policy-Making in Britain.' In *Social Scientists, Policy, and the State,* ed. Stephen Brooks and Alain-G Gagnon, 53-78. New York: Praeger 1990

–. 'Policy Paradigms, Social Learning and the State: The Case of Economic Policy Making in Britain.' *Comparative Politics* 25.3 (1993): 275-96

Hamm, Keith E. 'Patterns of Influence Among Committees, Agencies, and Interest Groups.' *Legislative Studies Quarterly* 8 (1983): 415

Hanebury, J.B. 'Environmental Impact Assessment in the Canadian Federal System.' *McGill Law Journal* 36 (1991): 962-1005

Harris, Leslie. 'The East Coast Fisheries.' In *Resource and Environmental Management in Canada: Addressing Conflict and Uncertainty,* ed. Bruce Mitchell, 130-50. Toronto: Oxford University Press 1995

Harrison, Kathyrn. 'Prospects for intergovernmental Harmonization in Environmental Policy.' In *Canada: The State of the Federation 1994,* ed. Douglas Brown and Janet Hiebert, 179-99. Kingston: Institute of Intergovernmental Relations, Queen's University 1995

–. 'Is Co-operation the Answer: Canadian Environmental Enforcement in Comparative Context.' *Journal of Policy Analysis and Management* 14.2 (1995): 221-44

–. 'Environmental Protection in British Columbia: Postmaterial Values, Organized Interests and Party Politics.' In *Politics, Policy and Government in British Columbia,* ed. R.K. Carty, 290-309. Vancouver: UBC Press 1996

–. *Passing the Buck: Federalism and Canadian Environmental Policy.* Vancouver: UBC Press 1996

Harrison, Kathryn, and George Hoberg. 'Setting the Environmental Agenda in Canada and the United States: The Cases of Dioxin and Radon.' *Canadian Journal of Political Science* 24.1 (1991): 3-27

–. *Risk, Science, and Politics: Regulating Toxic Substances in Canada and the United States.* Montreal and Kingston: McGill-Queen's University Press 1994

Harrison, Kathryn, and W.T. Stanbury. 'Privatization in British Columbia: Lessons from the Sale of Government Laboratories.' *Canadian Public Administration* 33.2 (1990): 165-97

Harter, Philip J. 'Negotiating Regulations: A Cure for the Malaise?' *Environmental Impact Assessment Review* 3.1 (1982): 75-91

Hawkens, Paul. *The Ecology of Commerce.* New York: Harper Business 1993

Hayes, Michael T. 'The Semi-Sovereign Pressure Groups: A Critique of Current Theory and an Alternative Typology.' *Journal of Politics* 40 (1978): 134-61

–. *Incrementalism and Public Policy.* New York: Longmans 1992

Hays, Samuel P. *Conservation and the Gospel of Efficiency: The Progressive Movement in Conservation 1890-1920.* New York: Atheneum Press 1969

Healy, Robert G., and William Ascher. 'Knowledge in the Policy Process: Incorporating Environmental Information in Natural Resources Policy Making.' *Policy Sciences* 28 (1995): 1-19

Heclo, Hugh. 'Issue Networks and the Executive Establishment.' In *The New American Political System,* ed. Anthony King, 87-124. Washington, DC: American Enterprise Institute for Public Policy Research 1978

Heinz, John P., et al. 'Inner Circles or Hollow Cores.' *Journal of Politics* 52.2 (1990): 356-90

Heinz, John P., et al. *The Hollow Core: Private Interests in National Policy Making.* Cambridge: Harvard University Press 1993

Hernes, Gudmund. 'Structural Change in Social Processes.' *American Journal of Sociology* 82 (1976): 513-47

Heron, Craig, and Robert Storey. *On the Job: Confronting the Labour Process in Canada.* Montreal: McGill-Queen's University Press 1986

Hessing, Melody. 'Production of the Public Voice: Public Participation in the Hearing Process as Contemporary Democracy.' Ph.D. dissertation, University of British Columbia, 1984

–. 'Public Participation in the Okanagan Lakes Milfoil Issue: A Grassroots Struggle.' In *Community Organizing and the Canadian State,* ed. R. Ng, G. Walker, and J. Muller. Toronto: Between the Lines 1990

–. 'Environmental Protection and Pulp Pollution in British Columbia: The Challenge of the Emerald State.' *The Journal of Human Justice* 5.1 (Autumn 1993): 29-45

–. 'Making the Connections: Ecofeminist Perspectives on Women and Environment.' *Alternatives* 19.1 (June 1993): 14-21

Hibbs, Douglas A., Jr. *The Political Economy of Industrial Democracies.* Cambridge, MA: Harvard University Press 1987

Hilgartner, Stephen, and Charles L. Bosk. 'The Rise and Fall of Social Problems: A Public Arenas Model.' *American Journal of Sociology* 94 (1981): 53-78

Hiller, Harry. *Canadian Society: A Macro Analysis.* Scarborough: Prentice-Hall 1991

Hirst, Paul, and Grahame Thompson. 'The Problems of "Globalization": International Relations, National Economic Management and the Formation of Trading Blocs.' *Economy and Society* 21.4 (1992): 357-96

Hoberg, George. 'Technology, Political Structure and Social Regulation: A Cross-National Analysis.' *Comparative Politics* 18.3 (1986): 357-76

–. 'Risk, Science and Politics: Alachlor Regulation in Canada and the United States.' *Canadian Journal of Political Science* 23.2 (1990): 257-78

–. 'Representation and Governance in Canadian Environmental Policy.' At the Annual Meeting of the Canadian Political Science Association, Kingston, 1991

–. 'Sleeping with an Elephant: The American Influence on Canadian Environmental Regulation.' *Journal of Public Policy* 11.1 (1991): 107-31

–. 'Environmental Policy: Alternative Styles.' In *Governing Canada: Institutions and Public Policy*, ed. M.M. Atkinson, 307-42. Toronto: Harcourt Brace Jovanovich 1993

–. 'Governing the Environment: Comparing Canada and the United States.' In *Degrees of Freedom: Canada and the United States in a Changing World*, ed. Keith Banting, George Hoberg, and Richard Simeon, 341-88. Montreal: McGill-Queen's University Press 1997

Hoberg, George, and Kathyrn Harrison. 'It's Not Easy Being Green: The Politics of Canada's Green Plan.' *Canadian Public Policy* 20.2 (1994): 119-37

Hodgetts, J.E. *Pioneer Public Service.* Toronto: University of Toronto Press 1957

–. *The Canadian Public Service: A Physiology of Government 1867-1970.* Toronto: University of Toronto Press 1973

Hodgins, Bruce W., and Jamie Benidickson. *The Temagami Experience: Recreation, Resources and Aboriginal Rights in the Northern Ontario Wilderness.* Toronto: University of Toronto Press 1989

Hodgins, B.W., J. Benidickson, and P. Gillis. 'The Ontario and Quebec Experiments in Forest Reserves.' *Journal of Forest History* 26 (1982): 20-33

Hogg, P.W. 'The Supreme Court of Canada and Administrative Law 1949-1971.' *Osgoode Hall Law Journal* 11.2 (1973): 187-223

Hood, Christopher. 'Using Bureaucracy Sparingly.' *Public Administration* 61.2 (1983): 197-208

Hood, Christopher C. *The Tools of Government.* Chatham: Chatham House 1986

Howlett, Michael. 'Forest Policy in Canada: Resource Constraints and Political Interests in the Canadian Forest Sector.' Ph.D. dissertation, Queen's University, 1988

–. 'The 1987 National Forest Sector Strategy and the Search for a Federal Role in Canadian Forest Policy.' *Canadian Public Administration* 32.4 (1989): 545-63

–. 'The Round Table Experience: Representation and Legitimacy in Canadian Environmental Policy Making.' *Queen's Quarterly* 97.4 (1990): 580-601

–. 'The Politics of Constitutional Change in a Federal System: Institutional Arrangements and Political Interests in the Negotiation of Section 92A of the Canadian Constitution Act (1982).' *Publius: The Journal of Federalism* 21.1 (1991): 121-42

–. 'Policy Paradigms and Policy Change: Lessons from the Old and New Canadian Policies towards Aboriginal Peoples.' *Policy Studies Journal* 22.4 (1994): 631-51
–. 'Sustainable Development: Environmental Policy.' In *Canadian Public Policy: Globalization and Political Parties*, ed. A. Johnson and A. Stritch. Toronto: Copp Clark Longman 1996
–. 'Issue-Attention and Punctuated Equilibria Models Reconsidered: An Empirical Examination of the Dynamics of Agenda-Setting in Canada.' *Canadian Journal of Political Science* forthcoming 30.1 (1997)
Howlett, Michael, and Rebecca Raglon. 'Constructing the Environmental Spectacle: Green Ads and the Corporate Image 1910-1990.' *Environmental History Review* 16.4 (1993): 53-73
Howlett, Michael, and M. Ramesh. *Political Economy of Canada: An Introduction*. Toronto: McClelland and Stewart 1992
–. 'Patterns of Policy Instrument Choice: Policy Styles, Policy Learning and the Privatization Experience.' *Policy Studies Review* 12.1 (1993): 3-24
–. *Studying Public Policy: Policy Cycles and Policy Subsystems*. Toronto: Oxford University Press 1995
Howlett, Michael, and Jeremy Rayner. 'Do Ideas Matter? Policy Subsystem Configurations and Policy Change in the Canadian Forest Sector.' *Canadian Public Administration* 38.3 (1995): 382-410
–. 'The Framework of Forest Management in Canada.' In *Forest Management in Canada*, ed. Monique M. Ross, 43-118. Calgary: Canadian Institute for Resources Law 1995
Huestis, Lynne. 'Enforcement of Environmental Law in Canada.' In *Environmental Law and Business in Canada*, ed. G. Thompson, M. McConnell, and L. Huestis. Toronto: Canada Law Books 1993
Hunt, C. 'Approaches to Native Land Settlements and Implications for Northern Land Use and Resource Management Policies.' In *Northern Transitions*, ed. R.F. Keith and J.B. Wright, 5-41. Ottawa: Canadian Arctic Resources Committee 1978
Hurtig, Mel. *The Betrayal of Canada*. Toronto: Stoddart 1992
Hutton, Thomas A. *Visions of a 'Post-Staples' Economy: Structural Change and Adjustment Issues in British Columbia*. Vancouver: Centre for Human Settlements 1994
–. *Economic Implications of Environmental Enhancement: A Review and Interpretation of the Contemporary Literature*. Vancouver: University of British Columbia, Centre for Human Settlements 1995
Inglehart, Ronald. *The Silent Revolution*. Princeton: Princeton University Press 1977
–. 'Post-Materialism in an Environment of Insecurity.' *American Political Science Review* 75.3 (1981): 880-900
–. *Culture Shift in Advanced Industrial Society*. Princeton: Princeton University Press 1990
Ingram, Helen M., and Dean E. Mann. 'Policy Failure: An Issue Deserving Analysis.' In *Why Policies Succeed or Fail*, ed. H.M. Ingram and D.E. Mann, 11-32. Beverly Hills: Sage Publications 1980
Innis, Harold Adams. *The Fur Trade in Canada: An Introduction to Canadian Economic History*. New Haven: Yale University Press 1930
–. *Problems of Staple Production in Canada*. Toronto: Ryerson Press 1933
International Union for the Conservation of Nature and Natural Resources. *World Conservation Strategy*. Gland, Switzerland: International Union for the Conservation of Nature and Natural Resources 1980
–. *From Strategy to Action: How to Implement the Report of the World Commission on Environment and Development*. Gland, Switzerland: International Union for the Conservation of Nature and Natural Resources 1988
Ip, Irene. 'An Overview of Provincial Government Finance.' In *Provincial Public Finances*, ed. M. McMillan. Toronto: Canadian Tax Foundation 1991
Jacobs, Peter, and D.A. Munro, eds. *Conservation with Equity: Strategies for Sustainable Development*. Cambridge: International Union for the Conservation of Nature and Natural Resources 1987
Jacobs, Peter, Peter Mulvihill, and Barry Sadler. 'Environmental Assessment: Current Challenges and Future Prospects.' In *Law and Process in Environmental Management*, ed.

S.A. Kennett, 13-27. Calgary: Canadian Institute for Resources Law 1993

Jaffe, Louis L. *Judicial Control of Administrative Action.* Boston: Little Brown 1965

–. *English and American Judges as Lawmakers.* Oxford: Clarendon 1969

Jasonoff, Sheila. 'Procedural Choices in Regulatory Science.' *Technology and Society* 17.3 (1995): 279-93

Jeffery, M.I. 'Environmental Enforcement and Regulation in the 1980's: *Regina v. Sault Ste. Marie* Revisited.' *Queens Law Journal* 10.1 (1984): 43-70

Jegr K.M., and K.M. Thompson. *The Canadian Pulp and Paper Industry: Threats and Opportunities 1980-1990.* Montreal: Pulp and Paper Research Institute of Canada 1975

Jenkins-Smith, Hank C., and Paul A Sabatier. 'The Study of Public Policy Processes.' In *Policy Change and Learning: An Advocacy Coalition Approach*, ed. Paul A. Sabatier and Hank C. Jenkins-Smith, 5. Boulder, CO: Westview 1993

Jenkins-Smith, Hank C.J., Gilbert K. St. Clair, and Brian Woods. 'Explaining Change in Policy Subsystems: Analysis of Coalition Stability and Defection over Time.' *American Journal of Political Science* 35.4 (1991): 851-80

Jenson, Jane. 'Paradigms and Political Discourse: Protective Legislation in France and the United States Before 1914.' *Canadian Journal of Political Science* 22.2 (1989): 235-58

Johnson, Pierre Marc, and André Beaulieu. *The Environment and NAFTA: Understanding and Implementing the New Continental Law.* Washington, DC: Island Press 1996

Jones, Bryan D. *Reconceiving Decision-Making in Democratic Politics: Attention, Choice and Public Policy.* Chicago: University of Chicago Press 1994

Jones, Charles O. *An Introduction to the Study of Public Policy.* Monterey, CA: Brooks/Cole 1984

Jones, R.J. Barry. *Globalisation and Interdependence in the International Political Economy.* London: Pinter 1995

Jones, R., and R.E. Dunlap. 'The Social Bases of Environmental Concern: Have They Changed over Time?' *Rural Sociology* 57 (1992): 28-47

Jordan, Grant. 'Iron Triangles, Woolly Corporatism and Elastic Nets: Images of the Policy Process.' *Journal of Public Policy* 1 (1981): 95-123

–. 'Sub-governments, Policy Communities and Networks: Refilling the Old Bottles?' *Journal of Theoretical Politics* 2 (1990): 319-38

Kahler, Miles. *International Institutions and the Political Economy of Integration.* Washington, DC: Brookings Institution 1995

Kaplan, Robert D. 'The Coming Anarchy.' *Atlantic Monthly,* February 1994, 58

Katzenstein, Peter J. 'Conclusion: Domestic Structures and Strategies of Foreign Economic Policy.' *International Organization* 31 (1977): 879-920

–. *Between Power and Plenty: Foreign Economic Policies of Advanced Industrial States.* Madison: University of Wisconsin Press 1978

Kazis, Richard, and Richard L. Grossman. *Fear at Work: Job Blackmail, Labor, and the Environment.* New York: Pilgrim Press 1982

Keeping, J. *The Inuvialuit Final Agreement.* Calgary: Canadian Institute of Resources Law 1989

Keiper, Joseph S., Ernest Kurnow, and Clifford D. Clark, and Harry H. Segal. *Theory and Measurement of Rent.* Philadelphia: Chilton 1961

Kenis, Patrick. 'The Pre-Conditions for Policy Networks: Some Findings from a Three Country Study on Industrial Re-Structuring.' In *Policy Networks: Empirical Evidence and Theoretical Considerations*, ed. B. Marin and R. Mayntz, 297-330. Boulder, CO: Westview Press 1991

Kennett, Steven A. 'Hard Law, Soft Law and Diplomacy: The Emerging Paradigm for Intergovernmental Co-operation in Environmental Assessment.' *Alberta Law Review* 31 (1993): 644-61

–. 'Inter-jurisdictional Harmonization of Environmental Assessment in Canada.' In *Law and Process in Environmental Management*, ed. S.A. Kennett, 277-318. Calgary: Canadian Institute for Resources Law 1993

–. 'Environmental Assessment in Alberta Meets the Rule of Law.' *Resources* 52 (Fall 1995): 5-8

–. 'The Environmental Management Framework Agreement: Reforming Federalism in Post-Referendum Canada.' *Resources* 52 (Fall 1995): 1-5

–. 'Nova Pipeline Jurisdiction: Federal or Provincial?' *Resources* 54 (1996): 1-6

Keohane, Robert O. 'International Institutions: Two Approaches.' In *International Institutions and State Power: Essays in International Relations Theory*, ed. R.O. Keohane, 158-79. Boulder, CO: Westview 1989

–. 'Multilateralism: An Agenda for Research.' *International Journal* 45 (1990): 731-64

Keohane, Robert O., and Helen V. Milner, eds. *Internationalization and Domestic Politics*. Cambridge: Cambridge University Press 1996

Kernaghan, K. 'Power, Parliament and Public Servants in Canada: Ministerial Responsibility Reexamined.' *Canadian Public Policy* 5 (1979): 383-9

–. 'The Public and Public Servant in Canada.' In *Public Administration in Canada: Selected Readings*, ed. K. Kernaghan, 323-30. Toronto: Methuen 1985

–. 'Judicial Review of Administration Action.' In *Public Administration in Canada: Selected Readings*, ed. K. Kernaghan, 358-73. Toronto: Methuen 1985

Khosla, Punam. *Review of the Situation of Women in Canada*. Toronto: National Action Committee on the Status of Women 1994

Kingdon, John W. *Agendas, Alternatives and Public Policies*. Boston: Little, Brown and Company 1984

Kirton, J., and S. Richardson, eds. *Trade, Environment, and Competitiveness: Sustaining Canada's Prosperity*. Ottawa: National Round Table on Environment and Economy 1992

Klycza, Christopher McGrory, and Mlyn, Eric. 'Privileged Ideas and State Interests: Bombs, Trees and State Autonomy.' *Policy Studies Journal* 23.2 (1995): 203-17

Knoke, David. *Political Networks: The Structural Perspective*. Cambridge: Cambridge University Press 1987

Krasner, Stephen D. 'Approaches to the State: Alternative Conceptions and Historical Dynamics.' *Comparative Politics* 16:2 (1984): 223-46

–. ed. *International Regimes*. Ithaca: Cornell University Press 1983

Kuhn, Thomas S. 'Second Thoughts on Paradigms.' In *The Structure of Scientific Theories*, ed. Frederick Suppe, 459-82. Chicago: University of Chicago Press 1974

Kumar, P. 'Union Growth in Canada: Retrospect and Prospect.' In *Canadian Labour Relations*, ed. W.C. Riddell, 95-160. Toronto: University of Toronto Press 1986

Kuznets, Simon S. *Modern Economic Growth: Rate, Structure and Spread*. New Haven: Yale University Press 1966

La Forest, Gerard V. *Disallowance and Reservation of Provincial Legislation*. Ottawa: Department of Justice 1955

–. *Natural Resources and Public Property under the Canadian Constitution*. Toronto: University of Toronto Press 1969

Lacroix, R. 'Strike Activity in Canada.' In *Canadian Labour Relations*, ed. W.C. Riddell, 161-209. Toronto: University of Toronto Press 1986

Lake, Laura M. *Environmental Mediation: The Search for Consensus*. Boulder, CO: Westview Press 1980

Lambert, Richard S., and Paul Pross. *Renewing Nature's Wealth: A Centennial History of the Public Management of Lands, Forests, and Wildlife In Ontario 1763-1967*. Toronto: Department of Lands and Forests 1967

Lang, R., ed. *Integrated Approaches to Resource Planning and Management*. Calgary: University of Calgary Press 1986

Lauber, Volkmar. 'Ecology, Politics and Liberal Democracy.' *Government and Opposition* 13.2 (1978): 199-217

Laumann, Edward O., and David Knoke. *The Organizational State: Social Choice in National Policy Domains*. Madison: University of Wisconsin Press 1987

Law Reform Commission of Canada. *Policy Implementation, Compliance and Administrative Law*. Ottawa: Law Reform Commission 1986

Lederman, W.R. 'The Concurrent Operation of Federal and Provincial Laws in Canada.' *McGill Law Journal* 9.3 (1962-3): 185-99

–. 'The Offshore Reference.' In *The Courts and the Canadian Constitution: A Selection of Essays*, ed. William R. Lederman. Toronto: McClelland and Stewart 1964

Lenny, David M. 'The Case for Funding Citizen Participation in the Administrative Process.' *Administrative Law Review* 28 (1978): 487-500

Lertzman, K., J. Rayner, and J. Wilson. 'Learning and Change in the British Columbia Forest Policy Sector: A Consideration of Sabatier's Advocacy Coalition Framework.' *Canadian Journal of Political Science* 29.1 (1996): 111-34

Lester, James P., ed. *Environmental Politics and Policy: Theories and Evidence.* Durham: Duke University Press 1989

Leventhal, Harold. 'Environmental Decision Making and the Role of the Courts.' *University of Pennsylvania Law Review* 122.3 (1974): 509-55

Lewis, Martin. *Green Delusions: An Environmentalist Critique of Radical Environmentalism.* Durham: Duke University Press 1994

Liberal Party of Canada. *Creating Opportunity.* Toronto: Liberal Party of Canada 1993

Lindblom, Charles E. 'The Science of Muddling Through.' *Public Administration Review* 19.2 (1959): 79-88

–. *Politics and Markets: The World's Political Economic Systems.* New York: Basic Books 1977

–. 'Still Muddling, Not Yet Through.' *Public Administration Review* 39.6 (1979): 517-26

Linder, Stephen H., and B. Guy Peters. 'From Social Theory to Policy Design.' *Journal of Public Policy* 4.3 (1984): 237-59

–. 'The Analysis of Design or the Design of Analysis?' *Policy Studies Review* 7.4 (1988): 738-50

–. 'Instruments of Government: Perceptions and Contexts.' *Journal of Public Policy* 9 (1989): 35-58

–. 'Research Perspectives on the Design of Public Policy: Implementation, Formulation, and Design.' In *Implementation and the Policy Process: Opening up the Black Box*, ed. Dennis J. Palumbo and Donald J. Calista, 51-66. New York: Greenwood Press 1990

Lindquist, Evert A. 'What Do Decision Models Tell Us about Information Use?' *Knowledge in Society* 1.2 (1988): 86-111

Lipton, Charles. *The Trade Union Movement of Canada 1827-1959.* Montreal: Canadian Social Publications 1967

Liroff, Richard A. 'NEPA Litigation in the 1970s: A Deluge or a Dribble?' *Natural Resources Journal* 21.2 (1981): 315-30

List, Martin, and Volker Rittberger. 'International Environmental Management.' In *The International Politics of the Environment: Actors, Interests and Institutions*, ed. Andrew Hurrell and Benedict Kingsbury, 85-109. Oxford: Clarendon Press 1992

Livingston, John A. *The Fallacy of Wildlife Conservation.* Toronto: McClelland and Stewart 1981

Long, J.A. 'Political Revitalization in Canadian Native Indian Society.' *Canadian Journal of Political Science* 23 (1990): 751-74

Lowe, Philip, and Jane Goyder. *Environmental Groups in Politics.* London: Allen and Unwin 1983

Lowenthal, David. 'Awareness of Human Impacts: Changing Attitudes and Emphases.' In *The Earth as Transformed by Human Action*, ed. B.L. Turner II, 121-35. Cambridge: Cambridge University Press 1993

Lower, A.R.M., and H.A. Innis. *Settlement and the Forest Frontier in Eastern Canada.* Toronto: Macmillan 1936

Lowi, Theodore. *The End of Liberalism: Ideology, Policy and the Crisis of Public Authority.* New York: Norton 1969

Lucas, A. 'Water Pollution Control Law in British Columbia.' *University of British Columbia Law Review* 4 (1969): 4, 56

Lucas, Alistair. 'Legal Foundations for Public Participation in Environmental Decision-Making.' *Natural Resources Journal* 16 (1976): 73-102

–. 'Fundamental Prerequisites for Citizen Participation.' In *Involvement and Environment*, ed. B. Sadler, 43-57. Edmonton: Environment Council of Alberta 1978

–. 'Natural Resources and the Environment: A Jurisdictional Primer.' In *Environmental*

Protection and the Canadian Constitution, ed. D. Tingley. Edmonton: Environmental Law Centre 1987

–. 'The New Environmental Law.' In *Canada and the State of the Federation 1989*, ed. R. Watts and D.M. Brown, 167-92. Kingston: Queen's University Institute of Intergovernmental Relations 1989

–. 'Jurisdictional Disputes: Is "Equivalency" a Workable Solution?' In *Into the Future: Environmental Law and Policy for the 1990's*, ed. D. Tingley, 25-36. Edmonton: Environmental Law Centre 1990

–. 'Judicial Review of the Environmental Assessment Process: Has Federal Environmental Assessment Been Judicialized?' Paper presented to the 6th CIRL Conference on Natural Resources Law, Ottawa, 1993

Lucas, Rex A. *Minetown, Milltown, Railtown: Life in Canadian Communities of Single Industry*. Toronto: University of Toronto Press 1971

Luke, Tim. 'The Dreams of Deep Ecology.' *Telos* 76 (1988): 65-92

Lyon, Vaughan. 'The Reluctant Party: Ideology versus Organization in Canada's Green Movement.' *Alternatives* (December 1985): 3-9

–. 'Green Politics: Political Parties, Elections, and Environmental Policy.' In *Canadian Environmental Policy*, ed. R. Boardman, 144-63. Toronto: Oxford University Press 1992

Lysyk, K. 'Approaches to Settlement of Indian Title Claims: The Alaska Model.' *UBC Law Review* 8 (1973): 321-42

–. 'The Indian Title Question in Canada: An Appraisal in the Light of Calder.' *Canadian Bar Review* 51 (1973): 450-80

McAllister, M.L., ed. *Changing Political Agendas*. Kingston: Queen's University, Centre for Resource Studies 1992

McAllister, Mary Louise. 'Administrative Reform and "Shared Decision-Making": Prospects for the Mining Sector.' In *Proceedings of the First Annual Meeting*, ed. E.R. Black, M. Howlett, and P.J. Smith, 159-76. Vancouver: British Columbia Political Studies Association 1996

McBride, Stephen. *Not Working: State, Unemployment, and Neo-Conservatism in Canada*. Toronto: University of Toronto Press 1992

McConnell, W.H. 'The Calder Case in Historical Perspective.' *Saskatchewan Law Review* 38 (1974): 88-122

McCool, Daniel. 'Subgovernments and the Impact of Policy Fragmentation and Accommodation.' *Policy Studies Review* 8 (1989): 264-87

Macdonald, Doug. *The Politics of Pollution: Why Canadians Are Failing Their Environment*. Toronto: McClelland and Stewart 1991

Macdonald, Martha. 'Becoming Visible: Women and the Economy.' In *Limited Edition*, ed. Geraldine Finn, 167. Halifax: Fernwood Books 1994

McFarland, Andrew S. 'Interest Groups and Theories of Power in America.' *British Journal of Political Science* 17.2 (1987): 129-47

MacKay, Donald. *Heritage Lost: The Crisis in Canada's Forests*. Toronto: Macmillan 1985

McKenzie, Richard B. 'The Emergence of the "Service Economy": Fact or Artifact.' In *Conceptual Issues in Service Sector Research: A Symposium*, ed. H.G. Grubel, 73-97. Vancouver: Fraser Institute 1987

Mackintosh, W.A. *Prairie Settlement: The Geographical Setting*. Toronto: Macmillan 1934

Macklem, P. 'First Nations Self-Government and the Borders of the Canadian Legal Imagination.' *McGill Law Journal* 36 (1991): 382-486

MacLachlan, L. 'The Gwich'in Final Agreement.' *Resources* 36 (1991): 6-11

MacLellan, Duncan K. 'The Domestic Politics of the Federal-Provincial Eastern Canada Acid Rain Control Programme: A Case Study of Agenda-Building.' Paper presented to the Annual Meeting of the Canadian Political Science Association, Calgary, 1994

McMahon, Gerard. *Regulatory Negotiation: A Response to the Crisis of Regulatory Legitimacy*. Cambridge, MA: Harvard University Program on Negotiation 1985

McRoberts, K., and P. Monahan, eds. *The Charlottetown Accord: The Referendum and the Future of Canada*. Toronto: University of Toronto Press 1993

Majone, Giandomenico. *Evidence, Argument, And Persuasion In The Policy Process*. New

Haven: Yale University Press 1989

Mann, Dean E., ed. *Environmental Policy Implementation: Planning and Management Options and Their Consequences.* Lexington: Lexington Books 1982

Mann, Dean E., and Helen M. Ingram. 'Policy Issues in the Natural Environment.' In *Public Policy and the Natural Environment*, ed. H.M. Ingram and R.K. Godwin, 15-45. Greenwich: JAI Press 1985

Manning, E.W. 'Conservation Strategies: Providing the Vision for Sustainable Development.' *Alternatives* 16.4 (1990): 24-9

Manzer, Ronald. 'Policy Rationality and Policy Analysis: The Problem of the Choice of Criteria for Decision-making.' In *Public Policy and Administrative Studies*, ed. O.P. Dwivedi, 27-40. Guelph: University of Guelph 1984

Marchak, Patricia M. *Green Gold: The Forest Industry in British Columbia.* Vancouver: UBC Press 1983

-. 'Canadian Political Economy.' *Canadian Review of Sociology and Anthropology* 22.5 (1985): 673-709

-. 'What Happens When Common Property Becomes Uncommon?' *BC Studies* 80 (Winter 1988-9): 3-23

-. 'Uncommon property.' In *Uncommon Property: The Fishing and Fish-Processing Industries in British Columbia*, ed. Patricia Marchak, Neil Guppy, and John McMullan, 3-33. Vancouver: UBC Press 1989

Marcus, Alfred A. *Promise and Performance: Choosing and Implementing an Environmental Policy.* Westport: Greenwood 1980

Marin, Bernd, and Renate Mayntz, eds. *Policy Networks: Empirical Evidence and Theoretical Considerations.* Boulder, CO: Westview Press 1991

Martin, Chester. *'Dominion Lands' Policy.* Toronto: Macmillan 1938

Masterman, Margaret. 'The Nature of a Paradigm.' In *Criticism and the Growth of Knowledge*, ed. Imre Lakatos and Alan Musgrave, 59-89. Cambridge: Cambridge University Press 1970

May, Elizabeth E. 'Political Realities.' In *Endangered Spaces: The Future for Canada's Wilderness*, ed. Monte Hummel. Toronto: Key Porter Books 1989

-. *Paradise Won: The Struggle for South Moresby.* Toronto: McClelland and Stewart 1990

May, Peter J. 'Reconsidering Policy Design: Policies and Publics.' *Journal of Public Policy* 11 (1991): 187-206

Mazmanian, Daniel A., and Paul A. Sabatier, eds. *Implementation and Public Policy.* Glenview: Scott, Forseman 1983

Meekison, J.P., R.J. Romanow, and W.D. Moull, eds. *Origins and Meaning of Section 92(a): The 1982 Constitutional Amendment on Resources.* Montreal: Institute for Research on Public Policy 1985

Meny, Yves. 'The National and International Context of French Policy Communities.' *Political Studies* 37 (1989): 387-99

Merchant, Carolyn. *The Death of Nature: Women, Ecology and the Scientific Revolution.* San Francisco: Harper & Row 1983

Meredith, Thomas. 'Assessing Environmental Impacts in Canada.' In *Resource and Environmental Management in Canada: Addressing Conflict and Uncertainty*, ed. Bruce Mitchell, 335-59. Toronto: Oxford University Press 1995

M'Gonigle, M. 'Developing Sustainability: A Native/Environmentalist Prescription for Third-Level Government.' *BC Studies* 84 (1989): 65-99

Milbrath, Lester W. 'Environmental Beliefs and Values.' In *Political Psychology*, ed. M.G. Hermann, 97-138. San Francisco: Jossey-Bass 1986

Milward, H. Brinton, and Ronald A. Francisco. 'Subsystem Politics and Corporatism in the United States.' *Policy and Politics* 11.3 (1983)

Milward, H. Brinton, and Gary L. Walmsley, 'Policy Subsystems, Networks and the Tools of Public Management.' In *Public Policy Formation*, ed. Robert Eyestone, 3-25. Greenwich: JAI Press 1984

Minunzie, Natalie. 'The Chain-Saw Revolution: Environmental Activism in British Columbia.' MA thesis, Department of Political Science, Simon Fraser University, 1993

Mitchell, Bruce. 'The Provincial Domain in Environmental Management and Resource Development.' In *Resources and the Environment: Policy Perspectives for Canada*, ed. O.P. Dwivedi, 49-76. Toronto: McClelland and Stewart 1980
–. *Geography and Resource Analysis*. New York: Wiley 1989
–, ed. *Resource and Environmental Management in Canada: Addressing Conflict and Uncertainty*. Toronto: Oxford University Press 1995
Mitchell, Bruce, and Richard Turkheim. 'Environmental Impact Assessments: Principles, Practices and Canadian Experiences.' In *Managing Canada's Renewable Resources*, ed. Ralph R. Kreuger and Bruce Mitchell. Toronto: Methuen 1977
Moe, Terry M. *The Organization of Interests: Incentives and the Internal Dynamics of Political Interest Groups*. Chicago: University of Chicago Press 1980
Molot, Maureen A. 'Public Resource Corporations: Impetus and Evolution.' In *Public Disposition of Natural Resources*, ed. N. Bankes and J.O. Saunders, 285-305. Calgary: Canadian Institute of Resources Law 1984
Morantz, T. 'Aboriginal Land Claims in Quebec.' In *Aboriginal Land Claims in Canada*, ed. K. Coates, 101-30. Toronto: Copp Clark Pitman 1992
Morley, C.G. *The Legal Framework for Public Participation in Canadian Water Management*. Burlington, ON: Inland Waters Directorate, Ontario Region, Water Planning and Management Branch 1975
Morrison, J.C. 'Oliver Mowat and the Development of Provincial Rights in Ontario: A Study in Dominion-Provincial Relations 1867-1896.' In *Three History Theses*, ed. Ontario Department of Public Records and Archives. Toronto: Department of Public Records and Archives 1961
Mueller, Dennis C. *Public Choice II*. Cambridge: Cambridge University Press 1989
Mulroney, Brian. *Where I Stand*. Toronto: McClelland and Stewart 1983
Naess, Arne. 'Deep Ecology and Ultimate Premises.' *The Ecologist* 18.4/5 (1980): 128-35
–. *Ecology, Community, and Lifestyle: Outline of an Ecosophy*. Cambridge: Cambridge University Press 1989
Nash, Roderick. *Wilderness and the American Mind*. New Haven: Yale University Press 1967
National Task Force on Environment and Economy. *Progress Report of the National Task Force on Environment and Economy*. Toronto: Canadian Council of Resource and Environment Ministers 1988
Nelkin, Dorothy. *Controversy: Politics of Technical Decisions*. Beverly Hills: Sage 1979
Nelles, H.V. *The Politics of Development: Forests, Mines, and Hydro-Electric Power in Ontario 1849-1941*. Toronto: Macmillan 1974
Nelson, J.G. 'Canada's National Parks: Past, Present and Future.' In *Recreational Land Use: Perspectives on Its Evolution in Canada*, ed. J. Marsh and G. Wall. Ottawa: Carleton University Press 1982
Nemetz, Peter N. 'Federal Environmental Regulation in Canada.' *Natural Resources Journal* 26.3 (1986): 551-608
–. 'The Fisheries Act and Federal-Provincial Environmental Regulation: Duplication or Complementarity?' *Canadian Public Administration* 29.3 (1986): 401-24
Nesmith, Cathy, and Pamela Wright. 'Gender, Resources and Environmental Management.' In *Resource and Environmental Management in Canada: Addressing Conflict and Uncertainty*, ed. Bruce Mitchell, 80-98. Toronto: Oxford University Press 1995
Nichols, Alan B. 'Bioregionalism: Pragmatic or Idealistic.' *Water Environment and Technology* 3.3 (1991): 57-71
Niosi, Jorge. *Technology and National Competitiveness*. Montreal and Kingston: McGill-Queen's University Press 1991
Notzke, Claudia. *Aboriginal Peoples and Natural Resources in Canada*. Toronto: Centre for Aboriginal Management, Education and Training 1994
O'Connor, James. 'Capitalism, Nature, Socialism: A Theoretical Introduction.' *Capitalism, Nature Socialism* 1.1 (1988): 11-38
Oehlschlaeger, Max. *The Idea of Wilderness*. New Haven: Yale University Press 1991
Offe, Claus. 'Challenging the Boundaries of Institutional Politics: Social Movements Since the 1960's.' In *Changing Boundaries of the Political: Essays on the Evolving Balance*

between the State and Society, Public and Private in Europe, ed. C.S. Maier, 63-105. Cambridge: Cambridge University Press 1987

Olewiler, Nancy D. *The Regulation of Natural Resources in Canada: Theory and Practice.* Ottawa: Economic Council of Canada 1981

Olsen, Johan P. *Rediscovering Institutions: The Organizational Basis of Politics.* New York: Free Press 1989

Olson, Mancur. *The Logic of Collective Action: Public Goods and the Theory of Groups.* Cambridge: Harvard University Press 1965

–. 'A Theory of the Incentives Facing Political Organizations: Neo-Corporatism and the Hegemonic State.' *International Political Science Review* 7.2 (1986): 165-89

Ontario Law Reform Commission. *Report on the Law of Standing.* Toronto: Ministry of the Attorney General 1989

O'Reilly, J. 'The Courts and Community Values: Litigation Involving Native Peoples and Resource Development.' *Alternatives* 15 (1988): 40-8

Orton, David. 'Opposing Forest Spraying.' *Capitalism, Nature, Socialism* 2.1 (1991): 109-23

Ostrom, Elinor. *Governing the Commons: The Evolution of Institutions for Collective Action.* New York: Cambridge University Press 1990

Ostrom, Elinor, Roy Gardner, and James Walker. *Rules, Games, and Common-Pool Resources.* Ann Arbor: University of Michigan Press 1994

Paehlke, Robert. 'Democracy, Bureaucracy, and Environmentalism.' *Environmental Ethics* 10.4 (1989): 291-328

–. *Environmentalism and the Future of Progressive Politics.* New Haven: Yale University Press 1989

–. 'Democracy and Environmentalism: Opening a Door to the Administrative State.' In *Managing Leviathan: Environmental Politics and The Administrative State*, ed. R. Paehlke and D. Torgerson, 35-55. Peterborough, ON: Broadview Press 1990

–. 'Regulatory and Non-Regulatory Approaches to Environmental Protection.' *Canadian Public Administration* 33 (1990): 17-36

Paehlke, Robert, and Douglas Torgerson, eds. *Managing Leviathan: Environmental Politics and the Administrative State.* Peterborough, ON: Broadview Press 1990

Painter, An. 'The Future of Environmental Dispute Resolution.' *Natural Resources Journal* 28.1 (1988): 145-70

Pal, Leslie. *Interests of State.* Montreal and Kingston: McGill-Queens University Press 1994

–. 'Competing Paradigms in Policy Discourses: The Case of International Human Rights.' *Policy Sciences* 28 (1995): 185-207

Panitch, Leo, ed. *The Canadian State: Political Economy and Political Power.* Toronto: University of Toronto Press 1977

Parenteau, Rene. *Public Participation in Environmental Decision-Making.* Ottawa: Federal Environmental Assessment Review Office 1988

Parlour, James W. 'The Politics of Water Pollution Control: A Case Study of the Canadian Fisheries Act Amendments and the Pulp and Paper Effluent Regulations 1970.' *Journal of Environmental Management* 13 (1981): 127-49

Parlour, J.W., and S. Schatzow. 'The Mass Media and Public Concern for Environmental Problems in Canada 1960-72.' *International Journal of Environmental Studies* 13 (1978): 14

Pateman, Carole. *Participation and Democratic Theory.* Cambridge: Cambridge University Press 1970

Patterson, E.P. 'A Decade of Change: Origins of the Nishga and Tsimshian Land Protests in the 1880's.' *Journal of Canadian Studies* 18 (1983): 40-54

Pearse, Peter H. 'Property Rights and the Regulation of Commercial Fisheries.' In *Resource Policy: International Perspectives*, ed. P.N. Nemetz, 185-210. Montreal: Institute for Research on Public Policy 1980

–. 'Reconciling Competing Demands on Resources.' In *Public Disposition of Natural Resources*, ed. N. Bankes and J.O. Saunders, 343-54. Calgary: Canadian Institute of Resources Law 1984

Peters, E.J. *Existing Aboriginal Self-Government Arrangements in Canada: An Overview.* Kingston: Queen's University Institute of Intergovernmental Relations 1987

Phillips, Susan D. 'Making Change: The Potential for Innovation under the Liberals.' In *How Ottawa Spends 1994-95: Making Change*, ed. Susan D. Phillips, 1-38. Ottawa: Carleton University Press 1994

Piddington, Kenneth. 'The Role of the World Bank.' In *The International Politics of the Environment*, ed. A. Hurrell and B. Kingsbury, 212-27. Oxford: Clarendon Press 1992

Pierce, John C., Nicholas P. Lovrich, Jr., and Masahiko Matsuoka. 'Support for Citizen Participation: A Comparison of American and Japanese Citizens, Activists and Elites.' *Western Political Quarterly* 43.1 (1990): 39-59

Pinkerton, Evelyn, ed. *Cooperative Management of Local Fisheries: New Directions for Improved Management and Community Development*. Vancouver: UBC Press 1989

Plant, Christopher, and Judith Plant, eds. *Turtle Talk: Voices for a Sustainable Future*. Philadelphia, PA: New Society Publishers 1990

Pollock III, Philip H., Stuart A. Lilie, and M. Elliot Vittes. 'Hard Issues, Core Values and Vertical Constraint: The Case of Nuclear Power.' *British Journal of Political Science* 23.1 (1993): 29-50

Polsby, Nelson W. *Political Innovation in America: The Politics of Policy Initiation*. New Haven: Yale University Press 1984

Porter, Michael E. *Canada at the Crossroads: The Reality of a New Competitive Environment*. Ottawa: Business Council on National Issues/Ministry of Supply and Services 1991

Postel, Sandra. 'Carrying Capacity: Earth's Bottom Line.' In *State of the World 1994: A Worldwatch Institute Report on Progess Towards a Sustainable Society*, ed. Lester R. Brown, Janet Abramovitz, Chris Bright, Christopher Flavin, Gary Gardner, Hal Kane, Anne Platt, Sandra Postel, David Roodman, Aaron Sachs, and Linda Starke. New York: Norton 1994

Pratt, Larry. *The Tar Sands*. Edmonton: Hurtig 1973

Price Waterhouse Associates. *A Study of Taxation Practices Related to the Pulp and Paper Industry: Part II Phase II – Other Fiscal Measures*. Ottawa: Government of Canada 1973

Priest Margot, and Aron Wohl. 'The Growth of Federal and Provincial Regulation of Economic Activity 1867-1978.' In *Government Regulation: Scope, Growth, Process*, ed. W.T. Stanbury, 69-150. Montreal: Institute for Research on Public Policy 1980

Priscoli, J.D., and P. Homenuck. 'Consulting the Publics.' In *Integrated Approaches to Resource Planning and Management*, ed. R. Lang, 67-79. Calgary: University of Calgary Press 1986

Pross, A. Paul, Innis Christie, and John A. Yogis, eds. *Commissions of Inquiry*. Toronto: Carswell 1990

Pross, A.P. 'Canadian Pressure Groups in the 1970s: Their Role and Their Relations with the Public Service.' *Canadian Public Administration* 18 (1975): 121-35

–. *Group Politics and Public Policy*. Toronto: Oxford University Press 1992

Quebec. *The James Bay and Northern Quebec Agreement: Agreement between the Government of Quebec, the Societe d'Energie de la Baie james, the Societe de developpement de la Baie james, The Commission Hydroelectrique de Quebec (Hydro-Quebec) and the Grand Council of the Crees (of Quebec), the Northern Quebec Inuit Association and the Government of Canada*. Quebec: Editeur Officiel du Quebec 1976

Raglon, Rebecca. 'Women and the Great Canadian Wilderness: Reconsidering the Wild:' *Women's Studies* 25 (1996): 513-31

Rankin, Murray. 'Environmental Regulation and the Changing Canadian Constitutional Landscape.' In *Environmental Law and Business in Canada*, ed. G. Thompson, M.L. McConnell, and L.B. Huestis, 31-53. Aurora: Canada Law Book 1993

Raunet, D. *Without Surrender, Without Consent: A History of the Nishga Land Claims*. Vancouver: Douglas and McIntyre 1984

Reed, F.L.C., and Associates. *Forest Management in Canada*. Ottawa: Canadian Forestry Service, Environment Canada 1978

Rees, William. 'Ecological Footprints and Appropriated Carrying Capacity: What Urban Economics Leaves Out.' Paper presented to Globe '92, 16-20 March, Vancouver, 1992

Reif, Linda C. 'International Environmental Law.' In *Environmental Law and Business in Canada*, ed. G. Thompson, M.L. McConnell, and L.B. Huestis, 71-103. Aurora: Canada Law Book 1993

Resnick, Philip. 'B.C. Capitalism and the Empire of the Pacific.' *BC Studies* 67 1985: 29-46

Rhodes, R.A.W. 'Power-Dependence, Policy Communities and Intergovernmental Networks.' *Public Administration Bulletin* 49 (1984): 14-15

Richards, J. Howard. 'Lands and Policies: Attitudes and Controls in the Alienation of Lands in Ontario During the First Century of Settlement.' *Ontario History* 50.4 (1958): 193-209

Richardson, Jeremy, Gunnel Gustafsson, and Grant Jordan. 'The Concept of Policy Style.' In *Policy Styles in Western Europe*, ed. Jeremy J. Richardson, 13. London: George Allen and Unwin 1982

Ripley, Randall B., and Grace A. Franklin. *Congress, the Bureaucracy, and Public Policy.* Homewood, IL: Dorsey Press 1980

Rittberger, Volker, and Peter Mayer, ed. *Regime Theory and International Relations.* Oxford: Clarendon Press 1993

Roberts, Tim. *Pesticides: The Legal Questions.* Vancouver: Legal Services Society 1981

Robin, Martin. *Radical Politics and Canadian Labour 1880-1930.* Kingston: Industrial Relations Centre, Queen's University, 1968

Rochefort, David A., and Roger W. Cobb, 'Problem Definition, Agenda Access, and Policy Choice.' *Policy Studies Journal* 21.1 (1993): 56-71

Rochon, Thomas R., and Daniel A. Mazmanian. 'Social Movements and the Policy Process.' *The Annals of the American Academy of Political Science and Sociology* 528 (1993): 75-87

Rolfe, Chris. 'Federal Regulation of Systemic Pollution from the Pulp and Paper Industry in British Columbia: Barriers to Enforcement and Proposals for Reform.' Unpublished paper, Victoria, 1989

Roman, Andrew J. '*Locus Standi*: A Cure in Search of a Disease?' In *Environmental Rights in Canada*, ed. J. Swaigen, 11-59. Toronto: Butterworths 1981

Roman, Andrew J., and Kelly Hooey. 'The Regulatory Framework.' In *Environmental Law and Business in Canada*, ed. Geoffrey Thompson, Moira L. McConnell, and Lynne B. Huestis, 53-69. Aurora, ON: Canada Law Book 1993

Roman, Andrew J., and Mart Pikkov. 'Public Interest Litigation in Canada.' In *Into the Future: Environmental Law and Policy for the 1990's*, ed. D. Tingley, 165-84. Edmonton: Environmental Law Centre 1990

Rose, Richard. 'Comparative Policy Analysis: The Program Approach.' In *Comparing Pluralist Democracies: Strains on Legitimacy*, ed. M. Dogan, 219-41. Boulder, CO: Westview Press 1988

–. 'What is Lesson-Drawing?' *Journal of Public Policy* 11.1 (1991): 3-30

–. *Lesson-Drawing in Public Policy: A Guide to Learning across Time and Space.* Chatham: Chatham House 1993

Rostow, W.W. *The Stages of Economic Growth: A Non-Communist Manifesto.* Cambridge, UK: Cambridge University Press 1960

Royal Commission on Canada's Economic Prospects. *Final Report of the Royal Commission on Canada's Economic Prospects.* Ottawa: Queen's Printer 1957

Runge, C. Fred. *Freer Trade, Protected Environment: Balancing Trade Liberalization and Environmental Institutions.* Washington, DC: Council on Foreign Relations 1994

Sabatier, Paul A. 'Knowledge, Policy-Oriented Learning, and Policy Change.' *Knowledge: Creation, Diffusion, Utilization* 8.4 (1987): 649-92

–. 'An Advocacy Coalition Framework of Policy Change and the Role of Policy-Oriented Learning Therein.' *Policy Sciences* 21.2/3 (1988): 129-68

–. 'Toward Better Theories of the Policy Process.' *PS: Political Science and Politics* 24.2 (1991): 144-56

–. 'Policy Change Over A Decade or More.' In *Policy Change and Learning: An Advocacy Coalition Approach,* ed. P.A. Sabatier and H.C. Jenkins-Smith, 13-39. Boulder, CO: Westview 1993

Sabatier, Paul, and Hank Jenkins-Smith. 'The Advocacy Coalition Framework: Assessment, Revisions, and Implications for Scholars and Practitioners.' In *Policy Change and Learning: An Advocacy Coalition Approach,* ed. P.A. Sabatier and H.C. Jenkins-Smith, 211-35. Boulder, CO: Westview Press 1993

Sabatier, Paul A., and Hank C. Jenkins-Smith, eds. *Policy Change and Learning: An Advocacy Coalition Approach.* Boulder, CO: Westview Press 1993

Sachs, Ignacy. 'The Strategies of Ecodevelopment.' *Ceres* 17.4 (1984): 17-21

Sadler, Barry. 'Basic Issues in Public Participation: A Background Perspective. In *Involvement and Environment: Proceedings of the Canadian Conference on Public Participation,* ed. B. Sadler. Edmonton: Environment Council of Alberta 1978

-, ed. 'Environmental Conflict Resolution in Canada.' (Special Symposium) *Resolve* 18 (1986)

Salamon, Lester M. 'Rethinking Public Management: Third-Party Government and the Changing Forms of Government Action.' *Public Policy* 29.3 (1981): 255-75

Sale, Kirkpatrick. *Dwellers in the Land.* San Francisco: Sierra Club 1985

Salembier, G.E., A.R. Moore, and F. Stone. *The Canadian Import File: Trade, Protection and Adjustment.* Montreal: Institute for Research on Public Policy 1987

Salter, Liora, Debra Slaco, and Karin Konstantynowicz. *Public Inquiries in Canada.* Ottawa: Science Council of Canada 1981

Sandbach, F. 'A Further Look at the Environment as a Political Issue.' *International Journal of Environmental Studies* 12.2 (1978): 99-110

Sanders, D. 'The Nishga Case.' *BC Studies* 19 (1973): 3-20

-. 'An Uncertain Path: The Aboriginal Constitutional Conferences.' In *Litigating the Values of a Nation,* ed. J.M. Weiler and R.M. Elliot, 63-77. Toronto: Carswell 1986

-. 'The Supreme Court of Canada and the "Legal and Political Struggle" over Indigenous Rights.' *Canadian Ethnic Studies* 22 (1990): 122-9

Sanders, D.E. 'The Indian Lobby.' In *And No One Cheered: Federalism, Democracy and the Constitution Act,* ed. R. Simeon and K. Banting, 301-32 Toronto: Methuen 1983

Savoie, Donald J. *Regional Economic Development: Canada's Search for Solutions.* Toronto: University of Toronto Press 1986

Sax, Joseph L. 'The Public Trust Doctrine in Natural Resource Law: Effective Judicial Intervention.' *Michigan Law Review* 68 (1969-70): 473-566

-. *Defending the Environment: A Strategy for Citizen Action.* New York: Alfred A. Knopf 1971

Schaefer, Richard T. *Sociology.* New York: McGraw-Hill 1989

Scherer, Frederic M. *Industrial Market Structure and Economic Performance.* Chicago: Rand McNally 1970

Schmidt, Ray. 'Canadian Political Economy: A Critique.' *Studies in Political Economy* 6 (1981): 65-92

Schmitter, Philipe C. 'Reflections on Where the Theory of Neo-Corporatism Has Gone and Where the Praxis of Neo-Corporatism May Be Going.' In *Patterns of Corporatist Policy-Making,* ed. G. Lehmbruch and P.C. Schmitter, 259-79. London: Sage 1982

-. 'Interest Intermediation and Regime Governability in Western Europe and North America.' In *Organizing Interests in Western Europe,* ed. S. Berger, 287-330. Cambridge: Cambridge University Press 1983

Schnaiberg, Allan. *The Environment: From Surplus to Scarcity.* New York: Oxford University Press 1980

-. 'The Political Economy of Environmental Problems and Policies: Consciousness, Conflict, and Control Capacity.' In *Handbook of Environmental Sociology,* ed. Riley Dunlap and William Michelson, 2. Westport, CT: Greenwood Press 1991

Schnaiberg, Allan, and Kenneth Alan Gould. *Environment and Society: The Enduring Conflict.* New York: St. Martin's Press 1994

Schneider, Joseph W. 'Social Problems Theory: The Constructionist View.' *Annual Review of Sociology* 11 (1985): 209-29

Schrecker, Ted F. *Political Economy of Environmental Hazards: A Study Paper.* Ottawa: Law Reform Commission 1984

-. 'The Mobilization of Bias in Closed Systems: Environmental Regulation in Canada.' *Journal of Business Administration* 15.1-2 (1984-5): 43-63

–. 'Environmental Hazards: A Critical Approach to Policy Analysis.' In *Public Policy and Administrative Studies*, ed. O.P. Dwivedi and R.B. Woodrow, 143-54. Guelph: University of Guelph 1985

–. 'Resisting Regulation: Environmental Policy and Corporate Power.' *Alternatives* 13 (1985): 9

–. 'The Political Context and Content of Environmental Law.' In *Law and Society: A Critical Perspective*, ed. T. Caputo, 173-204. Toronto: Harcourt, Brace Jovanovich 1989

–. 'Resisting Environmental Regulation: The Cryptic Pattern of Business-Government Relations.' In *Managing Leviathan: Environmental Politics and the Administrative State*, ed. R. Paehlke and D. Torgerson, 165-99. Peterborough, ON: Broadview Press 1990

–. 'The Canadian Environmental Assessment Act: Tremulous Step Forward, or Retreat into Smoke and Mirrors.' *Canadian Environmental Law Reports* 5 (March 1991): 192

–. 'Of Invisible Beasts and the Public Interest: Environmental Cases and the Judicial System.' In *Canadian Environmental Policy: Ecosystems, Politics and Process*, ed. R. Boardman, 83-105. Toronto: Oxford University Press 1992

Schreuder, G.F., ed. *Global Issues and Outlook in Pulp and Paper*. Seattle: University of Washington Press 1988

Schumpeter, J.A. *Capitalism, Socialism, and Democracy*. New York: Harper and Row 1942

Scott, Anthony. *Natural Resources: The Economics of Conservation*. Toronto: University of Toronto Press 1955

Scott, A., and P.A. Neher, eds. *The Public Regulation of Commercial Fisheries in Canada*. Ottawa: Canadian Government Publishing Centre 1981

Scott, Anthony, John Robinson, and David Cohen, eds. *Managing Natural Resources in British Columbia: Markets, Regulations, and Sustainable Development*. Vancouver: UBC Press 1995

Sessions, George. 'Ecological Consciousness and Paradigm Change.' In *Deep Ecology*, ed. M. Tobias. San Marcos, CA: Avant Books 1988

Sharpe, L.J. 'Central Coordination and the Policy Network.' *Political Studies* 33 (1985): 361-81

Shiva, Vandana. *Staying Alive: Women, Ecology and Development*. London: Zed Books 1989

–. 'Development as a New Project of Western Patriarchy.' In *Reweaving the World: The Emergence of Ecofeminism*, ed. I. Diamond and G.F. Orenstein. San Francisco: Sierra Club Books

Shrybman, Steven. *Environmental Mediation: From Theory to Practice*. Ottawa: Environmental Protection Service 1989

–. 'International Trade and the Environment: An Environmental Assessment of Present GATT Negotiations.' *Alternatives* 17.2 (1990): 20-9

Shumacher, E.G. *Small Is Beautiful: Economics as if People Mattered*. New York: Harper and Row 1973

Simon, Herbert A. *Administrative Behavior: A Study of Decision-Making Processes in Administrative Organization*. New York: Macmillan 1957

Sinclair, William. *Controlling Pollution from Canadian Pulp and Paper Manufacturers: A Federal Perspective*. Ottawa: Environment Canada 1988

–. 'Controlling Effluent Discharges from Canadian Pulp and Paper Manufacturers.' *Canadian Public Policy* 17.1 (1991): 86-105

Singelmann, Joachim. *From Agriculture to Services: The Transformation of Industrial Employment*. Beverly Hills: Sage Publications 1978

Skogstad, Grace, and Paul Kopas. 'Environmental Policy in a Federal System: Ottawa and the Provinces.' In *Canadian Environmental Policy: Ecosystems, Politics and Process*, ed. R. Boardman. Toronto: Oxford University Press 1992

Slattery, B. 'The Constitutional Guarantee of Aboriginal and Treaty Rights.' *Queen's Law Journal* 8 (1983): 232-73

–. 'The Hidden Constitution: Aboriginal Rights in Canada.' *American Journal of Comparative Law* 32 (1984): 361-92

Smith, C.R., and D.R. Witty. 'Conservation Resources and Environment: An Exposition and Critical Evaluation of the Commission of Conservation, Canada.' *Plan Canada* 11.1 (1970): 55-71

–. 'Conservation Resources and Environment: An Exposition and Critical Evaluation of the Commission of Conservation, Canada.' *Plan Canada* 11.3 (1972): 199-216

Smith, Douglas A. 'Defining the Agenda for Environmental Protection.' In *How Ottawa Spends 1990-91: Tracking the Second Agenda*, ed. K.A. Graham, 113-36. Ottawa: Carleton University Press 1990

Smith, Gilbert, and David May. 'The Artificial Debate between Rationalist and Incrementalist Models of Decision-Making.' *Policy and Politics* 8 (1980): 147-61

Smith, Martin J. 'Pluralism, Reformed Pluralism and Neopluralism: The Role of Pressure Groups in Policy-Making.' *Political Studies* 38 (June 1990): 302-22

Sproule-Jones, Mark. 'Public Choice Theory and Natural Resources: Methodological Explication and Critique.' *American Political Science Review* 76 (1982): 790-804

Stallings, Barbara. 'International Influence on Economic Policy: Debt, Stabilization, and Structural Reforms.' In *The Politics of Economic Adjustment: International Constraints, Distributive Conflicts and the State*, ed. S. Haggard and R. R. Kaufman, 41-88. Princeton: Princeton University Press 1992

Standing Committee on the Environment and Sustainable Development. *Its About Our Health.* Electronic document available at <http://www.web.apc.org/cepa911/recoms.toc.html>

Statistics Canada. *Human Activity and the Environment.* Ottawa: Ministry of Industry, Science and Technology 1991

–. *Human Activity and the Environment.* Ottawa: Statistics Canada 1994

Stefanick, Lorna. 'The Green Wave: Canada's Environmental Lobby.' Paper presented to the Canadian Political Science Association, Calgary, 1994

–. 'From Protest to Participation: A Comparison of Environmental Activism in B.C. and Ontario.' Paper presented to the Annual Meeting of the Canadian Political Science Association, Montreal, 1995

Stewart, Jenny. 'Corporatism, Pluralism and Political Learning: A Systems Approach.' *Journal of Public Policy* 12.3 (1992): 243-56

Stewart, John. *The Canadian House of Commons: Procedure and Reform.* Montreal: McGill-Queen's University Press 1977

Stone, Christopher. *Should Trees Have Standing?: Toward Legal Rights for Natural Objects.* New York: Avon Books 1972

Stone, Deborah A. *Policy Paradox and Political Reason.* Glenview, IL: Scott, Foresman 1988

Stone, Frank. *Canada, the GATT and the International Trade System.* Montreal: Institute for Research on Public Policy 1984

Sutherland, Sharon L. 'The Public Service and Policy Development.' In *Governing Canada: Institutions and Public Policy,* ed. M. Michael Atkinson. Toronto: Harcourt Brace Jovanovich 1993

Swaigen, John. 'Environmental Law 1975-1980.' *Ottawa Law Review* 12.2 (1980): 439-88

Swinton, K. *Competing Constitutional Visions: The Meech Lake Accord.* Toronto: Carswell 1988

Switzer, Jacqueline. *Environmental Politics: Domestic and Global Dimensions.* New York: St. Martin's Press 1994

Taylor, Andrew J. *Trade Unions and Politics.* Basingstoke: Macmillan 1989

Taylor, Duncan M. *Off Course: Restoring the Balance Between Canadian Society and the Environment.* Ottawa: International Development Research Centre 1994

Tennant, P. *Aboriginal Peoples and Politics: The Indian Land Question in British Columbia 1849-1989.* Vancouver: UBC Press 1990

Thacher, Peter S. 'The Role of the United Nations.' In *The International Politics of the Environment,* ed. A. Hurrell and B. Kingsbury, 183-211. Oxford: Clarendon Press 1992

Thomas, C., and G.A. Tereposky. 'The NAFTA and the Side Agreement on Environmental Co-operation.' *Journal of World Trade* 27.6 (1993): 5-34

Thompson, Andrew R. *Environmental Regulation in Canada.* Vancouver: Westwater Research Institute 1980

–. *Energy Project Approval in British Columbia*. Vancouver: Westwater Research Centre, University of British Columbia 1981

Thompson, A.R., and H.R. Eddy. 'Jurisdictional Problems in Natural Resource Management in Canada.' In *Essays on Aspects of Resource Policy*, ed. W.D. Bennett et al., 67-96. Ottawa: Science Council of Canada 1973

Thompson, Geoffrey, Moira L. McConnell, and Lynne B. Huestis, eds. *Environmental Law and Business in Canada*. Toronto: Canada Law Book 1993

Thompson, I.D. 'The Myth of Integrated Wildlife/Forestry Management.' *Queen's Quarterly* 94.3 (1987): 609-21

Thorne, Stevenson, and Kellogg. *Funding Mechanisms for Forest Management*. Toronto: Canadian Council of Resource and Environment Ministers 1981

Titley, E. *A Narrow Vision: Duncan Campbell Scott and the Administration of Indian Affairs in Canada*. Vancouver: UBC Press 1986

Toner, Glen. 'The Politics of Energy and the National Energy Program: A Framework and Analysis.' Ph.D dissertation, Carleton University, 1984

–. 'The Green Plan: From Great Expectations to Eco-Backtracking ... to Revitalization?' In *How Ottawa Spends 1994-95: Making Change*, ed. S.D. Phillips, 229-60. Ottawa: Carleton University Press 1994

Torgerson, Douglas. 'Between Knowledge and Politics: Three Faces Of Policy Analysis.' *Policy Sciences* 19.1 (1986): 33-59

–. 'Power and Insight in Policy Discourse: Post-Positivism and Problem Definition.' In *Policy Studies in Canada: the State of the Art*, ed. L. Dobuzinskis, M. Howlett, and D. Laycock, 266-98. Toronto: University of Toronto Press 1996

Troyer, Warner. *No Safe Place*. Toronto: Clarke, Irwin 1977

Tuohy, Carolyn. *Policy and Politics in Canada: Institutionalized Ambivalence*. Philadelphia: Temple University Press 1992

Turpel, Mary Ellen. 'The Charlottetown Discord and Aboriginal Peoples' Struggle for Fundamental Political Change.' In *The Charlottetown Accord, The Referendum, and the Future of Canada*, ed. K. McRoberts and P. Monahan, 117-51. Toronto: University of Toronto Press 1993

Upton, L. 'The Origins of Canadian Indian Policy.' *Journal of Canadian Studies* 8 (1973): 51-61

Urquhart, Ian, and Larry Pratt. *The Last Great Forest*. Edmonton: NeWest Press 1994

Usher, P. 'Some Implications of the Sparrow Judgement for Resource Conservation and Management.' *Alternatives* 18 (1991): 20-2

Usher, P.J., F.J. Tough, and R.M. Galois. 'Reclaiming the Land: Aboriginal Title, Treaty Rights and Land Claims in Canada.' *Applied Geography* 12 (1992): 109-32

Van Waarden, Frans. 'Dimensions and Types of Policy Networks.' *European Journal of Political Research* 21 (1992): 29-52

Vander Zwaag, David, and Linda Duncan. 'Canada and Environmental Protection: Confident Political Faces, Uncertain Legal Hands.' In *Canadian Environmental Policy: Ecosystems, Politics and Process*, ed. R. Boardman, 3-23. Toronto: Oxford University Press 1992

Vander Zwaag, David, and Brenda McLuhan. 'Pulp and Paper Pollution: Shifting Legal Approaches and the Search for Sustainable Industries.' In *Environmental Law and Business in Canada*, ed. Geoffrey Thompson, Moira L. McConnell, and Lynne B. Huestis, 479-522. Aurora, ON: Canada Law Book 1993

Victor, Peter A. 'Economics and the Challenge of Environmental Issues.' In *Ecology versus Politics in Canada*, ed. W. Leiss, 34-56. Toronto: University of Toronto Press 1979

Victor, Peter, and Terrence Burrell. *Environmental Protection Regulation: Water Pollution and the Pulp and Paper Industry*. Technical Report No. 14. Ottawa: Economic Council of Canada 1981

Vogel, David. *National Styles of Regulation: Environmental Policy in Great Britain and the United States*. Ithaca: Cornell University Press 1986

von Beyme, Klaus. 'Do Parties Matter? The Impact of Parties on the Key Decisions in the Political System.' *Government and Opposition* 19.1 (1984): 5-29

Wagner, M.W. 'Footsteps Along the Road: Indian Land Claims and Access to Natural Resources.' *Alternatives* 18 (1991): 22-8

Walker, Jack L. 'The Diffusion of Knowledge and Policy Change: Toward a Theory of Agenda-Setting.' Paper presented at the Annual Meeting of the American Political Science Association, Chicago, 1974

Watkins, M.H. 'The Staple Theory Revisited.' *Journal of Canadian Studies* 12.5 (1977): 83-95

Watkins, Melville H. 'A Staple Theory of Economic Growth.' *Canadian Journal of Economics and Political Science* 29.2 (1963): 141-58

Watts, N., and G. Wandesforde-Smith. 'Postmaterial Values and Environmental Policy Change.' In *Environmental Policy Formation*, ed. D.E. Mann, 29-42. Lexington, MA: Lexington Books 1981

Weaver, R. Kent, and Bert A. Rockman. 'Assessing the Effects of Institutions.' In *Do Institutions Matter? Government Capabilities in the United States and Abroad*, ed. R.K. Weaver and B.A. Rockman, 1-41. Washington, DC: Brookings Institution 1993

Webb, Kernaghan. 'Between the Rocks and Hard Places: Bureaucrats, the Law and Pollution Control.' *Alternatives* 14.2 (1987): 4-13

-. 'On the Periphery: The Limited Role for Criminal Offenses in Environmental Protection.' In *Into the Future: Environmental Law and Policy for the 1990's*, ed. D. Tingley, 58-69. Edmonton: Environmental Law Centre 1990

Webb, Kernaghan, and John C. Clifford. *Pollution Control in Canada: The Regulatory Approach in the 1980s*. Ottawa: Law Reform Commission of Canada 1988

Webb, M.C., and M.W. Zacher. *Canada and International Mineral Markets: Dependence, Instability and Foreign Policy*. Kingston: Queen's University, Centre for Resource Studies 1988

Webber, David J. 'The Distribution and Use of Policy Knowledge in the Policy Process.' In *Advances in Policy Studies Since 1950*, ed. W.N. Dunn and R.M. Kelly. New Brunswick, NJ: Transaction Publishers 1992

Weeks, E.P., and L. Mazany. *The Future of the Atlantic Fisheries*. Montreal: Institute for Research on Public Policy 1983

Weir, Margaret. 'Ideas and the Politics of Bounded Innovation.' In *Structuring Politics: Historical Institutionalism in Comparative Analysis*, ed. S. Steinmo, K. Thelen, and F. Longstreth, 188-216. Cambridge: Cambridge University Press 1992

Wengert, N. 'Citizen Participation: Practice in Search of a Theory.' In *Natural Resources for a Democratic Society: Public Participation in Decision-Making*, ed. A.E. Utton, 23-40. Boulder, CO: Westview Press 1976

Wengert, Norman I. *Natural Resources and the Political Struggle*. New York: Random House 1955

Wenner, Lettie M. *The Environmental Decade in Court*. Bloomington: Indiana University Press 1982

Whalley, John, ed. *Canada's Resource Industries*. Toronto: University of Toronto Press 1986

Whalley, John. 'Regional Trade Arrangements in North America: CUSTA and NAFTA.' In *New Dimensions in Regional Integration*, ed. J. de Melo and A. Panagariya, 352-89. Cambridge: Cambridge University Press 1993

Wheare, Kenneth. *Federal Government*. New York: Oxford University Press 1964

White, J.H. *Forestry on Dominion Lands*. Ottawa: Commission of Conservation 1915

Whittington, Michael. *CCREM: An Experiment in Interjurisdictional Co-ordination*. Ottawa: Science Council of Canada 1978

Whyte, John D. *The Constitution and Natural Resource Revenues*. Kingston: Institute of Intergovernmental Relations, Queens University 1982

Wildsmith, B.H. *Aboriginal People and Section 25 of the Canadian Charter of Rights and Freedoms*. Saskatoon: University of Saskatchewan Native Law Centre 1988

Wilkinson, Bruce W. 'Canada's Resource Industries: A Survey.' In *Canada's Resource Industries and Water Export Policy*, ed. J. Whalley, 1-159. Toronto: University of Toronto Press 1986

Wilks, Stephen, and Maurice Wright. 'Conclusion: Comparing Government-Industry Relations: States, Sectors, and Networks.' In *Comparative Government-Industry Relations:*

Western Europe, the United States, and Japan, ed. Stephen Wilks and Maurice Wright, 298. Oxford: Clarendon Press 1987

Williams, Glen. *Not for Export: Toward a Political Economy of Canada's Arrested Industrialization.* Toronto: McClelland and Stewart 1983

–. 'Greening the New Canadian Political Economy.' *Studies in Political Economy* 37 (1992): 5-30

Williams, P.W. 'Tourism and the Environment: No Place to Hide.' *World Leisure and Recreation* 34.2 (Summer 1992): 1-9

–. 'Ecotourism: An Emerging Tourism Product with Emerging Management Challenges.' *Texas Tourism Trends* 5.3 (1993): 1-5

Wilson, Graham K. *Business and Politics: A Comparative Introduction.* London: Macmillan 1990

Wilson, Jeremy. 'Wilderness Politics in B.C.' In *Policy Communities and Public Policy in Canada: A Structural Approach,* ed. William D. Coleman and Grace Skogstad. Toronto: Copp Clark Pitman 1990

–. 'Green Lobbies: Pressure Groups and Environmental Policy.' In *Canadian Environmental Policy,* ed. R. Boardman, 109-25. Toronto: Oxford University Press 1992

Winfield, Mark S. 'The Ultimate Horizontal Issue: The Environmental Policy Experience of Alberta and Ontario 1971-1993.' *Canadian Journal of Political Science* 27.1 (1994): 129-52

–. 'Achieving the Holy Grail? A Legal and Political Analysis of Ontario's Environmental Bill of Rights.' Paper presented to the Annual Meeting of the Canadian Political Science Association, Montreal, 1995

Wolf, Edward C. *On the Brink of Extinction: Conserving the Diversity of Life.* Worldwatch Paper 78. Washington, DC: Worldwatch Institute 1987

World Commission on Environment and Economy. *Our Common Future.* Oxford: Oxford University Press 1987

Young, Oran. *International Environmental Regimes.* Ithaca: Cornell University Press 1989

–. 'The Politics of International Regime Formation: Managing Natural Resources and the Environment.' *International Organization* 43.3 (1989): 349-76

Yudelman, David. *Canadian Mineral Policy Past and Present: The Ambiguous Legacy.* Kingston, ON: Centre for Resource Studies, Queen's University 1985

Zahariadis, Nikolas, and Christopher S. Allen. 'Ideas, Networks and Policy Streams: Privatization in Britain and Germany.' *Policy Studies Review* 14.1/2 (1995): 71-98

Zuker, Richard C. *Blue Gold: Hydro-Electric Rent in Canada.* Ottawa: Ministry of Supply and Services Canada 1984

Index

Deep ecology, 15, 16, 247-9
Democracy: eroded by NAFTA, 243; parliamentary system, and strength of executive, 53, 143-4; and policy subsystems, 74; and public participation, 73, 106
Demographics. *See* Population
Department of Energy, Mines and Resources (federal), 62
Department of Environment Act (Newfoundland), 63
Department of Indian and Northern Affairs. *See also* Aboriginal land claims; First Nations
Department of Indian and Northern Affairs (federal), 62
Department of the Environment (DOE) (federal), 60-1, 168. *See also* Environment Canada
Department of Transport (federal), 62
'Dependency' approach, in economic development theory, 44, 45
DOE. *See* Department of the Environment
Doern, G. Bruce, 94, 95

EARP. *See* Environmental Assessment Review Process
Ecofeminism, 247, 249-50
Ecological economics, 251-3
Ecological systems: effect of economic growth on, 244-5; and philosophy of deep ecology, 16, 249; as resource systems, 40-1; viability, and ecological economics, 252
Economic and Regional Development Agreement (ERDA), 167
Economy: capitalist, and business interest groups, 83-4; capitalist, and natural resource policy, 95; development, environmental implications of, 42-3; development, theories, 43-5; economic transition models, 43; effect on policy implementation, 173; frontier, and resource management, 14; growth stages (Rostow), 23-4; neoclassical models, 10-11, 251; political economic perspective, 11-14, 21, 46, 235-7; poststaples, 238-40; primary sector, 22, 24; secondary sector, 24; staples, 22-6, 43-4, 45; and sustainability, 251-3
Economy, Canadian: boom and bust cycles, 34; changes in, and environmental policy, 236-7; dependence on

natural resources, 8, 10-14, 22-35, 69; dependence on trade, 26; diversification of, future, 253-4; diversity, lack of, 43-4, 46; ecological dimensions, 40-3, 244-5; and environmental policy, constraints on, 46, 68-9; globalization of, 243; history, 6, 27; and international markets, 34; and lack of value-added finishing, 22; new industries, and poststaples economy, 240; poststaples, 238-40; regional differences, 26, 31-5, 43; resource-based manufacturing, 34; social dimensions of, 36-40; and stages of economic growth, 23-4; staples, 22-6, 43-4; tertiary sector, 24, 238-40; trade balances, 29. *See also* Canada-US Free Trade Agreement (CAFTA); Corporations; Exports; General Agreement on Tariffs and Trade (GATT); Imports; North American Free Trade Agreement (NAFTA)
Economy, international: Canada as price-taker for natural resources, 34; and Canadian trade balance, 29; and environmental policy, 13-14
Ecosystems: interdependence of, 3; and policy-making jurisdictions, 41-3
Ecotourism, 245
Education, as activity of environmental groups, 82, 115, 118, 139
Endangered Species Act (federal), 175
Energy, Mines and Resources Canada (federal), 41
Energy industry: affected by NAFTA, 66-7; alternative energy sources, 240; and Canadian economy, 25; trade balances, 29. *See also* Hydroelectric power generation
ENGOs (Environmental non-government organizations). *See* Environmental groups
Environment: attitude towards, 8, 13, 16, 26, 36, 108-9, 113-14, 115-16; issues, multiple jurisdictions, 7
Environment 2001, 227
Environment Act (Manitoba), 63
Environment Assessment Act (Ontario), 165
Environment Canada, 52, 62, 198. *See also* Department of the Environment (DOE) (federal)
Environment Management Act (British Columbia), 51, 63
Environment Quality Act (Quebec), 63

Set in Stone by Tesfa Design

Printed and bound in Canada by Friesens

Copy-editor: Dallas Harrison

Proofreader: Andy Carroll

Indexer: Annette Lorek

Books of Related Interest

The following titles are also available from UBC Press. Prices listed are in effect as of Spring 1997 and are subject to change.

Passing the Buck:
Federalism and Canadian
Environmental Policy
Kathryn Harrison
1996
0-7748-0557-9, hc, $70.00
0-7748-0558-7, pb, $29.95

Managing Natural Resources in
British Columbia:
Markets, Regulations, and
Sustainable Development
Anthony Scott, John Robinson,
and David Cohen, eds.
1996
0-7748-0534-X, hc, $65.00
0-7748-0550-1, pb, $34.95

Life in 2030:
Exploring a Sustainable Future
for Canada
John B. Robinson et al.
1996
0-7748-0562-5, hc, $65.00
0-7748-0569-2, pb, $25.95

Achieving Sustainable
Development
Anne Dale and
John B. Robinson, eds.
1996
0-7748-0556-0, hc, $75.00
0-7748-0540-4, pb, $25.95

Balancing Act:
Environmental Issues in
Forestry
Second Edition
Hamish Kimmins
1997
0-7748-0574-9, pb, $29.95

Dictionary of Natural Resource
Management
Julian and Katherine Dunster
1996
0-7748-0503-X, hc, $90.00
0-7748-0567-6, pb, $34.95

The Language of the
Environment:
A New Rhetoric
George Myerson and Yvonne Rydin
1996
1-85728-331-7, pb, $24.95
Canada only

Collaborative Planning:
Shaping Places in Fragmented
Societies
Patsy Healey
1997
0-7748-0597-8, hc, $75.00
0-7748-0598-6, pb, $29.95

The Green Economy:
Environment, Sustainable
Development, and the Politics
of the Future
Michael Jacobs
1995
0-7748-0474-2, pb, $22.95
Canada only

Biodiversity in British
Columbia:
Our Changing Environment
Lee E. Harding and Emily
McCullum, eds.
1994
*published by Canadian Wildlife
Service*
0-662-20671-1, pb, $34.95

A Stake in the Future:
Redefining the Canadian
Mineral Industry
Mary Louise McAllister and
Cynthia J. Alexander
1997
0-7748-0603-6, hc, $75.00
0-7748-0602-8, pb, $29.95

The International Politics of
Whaling
Peter J. Stoett
1997
0-7748-0605-2, hc, $65.00
0-7748-0604-6, pb, $24.95

Order Information

For information on how to place an order or receive a catalogue please
contact:

UBC Press
University of British Columbia
6344 Memorial Road
Vancouver, BC V6T 1Z2

(604) 822-5959
Fax: 1-800-668-0821
E-mail: orders@ubcpress.ubc.ca

Payment must accompany orders from individuals.

Shipping $5.00. For Canadian orders please add 7% GST to total order,
including shipping.

Outside Canada all prices are in US funds.

Visit the UBC Press World Wide Web site at:

http://www.ubcpress.ubc.ca

for detailed information on forthcoming and backlist titles in all subject
areas.